CONSTRUCTING MODERN SLAVERY

Modern slavery laws are a response to global capitalism, which undermines the distinction between free and unfree labour and poses intense challenges to state sovereignty. Instead of being a solution, *Constructing Modern Slavery* argues that modern slavery laws divert attention from the underlying structures and processes that generate exploitation. Focusing on unfree labour associated with international immigration and global supply chains, it provides a novel sociolegal genealogy of the concept of 'modern slavery' through a series of linked case studies of influential actors associated with key legal instruments: the United Nations, the United States, the International Labour Organization, the European Union, the United Kingdom, and Walk Free Foundation. *Constructing Modern Slavery* demonstrates that despite the best efforts of academics, advocates, and policymakers to develop a truly multifaceted approach to modern slavery, it is difficult to uncouple antislavery initiatives from the conservative moral and economic agendas with which they are aligned. This title is also available as Open Access on Cambridge Core.

Judy Fudge is Professor in the School of Labour Studies at McMaster University and a Fellow of the Royal Society of Canada. She takes a sociolegal approach to studying work and labour and has published extensively on employment and labour law from a range of critical perspectives.

Constructing Modern Slavery

LAW, CAPITALISM, AND UNFREE LABOUR

JUDY FUDGE
McMaster University

CAMBRIDGE
UNIVERSITY PRESS

CAMBRIDGE
UNIVERSITY PRESS

Shaftesbury Road, Cambridge CB2 8EA, United Kingdom

One Liberty Plaza, 20th Floor, New York, NY 10006, USA

477 Williamstown Road, Port Melbourne, VIC 3207, Australia

314–321, 3rd Floor, Plot 3, Splendor Forum, Jasola District Centre, New Delhi – 110025, India

103 Penang Road, #05-06/07, Visioncrest Commercial, Singapore 238467

Cambridge University Press is part of Cambridge University Press & Assessment, a department of the University of Cambridge.

We share the University's mission to contribute to society through the pursuit of education, learning and research at the highest international levels of excellence.

www.cambridge.org
Information on this title: www.cambridge.org/9781108473422

DOI: 10.1017/9781108562058

First published 2024

A catalogue record for this publication is available from the British Library.

A Cataloging-in-Publication data record for this book is available from the Library of Congress

ISBN 978-1-108-47342-2 Hardback

Contents

Acknowledgements

This book has been a long time in the making. I started thinking and writing about the relationship between unfree labour and modern slavery in 2013 when I moved to the United Kingdom. My initial focus was on how different forms of unfree labour and labour exploitation came to be seen as modern slavery. But I hit an impasse. As a feminist who studies what the law treats as labour, I felt it was incumbent on me to address sex work and its relationship to unfree labour and modern slavery. But most of the literature on human trafficking and modern slavery treats labour and sexual exploitation separately even though many forms of work are exploitative, and gendered forms of exploitation – which include sexual violence and harassment – permeate many occupations. My challenge was to find a way to discuss sexual and labour exploitation and the different governance strategies associated with them without either treating them as essentially different or becoming mired in an unhelpful debate about whether commercial sex work is exploitative. It took me a while to figure my way out of this deadlock, which I did by treating the distinction between labour and sexual exploitation as an artefact of law and governance. This solution gave me the clue to approaching modern slavery as a construct of law and governance – hence the title of this book.

Having written a book about how 'modern slavery' was constructed, it is obvious that I think words and terminology matter. Thus, I want to explain my decision to use the term 'victim' of trafficking instead of 'survivor', 'illegal' migrant rather than 'undocumented', and both 'sex work' and 'prostitution' to describe the sale of sexual services. I borrowed the terms used in the legal and political debates and legal instruments I examined. My goal was to put them in their context and explore their meaning in that context.

During the book's lengthy gestation, I had the good fortune to discuss some of my ideas with a great many people, who I would like to thank. I enjoyed a fruitful collaboration with Kendra Strauss, a feminist geographer, using the concept of legal jurisdiction in combination with feminist political economy to explain how characterising migrant domestic workers' unfreedom in the United Kingdom as modern slavery resulted, paradoxically, in more restrictive visa conditions and constraints on their freedom. Working at Kent Law School between 2013 and 2018 not only introduced me to the concept of 'modern slavery' but helped to shape my approach to the topic. I benefited from a lively and convivial group of sociolegal scholars interested in critical theory, feminism, and political economy. I owe them a debt of gratitude for reminding me that theory matters and how to do it clearly.

I worked out some of my ideas in early articles, chapters, briefs, blog posts, and presentations. I am very grateful to the individuals and institutions who gave me an opportunity to discuss my ideas and receive extremely useful feedback. I want to thank: Prabha Kotiswaran for inviting me to contribute to an international workshop on 'Shaping the Definition of Trafficking in the Palermo Protocol' at King's College London in May 2014; Johanna Howe and Rosemary Owens for their invitation to participate in the workshop 'Temporary Labour Migration in the Global Era; The Regulatory Challenges', which was held at the International Institute for the Sociology of Law in Oñati, Spain, in June 2015; Ruth Dukes for including me in a workshop on 'Labour Laws and Labour Markets: New Methodologies' at the University of Glasgow in November 2016; Amir Fuchs for inviting me to present at the workshop for the Foundation for Law, Justice and Society held at Wolfson College, Oxford, in March 2017; Bernard Ryan for his invitation to participate in a workshop on the nexus between immigration and labour law at the University of Leicester in September 2017; Karin Engels for inviting me to present my work at the Rapoport Centre for Human Rights, University of Texas, Austin, in October 2017; and Eva Kocher and the B/orders in Motion Research Factory for inviting me to share my work in progress at the European University Viadrina Frankfurt, (Oder), Germany, in January 2018. I also had the pleasure of learning about unfree labour from an amazing group of scholars from a variety of disciplines at Re:work: Work and Human Life Cycle in Global History, an international research centre at Humboldt University, where I was the guest of the director, Andreas Ecker, from December 2017 to July 2018. These conversations provided intellectual camaraderie and inspiration.

When I returned to Canada in 2018, I took up a position in the School of Labour Studies at McMaster University, which challenged me to be truly transdisciplinary and explain my ideas about law to people interested in labour who did not have legal training. I am grateful to my McMaster graduate students for their contributions in the various iterations of my unfree labour course, and the Laborers' International Union of North America (LIUNA) Enrico Henry Mancinelli Chair of Global Labour Issues for financial support and research time.

I want to give special thanks to the colleagues and institutions that invited me to present the first two chapters and part of the conclusion of the book: the Graduate Student Organizing Committee for inviting me to speak at the conference, 'Mapping the Global Dimensions of Policy' at McMaster University, Hamilton, in March 2019; Beth Gaze and Joo-Cheong Tham for asking me to present a seminar to the Melbourne Centre of Employment and Labour Rights at Melbourne Law School, in May 2019; Raphael Gomez for inviting me to give the Sefton-Williams Annual Lecture, Centre for Industrial Relations and Human Resource Management and Woodsworth College, University of Toronto, in March 2019; Guy Mundlak and Hila Shamir for asking me to present my work in progress to their advanced labour law seminar at Tel Aviv Law School in November 2020; Liz Oliver and Kate Hardy for their invitation to give a seminar to the Centre for Employment Relations, Innovation and Change, Leeds Business School, in December 2020; and Rianne Mahon for her invitation to present to the Gender and Governance Group at Carleton University, Ottawa, in May 2021. These different audiences, with different interests and drawn from different disciplines, forced me to be clear about my arguments and analysis. I am also very grateful to Oxford University Press for allowing me to republish a revised version of 'Bad for business: The construction of modern slavery and the reconfiguration of sovereignty' initially published in *London Review of International Law* (Vol. 10, Issue 1, March 2022, 3–31) as Chapter 2 of this book.

Writing is an engaging, but lonely endeavour. Leila Kawar, Rianne Mahon, and Tony Porter, who read and gave me comments on earlier drafts of the Introduction and Chapter 1, deserve a special thanks as they had to wade through inchoate ideas. Lesley Erikson, a fantastic editor, gave me great advice about what to cut and how to make this book more readable and Lisa Fedorak provided a very helpful index. Judith Onwubiko, Moritz Neugebauer, Jonelle Humphrey, and Siena Mcilwraith-Fraticelli provided helpful research and good cheer along the way. Tobias Ginsberg and Gemma Smith of Cambridge University Press helpfully navigated this book through the publication process. I would also like to thank the many individuals in the United Kingdom who I interviewed for this project. Although I did not quote or name you, you offered me your insights and provided me with leads. Thank you for being generous with your time.

Three friends in particular deserve special acknowledgement for not letting me drop this book when it was tempting to do so: Anna Konik, Guy Mundlak, and Susan Russell. And finally, I would like to acknowledge and thank Millie and Bern Fudge, my parents, who cultivated an environment in which I was free to pursue what was meaningful to me and Ken Massicotte, my fellow traveller, for his company on that journey.

International Conventions

1921 International Convention for the Suppression of the Traffic in Women and Children, adopted on 30 December 1921, 9 LNTS 415

1926 Slavery, Servitude, Forced Labour and Similar Institutions and Practices Convention of 1926 (Slavery Convention of 1926), in force 9 March 1927, 60 LNTS 253

1930 International Labour Organization, ILO Forced Labour Convention, 1930 (No. 29), 28 June 1930

1934 International Convention for the Suppression of the Traffic in Women of Full Age, Geneva, 11 October 1933, in force 24 August 1934, 150 LNTS 431

1949 International Convention for the Suppression of the Traffic in Persons and the Exploitation of the Prostitution of Others, 2 December 1949, in force on 25 July 1951, 96 UNTS 271

1956 UN Economic and Social Council (ECOSOC), Supplementary Convention on the Abolition of Slavery, the Slave Trade, and Institutions and Practices Similar to Slavery, 7 September 1956

1957 International Labour Organization (ILO), Abolition of Forced Labour Convention, C105, 25 June 1957

1975 International Labour Organization, Migrant Workers (Supplementary Provisions) Convention, 1975 (No. 143)

1993 UN General Assembly, Vienna Declaration and Programme of Action, 12 July 1993, A/CONF.157/23

1998 International Labour Organization, ILO Declaration on Fundamental Principles and Rights at Work, June 1988

2000 UN General Assembly, United Nations Convention against Transnational Organized Crime: Resolution, adopted by the General Assembly, 8 January 2001, A/RES/55/25

UN General Assembly, Protocol to Prevent, Suppress and Punish Trafficking in Persons, Especially Women and Children, Supplementing the United Nations Convention against Transnational Organized Crime, 15 November 2000, A/RES/55/25

UN General Assembly, Protocol against the Smuggling of Migrants by Land, Sea and Air, Supplementing the United Nations Convention against Transnational Organized Crime, 15 November

2007 Human Rights Council, Resolution 6/14, Special Rapporteur on Contemporary Forms of Slavery, 28 September 2007, https://ap.ohchr.org/documents/E/HRC/resolutions/A_HRC_RES_6_14.pdf

2014 International Labour Organization, Protocol of 2014 to the Forced Labour Convention, 1930 (no. 29)

Council of Europe Conventions

1950 Council of Europe. "Convention for the Protection of *Human Rights* and Fundamental Freedoms." Council of Europe Treaty Series 005, 4 November 1950.

2005 Council of Europe Convention on Action against Trafficking in Human Beings, Council of Europe Treaty Series - No. 197, 16 May 2005.

2014 Council of Europe, Parliamentary Assembly, 'Prostitution, trafficking and modern slavery in Europe, Resolution 1983 (2014), Final version'.

2020 Council of the European Union, 'Council conclusions on human rights and decent work in global supply chains', Brussels, 1 December 2020 (OR.), 13512/20 SOC 772, EMPL 542.

European Union Treaties, Directives, and Agreements

1985 Agreement on the Gradual Abolition of Checks at Common Borders of the Benelux, the Federal Republic of Germany and France, June 14, 1985.

Convention Implementing the Schengen Agreement of 14 June 1985 between the Governments of the States of the Benelux Economic Union, the Federal Republic of Germany and the French Republic, on the Gradual Abolition of Checks at Their Common Borders "Schengen Implementation Agreement" (1985).

1989 Resolution on the Exploitation of Prostitution and the Traffic in Human Beings, 1989 OJ (C 120), Eur. Parl. Doc. (A2-52/89) 352–354 (1989)

1992 European Union, *Treaty on European Union (Consolidated Version), Treaty of Maastricht*, 7 February 1992, *Official Journal of the European Communities*, C 325/5

2001 European Union, '2001/220/JHA: Council framework decision of 15 March 2001 on the standing of victims in criminal proceedings'

2002 Council of Europe, Parliamentary Assembly, 'Recommendation No 1545 (2002) on a campaign against trafficking in women' (21 January 2002)

Council of the European Union, 'Proposal for a comprehensive plan to combat illegal immigration and trafficking of human beings in the European Union', 2002/C 142/02, *Official Journal*, C142, 14 June 2002

European Union, *Brussels Declaration on Preventing and Combating Trafficking in Human Beings*, 29 November 2002, 14981/02

European Union, '2002/629/JHA: Council framework decision of 19 July 2002 on combating trafficking in human beings', *Official Journal of the European Communities*, L 203/1

European Union, '2002/946/JHA: Council framework decision of 28 November 2002 on the strengthening of the penal framework to prevent the facilitation of unauthorised entry, transit and residence', *Official Journal of the European Communities*, L 328/1

European Union, 'Council directive 2002/90/EC of 28 November 2002 defining the facilitation of unauthorised entry, transit and residence', *Official Journal of the European Communities*, L 328/17

European Union, 'Council framework decision of 19 July 2002 on combating trafficking in human beings', *Official Journal of European Communities*, L 203/1

2004 European Union, 'Council Directive 2004/80/EC of 29 April 2004 relating to compensation to crime victims', *Official Journal of the European Union*, L 261/15

2005 Commission of the European Communities, 'Communication from the commission to the European Parliament and the council: Fighting trafficking in human beings – An integrated approach and proposals for an action plan', Brussels, 18 October 2005, COM(2005) 514 final

Council of Europe, Council of Europe Convention on Action against Trafficking in Human Beings, 16 May 2005, CETS 197

2007 *Consolidated Version of the Treaty on the Future of the European Union*, 13 December 2007, 2008/C 115/01, Article 50(1) and (2)(g)

European Union, *Treaty of Lisbon Amending the Treaty on European Union and the Treaty Establishing the European Community*, 13 December 2007, 2007/C 306/01

2009 European Union, 'Directive 2009/52/EC of the European Parliament and of the council of 18 June 2009 providing for minimum standards on sanctions and measures against employers of illegally staying third-country nationals', *Official Journal of the European Union*, 30 June 2009

Opinion of the Group of Experts on Trafficking in Human Beings set up by the European Commission, On the Commission Proposal for a Council Framework Decision on preventing trafficking in human beings, and protecting victims, repealing Framework Decision 2002/629/JHA, COM (2009)

2010 European Commission, 'Proposal for a directive of the European Parliament and of the council on preventing and combating trafficking in human beings, and protecting victims, repealing Framework Decision 2002/629/JHA', Brussels, 29 March 2010, COM (2010)95 final, 2010/0065 (COD)

European Union, 'European Parliament resolution of 10 February 2010 on preventing trafficking in human beings', P7TA(2010)0018, www.europarl.europa.eu/doceo/document/TA-7-2010-0018_EN.html

2011 European Union, 'Directive 2011/36/EU of the European Parliament and of the Council of 5 April 2011 on preventing and combating trafficking in human beings and protecting its victims, and replacing Council Framework Decision 2002/629/JHA', *Official Journal of the European Union*, L 101/1, 1–11

2012 European Commission, 'Communication from the Commission to the European Parliament, the Council, the European Economic and Social Committee and the Committee of the Regions: The EU Strategy towards the Eradication of Trafficking in Human Beings, 2012–2016', Brussels, 19 June 2012, COM (2012) 286 final

European Union, 'Directive 2012/29/EU of the European Parliament and of the Council of 25 October 2012 establishing minimum standards on the rights, support, and protection of victims of crime, and replacing Council Framework Decision 2001/220/JHA', *Official Journal of the European Union*, L 315/57

2014 European Commission, 'Mid-term Report on the Implementation of the EU Strategy towards the Eradication of Trafficking in Human Beings', Brussels, 17 October 2014, COM (2014) 635 final

European Union, 'Directive 2014/95/EU of the European Parliament and of the council of 22 October 2014 amending Directive 2013/34/EU as regards disclosure of non-financial and diversity information by certain large undertakings and groups', *Official Journal of the European Union*, L 330/1

European Union, 'European Parliament resolution of 26 February 2014 on sexual exploitation and prostitution and its impact on gender equality', 2013/2103(INI)

2016 European Commission, 'Report from the commission to the European Parliament and the Council assessing the extent to which member states have taken the necessary measures in order to comply with directive 2011/36EU on preventing and combating trafficking in human beings and protecting its victims in accordance with Article 23 (1), Brussels, 2 December 2016, COM(2016) 722 final

European Commission, 'Report from the commission to the European Parliament and the council assessing the impact of existing national law, establishing as a criminal offence the use of services which are the objects of exploitation of trafficking in human beings, on the prevention of trafficking in human beings, in accordance with

Article 23 (2) of the Directive 2011/36/EU', Brussels, 2 December 2016, COM(2016) 719 final

European Commission, 'Report from the commission to the European Parliament and the council on the progress made in the fight against trafficking in human beings (2016) as required under Article 20 of Directive 2011/36EU on preventing and combating trafficking in human beings and protecting its victims', Brussels, 19 May 2016, COM(2016) 267 final, 4

European Union, 'European Parliament resolution of 5 July 2016 on the fight against trafficking in human beings in the EU's external relations (2015/2340(INI))', para. 12, (2018) O.J. (C 101) 47 (5 July 2016).

European Union, 'European Parliament resolution of 25 October 2016 on corporate liability for serious human rights abuses in third countries', 2015/2315(INI).

2017 European Commission, 'Communication from the commission to the European Parliament and the council, reporting on the follow-up to the EU strategy towards the eradication of trafficking inhuman beings and identifying further concrete actions', Brussels, 4 December 2017, COM(2017) 728 final

European Union, 'Regulation (EU) No 2017/821 of the European Parliament and of the council of 17 May 2017', *Official Journal of the European Union*, L 130/1.

2021 European Commission, 'Communication from the commission to the European Parliament, the council, the European Economic and Social Committee, and the Committee of the Regions, on the EU Strategy on Combatting Trafficking in Human Beings, 2021–2025', Brussels, 14 April 2021 COM(2021) 171 final

European Union, 'European Parliament resolution of 10 March 2021 with recommendations to the Commission on corporate due diligence and corporate accountability', Brussels, 10 March 2021, 2020/2129 (INL)

2022 European Commission, 'Commission staff working document: Executive summary of the impact assessment report,' accompanying the document, 'Proposal for a Directive of the European Parliament and of the Council amending Directive 2011/36/EU on preventing and combating trafficking in human,' Brussels, 19 December 2022, COM(2022) 732 final, SWD(2022) 425 final

European Commission, 'Proposal for a directive amending directive 2011/36/EU on preventing and combating trafficking in human beings and protecting its victims', Brussels, 19 December 2022, COM (2022) 732 final, 2022/0426 (COD)

European Commission, 'Proposal for a directive of the European Parliament and of the council on corporate sustainability due diligence and amending directive (EU) 2019/1937', Brussels, 23 February 2022, COM(2022) 71 final, 2002/0051 (COD)

European Commission, 'Proposal for a regulation of the European Parliament and of the council on prohibiting products made with forced labour on the Union market', Brussels, 14 September 2022. COM(2022) 453 final, 2022/0269 (COD)

Statutes

AUSTRALIA

Modern Slavery Act 2018 (No. 153, 2018)

FRANCE

Duty of Vigilance of Parent and on Its Affiliated Entities, Law No. 2017-399 (27 March 2017)

Loi no. 2017-399 du 27 Mars 2017 relative au devoir de vigilance des sociétés mères et des entreprises donneuses d'ordre

UNITED KINGDOM

Combination Act 1799, 39 Geo. III, c. 81

An Act for the Abolition of the Slave Trade, 47 Geo. III, sess. 1, c. 36 (Hansard, 10 February 1807)

Gang Act, 1867, 30 & 31 Vict., c. 130

Immigration Act 1971 (1971, c. 77)

Employment Agencies Act 1973 (1973, c. 35)

Human Rights Act 1998 (1998, c. 42)

National Minimum Wage Act 1998 (1998, c. 39)

Nationality, Immigration and Asylum Act 2002 (2002, c. 41)

Proceeds of Crime Act 2002 (2002, c. 29)

Sexual Offences Act 2003 (2003, c. 42)

Asylum and Immigration (Treatment of Claimants, etc.) Act 2004 (2004, c. 19)

The Gangmasters (Licensing) Act 2004 (2004, c. 11)

Identity Cards Act 2006 (2006, c. 15)
Immigration, Asylum and Nationalities Act 2006 (2006, c. 13)
Immigration (Restrictions on Employment) Order 2007 (2007, No. 3290)
The UK Borders Act 2007 (2007, c. 30)
Coroners and Justice Act 2009 (2009, c. 25)
Policing and Crime Act 2009 (2009, c. 26)
Bribery Act 2010 (2010, c. 23)
Immigration Act 2014 (2014, c. 22)
Modern Slavery Act 2015 (2015, c. 30)
Immigration Act 2016 (2016, c. 19)
National and Borders Act 2022 (2022, c. 36)
Illegal Migration Act 2023 (2023, c. 37)

UNITED STATES

Victims of Trafficking and Violence Protection Act of 2000, Pub. L. No. 106-385, 114 Stat. 1464 (2000) (codified and amended in scattered sections of 8, 18, 22 USC)

William Wilberforce Trafficking Victims Protection Reauthorization Act of 2008, Pub. L. No. 110-457 (2008), 22 USC 7101

California Transparency in Supply Chains Act of 2010, California Civil Code, sec. 171443

Dodd–Frank Wall Street and Consumer Protection Act of 2010, Pub. L. No. 111-203, 124 Stat. 1376 (2010), 12 USC 53

Strengthening Protection Against Trafficking in Persons in Federal Contracts, Executive Order 13627, 25 September 2012

Trade Facilitation and Trade Enforcement Act of 2015, Pub. L. No. 114-125, 19 USC 4301

Allow States and Victims to Fight Online Sex Trafficking Act of 2017, Pub. L. No. 115-164, 132 Stat. 1253, 18 USC 1 note, 47 USC 230 note

Frederick Douglass Trafficking Victims Prevention and Protection Reauthorization Act of 2018, Pub. L. No. 115-425, 132 Stat. 5472, 22 USC 7101 note

United States–Mexico–Canada Implementation Agreement, 13 March 2020, Pub. L. No. 116-113, 19 USC 29

Uyghur Forced Labor Prevention Act, 23 December 2021, Pub. L. No. 117-78, 135 Stat. 1525, 22 USC 6901

Jurisprudence

COUNCIL OF EUROPE

Chowdury and Others v. Greece, 21884/15, European Union: European Court of Human Rights, 30 March 2017

CN v. UK, 4239/08, Council of Europe: European Court of Human Rights, 13 November 2012

Rantsev v. Cyprus and Russia, 25965/04, Council of Europe: European Court of Human Rights, 7 January 2010

Siliadin v. France, 73316/01, Council of Europe: European Court of Human Rights, 26 July 2005

UNITED KINGDOM

CN v. UK (2013) 56 EHRR 24

K (Ghana) v. Secretary of the State for the Home Department [2018] EWCA Civ 98

UNITED STATES

Agency for International Development v. Alliance for Open Society International, Inc., 570 U.S. 205 (2013).

USAID v. Alliance for Open Society (or *Alliance for Open Society II*), 591 U.S. (2020)

Abbreviations

APPG	All-Party Parliamentary Group
ATMG	Anti-Trafficking Monitoring Group
CATW	Coalition Against Trafficking in Women
CEACR	Committee of Experts on the Application of Conventions and Recommendations
COP	Conference of Parties
CPS	Crown Prosecution Service
CSJ	Center for Social Justice
DEFRA	Department of Environment, Food and Rural Affairs
EFRA	Parliament Select Committee on Environment, Food and Rural Affairs
Eurofound	European Foundation for the Improvement of Living and Working Conditions
FAST	Finance Against Slavery and Trafficking
FRA	European Union Agency for Fundamental Rights
FRI	Fair Recruitment Initiative
GAATW	Global Alliance Against Traffic in Women
GB	Governing Body
GEMS	Global Estimates of Modern Slavery
GFEMS	Global Fund to End Modern Slavery
GLAA	Gangmasters Labour Abuse Authority
GLA	Gangmasters Licensing Authority
GRETA	Group of Experts on Action against Trafficking in Human Beings
GSI	Global Slavery Index
HMICFRS	Her Majesty's Inspectorate of Constabulary, Fire Rescue Services

HRDD	human rights due diligence
ICAT	Inter-Agency Coordination Group against Trafficking in Persons
IDMG	Inter-Departmental Ministerial Group
ILC	International Labour Conference
ILO	International Labour Organization
IOE	International Organization of Employers
IOM	International Organization for Migration
IPEC	International Programme on the Elimination of Child Labour
ITUC	International Trade Union Confederation
MNE	Tripartite Declaration of Principles Concerning Multinational Enterprises and Social Policy
MSA	Modern Slavery Act
NAO	National Audit Office
NCA	National Crime Agency
NRM	National Referral Mechanism
ODLME	Office of the Director of Labour Market Enforcement
ODW	Overseas Domestic Worker
OECD	Organisation for Economic Co-operation and Development
OHCHR	Office of the High Commissioner for Human Rights
SAP-FL	Special Action Programme to Combat Forced Labour
STRIP	Special Rapporteur on Trafficking in Persons
TFEU	Treaty on the Functioning of the European Union
TIP	trafficking in persons
TIP Office	Office to Monitor and Combat Trafficking in Persons
TVPA	Victims of Trafficking and Violence Protection Act
UKIP	United Kingdom Independence Party
UN.GIFT	UN Global Initiative Against Trafficking
UNGP	United Nations Guiding Principles on Business and Human Rights
UNHRC	UN Human Rights Council
UNICEF	United Nations International Children's Emergency Fund
UNODC	United Nations Office on Drugs and Crime

Introduction

No country in the world is exempt from modern slavery. Regardless of size, population or wealth, this insidious crime permeates national borders and global supply chains.

—Walk Free, *Measurement, Action, Freedom*

At base, the border is a line of jurisdiction – a legal topographical instantiation of authority.

—Longo, *The Politics of Borders*

Modern slavery is widely regarded as a global problem of epic proportions. According to the 2021 Global Estimates, on any given day, there are 50 million people in situations of modern slavery, of whom 27.6 million are in forced labour and 22 million are in forced marriage. Despite the growth of a large web of antislavery laws and key political actors' commitment to eradicating modern slavery, the number of slaves grew by 9.3 million people (about the population of Austria) between 2016 (the year the UN set a target to eliminate modern slavery by 2030) and 2021.[1] Putting these figures into historical perspective, George Ramos, chief of staff of the Organisation for Economic Co-operation and Development (OECD), claimed that in 2015 the number of modern slaves in the world was 'nearly four times the total number of Africans sold in the Americas during the four centuries of the transatlantic slave trade'.[2]

1 This increase could, in part, be attributed to the different methodology used in this installment of the estimates or to the social and economic disruption unleashed by the COVID-19 pandemic. ILO, Walk Free Foundation and IOM, *Global Estimates of Modern Slavery*, 2022, 1, 2, 12.

2 Ramos, 'Abolish modern slavery!'

These numbers are astonishing, and they help to explain why modern slavery has become a prominent issue on the global governance agenda.[3] Although there is a growing literature challenging these figures,[4] this book is not concerned with how many modern slaves there *really* are.[5] Instead, it focusses on law's role in constructing modern slavery as a global problem. Modern slavery is an amalgam of legal concepts (including chattel slavery, forced labour, and human trafficking for labour exploitation and prostitution) defined in international law.[6] What unites these concepts is a shared characteristic – they are all forms of unfree labour: one person deprives 'another person of their freedom for profit'.[7] This book explains how modern slavery's legal expression – how it is defined in law, and the legal domains and jurisdictions to which it is assigned – shapes what we 'see' when we see modern slavery and how we go about getting rid of it.

THE LEGAL CONSTRUCTION OF MODERN SLAVERY

This book provides a genealogy of modern slavery by tracing the evolution over time of its component legal concepts and how they came together under a single umbrella.[8] It grew out of my puzzlement with developments in the UK. When I moved there in 2013, I encountered a lively legal and political debate about how to define and combat modern slavery. In Canada, where

3 I am using 'governance' to refer to regulatory practices (by public and private actors) and their effects. My approach is compatible with Foucauldian concepts of sovereignty, discipline, and governmentality, although I am not using this terminology in this book. See Fudge, 'Bad for business' where I explicitly use Foucauldian concepts.

4 Phillips, 'The politics of numbers'; LeBaron, 'The coming and current crisis', 1; Kessler, 'The false claim that human trafficking is a "$9.5 billion business"'; Mügge, '40.3 million slaves?'; Gallagher, 'What's wrong with the Global Slavery Index?'; Brankovic, 'Measure of shame'; and Feingold, 'Trafficking in numbers'.

5 My adoption of a sociolegal constructivist (constitutive) approach does not mean that I think that labour exploitation and labour abuse are not real problems and that individuals are not harmed by a range of abusive practices. Indeed, they are real problems, and the need to address them is urgent. But labelling these practices as instances of modern slavery, this book argues, does not help to eradicate them.

6 International Labour Organization, ILO Forced Labour Convention, 1930 (No. 29), 28 June 1930; Slavery, Servitude, Forced Labour and Similar Institutions and Practices Convention of 1926 (Slavery Convention of 1926), in force 9 March 1927, 60 LNTS 253; and UN General Assembly, Protocol to Prevent, Suppress and Punish Trafficking in Persons, Especially Women and Children.

7 Walk Free, 'What is modern slavery?'.

8 For discussions of genealogy as a method see, Foucault, *Language, Counter-Memory, Practice*; Christodoulidis, 'Labour constitutionalism in a genealogical key'; Adams, *Labour and the wage*; and Somers, *Genealogies of Citizenship*.

I had been living and working, 'modern slavery' was used occasionally as a political rhetoric to vilify instances of exploitation. I was, however, familiar with the term 'unfree labour', used as an analytic concept for work relations in which direct physical, political, and legal compulsion is used to acquire and exploit labour.[9] In the UK, modern slavery became a quasi-legal concept with the enactment of the UK Modern Slavery Act, 2015. This act combines wide-ranging criminal prohibitions against human trafficking for sexual and labour exploitation with business regulations designed to create incentives for large transnational corporations to eliminate modern slavery in their businesses and supply chains.

I was curious about how modern slavery came to be the predominant legal lens for characterising unfree labour in the UK. I traced the origins of the UK's Modern Slavery Act to the UN's Protocol to Prevent, Suppress and Punish Trafficking in Persons Especially Women and Children against Trafficking in Persons, which was adopted in 2000 and came into effect in 2003. I turned to legal scholarship to identify the provenance of the legal concepts (such as human trafficking and forced labour) that comprise modern slavery. Doctrinal scholarship is concerned with identifying the key elements of different legal concepts – their history, interpretation, and application.[10] Legal scholars debate the 'best' interpretation of these concepts and how they fit together. Some claim that it is critical to place each concept in its appropriate legal domain because the legal context will influence the concept's meaning and legal strategies.[11] For example, some legal researchers argue that freedom from human trafficking should be treated as a human right, not simply a criminal prohibition.[12]

Although doctrinal legal scholarship is essential for identifying the origins of modern slavery's legal components and technicalities, it can't explain why a specific definition was crafted or why it was lodged in one legal domain instead of another. To answer these questions, we must move from legal analysis to study the social world.

In the fields of political science, sociolegal studies, and sociology, scholars have shown that how the problem of modern slavery is framed influences the different legal domains (criminal, human rights, immigration, or labour law)

[9] Fudge, '(Re)conceptualising unfree labour'.
[10] Allain, 'The legal definition of slavery'; Costello, 'Migrants and forced labour'; Stoyanova, *Human Trafficking and Slavery Reconsidered*; Paz-Fuchs, 'Badges of modern slavery'; and Jovanovic, 'The essence of slavery'.
[11] Krieg, 'Trafficking in human beings', 775; Fitzpatrick, 'Trafficking and a human rights violation'; and Huckerby, 'Same, but different'.
[12] Jovanovic, *State Responsibility for Modern Slavery in Human Rights Law*.

selected to address it.[13] Frames are the mental structures we use to make sense of the world. They are the (often unconscious) constructs that shape the way we see the world; they tell us how different pieces of information connect, what is right and wrong, and how to make sense of this information and suggest solutions to correct perceived wrongs.[14]

To understand how frames work, consider the sale of sexual services (prostitution) and human trafficking for sexual exploitation. For many people, the exchange of sexual services for money is an anathema; it is an essentially exploitative activity that undermines human dignity. Under this frame, the purchase and sale of sexual services should be banned by criminal law. But for other people, the gendered nature of commercial sexual services – the fact that most sellers are women and most purchasers men – reflects the sexual objectification and subordination of women. This 'women's equality' frame treats prostitution as a form of violence against women, and the solution is to prohibit the purchase of sexual services. According to both these frames, prostitution is exploitation, and exploitation is a key element of the international definition of human trafficking. By contrast, some people (including many feminists) see the sale of sexual services as a livelihood strategy in the context of constrained choices; for this reason, the sale of sexual services should be regulated by labour law to prevent exploitation.

Laden with assumptions and meanings, frames are devices that help us select and categorise information and imbue it with moral significance. Thus, the literature on how societies frame modern slavery is critical for understanding how different forms of exploitation are conceptualised within public policy and how this influences what is considered to be the appropriate legal response. This literature is also useful for unpacking the social, economic, and political relations that result in specific legal strategies.

There is also a lively debate about the political work that the concept of 'modern slavery' performs. Annie Bunting and Joel Quirk argue that it harnesses the moral outrage once associated with the transatlantic slave trade and directs it at 'an unstable amalgamation of a wide range of diverse practices that go well beyond both legal definition and historical experiences of slavery'.[15] Researchers have shown that antislavery rhetoric is a 'powerful lodestone' for competing interests that potentially align with other ideological, political, and

[13] Edwards, 'Traffic in human beings'; Chuang, 'Exploitation creep'; Krieg, 'Trafficking in human beings'; Charnysh, Lloyd, and Simmons, 'Frames and consensus formation'; and Kotiswaran 'From sex panic to extreme exploitation'.

[14] Kenway, *The Truth about Modern Slavery*, 2. Frame analysis is a method of discourse analysis concerned with dissecting how an issue is defined and problematized.

[15] Bunting and Quirk, 'Contemporary slavery as more than rhetorical strategy?', 6.

economic agendas.[16] Antislavery rhetoric has been used to support a conservative moral approach to commercial sex, stronger border and immigration controls, and a national security agenda that emphasises borders and policing.[17]

Others point out that 'modern slavery' has been used to focus attention on labour exploitation and to support forms of labour regulation.[18] Some researchers dig deeper to investigate the 'traditions of thought, conceptual schema, and collective memories' that frame the very idea of modern slavery.[19] They question whether the term 'modern slavery' should be used at all. Lyndsey Beutin, for example, argues that the concept's rhetoric and imagery functions as a racial mnemonic 'to circumvent historical Western responsibility for racial chattel slavery'.[20]

I draw on the critical modern slavery literature to place key legal concepts in their cultural, political, and economic context and to trace their use and evolution over time. I bring the legal and social-political literature into conversation to show how social and political context shapes legal meaning and how legal concepts and technicalities, in turn, shape how we see our world. Since the relationship between the social and the legal is recursive and co-evolving, this dual approach is necessary for understanding why antislavery laws and policies have risen on the political agenda and the broader governance work they do.

'Modern slavery' covers a wide range of different kinds of exploitation, including sex trafficking, child sex trafficking, forced labour, forced marriage, the compelled sale of organs and body parts, debt bondage, domestic servitude, forced child labour, and the unlawful recruitment and use of child labour. I focus on a subset of modern slavery – forms of unfree labour associated with international labour migration and transnational supply chains – for two reasons. To offer insight into the relationship between unfree labour and capitalism, on the one hand, and to explore how sovereignty is being reconfigured, on the other.

16 Quirk, 'When human trafficking means everything and nothing', 85–86.

17 Broad and Turnbull, 'From human trafficking to modern slavery'; Broad and Gadd, *Demystifying Modern Slavery*; Kenway, *The Truth about Modern Slavery*; Chuang, 'Rescuing trafficking from ideological capture'; Doezema, 'Loose women or lost women?'; Andrijasevic, *Migration, Agency and Citizenship*; Beutin, *Trafficking in Antiblackness*; Brace and O'Connell-Davidson, 'Slavery and the revival of antislavery activism'; Fukushima, *Migrant Crossings*; Lobasz, *Constructing Human Trafficking*; and O'Connell-Davidson, *Modern Slavery*.

18 Feasely, 'Eliminating corporate exploitation'.

19 O'Connell-Davidson, *Modern Slavery*, 3.

20 Beutin, *Trafficking in Antiblackness*, 7.

UNFREE LABOUR AND TRANSNATIONAL LAW

The discovery of modern slavery as a global problem both coincided with and reinvigorated debates about how to conceptualise unfree labour in relation to capitalism. Historically associated with precapitalist forms of economic organisation, unfree forms of labour (such as chattel slavery, indenture, debt bondage, and servitude) were regarded as the antithesis of free wage labour.[21] According to prevailing economic wisdom, unfree labour was supposed to disappear as capitalism deepened and expanded. Recently, however, unfree forms of labour have attracted increasing attention as neoliberal policy regimes, which promote labour flexibility and see the market as the key governance mechanism, have become embedded across the globe.[22] The persistence and proliferation of unfree forms of labour across developed, emerging, and developing countries has been linked to different aspects of contemporary globalisation – dispossession through war, ecological degradation, structural adjustment policies, transnational criminal activity, international migration, neoliberal capitalism, and state corruption and the breakdown of the rule of law.[23] By investigating attempts to address forms of unfree labour linked to international migration and global supply chains, I reveal the extent to which antislavery initiatives are linked to the fading legitimacy of contemporary neoliberal capitalism.[24]

Modern slavery involving migrant workers and supply chains is a transnational problem because it crosses national borders. But nation-states lack the legal authority – the jurisdiction – to deal with it. International law supports national sovereignty and frames it in territorial terms.[25] A state has jurisdiction, the authority to exercise legal power, over its territory.[26] Initiatives to combat unfree labour linked to transnational processes do not fit with territorial understandings of jurisdiction tied to the territory of the nation-state.

[21] LeBaron, 'Unfree labour beyond binaries'.

[22] Rittich, 'Making natural markets'.

[23] Bales, *Disposable People*; Morgan and Olsen, 'Forced and unfree labour'; Peksen, Blanton, and Blanton, 'Neoliberal policies and human trafficking for labor'; Mezzadri, *The Sweatshop Regime*; Fraser, 'From exploitation to expropriation'; Gordon, 'Capitalism, neoliberalism, and unfree labour'; and Phillips, 'Unfree labour and adverse incorporation', 171–196.

[24] Neoliberalism is an economic, political, and social project that is committed to the expansion of the market as the logic of social ordering. It promotes profitability and accumulation as *the* measures of economic and social activities, which are encouraged through a core set of policies, including liberalisation, deregulation, privatisation, recommodification, and globalisation. Harvey, *A Brief History of Neoliberalism*; Jessop, 'Neoliberalization, uneven development, and Brexit', 1729–1733; and Davies, *The Limits of Neoliberalism*.

[25] Ryngaert, *Jurisdiction in International Law*.

[26] Ford, 'Law's territory (A history of jurisdiction)'.

Consequently, a thick web of international, regional, national, and local legal instruments, policies, techniques, and practices has been fabricated to eradicate the 'global' problem of modern slavery.[27] An antislavery network composed of key states, advocacy groups, nongovernmental organisations, faith groups, trade unions, transnational corporations and their charitable foundations, and national, international, and supranational institutions and organisations grew alongside it. This network advocates using a wide variety of legal approaches and instruments to tackle modern slavery, including criminal, immigration, human rights, labour, and business law.[28]

In this context, the nation-state, which used to be the primary actor, is now but one among an assemblage of actors, what I call the 'global antislavery governance network'. Terrance Halliday and Gregory Shaffer's processual conception of transnational law is useful for understanding this multiscalar network and the web of antislavery laws it has generated. Their approach places 'processes of local, national, international, and transnational public and private lawmaking and practice in dynamic tension within a single analytic'.[29] In doing so, it offers a way to distinguish law from other forms of social ordering by emphasising law's distinctive institutions (courts, legislatures, agencies, tribunals, and executive departments) and forms (statutes, regulations, codes, case law, treaties, model laws, and court decisions) and its alignment with state and juridical-sovereign power.[30] Halliday and Shaffer's approach also captures the multiscalar dimension of transnational law since the institutions and organisations involved in its production must 'transcend or span' the nation-state, even though the approach recognises that these laws are generally directed at the nation-state since national sovereignty continues to be accepted as the predominant form of legitimate authority.

Modern slavery laws exemplify transnational law since they combine international, national, and sometimes regional laws.[31] To make sense of this tangle, I provide case studies of what can be called 'transnational modern slavery law'.[32] I selected five cases because they involve the international laws upon which the concept of modern slavery is based, they include key actors in the global antislavery governance network, they illustrate the scalar interaction

[27] Gómez-Mera, 'The global governance of trafficking in persons'; and Kotiswaran, 'From sex panic to extreme exploitation'.

[28] Gómez-Mera, 'The global governance of trafficking in persons', 303.

[29] Halliday and Shaffer, 'Transnational legal orders', 8.

[30] Ibid., 15–20.

[31] Kotiswaran, 'From sex panic to extreme exploitation'.

[32] For a comprehensive discusson of transnational labour law, including modern slavery, see Blackett and Trebilcock, *Research Handbook on Transnational Labour Law*.

of transnational law, and they exemplify different approaches to combatting modern slavery.

Three chapters focus on the international scale. Chapter 1 describes how the UN and United States developed an international criminal-law instrument to define human trafficking, subsequent attempts by US administrations to pin down the meaning of human trafficking, and the development of a multifaceted approach to the problem. Chapter 2 examines how Walk Free, a private foundation, has become a key global governance actor by producing knowledge about modern slavery and promoting business-led forms of governance to eliminate it from global supply chains. Chapter 3 investigates how the International Labour Organization (ILO) used its jurisdiction over forced labour to stake a claim in the global antitrafficking assemblage and to steer global antislavery policy away from criminal and immigration law towards labour and human rights. Shifting from the international scale, Chapter 4 studies the European Union (EU), a site of multiscalar governance that has led the way in adopting binding, region-wide legal norms to address human trafficking. These norms augment the human rights of victims and fill the gap surrounding victim protection left in the UN's Human Trafficking Protocol.

Chapters 5 and 6 focus on the United Kingdom to provide an in-depth account of how antislavery governance strategies involving transnational forms of unfree labour have changed over time at the national scale. Although international and transnational legal instruments define the main legal categories of unfree labour, nation-states must implement them and give them meaning. As antitrafficking scholar Kiril Sharapov notes, 'The role of national framing contexts and of larger frameworks of neoliberal movements of labour, resources, and capital globally remain largely unacknowledged within official antitrafficking discourses.'[33] As this book shows, how a country filters international norms and approaches through its distinctive cultural political economy shapes its governance strategy.[34] I focus on the UK for several reasons: it was the first country to enact a modern slavery law that combined criminal law with business regulation; as a member of the EU until early 2020, it was embedded in a multiscalar legal regime governing human trafficking; and it is a prominent member of the global antislavery governance network.

33 Sharapov, 'Giving us the "biggest bang for the buck"', 23.

34 Cultural political economy is an analytical approach that tries to synthesize contributions from critical political economy and the critical analysis of discourse with the field of policy studies. It highlights the relevance of the cultural dimension (understood as meaning making) in the interpretation and explanation of policies. See Sum and Jessop, *Towards a Cultural Political Economy*; and Paul, *The Political Economy of Border Drawing*.

JURISDICTION MATTERS

When it comes to transnational law and modern slavery, jurisdiction matters. 'Jurisdiction' in this context is not simply a technical question concerned with whether a particular sovereign state or judicial or quasi-judicial body can exercise legal authority over a territory, dispute, person, or issue.[35] Rather, the transnational legal governance of modern slavery demands a multidimensional understanding of jurisdiction. The scalar dimension of jurisdiction is the most familiar. Take federal states, for example, where jurisdiction operates to determine which level of government has authority over a particular matter. The treaties that make up the EU also allocate competences (governance authority) on a scalar basis between EU institutions and Member States. But 'jurisdiction' has another important meaning: it refers to the power of the law to act and the scope of a legal institution's authority in relation to other institutions.[36] This is the governance dimension of jurisdiction. By combining the governance and scalar dimensions of jurisdiction, Marianna Valverde treats jurisdiction as a complex legal assemblage that operates as a kind of sorting mechanism that allocates a problem – a particular form of unfree labour, for example – to an authority for resolution.[37] Jurisdiction establishes which state has legal authority over a particular issue, whether the delegation of authority to other systems and apparatuses is lawful or unlawful, and which of the different subsystems or domains within a legal system and its institutions (a criminal court, or human-rights tribunal, for example) has authority over a specific matter.[38]

Modern legal systems are a quilt of different legal domains, such as criminal law, commercial law, and constitutional law. Each legal domain involves assumptions about the nature and causes of a problem and the goals, strategies, and techniques for governing it, including burden of proof, remedies, operatives, and forms and processes of adjudication and dispute resolution.[39] By assigning a subject to one of the legal domains that makes up a legal system, jurisdiction settles the political question of how a problem is to be resolved. If, for example, human trafficking is seen primarily as a problem of

[35] Pahuja, 'Laws of encounter', 63; and Chimni, 'The international law of jurisdiction', 31–32.

[36] Richland, 'Jurisdiction'; Strauss, 'Sorting victims from workers'; Dorsett and McVeigh, *Jurisdiction*; and Kaushal, 'The politics of jurisdiction', 762.

[37] Valverde, 'Jurisdiction and scale'.

[38] Pratt and Templeman, 'Jurisdiction, sovereignties and Akwesasne', 338; and Valverde, *Chronotopes of Law*, 83.

[39] Shamir, 'A labor paradigm'; Thomas, 'Convergences and divergences in international legal norms'; and Fudge, 'Migrant domestic workers in British Columbia, Canada'.

criminal activity, then the criminal-law jurisdiction is set in motion. Criminal law is replete with its own focus (the guilt or innocence of the perpetrator), principles (innocent until proven guilty), precepts (proof beyond reasonable doubt), technicalities (rules of evidence), and officials (police, prosecutors, and courts) with a range of powers (search, arrest, confiscation of assets). By contrast, if human trafficking is regarded primarily as a matter of human rights, the institutional goals and practices of that legal domain are quite different from those of the criminal law. The goal of human-rights law is to safeguard the rights of victims of trafficking from infringement by state policies and practices. The prevailing principle or legal norm is to preserve human dignity, and states are required to develop mechanisms to identify victims and offer them redress. The relevant institutions are human-rights agencies and tribunals that exercise administrative powers. The legal assemblage of jurisdiction operates as a sorting mechanism that allocates a problem – a particular form of unfree labour, for example – to an authority for resolution and keeps the different domains from clashing.[40]

The assignment of jurisdiction over a social problem means that questions about the nature of the problem or how best to deal with it are no longer relevant.[41] Once human trafficking is assigned to the criminal law, the political contest over the goals and techniques of governance is transformed into an 'apolitical' process of sorting subjects into legal categories such as 'victim of trafficking' or 'smuggled migrant'. Ascertaining the appropriate jurisdiction becomes habitual and path-dependent; in the process, jurisdictional questions are classified as simply 'technical'. Legal officials draw the borders between different legal categories such as 'victims of trafficking' and 'illegal migrant', and, in turn, these categories come to be seen by ordinary people as common sense and, as such, come to be used to describe the people to whom the legal categories apply.[42] In this way, legal categories help to construct what we see as unfree labour.

Jurisdiction also resolves scalar questions about which institution – international, transnational, nation-state, or subcomponent of a nation-state – has authority. The scalar dimension of jurisdiction can also operate as a technique of governance: one that challenges territorial notions of national sovereignty. Increasingly, states must negotiate with various other agents (such as local governments, international institutions, and transnational corporations that

[40] Valverde, 'Jurisdiction and scale', 139–157; and Valverde, 'Analyzing the governance of security', 6.

[41] Richland, 'Jurisdiction', 214.

[42] Berman, 'From international law to law and globalization', 494.

wield power) and other sources of law to retain or exercise sovereignty. This partial detachment of authority from territory – or deterritorialisation – requires private actors to enforce border and immigration control.[43] Saskia Sassen points to trade and investment treaties as a 'new type of bordering' that allow 'firms and markets to move across conventional borders with the guarantee of multiple protections as they enter national territories'.[44] What international trade and investment law does is allow firms to rescale, to shift from national to international law, to enforce contracts. But nations have no similar recourse should contractual terms end up harming workers or being unfavourable to the socioeconomic interests of their citizens.[45] States in the Global North have begun to respond to this jurisdictional conundrum by enacting laws that require large transnational corporations to exercise due diligence to keep their global supply chains free of modern slavery. In this way, states use corporations residing in their territorial jurisdiction to extend legal norms beyond their territory. This rescaling is part of the game of jurisdiction, in which states, the EU, and corporations seek to manipulate the law to their advantage.[46] Approaching scale in this way helps to illuminate how processes of globalisation reconfigure rather than simply weaken state sovereignty.[47]

Understanding jurisdiction as an assemblage enables us to see how jurisdiction can be 'unbound' from territory.[48] One implication of states using transnational corporations as a 'territorial extension' of their jurisdiction is, as Nico Krisch notes, the possiblity for multiple states to have valid claims to have

43 Borders are epistemological devices of inclusion that filter, sort, and channel the movement of people and, by doing so, construct and maintain social and political order. Not only state officials but a host of 'private' actors engage in constructing, maintaining, and reinforcing borders that extend both within and outside the territorial frontiers of the nation state. Mezzadra and Neilson, *Border as Method*; Balibar, *Politics and the Other Scene*; Dehm, 'Framing international migration'; Van Houtum, 'The geopolitics of borders and boundaries'; Paul, *The Political Economy of Border Drawing*; Nail, *Theory of the Border*; Longo, *The Politics of Borders*; Yuval-Davis, Wemyss, and Cassidy, *Bordering*; and Vaughan-Williams, 'Borders, territory, law.'

44 Sassen, 'When territory deborders territoriality', 39. The distinction between 'territory', which is a spatial concept, and 'territoriality', which is a legal construct, is critical. Although sovereignty and jurisdiction have come to be linked to territory, territoriality, as Hannah Buxbaum claims, is constructed 'within individual legal regimes, and must be understood as contingent upon the specific legal and institutional frameworks in which they are embedded'. Buxbaum, 'Territory, territoriality, and the resolution', 635.

45 Alessandrini, 'Global value chains, development and the *long durée*'.

46 Valverde, 'Jurisdiction and scale', 145; Iossa and Persdotter, 'Cross-border social dumping as a "game of jurisdiction"'.

47 Legg, 'Of scales, networks and assemblages', 2; Legg, *Prostitution and the Ends of Empire*; and Mezzadra and Neilson, *Border as Method*, 188.

48 Krisch, 'Jurisdiction unbound,' 481.

jurisdiction over an issue without an established legal method for resolving which should prevail.[49] In such cases, the exercise of jurisdiction 'depends above all on states' political, institutional weight', exacerbating power inequalities that were forged as capitalism advanced along with European imperialism.[50] The result is that the jurisdictional claims of some states matter more than others.

QUESTIONS AND APPROACH

This book argues that modern slavery laws are a response to global capitalism, which undermines the traditional understandings of the distinction between free and unfree labour and poses intense challenges to state sovereignty. Instead of being a solution to the problem of labour exploitation, modern slavery laws divert attention from the underlying structures and processes that generate exploitation in the first place. Despite the best efforts of academics, advocates, and policymakers to develop a truly multifaceted approach to modern slavery, it is difficult to dislodge modern slavery initiatives from the domains of criminal and immigration law and uncouple them from the conservative moral and economic agendas with which antislavery initiatives are aligned. The problem with the concept of modern slavery, as Julia O'Connell-Davidson shows, is that it provides a 'highly selective lens through which to view restraints on human freedom'.[51]

How did modern slavery emerge on the global political agenda? Where do key actors in the global antislavery network draw the boundary between free and unfree labour? How does the multifaceted approach to modern slavery keep the different legal domains to which unfree labour is assigned from clashing? How do attempts to govern transnational forms of unfree labour reconfigure sovereignty? The book answers these questions by crafting a genealogy of modern slavery based on secondary sources, primary legal and policy documents, government documents, media accounts, grey literature, advocacy material, websites, and key informant interviews. Its case studies cover a period of just over twenty-five years, from the late 1990s, when human trafficking was identified as a global problem requiring international action, to September 2023. I conclude by summarising the book's main arguments and considering the vexed problem: What makes labour free?

[49] Ibid., 498.
[50] Ibid., 512; and Chimni, 'The international law of jurisdiction', 29.
[51] O'Connell-Davidson, *Modern Slavery*, 2.

1

From White Slavery to Human Trafficking

Each year an estimated 800,00 to 900,000 human beings are bought, sold, or forced across the world's borders ... There's a special evil in the abuse and exploitation of the most innocent and vulnerable. The victims of sex trade see little of life before they see the very worst of life – an underground of brutality and lonely fear. Those who create these victims and profit from their suffering must be severely punished. Those who patronize this industry debase themselves and deepen the misery of others. And governments that tolerate this trade are tolerating a form of slavery.

—George W. Bush, Address to the UN, 2003

All bordering processes are a combination of ordering and othering.

—Nira Yuval-Davis, Georgie Wemyss, and Kathryn Cassidy, *Bordering*

In his February 2019 State of the Union Address to Congress, US president Donald Trump warned that 'human traffickers and sex traffickers take advantage of the wide-open areas between our ports of entry to smuggle thousands of young girls and women into the United States and to sell them into prostitution and modern-day slavery'.[1] Throughout his presidency, Trump repeatedly linked human trafficking to the need to strengthen the US border with Mexico. This trope of criminal gangs transporting vulnerable women and children across borders to prostitute them has been an enduring feature of human-trafficking discourse since the turn of the twentieth century when the first international treaties were adopted to end the 'white slave trade'.[2]

Historically, antitrafficking campaigns reflected anxieties over women's mobility and coincided with intense periods of globalisation.[3] 'White slavery' and

[1] Trump, 'State of the Union Address'.
[2] Legg, 'The life of individuals', 647–664.
[3] Day, 'The re-emergence of "trafficking"', 822.

'trafficking' functioned, as many historians have shown, as moral panics. During these panics, states gave immigration bureaus and police the power to patrol borders and surveil the marginalised, and often racialised, women who were labelled as 'prostitutes' and 'victims' of men who were called 'traffickers' and 'pimps'.[4] Then, as now, white slavery and human trafficking functioned as cultural myths that constructed particular conceptions of migration and expressed anxieties about 'national identity, women's increasing desire for autonomy, foreigners, immigrants, and colonial peoples'.[5] Stereotypes about race, gender, sexuality, and mobility are enduring features of antitrafficking policies. But today the fear no longer is of 'white' European women being trafficked to the colonies; now, the concern is of 'non-Western' women being transported into 'Western' countries.[6]

This shift occurred in the early 1990s when many states believed the political instability caused by the collapse of the Soviet Union, economic liberalisation, and globalisation was fuelling transnational criminal networks engaged in trafficking in drugs, people, and weapons, and associated crimes such as money laundering, corruption, and possibly even terrorist financing.[7] Destination countries in Europe, North America, and Australia were also apprehensive that illegal migration and migrant smuggling were undermining national sovereignty.[8] Globalisation and mass mobility fuelled fears over border insecurity.

In 1994, when the UN discussed the need for an international convention to foster interstate cooperation to combat organised crime, the United States promoted the idea of a separate protocol dedicated to human trafficking.[9] In 2000, the United Nations General Assembly adopted the Convention against Transnational Organized Crime, which was supplemented by three specific optional protocols devoted to firearms, migrant smuggling, and human trafficking, respectively. These international criminal-law instruments were intended to address the 'dark side' of globalisation, which one UN official described as the 'unrelenting growth of cross-border illegal activities ... that threaten the institutions of the State and civil society in many countries'.[10]

4 Hetherington and Laite, 'Introduction to the issue of trafficking', 18.
5 Doezema, 'Loose women or lost women?', 24.
6 Ibid., and Fukushima, *Migrant Crossings*, 40.
7 Thachuk, *Transnational Threats.*
8 Gallagher, *The International Law of Human Trafficking*; and Lloyd and Simmons, 'Framing for a new transnational legal order', 400–438.
9 Charnysh, Lloyd, and Simmons, 'Frames and consensus formation', 323–351.
10 Heine and Thakar, *The Dark Side of Globalization.* Sandro Calvani was the UN representative in East Asia and the Pacific for drug control and crime prevention, based in Bangkok.

The Protocol to Prevent, Suppress and Punish Trafficking in Persons, especially Women and Children (the Trafficking Protocol) is the linchpin of what has become the global campaign to end modern slavery. In 2016, the UN made this campaign official when it adopted the eradication of forced labour, human trafficking, and modern slavery by 2030 Target 8.7 of its Sustainable Development Goals. Over the past twenty years, human-trafficking policy has expanded from an initial state-centred focus on using the criminal law to prosecute traffickers who transport women and children across international borders for the purpose of sexual exploitation to a multifaceted and transnational ensemble of private and public actors united by the goal of eradicating modern slavery. This global antislavery network deploys a range of governance strategies from criminal laws prohibiting the purchase of sexual services and strict border controls to supply-chain transparency and due-diligence legislation requiring large corporations to engage in social responsibility initiatives (such as reporting, social auditing, and remediation) to trade rules banning the importation of slave-made goods.

How did this governance shift happen, and what are its implications for how we understand unfree labour? To answer these questions, this chapter explores how influential public actors, especially key states such as the United States and prominent international organisations associated with the UN, framed and sought a legal solution to the problem of human trafficking at the international level. As we shall see, to accommodate sharp disagreements over the meaning of human trafficking and to facilitate the protocol's speedy adoption, the UN's definition was broad. This manoeuvre accommodated, but did not resolve, social contestation over the meaning of 'human trafficking.' The legal instability that resulted generated a policy spiral and the proliferation of governance strategies.[11]

The United States stepped in to stabilise the definition of human trafficking and steer antitrafficking policy. It constructed an apparatus to discipline states that did not follow its lead to stop transnational sexual exploitation. UN-related institutions responded by insisting on an approach to human trafficking that included labour exploitation and offered greater protection for the rights of victims. The governance strategies for tackling different types of human trafficking were deeply gendered. Sexual exploitation was seen as primarily involving women and girls, and the key issue was whether the purchase of sexual services should be abolished using criminal law. Labour exploitation, by contrast, was seen as involving mostly men, and the goal was to regulate and improve, not to abolish, this labour.

[11] Broad and Turnbull, 'From human trafficking to modern slavery', 121.

Policy actors and stakeholders endorsed what has come to be known as a multifaceted or 'holistic' approach to human trafficking and modern slavery. This approach emphasises the alignment of different legal domains – criminal, immigration, labour, human rights, business regulation, and trade – to address different aspects of the problem of modern slavery.[12] Under this approach, different agencies and actors draw on their expertise and governance tools to tackle different aspects of the problem. Combined, they draw the borders between free and unfree labour and between sexual and labour exploitation while the legal assemblage of jurisdiction keeps these different domains from clashing .

TRAFFICKING IN HUMAN BEINGS: CRIME, PROSTITUTION, AND MIGRATION

The collapse of the Soviet Union in the early 1990s triggered fears that organised crime was threatening national security by undermining governance and territorial integrity.[13] Increasing economic integration across borders through trade liberalisation, structural adjustment policies in developing countries, and a seemingly insatiable demand for low-wage labour in developed and developing countries also fuelled the movement of people internationally. Legal and illicit cross-border flows of goods, money, and people increased, and states associated much of this cross-border movement with organised crime, which they viewed as a threat to local economies and the rule of law.[14]

Sensational media reports of women and children trafficked into prostitution by criminal gangs circulated widely in the mid-1990s.[15] Developed states, especially the United States and in the European Union, linked human trafficking to other crimes, treating it as part of a broader problem of combatting transnational crime and criminal networks.[16] Tackling the problem of human trafficking also coincided with destination countries' concern to stop irregular migrants from crossing their borders.[17]

[12] Edwards, 'Traffic in human beings', 9–53; and Gallagher, *The International Law of Human Trafficking*.

[13] Charnysh, Lloyd, and Simmons, 'Frames and consensus formation', 326.

[14] Shelley, *Human Trafficking*; and Anderson, *Us and Them?*, 139.

[15] Andrijasevic, 'Beautiful dead bodies', 24–44; and Sanford, Martínez, and Weitzer, 'Framing human trafficking', 142.

[16] Lloyd and Simmons, 'Framing for a new transnational legal order', 400–438.

[17] Dottridge, 'Trafficked and exploited', 63.

In 1994, the UN responded to these fears by convening a World Ministerial Conference on Organized Transnational Crime. Attended by 142 countries, it led to the establishment of a group of experts with a mandate to draft a multilateral convention to promote cooperation in combatting transnational crime.[18] Optional protocols devoted to firearms, migrant smuggling, and human trafficking, respectively, augmented the transnational crime convention. The United States, which was considered a major destination country, strongly influenced the process. The international expert group operated out of the United Nations Office on Drugs and Crime (UNODC), and it, along with the Clinton administration, developed and promoted a prosecutorial and criminal-law approach to resolving the problem of human trafficking.[19]

The Clinton administration's emphasis on putting a stop to the trafficking of women and children as part of the government's violence against women agenda overshadowed its recognition that trafficking also included sweatshop labour and domestic servitude.[20] This legal and policy frame shaped the approach of the intergovernmental Ad Hoc Committee, which was charged with drafting the protocol. It resonated with existing international antitrafficking treaties and fit within the established transnational crime-policy domain. It also made human trafficking easy to 'securitize', and it could be used to justify stronger law enforcement and border regimes.[21]

The 2000 Human Trafficking Protocol was a palimpsest; a series of international treaties adopted at the turn of the twentieth century formed the gendered and racialised canvas upon which it was drawn.[22] Beginning in 1904, a handful of mostly northern European countries proposed a series of international conventions to address the problem of 'white slavery'. The spark was a panic focused on European women procured to work as prostitutes in the colonies, which erupted in the context of ongoing moral and public health crusades to stop prostitution.[23] These international laws were informed by a highly gendered notion of moral purity and a view of migration as a corrupting influence. The term 'white slavery', with its racialised

[18] Charnysh, Lloyd, and Simmons, 'Frames and consensus formation', 327.

[19] Chuang, 'The United States as global sheriff', 442; Gallagher, *The International Law of Human Trafficking*, 56–59; and Lloyd and Simmons, 'Framing for a new transnational legal order', 422.

[20] Lobasz, *Constructing Human Trafficking*, 71.

[21] Charnysh, Lloyd, and Simmons, 'Frames and consensus formation', 345. After 9-11, border security became even more important.

[22] Miller and Zivkovic, 'Orwellian rights', 33.

[23] Quirk, *The Anti-Slavery Project*, 222; and Legg, 'The life of individuals', 647–664.

connotations, was dropped in 1921 by the League of Nations when it adopted the International Convention for the Suppression of the Traffic in Women and Children.[24] The idea behind the 1921 convention was to use the criminal law to reduce the supply of trafficked women and girls by making trafficking a criminal offence and to 'rescue' them from a life of prostitution. It was only in 1949, when the UN adopted the Convention for the Suppression of the Traffic in Persons and of the Exploitation of the Prostitution of Others, that men were treated along with women and children as potential victims.[25] At the same time, this convention also removed the transnational dimension and criminalised all forms of procurement and exploitation for the purposes of prostitution regardless of the consent of the person involved.

The legacy of these early antitrafficking conventions on the 2000 protocol is easy to see; all are lodged in the domain of international criminal law and animated by concerns about prostitution and migration. Anxieties over women's sexuality and mobility were once again tied up with notions of national identity and sovereignty. But what distinguished the twenty-first-century protocol from its forebearers was its alignment of criminal law with women's rights and its emphasis on human rights.

Influential women's rights organisations that advocated using the criminal law to tackle sexual violence and protect women's rights were instrumental in forging the connections between sex trafficking, violence against women, and human rights in international law in the early 1990s.[26] The 1993 Vienna Declaration and Programme of Action was the first UN document to set sex trafficking within the broader frame of violence against women.[27] Two years later, eliminating trafficking in women and assisting victims of violence were planks in the UN's Fourth World Congress on Women's Action Platform in Beijing.[28] These initiatives helped to elevate human trafficking on the global policy agenda and to equate its elimination with women's rights. However,

[24] International Convention for the Suppression of the Traffic in Women and Children, adopted on 30 December 1921, 9 LNTS 415.

[25] Legg, 'The life of individuals', 647–664; Edwards, 'Traffic in human beings', 13; and Allain, 'White slave traffic', 12–13. Under the 1933 convention, the element of coercion was removed. See International Convention for the Suppression of the Traffic in Women of Full Age, Geneva, 11 October 1933, in force 24 August 1934, 150 LNTS 431; International Convention for the Suppression of the Traffic in Persons and the Exploitation of the Prostitution of Others, 2 December 1949, in force on 25 July 1951, 96 UNTS 271.

[26] In 'Militarized humanitarianism meets carceral feminism', Elizabeth Bernstein dubs women's rights' advocates who took this approach 'carceral feminists'.

[27] UN General Assembly, Vienna Declaration and Programme of Action, 12 July 1993, A/CONF.157/23.

[28] Suchland, *Economies of Violence*, 49.

they failed to address the controversial relationship between prostitution and human trafficking.

This issue is so divisive that it threatened to derail the drafting process for the protocol. The crux of disagreement was over consent in relation to the sale and purchase of sexual services, otherwise known as prostitution. States had a range of views on the treatment of prostitution, and so did social actors. The debate among self-defining feminist proponents of women's rights exemplifies the stark contrast in positions. Feminists affiliated with the Coalition Against Trafficking in Women (CATW) claimed that all prostitution, not simply coerced sexual services, was exploitative. CATW joined with Christian evangelicals and conservative groups to urge governments to criminalise the purchase of sexual services and to abolish prostitution as the best way of combatting human trafficking and protecting the rights of women.[29]

By contrast, another influential feminist group, the Global Alliance Against Traffic in Women (GAATW), distinguished between exploitative sex work that should be prohibited and sex work as a form of labour. It claimed that laws criminalising various aspects of the purchase of sexual services stigmatised sex workers and made them more, not less, vulnerable to exploitation. Indeed, GAATW and the broader Human Rights Caucus, which also included labour and human-rights advocates, initially wanted all mention of prostitution removed from the definition of trafficking. It insisted that not all sexual services were exploitative and that sexual and labour exploitation should be treated the same way.[30] However, it abandoned this position in the face of fierce opposition.[31]

The impasse over the status of prostitution was broken by the adoption of a definition of 'trafficking in human beings' that expanded 'exploitation' beyond prostitution to include forms of exploitation such as slavery and forced labour.[32] Article 3 of the Trafficking Protocol defines the crime of 'trafficking in persons' as

> the recruitment, transportation, transfer, harbouring or receipt of persons, by means of threat or use of force or other forms of coercion, of abduction, of fraud, of deception, of the abuse of power or of a position of vulnerability or of the giving or receiving of payments or benefits to achieve the consent of a person having control over another person, for the purpose of exploitation.

29 Chuang, 'Exploitation creep', 609–649.

30 Munro, 'A tale of two servitudes', 91–114; and Kotiswaran, *Dangerous Sex, Invisible Labour*, 36–37.

31 Doezema, 'Now you see her, now you don't', 79.

32 Chuang, 'The United States as global sheriff', 443–445.

> Exploitation shall include, at a minimum, the exploitation of the prostitution of others or other forms of sexual exploitation, forced labour or services, slavery or practices similar to slavery, servitude or the removal of organs.[33]

According to this definition, human trafficking consists of three elements: an action, a means, and a purpose. The *action* requires some type of movement (recruitment, transportation, transfer, harbouring, or receipt of a person). The *means* requires some form of coercion or abuse of power. But instead of defining 'exploitation', which is the *purpose* element of the crime, the protocol simply lists specific examples of exploitation, some of which are defined in other international legal instruments that function as minimum requirements.[34] The definition, which refers to both prostitution and sexual exploitation, is equivocal about the relationship between them. Essentially, the protocol's broad definition of human trafficking delegates the resolution of these controversial issues to member states.

The protocol's reference to forms of exploitation (such as slavery and forced labour) defined and prohibited in other international instruments partly allayed international human-rights institutions' and activists' concern that the international human-trafficking law was too focused on prosecuting sex trafficking at the expense of other forms of exploitation.[35] Groups and institutions such as Amnesty International, the Office of the High Commissioner for Human Rights, the United Nations International Children's Emergency Fund (UNICEF), and the International Organization for Migration (IOM) framed trafficking as a problem of victim protection and emphasised the rights of trafficked persons to work and migrate with dignity.[36]

This advocacy led to the protocol's explicit recognition of the human rights of victims of trafficking. However, unlike mandatory criminalisation of human trafficking, state obligations regarding the human rights of victims are discretionary and linked to the willingness of victims to assist with prosecuting their

[33] UN General Assembly, Protocol to Prevent, Suppress and Punish Trafficking in Persons, Especially Women and Children, Supplementing the United Nations Convention against Transnational Organized Crime, 15 November 2000, Art. 3.

[34] The definition goes on to provide that the consent of the victim to the intended exploitation is irrelevant in cases where any of the means set out in the definition are used. In 'Exploitation creep and the unmaking of human trafficking law', Janie Chuang explains that this subparagraph was intended to ensure that traffickers would not use a victim's consent as a defence. However, the group arguing for the abolition of prostitution claimed that this provision meant that all prostitution, regardless of whether it is consensual, is caught in the definition of 'exploitation'.

[35] Gallagher, *The International Law of Human Trafficking*.

[36] Gallagher, 'Human rights and the new UN protocols', 975–1004; and Charnysh, Lloyd, and Simmons, 'Frames and consensus formation', 330.

traffickers. States also objected to protecting victims of trafficking from prosecution for status-related offences involving illegal migration, undocumented work, and prostitution. They claimed mandatory protection would invite victims to raise such a defence, thus interfering with a state's ability to use criminal law to combat irregular migration and prostitution.[37]

The protocol's conditional and tepid commitment to the human rights of victims resulted from states' unwillingness to agree to an international legal instrument that would require them to recognise the rights of trafficking victims. These rights raised controversial questions about victims' access to public benefits and their immigration status, residency, and repatriation, questions that relate to the essence of state sovereignty. In a context where states were jealous in guarding their sovereignty, human-rights advocates regarded the explicit incorporation of the human rights of trafficking victims in the protocol as an achievement. They believed they could build on these references to construct binding obligations on states to protect them.[38]

The relationship between human trafficking and illegal migration facilitated by others, commonly known as human smuggling, was another contentious issue. States saw human trafficking as part of the broader problem of illegal migration, and they wanted to draw clear and rigid borders between victims of human trafficking, who deserved protection, and illegal migrants, who ought to be prosecuted and deported. Human-rights advocates, by contrast, were concerned that illegal migrants, who often rely on others to cross borders, are also vulnerable to exploitation. They argued that it is difficult to sort out victims of trafficking from migrants who are smuggled since, in practice, human trafficking and migrant smuggling are often entwined processes.[39]

The UN's solution was to provide two separate protocols, one that dealt with human trafficking and the other with smuggling. They were adopted by the UN General Assembly on the same day.[40] The two protocols were intended to do different things. The Trafficking Protocol protects individuals from another's predation, whereas the Smuggling Protocol safeguards the state from individuals who violate their immigration laws. Coercion is central to the definition of trafficking (it is the means element of the crime) whereas illegal

37 Gallagher, 'Human rights and the new UN protocols', 991.

38 Fitzpatrick, "Trafficking and a human rights violation'.

39 Ibid.

40 UN General Assembly, Protocol against the Smuggling of Migrants by Land, Sea and Air, Supplementing the United Nations Convention against Transnational Organized Crime, 15 November 2000.

migration is the crux of smuggling.[41] Article 3 of the Smuggling Protocol defines migrant smuggling as 'the procurement, in order to obtain, directly or indirectly, a financial or other material benefit, of the illegal entry of a person into a State Party of which the person is not a national or a permanent resident'.

But even though the Trafficking Protocol's definition of trafficking makes no reference to the migration status of the person being trafficked, its focus is transnational trafficking involving organised crime (Article 4). Article 11 explicitly calls on states to strengthen border controls and provides them with a great deal of discretion on how to implement them. It even requires commercial carriers to conduct immigration-related checks at airports outside their territory.[42] Indeed, both protocols reinforce the idea that irregular migration is a crime and affirm the right of states to control their borders and to extend their border controls beyond their national territory.[43]

The Trafficking Protocol reflects a state-centric understanding of human trafficking that diagnoses the problem as a combination of organised crime and illegal migration. In the state-dominated process of the UN, the criminal-law and immigration-control approach to human trafficking easily prevailed over approaches concerned with the human rights of victims and the need for safe migration paths. The United States insisted on this approach, key international institutions promoted it, it resonated with earlier approaches to trafficking, it fit within an existing transnational criminal-law framework, and it coincided with the interests of states to preserve their sovereignty in the face of organised transnational crime.

Yet the speed with which the protocol was negotiated, within two years, is attributable to both its soft nature (there was no oversight mechanism to ensure that states fulfilled their obligations once they ratified the protocol) and to its flexibility (the definition of exploitation allowed states to develop their own definitions of human trafficking). While these features were necessary to accommodate conflict and co-opt criticism, ensuring the protocol's rapid adoption, they shifted debate from an international arena involving nation-states and international institutions, agencies, committees, and experts to individual nation-states. The resulting legal instability meant that the problem of human trafficking could be hitched to a range of different governance agendas.[44]

41 Gallagher, *The International Law of Human Trafficking*, 31.

42 Rodríguez-López, '(De)constructing stereotypes', 61–72.

43 Miller and Baumeister, 'Managing migration', 15–32.

44 McCarthy, 'Human trafficking and the new slavery', 223; and Kotiswaran, *Revisiting the Law*, 4.

THE UNITED STATES' WAR ON SEX TRAFFICKING: EXERCISING DISCIPLINARY POWER ACROSS BORDERS

The Trafficking Protocol was intended to provide a framework for states to implement their own criminal laws and to develop coordinated approaches with other states and international institutions to tackle a global problem. However, the broad definition of human trafficking and the absence of a mechanism to insist on human-trafficking legislation undermined that goal. The United States stepped in to fill the governance gap by putting in place an oversight mechanism designed to have a global reach. The United States' attempt to become what Janie Chuang so aptly calls the 'global sheriff' of antitrafficking law and policy, in turn, prompted UN agencies and institutions to develop their own monitoring, reporting, and ranking systems.[45] This competition over global governance led to a thickening of institutions involved in antitrafficking and a proliferation of governance strategies, mechanisms, and goals.

Just weeks before the UN General Assembly adopted the Trafficking Protocol, the United States implemented the Victims of Trafficking and Violence Protection Act of 2000 (TVPA), signed into law by President Clinton. This law was hailed as 'a shining example of bipartisan consensus'.[46] Indeed, Republican congressman Chris Smith declared that the law 'has attracted such broad support not only because it is pro-women, pro-child, pro-human rights, pro-family values and anti-crime, but because it addresses a problem that absolutely cries out for a solution'.[47] Despite its name and the Clinton administration's promotion of the 'three P approach' to human trafficking (*preventing* human trafficking, *prosecuting* traffickers, and *protecting* victims), the TVPA was primarily a criminal-law initiative, and the victim-protection elements, especially when it came to migrants, were limited to deserving victims who assisted with prosecution.[48] The TVPA profoundly shaped the global approach to human trafficking, even though its definition of human trafficking differed from that in the protocol.[49]

45 Chuang, 'The United States as global sheriff', 437–494.

46 Victims of Trafficking and Violence Protection Act of 2000, Pub. L. No. 106-385, 114 Stat. 1464 (2000) (codified and amended in scattered sections of 8, 18, 22 USC); and Grant, 'Strange bedfellows', 11.

47 Lobasz, *Constructing Human Trafficking*, 198.

48 The protection offered to migrants was especially contentious. At the last minute, Republicans insisted that the number of visas available to victims of trafficking, who were required to assist with prosecutions to be eligible, be capped at 5,000. See Doonan, 'A house divided', 273–293.

49 The TVPA's definition of trafficking is more limited than that provided in the protocol as it only covers serious exploitation. However, it also includes involuntary servitude, which is not

The TVPA established a comprehensive domestic antitrafficking regime, but what distinguished it from antitrafficking laws in other countries was its extraterritorial reach. The TVPA set up a monitoring and compliance system to 'persuade' other states to introduce and enforce their own antitrafficking legislation.[50] The State Department established the Office to Monitor and Combat Trafficking in Persons (TIP Office), led since 2003 by the United States Ambassador-at-Large to Monitor and Combat Trafficking in Persons. The TIP Office began issuing annual *Trafficking in Persons Reports* (TIP Reports) in 2001, two years before the UN's Human Trafficking Protocol received enough ratifications to be brought into effect in December 2003.

From the beginning, the TIP Reports ranked countries into three tiers (they subsequently added a tier two watch category) depending on the extent of meeting the minimum standards for eliminating trafficking. These standards include a range of mostly criminal-law and law-enforcement provisions and activities, although there are references to the rights of victims and prevention.[51] Countries that fail to comply with these minimum standards or to make 'significant' efforts to bring themselves into compliance run the risk of financial sanctions. The TVPA authorises the president to withdraw US financial assistance unrelated to trade or humanitarian goals to countries the United States considers not to have complied and to oppose them if they apply for funds from multilateral financial institutions such as the World Bank and International Monetary Fund.[52] The TVPA also offers incentives in the form of hundreds of millions of dollars to finance technical assistance to other states and antitrafficking work by international and domestic nongovernmental organisations (NGOs).[53] In this way, the US government set up a global antitrafficking apparatus to discipline states that did not meet its minimum standards and to reward those states that did.

President George W. Bush launched a crusade against human trafficking, declaring that 'human life is the gift of the Creator, and it should never be for sale'.[54] Under his administration, the US TIP Reports concentrated almost exclusively on cross-border trafficking for the purposes of prostitution, which

listed as a form of exploitation in the Trafficking Protocol's definition. See Dottridge, 'Trafficked and exploited', 64.

50 Chuang, 'The United States as global sheriff', 439; and Gallagher, *The International Law of Human Trafficking*, 480.

51 McGrath and Watson, 'Anti-slavery as development', 26.

52 Gallagher, *The International Law of Human Trafficking*, 484–485.

53 Chuang, 'The United States as global sheriff', 470; Weitzer, 'Moral crusade against prostitution', 33–38; and Merry, 'Counting the uncountable', 280.

54 Lobasz, *Constructing Human Trafficking*, 174.

had a trickle-down effect on other states.[55] News media in the United States focused on sex trafficking, and there was a dynamic and reciprocal relationship between the media, public perception, and policymaking.[56] Narratives of women and children transported across borders for the purposes of prostitution circulated broadly in support of this agenda: 'The stereotypical image of the victim is of a young, innocent, foreign woman tricked into prostitution abroad.'[57] The media highlighted lurid cases, presenting them as typical, and NGOs in the trafficking policy field had a vested interest in attracting media attention, funding, public involvement, and government support.[58] This depiction contributed to the creation of 'hierarchies of victims who are seen as deserving or undeserving of the state's protection and enforcement resources based on whether or not they fit this ideal type'.[59]

Supported by abolitionist feminists, mainline churches, evangelicals, and conservatives, the Bush administration's stance was that prostitution was per se exploitative and should be abolished.[60] Under Bush, the US government opposed 'prostitution and any related activities', maintaining 'that these activities should not be regulated as a legitimate form of work for any human being'.[61] It also imposed what came to be known as the 'prostitution pledge', denying US government funds to any programme that advocated for the legalisation of prostitution.[62] Antiprostitution organisations and activists rejected approaches to human trafficking that regarded exploitation as a result of labour-market inequalities for fear they would have the effect of legitimising prostitution as work.[63] Consent and choice were simply irrelevant when it came to sex work, when these were the features that made other forms of labour free. Sexual exploitation and prostitution were coded in gendered terms as women and children were seen as the primary victims. Law and policy focused on vigorously investigating and prosecuting sex trafficking, punishing traffickers, and strengthening borders.[64] Through the

55 Berman, 'The left, the right, and the prostitute', 269–294; Chuang, 'The United States as global sheriff'; and Kotiswaran, 'Beyond sexual humanitarianism', 377.

56 Sanford, Martínez, and Weitzer, 'Framing human trafficking', 153; and Bonilla and Mo, 'The evolution of human trafficking', 201–234.

57 Andrijasevic and Mai, 'Trafficking (in) representations', 2.

58 Weitzer, 'New directions in research on human trafficking', 6–24.

59 McCarthy, 'Human trafficking and the new slavery', 227.

60 Grant, 'Strange bedfellows', 14.

61 United States, Department of State, *Trafficking in Persons Report, June 2008*, 24.

62 Chuang, 'The United States as global sheriff', 469; and Milivojevic and Pickering, 'Trafficking in people', 594–595.

63 Huckerby, 'Same, but different', 630.

64 Milivojevic and Pickering, 'Trafficking in people', 595; and Chuang, 'Exploitation creep', 618.

TIP Reports and this system of sanctions, the United States influenced the legal status of the commercial sex industry within other states.[65]

The United States planted itself firmly at the centre of the global governance of human trafficking by providing a comprehensive disciplinary apparatus. The TIP Reports are the hub of knowledge production about human trafficking, and despite extensive criticisms of their methodology, even by the US Government Accountability Office, they continue to circulate and influence policy.[66] The sanctions and incentives that constitute the TVPA's ranking regime had a profound influence on the way states and other social actors framed the problem of human trafficking. The United States' minimum standards effectively functioned as the global antitrafficking norm. Not only were they taken up by civil-society actors, by 2013, 182 countries had criminal laws fully or partially prohibiting trafficking.[67]

From 2001 to 2009, the Bush administration steered the global antitrafficking policy towards fighting organised crime, illegal migration, and prostitution. In doing so, it amplified the criminal and immigration legal domains in the global governance of human trafficking. Prostitution policy was regarded as the key contributing factor to human trafficking, while the possible impact of migration and labour policy was ignored.[68] Sex trafficking was portrayed as a form of sex slavery, and victim protection was seen almost exclusively in terms of rescue and redemption. The UN Protocol's broad definition of human trafficking was operationalised in ways that limited it to ideal victims – women and children who were clearly coerced into sexual exploitation.[69] Human rights were narrowly conceived as belonging to deserving victims, and a centrepiece of this 'victim-centred' approach was to hold human traffickers accountable through criminal investigations and prosecutions.[70] The Bush administration drew clear borders between sexual and labour exploitation even as it collapsed the borders between a human-rights and criminal-law approach to human trafficking.

65 O'Brien and Wilson, 'Clinton, Bush and Obama', 123–137.
66 Merry, 'Counting the uncountable', 282.
67 McCarthy, 'Human trafficking and the new slavery', 233; and Merry, 'Counting the uncountable', 270.
68 McCarthy, 'Human trafficking and the new slavery', 227.
69 Hoyle, Bosworth, and Dempsey, 'Researching trafficked women', 769–779.
70 Peters, *Responding to Human Trafficking.*

PROLIFERATING JURISDICTIONS: FROM SEXUAL TO LABOUR EXPLOITATION

Faced with the United States' attempt to take over the governance of human trafficking policy, the UN and related institutions established their own governance mechanisms and attempted to influence the policy agenda, emphasising their different understandings of, and approaches to, human trafficking.[71] The UNODC, the protocol's home institution, treated human trafficking as a problem of transnational crime. Other international agencies such as the Office of the High Commission on Human Rights (OHCHR), the International Organization for Migration (IOM), and the International Labour Organization (ILO) adopted a human-rights approach, which they interpreted through their own institutional lens. The UN-related institutions assembled a global antitrafficking network that adopted a multifaceted approach.

In 2004, the UN set up an oversight mechanism for the Trafficking Protocol to act as a multilateral rival to the United States' system. It broadened the mandate of the Conference of Parties (COP) for the Convention against Transnational Organized Crime (the parent convention of the human trafficking protocol) to include monitoring, information exchange, and cooperation regarding human trafficking.[72] Made up of all states that ratified the protocol, COP was coordinated by UNODC, which supported a prosecutorial and criminal-law approach to human trafficking. While considerably more accountable than the TIP regime, which was backed by unilateral US sanctions, the UN's governance regime was substantially less effective. The COP lacks sanctioning powers, and its Implementation Review, which utilises a supportive peer-review process, was only fully in place in 2020.

The OHCRC, which was established by the UN in 1946 with a mandate to protect fundamental rights and freedoms, tried to pull antitrafficking initiatives into its domain. During the drafting stage of the Trafficking Protocol, the OHCHR had played a key role in expanding the definition of human trafficking beyond sexual exploitation and stressing the need to protect the human rights of victims.[73] Once the protocol was adopted, the OHCHR continued to

[71] Huckerby, 'Same, but different', 593–645; and Edwards, 'Traffic in human beings', 9–53.

[72] Gallagher, 'Human rights and human trafficking', 185–186.

[73] UN General Assembly, United Nations Convention against Transnational Organized Crime: Resolution, adopted by the General Assembly, 8 January 2001, A/RES/55/25; Charnysh, Lloyd, and Simmons, 'Frames and consensus formation', 329; and Gallagher, *The International Law of Human Trafficking*.

fortify the human-rights approach to human trafficking. Its high commissioner, Mary Robinson, declared that the human rights of trafficked persons should be at the centre of all efforts to prevent and combat human trafficking.[74] In 2002, the OHCHR released the Guidelines on Human Rights and Human Trafficking, designed to promote the integration of a human-rights perspective into national, regional, and international antitrafficking laws, policies, and interventions. Two years later, it appointed a Special Rapporteur on Trafficking in Persons (STRIP), who had a mandate to focus on the human rights of victims, especially those of women and children,.[75] Unlike the regular reporting requirements imposed by the TIP and the COP, the special rapporteur's role was investigatory and ad hoc, the idea being that by documenting and exposing human-rights violations governments would be more likely to be held to account.[76] The OHCHR and its successor, the UN Human Rights Council (UNHRC), produced a substantial body of soft law embedding trafficking within the broader web of international human-rights instruments.[77]

The IOM (the leading intergovernmental organization in the field of migration since 1951) stressed the immigration aspects of human trafficking. In the mid-1990s, it was concerned that women were being transported across borders to work in the commercial sex sector, confounding smuggling, which is voluntary, with trafficking, which is not.[78] During the protocol's drafting process, the IOM, along with other members of the UN interagency group, repeatedly stressed the difficulty of distinguishing between the victims of trafficking and migrants who are smuggled as well as the importance of protecting victims' rights. Highlighting the role of irregular and forced migration in creating the conditions for exploitation, the IOM called on its member states to open up more opportunities for legal migration as a way of preventing human trafficking.[79] The IOM also developed a broad suite of countertrafficking initiatives,

74 Dottridge, 'Collateral damage', 343.

75 The STRIP is part of a system of investigatory mechanisms, charged with monitoring, advising, and publicly reporting on a human rights situation in a specific country or on a particular issue.

76 Gallagher and Ezeilo, 'The UN Special Rapporteur', 916.

77 Gallagher, *The International Law of Human Trafficking*. The council is made up of forty-seven United Nations member states, which are elected by the UN General Assembly. In 2007, it set up a set of procedures and mechanisms, including a complaints procedure, to ensure states meet their obligations. The council assumed the special procedures established by the former commission, including the special rapporteurs.

78 The IOM is not a UN institution governed by the UN constitution, although it joined the UN system in 2016. IOM, *International Response to Trafficking*; Andrijasevic, 'Beautiful dead bodies', 24–44; and Gallagher, *The International Law of Human Trafficking*, 19.

79 Huckerby, 'Same, but different', 627.

assisting governments and nongovernmental organisations in strengthening policies and procedures to facilitate the identification, referral, protection, assistance, and repatriation of trafficked persons.[80]

For the ILO, the Trafficking Protocol was an opportunity to focus greater attention on forced labour, explicitly enumerated in the Trafficking Protocol as an example of exploitation. Founded in 1919, the ILO is regarded as the international 'House of Labour'. It became the first specialist institution of the UN in 1946 and it is the only UN organisation that is not comprised exclusively of member states as it also includes representatives of employers and workers. An observer in the process leading up to the Trafficking Protocol, the ILO stressed the linkages between its existing conventions, especially the two on forced labour, and the proposed protocol, which it regarded as necessary for combatting transnational organised crime.[81]

Initially, the ILO regarded human trafficking as a problem of crime and illegal immigration. However, in its 2005 report, *A Global Alliance against Forced Labour*, the ILO characterised trafficking as a subset of forced labour on the ground that the definition of trafficking includes the additional element of *movement* by the action of a third party *into* forced labour.[82] Estimating that 12.3 million people were in forced labour, of which trafficking accounted for 20 per cent and an estimated US$32 billion of illicit profits, the report contributed to a flurry of efforts to quantify both the number of people exploited by human trafficking and the profits that this exploitation generated.[83] Most significantly, the ILO's report on forced labour prompted other powerful social actors to consider labour as well as sex trafficking a major cause for concern.[84] As we shall see in Chapter 3, the ILO's entry into the antitrafficking policy terrain fuelled an approach to human trafficking and modern slavery that sees exploitation as rooted in labour-market structures that are best addressed using labour and market-based tools to enhance workers' bargaining power and capacities to resist.[85]

80 Andrijasevic and Walters, 'The International Organization for Migration', 977–999; and Vigeswaran, 'Methodological debates', 199.
81 Andrees and Aikman, 'Raising the barr', 362.
82 ILO, *A Global Alliance against Forced Labour*, 7, 14. The Committee of Experts, one of the ILO's key supervisory bodies, confirmed that abusive practices such as slavery and human trafficking fall within the scope of the ILO's forced labour conventions, thereby expanding the reach of the ILO's initiatives. See ILO, *Eradication of Forced Labour*, 41.
83 Plant, 'Trafficking for labour exploitation', viii; and Merry, 'Counting the uncountable', 273–304.
84 Chuang, 'Exploitation creep', 619.
85 Ibid., 620–622; Shamir, 'A labor paradigm', 76–135; and Andrees and Aikman, 'Raising the bar', 359–394.

To impose some order and cooperation among its affiliate organisations, the UN in 2007 established the Inter-Agency Coordination Group against Trafficking in Persons (ICAT). While ICAT formally broadened the international approach to human trafficking beyond the criminal law to include the United Nations High Commissioner for Human Rights (UNHCHR), the ILO, and the IOM, the UNODC was assigned the coordinating role, further reinforcing the centrality of the criminal law. However, ICAT was unable to develop an overarching strategy capable of coordinating the different approaches to tackling human trafficking. Another UN initiative, the Global Initiative Against Trafficking (UN.GIFT), a network of predominantly UN institutions funded by a large donation from the Emirate of Abu Dhabi, supplanted ICAT by financing different UN institutions' antitrafficking efforts.[86]

The UN's multifaceted approach to human trafficking did not result in a coherent division of labour among the different international institutions.[87] Even within one organisation, there were overlapping institutions with different concerns. For example, the UNHCR had appointed a Special Rapporteur on trafficking in persons, especially women and children in 2004. Five years later, the UNHCR appointed a Special Rapporteur on contemporary forms of slavery.[88] In 2010, the General Assembly of the UN adopted a Global Plan of Action to Combat Trafficking in Persons that sought to integrate states' obligations to criminalise and prosecute traffickers with their obligations to respect the human rights of victims and it added a fourth 'p', *partnerships* between actors involved in antitrafficking action, to its strategic agenda.[89] But this plan did not resolve the differences in approaches to human trafficking taken by the international institutions.[90] While the ILO treated trafficking as a subset of forced labour and identified the need to regulate labour markets, the UNODC regarded forced labour as a subset of trafficking and stressed the need to strengthen criminal laws and border controls.[91]

86 Dottridge, 'Trafficked and exploited', 75.

87 Kotiswaran, *Revisiting the Law*, 28; and Dottridge, 'Trafficked and exploited', 64.

88 Human Rights Council, Resolution 6/14, Special Rapporteur on contemporary forms of slavery, 28 September 2007, https://ap.ohchr.org/documents/E/HRC/resolutions/A_HRC_RES_6_14.pdf.

89 In July 2010, the United Nations General Assembly adopted Resolution 64/293, endorsing the United Nations Global Plan of Action to Combat Trafficking in Person, which called ICAT to improve coordination and cooperation amongst relevant UN bodies, including UN human rights treaty bodies and mechanisms, and international organizations.

90 Huckerby, 'Same, but different', 593–645; Dottridge, 'Trafficked and exploited', 342–353; and Kotiswaran, *Revisiting the Law*.

91 Merry, 'Counting the uncountable', 273–304.

These different institutions are not only lodged in different legal domains, but they also have different understandings of the cause of the problem of human trafficking and the groups most likely to be its victims. The organised crime frame focuses on the actions of individual criminals and ignores the structural problems that may encourage migration and exploitation in the first place, whereas a labour approach concentrates on labour-market structures and imbalances of power.[92] Different governance strategies and mechanisms were adopted for sexual and labour exploitation, reinforcing, in turn, that they are different kinds of exploitation. A dense assemblage of institutions, social actors, and discourses involved in antitrafficking initiatives and policies with different agendas, priorities, and ideologies emerged at the global level.[93]

THE SHIFTING AXIS OF THE UNITED STATES' ANTITRAFFICKING GOVERNANCE STRATEGY

In 2012, President Obama embraced 'modern slavery' as the true name of human trafficking. Proclaiming January as the National Slavery and Human Trafficking Prevention Month, he drew an explicit parallel with Abraham Lincoln's Emancipation Proclamation. Although he acknowledged the country's historical 'stain' of slavery, Obama cast the United States as 'a leader in the global movement to end slavery' and a 'beacon of hope to people everywhere who cherish liberty and opportunity'.[94] By reframing human trafficking as modern slavery, his administration expanded the US governance initiatives to include forced labour, adding them to existing measures designed to tackle sexual exploitation and prostitution, thereby bringing US antitrafficking policy into alignment with the multifaceted approach adopted by UN institutions.

The Obama administration did not repeal the Bush administration's anti-prostitution pledge. In fact, it attempted unsuccessfully to defend the ban against a legal challenge brought by two NGOs that it violated their first amendment right to free speech.[95] Over time, the Obama administration

92 Kempadoo, 'Abolitionism', vii–ix; and Shamir, 'A labour paradigm', 76–136.

93 Gómez-Mera, 'The global governance of trafficking in persons', 302–326.

94 Obama, 'Presidential Proclamation', 2015.

95 *Agency for International Development v. Alliance for Open Society International, Inc.*, 570 U.S. 205 (2013). The Supreme Court struck down the ban as it pertained to domestic individuals and organizations. However, seven years later, it upheld the ban as it applies to foreign organisations on the ground that they are not entitled to protection under the US Constitution. *USAID v. Alliance for Open Society* (alternatively called *Alliance for Open Society II*), 591 U.S. (2020).

moved away from a position that equated prostitution with trafficking.[96] Accommodating diverse groups with different policy orientations under the broad rubric of 'modern slavery' enabled the Obama administration to maintain a bipartisan consensus over antitrafficking policy in the face of growing Republican opposition to visas for trafficking victims as part of their increasingly hardline anti-immigration policies.[97]

The new elements in the US government's approach to human trafficking were its emphasis on labour trafficking in the United States and forced labour in transnational supply chains. Obama appointed Luis C. de Baca to the post of antitrafficking ambassador because of his record in prosecuting US agricultural employers for using forced labour. Together with the Department of Labour and the Equal Employment Opportunities Commission, the Office to Monitor and Combat Trafficking in Persons targeted traffickers in the United States who exploited migrant workers.[98] The Dodd–Frank Wall Street Reform and Consumer Protection Act, which was signed into law by Obama in 2010, contained a provision imposing an obligation on companies to conduct supply-chain due diligence and, where necessary, perform third-party verification to ensure that they had not sourced 'conflict minerals', which were likely to have been obtained by using forced labour, needed for the fabrication of their products.[99]

Attention to labour trafficking increased during Obama's second term. In 2012, Obama issued an executive order strengthening the protections against trafficking in federal contracting by forbidding federal contractors from charging recruitment fees to workers and confiscating identity documents. The order also required federal contractors to undertake antitrafficking compliance measures, including awareness training, whistle-blower protection, and housing and recruitment plans. Contractors who performed work abroad

96 O'Brien and Wilson, 'Clinton, Bush, and Obama', 195, 204.

97 Doonan, 'A house divided', 273–293. The Wilberforce Act 2008 prefigured a more accepting attitude to migrants who are victims of trafficking by protecting unaccompanied child minors and extending visas to those who were unwilling or unable to assist prosecutors.

98 Chuang, 'Exploitation creep', 609–649.

99 'Conflict minerals' refers to raw materials or minerals that come from a particular part of the world where conflict is occurring and affects the mining and trading of those materials. Dodd–Frank Wall Street and Consumer Protection Act of 2010, Pub. L. No. 111-203, 124 Stat. 1376 (2010), 12 USC 53. In 2010, the California legislature passed the California Transparency in Supply Chains Act of 2010, Californian Civil Code, sec. 1714.43, with the goal of informing consumers and businesses about companies 'efforts to address slavery and human trafficking in the supply chain, so that customers can consider this information when making their purchasing decisions.' The legislation does not require companies to make efforts to eliminate slavery and human trafficking.

worth over US$500,000 had to develop human-trafficking and forced-labour risk assessments and compliance plans.[100]

The US government's focus on forced labour fuelled the efforts of labour advocates to frame their initiatives in the language of trafficking.[101] In 2015, Secretary of State John Kerry presented the 2015 Presidential Award for Extraordinary Efforts to Combat Trafficking in Persons to the Coalition of Immokalee Workers for pioneering a worker-driven governance model that eradicated labour trafficking in farms participating in its Fair Food Program.[102] That year, Congress closed the 'consumptive demand' loophole in Section 307 of the US Tariff Act, which permitted the import of products mined, produced, or manufactured wholly or in part by forced labour so long as they were not domestically produced in such quantities as to meet US consumption needs. With the removal of this clause, the import of all goods into the United States made with forced labour was prohibited.[103] This initiative led to a flurry of 'withhold release orders' barring goods such as tobacco from Malawi and cotton from Turkmenistan from entering the United States on the ground that these products were made with forced labour.[104] On the cusp of leaving office, Obama called on the United States to address forced labour in supply chains, encouraging citizens to be 'conscientious consumers'.[105]

The change in the United States' domestic antitrafficking policy under Obama was also reflected in the TIPS' naming, shaming, and sanctioning regime. The TIP Reports were no longer predominantly preoccupied with transnational sex trafficking and prostitution; they began to concentrate much more on labour exploitation.[106] With the switch in focus of antitrafficking policies, the identities of the reported victims changed as men outstripped women and children as the majority of victims.[107] Under Obama, the TIP Reports adopted a much more 'holistic approach' to the problem of human

100 Strengthening Protections Against Trafficking in Persons in Federal Contract, Executive Order 13627, 25 September 2012.

101 Chuang, 'Exploitation creep', 609–649.

102 John Kerry, 'Remarks at the White House Forum'.

103 In February 2016, President Obama signed the US Trade Facilitation and Trade Enforcement Act of 2015, Pub. L. No. 114-125, 19 USC 4301, into law. Section 910 of the Act closed a loophole in the Tariff Act of 1930, by removing the 'consumptive demand' clause.

104 Cimino-Isaacs, Casey, and O'Reagan, 'Section 307 and U.S. imports of products of forced labor', 7.

105 Obama, 'Presidential Proclamation', 2017.

106 Chuang, 'Exploitation creep', 609–649; Kotiswaran, *Revisiting the Law*, 2017; and Quirk, 'When human trafficking means everything and nothing', 69–96.

107 Sanford, Martínez, and Weitzer, 'Framing human trafficking', 151.

trafficking in which different types of human trafficking – such as sexual exploitation, child soldiers, and forced labour – are sorted into the appropriate legal domain.

But the US government's emphasis on labour exploitation did not survive the 2016 federal election. The Trump administration favoured criminalising the demand for sexual services, which curried favour with evangelical and conservative groups. Endorsed by Ivanka Trump, in 2018, the Fight Online Sex Trafficking Act–Stop Enabling Sex Traffickers Act (FOSTA-SESTA) was passed into law with bipartisan support.[108] By holding websites accountable for sex work facilitated on their platforms, this law was designed to disrupt the market for commercial sex.[109]

The Trump administration also sought to repeal the disclosure and due-diligence provisions in the Dodd–Frank Act, and the secretary of labour recommended slashing funding for the Department of Labor's International Labor Affairs Bureau, charged with countering human trafficking, child labour, and forced labour across the United States and the world. Meeting strong resistance, including from businesses such as Apple and Intel, the administration backpedalled on these proposals.[110]

Trade initiatives and import controls were the Trump administration's preferred methods for addressing forced labour.[111] The prohibition against forced labour in the labour chapter of the United States–Mexico–Canada Agreement, which entered into force in 2020, served to strengthen enforcement efforts relating to Section 307 of the Tariff Act, which US Customs officials were using to issue broad industry and countrywide importation ban orders.[112] The Uyghur Forced Labor Prevention Act, passed by the House in September 2020, includes a rebuttable presumption that all goods produced

[108] Allow States and Victims to Fight Online Sex Trafficking Act of 2017, Pub. L. No. 115-164, 132 Stat. 1253, 18 USC 1 note, 47 USC 230 note.

[109] The administration's record on human-trafficking prosecutions belies its rhetoric. While there were over ten times as many federal prosecutions for sex trafficking as for labour trafficking in 2018, the number of prosecutions was minuscule: 213 federal prosecutions for sex trafficking and 17 for labour trafficking. See Krajeski, 'The hypocrisy of Trump's antitrafficking discourse', 43–65.

[110] Pilkington, 'Trump labour secretary'; and Ganesan, 'Business and human rights during Trump', 264–270.

[111] The Frederick Douglass Trafficking Victims Prevention and Protection Reauthorization Act of 2018 encouraged enforcement of the Tariff Act of 1930's prohibition on the importation of goods made with forced labour. Cimino-Isaacs, Casey, and O'Reagan, 'Section 307 and U.S. imports of products of forced labor', 7.

[112] United States–Mexico–Canada Implementation Agreement, 13 March 2020, Pub. L. No. 116-113, 19 USC 29; and International Labor Rights Forum, 'Trade Subcommittee Hearing'.

or manufactured in Xinjiang are made with forced labour, and thus prohibited under Section 307.[113]

Throughout his presidency, Trump identified the problem as criminal gangs of dangerous foreigners trafficking women and children across the United States' borders for the purpose of sexual exploitation and prostitution. His administration eventually broke the two-decade-old bipartisan consensus over human trafficking: it resisted granting victims without lawful immigration status temporary visas (T-visas) to protect them from immediate deportation.[114] In 2020, eight prominent nongovernmental antitrafficking organisations, including the Human Trafficking Legal Centre and Polaris, shunned a White House summit hosted by Ivanka Trump to end 'National Slavery and Human Trafficking Prevention Month' to protest the government's antitrafficking policy. A member of the boycott, Jean Bruggeman, executive director of Freedom Network (the United States' largest coalition of antitrafficking service organisations), explained that 'it's incredibly difficult now to support, assist, and protect immigrant survivors of trafficking, who make up most of the labour-trafficking survivors'.[115] Moreover, the consenus among antitraffickng organisations that prostitution should be treated as a crime to minimise trafficking was beginning to erode. When the Supreme Court struck down the prostitution pledge for domestic organisations, the Freedom Network no longer faced the risk of defunding and it announced its support for the decriminalisation of sex work to reduce opportunities for exploitation.[116]

The Trump White House used human trafficking to further its crusade to outlaw prostitution and eradicate illegal immigration, and its solution to the problem of labour trafficking and forced labour was simply to close the US borders to goods and people. In the 2019 TIP Report, the United States stressed the need for other governments to embrace a carceral approach to human trafficking, warning them that 'penalizing human traffickers for labour

[113] Uyghur Forced Labor Prevention Act, 23 December 2021, Pub. L. No. 117-78, 135 Stat. 1525, 22 USC 6901; and Cimino-Isaacs, Casey, and O'Reagan, 'Section 307 and U.S. imports of products of forced labor', 7.

[114] The T-visa lets trafficking victims without lawful migration status stay in the country and receive government benefits. It opens a path to US citizenship.

[115] Grant, 'The Trump administration'. Under the Trump administration, the number of approvals for the specialized visas for immigrant victims of trafficking, which allows them to reside in the US, was the lowest in nearly a decade. See Grant, 'The Trump administration'.

[116] *Agency for International Development v. Alliance for Open Society International, Inc.* (2013); Kotiswaran, 'The sexual politics', 44. In 2020, in *USAID v. Alliance for Open Society International* (2020), the US Supreme Court upheld the ban on funding foreign affiliates of US organizations that supported the decriminalisation of prostitution.

violations under employment law instead of charging them for labour trafficking, may mean that traffickers are given penalties substantially lower than those prescribed under antitrafficking law, limiting their potential deterrent effects'.[117] However, in spite of the Trump administration's call for criminal prosecution as the best strategy to deal with human trafficking, in the 2018 fiscal year, federal investigations in the Justice Department decreased from 783 to 657, and the number of defendants charged with human trafficking also fell.[118]

The election of Joe Biden as president in 2020 marked another change in US antitrafficking policy. A coalition of antitrafficking groups pushed his administration to focus more on labour than sex trafficking and to approve more T-visa applications by victims of human trafficking.[119] The shift in presidential rhetoric was stark; instead of using antitrafficking policy to vilify foreign traffickers, Biden identified the disproportionate impact of trafficking on 'racial and ethnic minorities, women and girls, LGBTQI+ individuals, vulnerable migrants, and other historically marginalized and underserved communities'. He linked antitrafficking initiatives 'to our broader efforts to advance equity and justice across our society'.[120] While efforts to eradicate sex trafficking would continue, the United States' 2021 National Action Plan to Combat Human Trafficking promised to increase efforts to investigate and prosecute forced labour and to devise means to encourage law-enforcement officials to request visas any time they encountered a foreign national likely to be a victim of human trafficking.[121]

The Biden administration also adopted what it called a 'worker-centred' trade policy, which reflects its 'commitment to use trade agreements, tools, and relationships to empower workers'.[122] Endorsing 'competition in a global market', the President's 2022 Trade Policy Agenda identified the 'exploitation of workers' as a form of unfair practice that distorts global trade at the expense of Americans.[123] The United States, Mexico, and Canada Free Trade Deal is a prime example of the President's worker-centred trade policy; it contains the 'strongest labour provisions in any trade agreement', strengthens the US ban on goods made with forced labour, and requires Mexico and Canada to

[117] United States, Department of State, *Trafficking in Persons Report, June 2019*, 8.
[118] Krajeski, 'The hypocrisy of Trump's antitrafficking discourse', 45.
[119] Murray, 'U.S. anti-trafficking groups urge Biden to shift focus from sex to labor'.
[120] Biden, 'Presidential Proclamation on National Human Trafficking Prevention Month'.
[121] US, *The National Action Plan to Combat Human Trafficking, 2021*, 47, 22.
[122] United States, Office of the U.S. Trade Representative, *The President's 2022 Trade Policy Agenda*, 1.
[123] Ibid.

impose similar bans.[124] The extent to which this trade deal and its enforcement mechanisms actually protect workers outside of the United States is an open question.[125]

Take import bans against goods produced with forced labour, which increased under Trump and Biden, as an example.[126] The United States' 2021 antitrafficking plan justified them on the grounds they protected domestic markets from unfair competition. It stated:

> Globally and in the United States, forced labor and associated harmful employment practices hide the true cost of labor and subvert the legitimate job market, such as displacing American workers, driving down wages, and corrupting the domestic and global economy. These practices create an uneven playing field for responsible businesses that invest in measures to prevent forced labor in their product supply chains.[127]

While these bans might level the playing field for American workers, since the US import ban does not require any form of remediation to protect 'foreign' workers who work in situations of forced labour, its impact on them could be detrimental as suppliers could lose orders and dismiss or squeeze workers in response.[128]

CONCLUSION

Beginning in the early 1990s, key states and international institutions depicted human trafficking as a problem of transnational criminals who exploit women and children, which provided states with a useful metaphor for violations of their territorial borders.[129] A desire to protect their sovereignty made states willing to adopt an international protocol that encouraged them to strengthen their criminal laws. It also explains their resistance to a precise and targeted definition of human trafficking and to mandatory obligations to protect victims' rights. These ideological and political dynamics account for the choice of criminal law as the Trafficking Protocol's legal home, its broad definition of human trafficking, and the weak obligations it imposes on states

[124] Ibid., 2.
[125] LeClercq, 'A worker-centred trade policy', 732.
[126] Indeed, Biden signed into law the Uyghur Forced Labor Prevention Act (UFLPA), and see US Customs and Border Protection, *Withhold Release Orders and Findings List*.
[127] US, *The National Action Plan to Combat Human Trafficking*, 2021, 15.
[128] Fudge and LeBaron, 'Regulatory design and interactions in worker-driven social responsiblity initiatives'; and Ebert, Francavilla and Guarcello, 'Tackling forced labour in supply chains'.
[129] Hubbard, Matthews, and Scoular, 'Regulating sex work', 14; and FitzGerald, 'Vulnerable geographies', 185.

to protect the rights of victims. A strong advocate for the international protocol and active in its drafting, the United States portrayed itself as a global humanitarian leader on the issue of human trafficking.[130] The TIP regime was effectively a form of extraterritorial governance, and it helped to propagate a dense network of criminal laws against human trafficking. The number of states making human trafficking a specific crime increased from 20 per cent in 2000 to 90 per cent in 2015.[131] This antitrafficking legal web reinforced the exercise of territorial sovereignty over national borders.

The protocol's broad definition of human trafficking provided an opportunity for states to deploy different governance strategies to deal with different kinds of human trafficking. The reference to prostitution and sexual exploitation was treated by some states, most notably the United States, as a justification for strengthening the borders between sexual and labour exploitation and providing different governance approaches to what it considered to be discrete, and highly gendered, forms of exploitation. Abolishing prostitution by criminalising demand for sexual services was seen as the appropriate solution to the problem of sexual exploitation, whereas strengthening the rights of migrant workers and enforcing labour standards were regarded by several UN organisations and the Obama and Biden administrations as the best ways to deal with labour exploitation.

Together with its companion protocol on human smuggling, the Trafficking Protocol also allocates migrants into distinct legal subcategories or statuses with different rights.[132] The borders between victims of trafficking and illegal migrants are drawn by national authorities as they sort individual migrants into their appropriate legal category and associated legal domain. Since trafficking victims are provided with better protection than migrants who are smuggled, national authorities have an incentive to identify irregular migrants as smuggled rather than trafficked.[133] Moreover, the dominant frame of trafficking, which depicts it as a matter of individual criminality, tends to obscure the broader economic inequalities and political forces that both create pressures for people to migrate across international borders and for states to strengthen borders against migration, which, in turn, make migrants vulnerable to abuse and exploitation.[134]

The ambiguous definition of trafficking spawned attempts by international institutions to reframe the problem of human trafficking through a human-

130 Doonan, 'A house divided', 273–293.

131 Lloyd and Simmons, 'Framing for a new transnational legal order', 436.

132 Anderson and Andrijasevic, 'Sex, slaves and citizens', 143.

133 Strauss, 'Sorting victims from workers', 140–158; and Fudge, 'Illegal working', 557–584.

134 O'Connell-Davidson, 'New slavery, old binaries', 256.

rights lens, with each institution emphasising its own capacities and rationalities. Over the past twenty years, social actors have recast the meaning of human trafficking and advocated several different policy frames and legal domains for resolving the problem. When the UN adopted Target 8.7 (ending human trafficking, modern slavery, and the worst forms of child labour by 2030) as one of its sustainable development goals, it placed the target under the broad themes of development and decent work. Labelling human trafficking a 'multifaceted crime', the UNODC endorsed a multidisciplinary approach that included criminal-law initiatives, protecting the rights of victims, and incentives for corporations to prevent human trafficking and forced labour in their supply chains.[135]

The multifaceted approach to tackling modern slavery has added legal domains and associated governance strategies to the global antislavery network. But not every legal domain or governance strategy has equal power. In the global governance network that assembled around the UN's Trafficking Protocol, criminal law has exerted a gravitational force, pulling human rights and immigration matters closer to it and out of administrative law's orbit. In the process, the human rights of trafficking victims have been narrowly construed as aids to criminal prosecution. In this context, human rights have been interpreted in carceral terms so that prosecuting criminals is seen as protecting the rights of victims, who are depicted in highly gendered terms.

Social and political forces can amplify the power of one legal domain or governance strategy over another. As the Obama administration dampened the focus on prostitution and illegal migration, the ILO and labour-rights activists were able to advocate a labour-regulation approach. But political and social forces also operated in the opposite direction. Under the Trump administration, there was an increased emphasis on sex trafficking, illegal migrants, and insecure borders, which amplified the criminal law and subsumed immigration within it. Despite the proliferation of international institutions, governance strategies, and legal domains that address human trafficking and modern slavery, global governance remains firmly anchored in the criminal law, a legal domain that can easily be galvanised by social actors to reinforce sovereign control over national borders and to vilify outsiders.

However, the effects of international lawmaking are not predetermined. Principles of state sovereignty and subsidiarity, combined with the need for most states to incorporate the norms and obligations of international law into domestic legal systems, means that there are regional, national, and

[135] UNDOC, *Global Report on Trafficking*, 18.

subnational effects of international lawmaking.[136] As we will see, different international institutions (the ILO, in Chapter 3), different regions (the EU, in Chapter 4), and different states (the UK, in Chapters 5 and 6) are subject to diverse social and political forces. They define the crime of human trafficking in different ways, empower some governance strategies more than others, and draw the legal border between victims of trafficking and illegal migrants in different places. Moreover, the meaning and efficacy of any governance strategy depend on how it fits into the multifaceted approach adopted by the global antislavery governance network.[137] The next chapter traces the role of private actors in the global antislavery governance network and the rise of market-based mechanisms to rid global supply chains of modern slavery.

[136] Strauss, 'Sorting victims from workers', 149.
[137] Goméz-Mera, 'The global governance of trafficking', 303–326.

2

Philanthrocapitalism's Market-Friendly Solution

From the experience of all ages and nations, I believe, that the work done by free men comes cheaper in the end than the work performed by slaves.

—Adam Smith, *An Inquiry into the Nature and Causes of the Wealth of Nations*

The realities of global trade and commerce make it inevitable that products generated by modern slavery will travel across borders and into higher income countries where the prevalence of modern slavery is low.

—Walk Free, *Global Slavery Index*, 2018

Created by Australian Christian philanthropist and mining magnate Andrew 'Twiggy' Forrest and his wife, Nicola, in 2012, Walk Free Foundation (Walk Free), an initiative of his Minderoo Foundation, quickly became the key player in the new abolitionist network formed to combat modern slavery and a pivotal global governance actor. Walk Free exemplifies the role and significance of philanthrocapitalists, who use their money, business savvy, and elite contacts to shape global policy in general and modern slavery policy in particular.[1] Philanthrocapitalists purport to inject philanthropy with the dynamism of capitalist enterprise by mobilising market forces and imposing business management models. They support projects with outcomes that can be quantified and measured.[2] Philanthrocapitalists exemplify the use of the market as a logic of social ordering, one of the key features of neoliberalism. They claim they are reinvesting the rewards of the rich for the benefit of the

[1] Chuang, 'Giving as governance?', 1516–1556.

[2] Mediavilla and Garcia-Arias, 'Philanthrocapitalism as a neoliberal (development agenda) artefact', 857; McGoey, 'Philanthrocapitalism and its critics', 185; and Bishop and Green, *Philanthro-Capitalism*.

poor by using business strategies to create resources for, and solutions to, problems that governments have been unable to solve.

'Harnessing the power of businesses and faiths', Walk Free seeks to drive legislative change in key countries to end modern slavery.[3] Its strategy has three interwoven strands: (1) defining, depicting, and measuring the problem; (2) establishing an elite network to influence policy and legislation; and (3) financing antislavery initiatives. These strategies have had a profound influence on the shape and orientation of recent attempts to govern the global problem of slavery. Either directly or through the charitable foundations they control, philanthropists who head transnational corporations have taken the lead in defining the problem of modern slavery, identifying the appropriate solutions, and steering the direction of development funds towards eradicating it. They portray slavery in supply chains as resulting from market failure and depict the control large transnational corporations have over their supply chains as an antidote to the limits of state sovereignty in the context of global capitalism. Thus, they advocate for market-based solutions to the problem of modern slavery – such as supply chain transparency and mandatory human-rights due-diligence legislation – that enlist transnational corporations located in the Global North to enforce international legal standards against contractors located primarily in the Global South. Laws that target modern slavery in supply chains partially detach sovereign authority from territory by delegating such authority to corporations to enforce the standards extraterritorially, projecting struggles against labour exploitation into a 'privatised sphere of corporate self-governance'.[4] Circulated through an elite network, this solution is widely accepted by such key states as Australia, the UK, and the United States, international organisations, religious institutions, and civil society organisations.

In contrast to the philanthrocapitalist's account of modern slavery, those who adopt a critical political-economy perspective argue that international and transnational trade and financial agreements have created conditions for multinational corporations to lower labour costs by outsourcing production and increase their control over the labour supply.[5] Instead of depicting the governance problem as a gap in the authority of states in the Global North to control bad actors in the Global South, critical political economists view the current multiscalar economic governance regime as creating a set of rules that

[3] Walk Free, *Global Slavery Index*, 2018, 6.

[4] Prentice, 'Labour rights from labour wrongs?', 1780; and Sarfaty, 'Shining light on global supply chains', 421.

[5] LeBaron, *Combatting Modern Slavery*, 1–22.

enable transnational corporations in the Global North to shift competitive pressures down the chain, thereby cultivating conditions that produce modern slavery in the Global South. Seen from this angle, modern slavery laws shore up the legitimacy of the global economic order by aligning transnational corporations with individual morality and by celebrating individual freedom, which is equated with free contracting.

How did Walk Free become an influential actor in the global antislavery governance network? What governance strategies did it promote? To answer these questions, this chapter shows how Walk Free assembled an ethical business alliance that positioned transnational corporations (mainly from the Global North) as the key actors in combatting modern slavery in supply chains. It concentrates on Walk Free's business-led proposals to tackle slave-made goods transmitted across national borders through supply chains and how Walk Free portrayed the transnational scale of the problem and the limited territorial jurisdiction of states as reasons to support business-led solutions. Walk Free's attempt to shape the global consensus on how best to rid supply chains of modern slavery illuminates the critical role philanthrocapitalists have come to play in global governance strategies.

THE NEW ABOLITIONISTS AND THE GLOBAL PROBLEM OF MODERN SLAVERY

The antislavery governance network emerged in the late 1990s out of a struggle over how to frame the problem of human trafficking. Before that decade, human trafficking was approached as a problem of organised crime and unlawful migration rather than a human rights or labour rights issue. Human rights institutions and activists tried to expand how human trafficking was framed and advocated for a broader range of solutions.[6] Their explicit goal was to rethink 'trafficking as one form of contemporary slavery' and their emphasis was on exploitation, not movement or migration.[7]

They linked up with new abolitionists to focus initiatives less on sex and individual perpetrators and more on labour exploitation and its structural causes.[8] They took up the phrase 'new abolition' because they found in the history of the legal abolition of slavery (with its emphasis on the role of nineteenth-century British and American evangelicals in ending the trans-Atlantic trade in African slaves) a strategic framework, a prototype for tactics,

6 Brysk and Choi-Fitzpatrick, *From Human Trafficking to Human Rights*, 3.

7 Ibid.

8 Choi-Fitzpatrick, 'Rethinking trafficking', 13–24; and Chuang, 'Exploitation creep', 609–649.

and a source of ethical and political inspiration.[9] Located primarily in Australia, the UK, and the United States, new abolitionists mobilised the iconography and narratives of historical forms of slavery to highlight its new forms and emphasise slavery's continued moral repugnance.[10] They portrayed modern slavery as a form of evil[11] and characterised the early crusades against the slave trade as 'the world's first and oldest social movement for human rights'.[12]

Celebrated as the 'world's leading expert on contemporary forms of slavery', new abolitionist Kevin Bales is regarded as being responsible for the modern slavery frame.[13] An influential norm entrepreneur, he insisted on using the word 'slavery' instead of 'human trafficking'.[14] Through a series of influential books that began with *Disposable People: New Slavery in the Global Economy* (1999), he defined modern slavery as 'the total control of one person by another for the purpose of economic exploitation'.[15] In 2000, he founded the US-based Free the Slaves, one of the most prominent antislavery organisations, and continues to be a key player in the global antislavery network: he sits on the boards of influential private funders, consults for private foundations, and directs the research of a key university human rights centre devoted to ending modern slavery. Bales emphasises that modern slavery is embedded in the global economy and connected across the world via supply chains.[16]

Faith-based groups are prominent actors in the global antislavery network.[17] Evangelical Christians were influential in shaping antitrafficking

9 Quirk, *The Anti-Slavery Project*; and Choi-Fitzpatrick, 'From rescue to representation', 486–503.

10 Bales, *Disposable People*; Bales, 'Slavery and the human right to evil', 53–63; Kara, *Sex Trafficking*; Quirk, *The Anti-Slavery Project*; and Gross and Thomas, 'The new abolitionism', 99–118.

11 Bales, 'Slavery and the human right to evil', 53–63.

12 Choi-Fitzpatrick, 'From rescue to representation', 487.

13 Ibid., 499; Dottridge, 'Global trafficking prevalence data', 161–164; Gross and Thomas, 'The new abolitionism', 99–118; and Quirk, *The Anti-Slavery Project*, 159.

14 Murphy, 'The new slave narrative', 382, 388.

15 Bales, 'Slavery and the human right to evil', 6.

16 Bales was a cofounder of Free the Slaves in Washington, DC, and he was the lead author of the *Global Slavery Index* (GSI) in 2013, 2014 and 2016. He now serves on the GSI Expert Working Group. He served as a consultant to the UN's Global Programme against Trafficking in Human Beings, and he edited an antihuman trafficking toolkit for the UN. In addition to *Disposable People*, his books include *Ending Slavery: How We Free Today's Slaves* (2007) and *Blood and Earth: Modern Slavery, Ecocide, and the Secret to Saving the World* (2016). He currently sits on the Freedom Fund and is the director of research at the Nottingham Human Rights Lab.

17 Bales and Gardner, 'Free soil, free producers, free communities', 85–88.

policy under the Bush administration, and they, along with other faith groups, were drawn to the broader fight against modern slavery.[18] The Catholic Church was involved in propagating the image of modern slavery as a pressing social problem.[19] And the emphasis on rescue and salvation was particularly appealing to the new abolitionists' Christian evangelical wing.[20] The International Justice Mission, which describes itself as the largest anti-slavery organisation in the world, is a US-based Christian evangelical organisation that mobilises churches and their members to support its model for ending slavery, which is to 'rescue and restore victims, bring criminals to justice, and strengthen justice systems'.[21] Developed by the Catholic Bishops' Conference of England and Wales in 2014, the Santa Marta Group is an alliance of international police chiefs and Catholic bishops who work with civil society to eradicate human trafficking and modern-day slavery.[22] Faith functions as a motivating force in the new abolitionists' network; it provides a framework for understanding the problem of modern slavery and imagining its solution.

The bicentenaries of the abolition of the slave trade (in Britain in 1807 and in the United States in 1808) fuelled campaigns to expand 'human trafficking' to include all forms of modern slavery. A flurry of antislavery organisations, many of which had strong ties to religious organisations, were established, including Stop the Traffik in 2006, Not for Sale and Alliance to End Slavery and Trafficking in 2007, and End Slavery Now, Unseen, and Justice and Care in 2008.[23] On their bicentenaries, the British and US governments linked the fight against human trafficking to the abolitionist movement to end the slave trade. The UK published an Action Plan on Trafficking, invoking as a historical precedent the Slave Trade Act 1807,[24] which abolished the slave trade in the British Empire.[25] The United States introduced the Wilberforce Trafficking Victims Protection Reauthorization Act of 2008,[26] named after the

[18] Choi-Fitzpatrick, 'To seek and save the lost', 119–140; and Leary, 'Religious organizations as partners', 51–60.
[19] Broad and Turnbull, 'From human trafficking to modern slavery', 127.
[20] Choi-Fitzpatrick, 'To seek and save the lost', 119–140; and Kurasawa, 'Show and tell', 170.
[21] International Justice Mission, 'Trafficking and slavery'.
[22] Santa Marta Group, 'About'.
[23] Chuang, 'Exploitation creep', 627; O'Connell-Davidson, *Modern Slavery*, 7; and LeBaron and Rühmkorf, 'Steering CSR through home state regulation', 15–18.
[24] An Act for the Abolition of the Slave Trade, 47 Geo III Sess. 1, c. 36 (*Hansard*, 10 February 1807).
[25] Fudge and Strauss, 'Migrants, unfree labour, and the legal construction', 160–179.
[26] William Wilberforce Trafficking Victims Protection Reauthorization Act of 2008, Pub. L. No. 110-457 (2008), 22 USC 7101.

evangelical British politician and philanthropist who championed the end of the British slave trade.[27]

The term 'modern slavery' was stretched to include chattel slavery ('old slavery'), forced labour, human trafficking for labour exploitation and prostitution, and forced marriage, among other practices, enabling new abolitionists to advocate for a multifaceted approach to modern slavery. They saw it not simply as a problem in need of a legal solution but also as 'a problem of economic development, migration, gender, prejudice, corruption, and political priorities and will'.[28] They emphasised the role of social movements, religious organisations, governments, and intergovernmental actors (from the UN to the World Bank) in the fight to end different forms of modern slavery, such as forced labour, sex trafficking, forced marriage, or child soldiers.

But what was distinctive about the new abolitionists' approach is that they regarded business and consumers as key actors in the fight against modern slavery. They proposed laws to confiscate goods or services made or provided by exploited labour and urged the adoption of naming and shaming campaigns to unleash consumer power to end modern slavery in supply chains.[29] Their emphasis on the role of Christian abolitionists and liberal nations in abolishing the Atlantic slave trade provided a historical prototype of benevolent paternalism that was irresistible to key actors in the emerging global governance network.[30] They cast modern slavery as a moral imperative that transcended political or economic interests.[31] By defining slavery as a 'unique moral aberration', the new abolitionist discourse, like that of their nineteenth-century forbearers, gave 'sanction to the prevailing economic order'.[32] Its focus is on the actions of individual evildoers rather than on the broader social relations and institutional configurations that create the conditions in which unfree labour is propagated.

The broad range of practices caught under the umbrella of 'modern slavery' also provided room for a diverse group of organisations and actors to take different approaches to the same problem and to focus on different types of modern slavery. The multifaceted approach favoured by international organisations accommodates a hardline criminal approach to prosecuting and incarcerating sex traffickers with a focus on the human rights of victims and the labour rights of migrant workers. The legal assemblage of jurisdiction sorts

[27] Chuang, 'Exploitation creep', 624.
[28] Bales and Choi-Fitzpatrick, 'The anti-slavery movement', 201.
[29] Ibid., 210–214.
[30] O'Connell-Davidson, *Modern Slavery*, 11–12; and Quirk, *The Anti-Slavery Project*, 248.
[31] Walk Free, *Measurement, Action, Freedom*, 10.
[32] Davis, 'The problem of slavery in the Age of Revolution', 63.

different governance projects such as transnational sex trafficking and forced labour in supply chains into different institutions and, in doing so, keeps them from clashing. It also reinforces gendered borders between different forms of unfree labour. Sexual exploitation and prostitution, which predominantly involve women and girls as victims, are treated differently from labour exploitation, where most of the victims are men.

In 2012, when he declared that modern slavery was the 'true name' of human trafficking, US president Barack Obama claimed that it 'ought to concern every business, because it distorts markets' and 'every nation, because it endangers public health and fuels violence and organized crime'.[33] In 2013, the Centre for Social Justice, a think tank established by a prominent Conservative politician, Ian Duncan-Smith, and influenced by the Catholic Church, released a report, which put pressure on the Conservative-Liberal Democrat coalition government to enact legislation.[34] As we will see in Chapter 6, the UK government passed the Modern Slavery Act 2015,[35] which requires large corporations to disclose the efforts they have made to detect and eliminate modern slavery in their businesses and supply chains.

While key states and activist networks were adopting the modern slavery frame, an epistemic community of experts on modern slavery was being established. Jean Allain, a professor of international law, set up the Research Network on the Legal Parameters of Slavery consisting of academic researchers, including Kevin Bales, and representatives of Free the Slaves and Anti-Slavery International. Its goal was to develop an understanding of the definition of slavery provided in the 1926 Convention for the Abolition of Slavery,[36] a definition suitable for the contemporary context that could be used by courts, states, civil society organisations, and international institutions.[37]

The challenge was to provide a meaningful definition of slavery in a context where abolition has already taken place and legal slavery no longer existed. Taking as its starting point the convention's definition of slavery as 'the status or condition of a person over whom any or all of the powers attaching to the right of ownership are exercised', the research network emphasised control

33 Obama, 'Remarks by the President to the Clinton Global Initiative'.

34 Broad and Turnbull, 'From human trafficking to modern slavery', 127. The report, *It Happens Here: Equipping the United Kingdom to Fight Modern Slavery*, was funded by Manpower Group and the Qatar Foundation.

35 Modern Slavery Act 2015, c. 30.

36 Slavery, Servitude, Forced Labour and Similar Institutions and Practices Convention of 1926 (Slavery Convention of 1926), in force 9 March 1927, 60 LNTS 253.

37 Allain, 'Contemporary slavery and its definition in law', 37.

tantamount to slavery as the critical element.[38] In 2012, it launched the Bellagio–Harvard Guidelines on the Legal Parameters of Slavery, which explained that the exercise of control is typically 'supported by and obtained through means such as violent force, deception and/or coercion' and that, to constitute slavery, the control must 'significantly deprive that person of his or her individual liberty, with the intent of exploitation through the use, management, profit transfer or disposal of that person'.[39] The goal of the guidelines was to 'unpack the 1926 definition of modern slavery' to give it heft both as a legal and advocacy tool.[40]

New abolitionists and the international human rights advocacy network recast human trafficking as a specific form of modern slavery. Key states such as the UK and the United States, along with international organisations such as United Nations Office on Drugs and Crime, adopted this broader framing of the problem,[41] and a community of scholars and prominent abolitionists provided legal and normative support.[42] Modern slavery was portrayed as a form of evil and a human rights violation that deprived individuals of their freedom. But it was the entry of philanthrocapitalists and the transnational corporations they represent that catalysed the creation of a strategic ethical business alliance committed to eliminating slavery in supply chains.

METRICS, NETWORKS, AND MONEY: WALK FREE'S GOVERNANCE STRATEGY

Since its inception, Walk Free has developed metrics, established an elite epistemic network, and used money to shape the global antislavery agenda. Andrew Forrest has demonstrated a keen understanding of the importance of counting, measuring, and valuing as techniques for identifying a social problem and taking ownership of it.[43] In this case, the challenge was how to make slavery – a 'hidden' crime – legible and measurable. Measurement has long been the core focus of Walk Free's work. Forrest subscribes 'to the belief that if you can't measure something, you can't fix it'.[44] As one of its first steps, Walk Free hired Kevin Bales to develop and produce a Global Slavery Index (GSI),

38 Ibid.

39 '2012 Bellagio-Harvard Guidelines on the Legal Parameters of Slavery', 375, Guideline 2.

40 Allain, 'Contemporary slavery and its definition in law', 37.

41 Gross and Thomas, 'The new abolitionism', 111.

42 Beutin, *Trafficking in Antiblackness*, 143–145.

43 Merry, *The Seductions of Quantification*; and Rittich, 'Representing, counting, valuing', 238, 255.

44 Walk Free, *Measurement, Action, Freedom*, 5.

which ranks countries based on the prevalence of modern slavery in their territories, their citizens' vulnerability to it, and their response.[45]

The first GSI, produced and published by Walk Free in 2013, explained that modern slavery encompasses human trafficking, forced labour, slavery, and slavery-like practices (a category that includes debt bondage, forced or servile marriage, and sale or exploitation of children, including in armed conflict).[46] According to Walk Free, what is common to these different practices is that 'victims of modern slavery have their freedom denied, and are used and controlled and exploited by another person for profit, sex, or the thrill of domination'.[47] The 2016 index also emphasised the element of control, noting that 'modern slavery' refers to situations 'with treatment akin to a farm animal'.[48] This understanding of modern slavery is similar to the definition of slavery in the Bellagio–Harvard Guidelines.

Initially, the GSI Index competed against the measuring and ranking systems of the US government, the International Labour Organization (ILO), and the International Organization for Migration (IOM). Each adopted a different approach to measuring trafficking, forced labour, and modern slavery, and each approach reflected different definitions that stemmed from political as much as conceptual and technical choices.[49] In 2013, the GSI's estimate of the extent of modern slavery – 29.8 million people globally – significantly exceeded the ILO's estimate of forced labour and human trafficking, which it pegged at 18.7 million.[50] In each subsequent edition of the GSI, the number of slaves in the world increased – from 35.8 million in 2014 to 45.8 million in 2016 as its methodology changed. Despite attracting a great deal of criticism for its flimsy methodology and earning a 'Pinocchio' ranking by the *Washington Post*'s Fact Checker column, the GSI was widely taken up by 'the global elite of governments, international organisations, philanthropists, and others'.[51]

45 Beutin, *Trafficking in Antiblackness*, 144.

46 Walk Free, *Global Slavery Index*, 2013. The ILO's Forced Labour Convention, 1930 (No. 29, Art. 2) defines forced labour as 'work or service which is exacted from any person under the menace of any penalty and for which said person has not offered himself voluntarily'. It identifies forced labour as a serious crime.

47 Walk Free, *Global Slavery Index*, 2013, 10.

48 Ibid., 2016, 10.

49 Merry, *The Seductions of Quantification*, 299; and Weitzer, 'New directions in research on human trafficking', 6–24; Rittich, 'Representing, counting, valuing', 238–270; Guth et al., 'Proper methodology and methods of collecting and analyzing slavery data', 14–22; and Gallagher, 'What's wrong with the Global Slavery Index?', 90–112.

50 Dottridge, 'Trafficked and exploited', 76; and Phillips, 'The politics of numbers', 44, 47.

51 Phillips, 'The politics of numbers', 46; LeBaron, 'The coming and current crisis', 1; and Kessler, 'The false claim that human trafficking is a "$9.5 billion business"'.

In the face of increasing criticism of its methodology, Walk Free joined forces with the ILO and IOM in 2017 to develop the joint Global Estimates of Modern Slavery.[52] This partnership significantly boosted the estimates' credibility and legitimacy. The ILO regards the 2017 Global Estimates as providing the 'benchmark figures against which progress of global efforts to eradicate modern slavery can be measured'.[53]

These estimates do not, however, rank countries according to their measures to combat modern slavery. The ILO is not involved in the GSI, which is a ranking exercise, but when it works with Walk Free to produce the Global Estimates on Modern Slavery, it lends an aura of legitimacy to the GSI. The GSI is now a leading global policy tool despite continued criticisms of its methods.[54] Moreover, it is widely cited in the media, which amplifies both the huge number of victims and the worst offenders.[55]

What is striking about the Global Estimates is the sheer enormity of the problem of modern slavery; an estimated 40 million people were victims of modern slavery in 2016. Of the total number of modern slaves, 25 million are in forced labour and 15 million are in forced marriage. Women and girls are estimated to account for 71 per cent of all victims of modern slavery, and debt bondage is estimated to have affected half of all victims of forced labour imposed by private actors. These estimates, which are treated as authoritative, help to construct the crime of modern slavery, its victims, and the extent of the problem.

The Global Estimates were the basis of Walk Free's revamped 2017 GSI, which is broken into two components. Its Vulnerability Model is widely treated as the source of 'official' statistics on the extent, types, and location of modern slavery.[56] It provides a risk score for 167 countries based on an analysis of data covering twenty-three risk variables across five major dimensions and functions as a 'measure of moral violation'.[57] These statistics are brought to life on Walk Free's website through vivid pictures of modern slaves in their work environment; information about the steps each government has taken to combat modern slavery; and maps of its distribution across the globe. Africa is covered in red, indicating the highest risk, and the Middle East and

52 ILO and Walk Free Foundation, *Global Estimates of Modern Slavery*.
53 Mügge, '40.3 million slaves?'
54 Ibid. For a discussion of the GSI methodology and estimates of modern slavery, see Landman, 'Measuring modern slavery', 303–331.
55 Brankovic, 'Measure of shame', 103–125.
56 LeBaron, 'The coming and current crisis', 43–52; and Phillips, 'The politics of numbers', 44–59.
57 Brankovic, 'Measure of shame', 103–125.

most of Asia are in shades of red and orange. Lighter shades in South America and white across western Europe, northern America, Australia, and New Zealand conjure an image of 'the Global North metaphorically shedding light onto the dark parts of the world where slavery still flourishes'.[58]

Walk Free also provides a Government Response Index that assesses the legal, policy, and programmatic actions that 181 governments are taking to respond to modern slavery. The index is in keeping with its self-proclaimed goal to become 'the leading non-government, non-business organisation to independently assess each country's progress towards United Nation's Sustainable Development Goal 8.7', which is to eliminate modern slavery and child labour by 2030.[59] Condemning the lack of official indicators to determine progress, in 2019 Walk Free released *Measurement, Action, Freedom*, which assesses the responses of 183 governments to modern slavery. Adopting 'situational crime prevention theory' as its conceptual frame for tracking progress, Walk Free assesses data relating to 102 indicators to evaluate and rank each county's progress.[60] These indicators tend to reflect modern slavery's antitrafficking heritage in criminal law. Most of the indicators refer to victim identification, criminal prosecution, and governmental coordination, although some address broader institutional and social risk factors and policies to prevent sourcing slave-made goods and services. The rankings tend to reinforce the image of richer countries in the Global North bringing pressure to bear on less civilised countries in the Global South, reformatting the old trope that ending slavery is the 'white man's burden'.[61] The UK, the Netherlands, and the United States lead the country rankings, with Australia not far behind. North Korea, Eritrea, Burundi, the Central African Republic, Afghanistan, Mauritania, South Sudan, Pakistan, Cambodia, and Iran hold the lowest ranks. By naming and shaming countries that tolerate slavery, the Government Response Index attributes moral blame and portrays slavery as a premodern problem that happens in evil or backward countries far away 'over there'.

Walk Free has assembled a global antislavery alliance that comprises governments, international organisations, religious leaders, NGOs, businesses, and academics. Its emphasis on recruiting both religious and business leaders is distinctive. Noting that over 80 per cent of the world's population is religious, it seeks to engage and unite faith leaders around the world to take

[58] McGrath and Watson, 'Anti-slavery as development', 22, 26.

[59] Walk Free, *Global Slavery Index*, 2018.

[60] Walk Free, *Measurement, Action, Freedom*, 28. This approach focuses on the setting for the crime rather than the characteristic of offenders.

[61] Kempadoo, 'Anti-slavery as development', 22–31.

spiritual and practical action to eradicate modern slavery. In 2014, Forrest established the Global Freedom Network, a faith-based group led by Pope Francis, Justin Welby (the archbishop of Canterbury), and Ahmed Mohamed Ahmed El-Tayeb (the grand imam of al-Ashar), in which religious leaders around the world unite to end modern slavery.[62] The network convened a meeting of key representatives of major global faith traditions at the Vatican on 2 December 2014, where they endorsed the Joint Declaration of Religious Leaders Against Modern Slavery, which pledged to eradicate modern slavery and human trafficking by 2020.[63] Walk Free is also the secretariat for the Bali Process Government and Business Forum, which brings together government ministers and senior business leaders to determine policies for addressing modern slavery and the worst forms of child labour in the Asia-Pacific region. This alliance of religion and business suggests that the goal of eradicating modern slavery transcends partisan approaches and traditional conflicts of interest; it is a moral question.[64] Walk Free has wide support, including from the UK, US, and Australian governments, the Association of Southeast Asian Nations (ASEAN), and the United Nations Inter-Agency Project on Human Trafficking.

Forrest and Walk Free are strong proponents of private initiatives and public–private partnerships. By 2011, governments had grown fatigued with funding antitrafficking initiatives; in response, the role of philanthrocapitalists and business increased.[65] In 2013, Forrest's charitable foundation, Minderoo, together with two private foundations (Humanity International, which was set up by the founder of eBay, and Legatum, the offspring of a Dubai-based private investment firm) established a new private Freedom Fund to support efforts to eradicate modern slavery. Allocating US$30 million to the fund, the three foundations set a goal of raising and spending US$100 million to combat slavery by 2020.[66] The fund's mission is to attract funding and innovative investors to frontline efforts to eradicate modern slavery in countries and sectors where it is most prevalent.[67] Bales, who is on the Freedom Fund's board of directors, estimated in 2007 that the cost of extirpating slavery would amount to about US$13.5 billion over a twenty-five-year period.[68] This

62 Chuang, 'Giving as governance?', 1533.
63 Walk Free, 'The Global Freedom Network'.
64 Bunting and Quirk, 'Contemporary slavery as more than rhetorical strategy?', 5, 19.
65 Dottridge, 'Private donors'.
66 Dottridge, 'Trafficked and exploited', 59, 76; and Ucnikova, 'OECD and modern slavery', 133–150.
67 Freedom Fund, 'Our vision is a world free of slavery'.
68 Bales, 'What predicts human trafficking?', 269–291.

figure has been cited by Walk Free researchers to castigate Organisation for Economic Co-operation and Development (OECD) member states for failing to provide sufficient funding.[69] As more money is distributed by this public–private partnership to frontline organisations, the call for metrics to determine the success of the initiatives escalates.

Walk Free created the Global Fund to End Modern Slavery (GFEMS) to 'coordinate a coherent global strategy to address modern slavery'.[70] The GFEMS's goal is to raise US$1.5 billion (£1.1 billion) to eliminate modern slavery by making it economically unprofitable. According to its first CEO, a former vice-president of global procurement for ExxonMobil, the organisation believes that 'sustainably ending modern slavery will require market-based solutions and proactive business leadership'.[71] The GFEMS was endorsed early on by the ILO, and in 2017 it received substantial funding from the US Department of State and the UK Department for International Development. Organisations (known as partners) that receive financial assistance from the GFEMS must support the fund's theory of change, which posits that 'there is demonstrable, long term economic value to be unlocked by eliminating forced labor from supply chains'.[72]

The idea is that once governments 'raise the cost of slavery by ending impunity (via effective laws/policies, civil remedies, and criminal proceedings) for all forms of trafficking', the private sector will be free to create and capture 'value by eliminating forced labour from supply chains'.[73] The dividends of freedom can then be used to provide alternative livelihoods for vulnerable individuals. This approach chimes with attempts to prove that 'slavery is bad for business'. Since Adam Smith wrote about the economic costs of slavery in the late eighteenth century, the assumption has been that chattel slavery is not as profitable as free wage labour. Kevin Bales, among others, has embraced this position, arguing that forced labour not only involves firm- and market-level inefficiencies but also imposes enormous opportunity costs and negative externalities on the population.[74]

69 Ucnikova, 'OECD and modern slavery', 146.

70 Mortimer, 'US and UK pledge millions'.

71 Ibid.

72 Global Fund to End Modern Slavery, 'Theory of change'.

73 Global Fund to End Modern Slavery, 'Funding principles', available at www.gfems.org/funding-principles (last visited 23 April 2021).

74 Datta and Bales, 'Slavery is bad for business', 205–223; Raigrodski, 'Creative capitalism and human trafficking', 71–134.

This emphasis on the market as a solution is a theme in other public–private partnerships established to combat modern slavery. Launched at the UN in 2017, the Financial Sector Commission on Modern Slavery and Human Trafficking, known as the Liechtenstein Initiative, was formed as a public–private partnership between Liechtenstein, Australia, and the Centre for Policy Research at the United Nations University. It has now established Finance Against Slavery and Trafficking (FAST) to develop initiatives to mobilise and promote responsible investment in the financial sector, such as tracking illicit financial flows to capture profits from modern slavery and making good-faith efforts to address forced labour risks in supply chains. The commission's 2019 report, *A Blueprint for Mobilizing Finance against Slavery and Trafficking*, depicts modern slavery as 'a tragic market failure'. Slavery, it argues, deprives those enslaved of an estimated US$150 billion for their labour each year and creates unfair competition by lowering labour costs.[75] It also represents a labour-market failure by failing to provide decent work and employment opportunities for all.[76] Emphasising the need for information about the risks of modern slavery to correct these market failures, the report recognises that additional regulatory interventions might be required to generate risk identification at the individual firm level, which could then be used to produce 'comparable market information' that would 'eventually impact pricing signals and costs of capital at the individual enterprise level'.[77]

Public–private partnerships, exemplified by the Freedom Fund, GFEMS, and FAST, consist of interlinking and overlapping individuals and organisations, and philanthrocapitalists such as Forrest and their charitable foundations are at their centre.[78] Together, they have assembled a strategic and purposeful ethical business alliance built on the idea that slavery is a market failure. The Global Slavery Index both identifies the problem of modern slavery and ranks governments in terms of their progress in solving it. It collects data, develops indicators, depicts the problem, and identifies best practices. It then circulates this knowledge through the larger global antislavery governance network. The ethical business alliance also creates financial incentives for other actors in the broader assemblage to adopt its understanding of the problem and its preferred solutions. It depicts modern slavery as 'a tragic result of market failure', the solution to which is corporate engagement

75 Liechtenstein Initiative, 'A blueprint for mobilizing finance', 2.
76 Ibid.
77 Ibid., 81.
78 Bales is on the board of the Freedom Fund, and Jean Baderschneider was a member of the Liechtenstein Initiative's commission.

and free markets.[79] Its goal is to persuade governments and other powerful governance actors that it has the best policy solutions for eliminating forced labour in supply chains.

THE ETHICAL BUSINESS ALLIANCE AND THE GOVERNANCE OF GLOBAL SUPPLY CHAINS

The twin goals of fostering decent work in global supply chains and taking action to eradicate modern slavery, forced labour, and human trafficking (as called for by SDG 8.7) moved onto the political stage at the May 2017 meeting of G20 labour and employment ministers in Bad Neuenahr, Germany.[80] Business-led initiatives had the greatest appeal, although other state-led measures were suggested.

In his keynote address to the meeting, John Ruggie (the UN Secretary-General's Special Representative for Business and Human Rights from 2005 to 2011) advised that the gap between the scale and impact of multinational corporations and the capacity of states to manage the adverse consequences of globalisation could be narrowed 'either through more effective cooperation or through roll-back, otherwise known as protectionism'.[81] Ruggie proposed the United Nations Guiding Principles on Business and Human Rights (UNGPs) as 'a roadmap for helping to bridge the governance gaps and imbalances that must be addressed for global supply chains and globalization itself to become socially sustainable'.[82]

The UNGPs were Ruggie's attempt to develop authoritative standards of expected behaviour from business regarding human rights. A form of 'soft' law, they offered human-rights due-diligence (HRDD) as a process for businesses to meet their obligation to respect human rights.[83] HRDD has three

[79] Cockayne, 'Working with the financial sector' 159–162. Cockayne was head of secretariat, Liechtenstein Initiative for FAST, is the Head of Office at the United Nations for the United Nations University, and the New South Wales Anti-slavery Commissioner.

[80] G20 Labour and Employment Ministers Meeting – Germany, 'Ministerial declaration'.

[81] Ruggie, '"Making economic globalization work for all"'.

[82] Ibid.

[83] The UNGP set out guidelines for implementing the 'Protect, Respect and Remedy' Framework, which consists of three complementary and interdependent pillars: (1) the state duty to protect against human rights abuses by third parties, including business enterprises, through appropriate policies, regulation, and adjudication; (2) corporate responsibility to respect human rights, which means that business enterprises should act with due diligence to avoid infringing on the human rights of others and to address adverse impacts with which they are involved; and (3) greater access by victims to effective remedy, judicial and nonjudicial.

interconnected components: (1) identifying actual or potential human-rights impacts; (2) preventing and mitigating those impacts; and (3) accounting for impacts and the responses to them. The UNGPs provide guidance about the scope and complexity of due-diligence obligations, how to prioritise redress for adverse human-rights impacts, and when and how to disclose information to stakeholders.[84] However, the guidelines are ambiguous about the extent to which states should supervise, or even mandate, corporate HRDD,[85] which help to explain their remarkable success. Adopted unanimously in 2011 by the forty-seven members of the Council of Human Rights (selected from member states of the UN General Assembly), the UNGPs have been widely taken up by large multinational corporations.

In their concluding declaration at the 2017 meeting, the G20 labour and employment ministers 'underlined the responsibility of businesses to exercise due diligence' in line with the UNGPs, the ILO Tripartite Declaration of Principles concerning Multinational Enterprises and Social Policy, and the OECD Guidelines for Multinational Enterprises, and 'encouraged businesses to report on these due-diligence procedures'.[86] They also committed to developing policy frameworks to foster decent work in sustainable, slavery-free global supply chains. These frameworks could include ratification of the ILO's 2014 Protocol to the Forced Labour Convention, incorporation of the ILO's Fundamental Rights and Principles at work in trade agreements, and the involvement of stakeholders (trade unions, workers, employers, companies, and consumers) in initiatives. In its follow-up Call to Action to End Forced Labour, Modern Slavery, and Human Trafficking, launched at the 2017 UN General Assembly, the UK government accentuated business-led initiatives, government procurement practices, and 'building a culture of consumer awareness which supports such action and promotes decent work'.[87]

It was in this political environment that Walk Free promoted a business-led approach to tackling modern slavery in supply chains within the broader global antislavery governance network. It created and distributed knowledge about modern slavery and how best to eradicate it from supply chains and

[84] Landau, *Human Rights Due Diligence and Labour Governance*. The UNGPs also provided guidance about the scope and complexity of due-diligence obligations, how to prioritise redress for adverse human rights impacts, and when and how to disclose information to stakeholders.

[85] Ibid.

[86] G20 Labour and Employment Ministers Meeting – Germany, 'Ministerial declaration'.

[87] United Kingdom, Department for International Development, 'A call to action to end forced labour'.

assembled an elite ethical business alliance to promote its solution.[88] Its 2018 Global Slavery Index examined 'the issue of modern slavery from the perspective of where ... the products of the crime are sold and consumed'.[89] Remarking that 'too often, the onus of eliminating modern slavery is placed only on the countries where the crime is perpetrated', Walk Free focused for the first time on key supply chains to G20 countries to understand 'the transfer of risk from source countries to consumer countries'.[90] This knowledge helped foster an elite consensus that the best way to tackle modern slavery in supply chains is through mandatory disclosure and due-diligence obligations. This solution rests on a specific understanding of the problem of modern slavery and of the role of supply chains in its production and circulation, one that characterises the cause of the problem as a combination of market failure and the territorial limits of the sovereign state.

The 2018 GSI defines, depicts, and measures the problem of modern slavery and the effects of state action – a form of governance by numbers. Its goal was to influence public opinion, policy, and legislation. It depicts modern slavery as a combination of market failure and the limited jurisdiction of nation-states to deal with social problems that cross national borders. Its solution calls on large multinational firms and their financial backers since only they are free to exercise their power across national borders.

Harnessing the Power of Business, released by Walk Free in 2016, exemplifies this way of thinking. In the foreword to the report, Forrest portrays himself as an ethical business leader. He explains that after his daughter learned of the extent of modern slavery in the Asia-Pacific region, he made a commitment as chairman of Fortescue Metals Group to deal with slavery in the mining conglomerate's global supply chain. Fortescue's suppliers were asked to review their first- and second-order supply chains and to ensure there was no forced labour or slavery-type practices in them. Verité, a labour auditing expert, was hired to verify the suppliers' reports.[91] However, the problem with these voluntary due-diligence initiatives is, Forrest notes, that business leaders who adopt them and disclose the results may be at competitive disadvantage against

88 In Foucauldian terms, Walk Free assembled a *dispostif* that created and then distributed knowledge about modern slavery and how best to eradicate it from supply chains (Foucault, *Society Must Be Defended*, 33–34). Ngai-Ling Sum and Bob Jessop define a *dispositif* as (1) a strategic and purposeful apparatus that comprises institutions, organisations, and networks; (2) a discourse with themes and objectives; (3) devices and technologies involved in producing power/knowledge; and (4) subject positions. Sum and Jessop, *Towards a Cultural Political Economy*, 208. See Fudge, 'Bad for business'.

89 Walk Free, *Global Slavery Index*, 2018, 102.

90 Ibid., 102, 103.

91 A global leader in iron ore, Fortescue generated over US$7.1 billion in revenue in 2016.

those who do nothing. They 'punish those who put the time and effort into ensuring they have clean supply chains, whilst rewarding those who do nothing'.[92] Forrest's solution is for governments to introduce legislation requiring businesses to prepare a yearly slavery statement disclosing the steps taken to ensure that their organisations and supply chains are slavery-free.

A guiding theme of Walk Free's approach to modern slavery is the role it sees for government, which is to create a level-playing field for ethical businesses. The beauty of mandatory disclosure, according to Walk Free, is that it enables 'the court of public opinion' to rank how organisations respond to the issues and permits investors and consumers to 'lead with their wallets'.[93] According to this view, once businesses disclose their and their suppliers' practices, consumers and investors can exercise their individual moral choices with confidence. Over time, firms that do not take adequate steps to end slavery will lose both customers and capital. Business leaders, consumers, and investors are cast as ethical subjects who want to follow their conscience and make ethical choices; the government's role is to ensure that they have the information to do so.

Walk Free also underscores the comparative governance advantage businesses have over governments: '[B]usinesses are very used to operating across borders', whereas 'the government capacity tends to be confined with national borders'.[94] Disclosure laws can have an extraterritorial effect by creating incentives for business to eradicate slavery transmitted through transnational supply chains. In this way, state sovereignty can be extended beyond territorial borders by requiring multinational enterprises to take steps to ensure that slave-made goods do not infiltrate their supply chains, thereby preventing such goods from crossing national borders. The imposition of mandatory-reporting obligations on firms is supposed to narrow the governance gap.

Advocates characterise modern slavery laws as a response to market failure, and they argue that eliminating slavery and thereby correcting market failure will be good for business.[95] Mandatory-reporting requirements purport to discipline business through market pressure. By making disclosure initiatives mandatory, public authorities exercise their sovereignty over lead firms located in their territorial jurisdiction in the Global North to 'leverage' private governance for public purposes in the Global South.[96] At the same time, states also

[92] Walk Free, *Harnessing the Power of Business*, 1.
[93] Ibid., 2.
[94] Ibid., 16.
[95] Ethical Trading Initiative, 'Modern slavery statement 2017/18'.
[96] Phillips, LeBaron, and Wallin, 'Mapping and measuring', 2.

augment and validate corporate authority by outsourcing governance to multinational enterprises.

Big business in Australia, the UK, and the United States has widely supported supply chain disclosure legislation, and it has been enacted by governments in countries that are key sites for new abolitionists through the 2010 California Supply Chain Act,[97] the United Kingdom's Modern Slavery Act 2015,[98] and Australia's Modern Slavery Act 2018.[99] Such legislation differs in terms of coverage; whether auditing is required; and the form, content, and stringency of disclosure requirements.[100] Yet a common theme of all of these laws is that they portray businesses as able to eradicate modern slavery that crosses national borders through supply chains while at the same time studiously avoiding imposing liability on them for business models and practices that cultivate unfreedom. As Walk Free's submission to the Australian government on its proposed modern slavery law declared: 'Our approach must be to encourage business to look and find, and to be open about what they discover. As a community, we must support not shame them'.[101]

Reporting and transparency obligations only require businesses to report what steps they have taken to ensure there is no modern slavery in their supply chain. They do not require businesses to take steps to eradicate modern slavery. They are a form of reflexive regulation: the goal is to provide incentives for business to regulate itself.[102] The purpose of these modern slavery laws is to enable consumers and investors in the Global North to align their ethical and economic choices. Devices such as the Global Slavery Index and techniques such as disclosure laws promote a neoliberal ethics based on individual responsibility.[103]

SHORING UP GLOBAL CAPITALISM?

Walk Free and the ethical business alliance it helped to coalesce played an important role in orienting global antislavery policy towards business and market-friendly forms of regulation to deal with slavery in global supply

97 California Civil Code, sec. 1714.43.

98 Modern Slavery Act 2015 (2015, c. 30).

99 Modern Slavery Act 2018 (No. 153, 2018); LeBaron, 'Slavery, human trafficking, and forced labour', 381–398; and Walk Free, *Harnessing the Power of Business*.

100 Phillips, LeBaron, and Wallin, 'Mapping and measuring'.

101 Wray-Bliss and Michelson, 'Modern slavery and the discursive construction'.

102 Wen, 'The cogs and wheels of reflexive law and business disclosure', 327–359.

103 Jessop, 'Neoliberalization, uneven development, and Brexit', 1729–1733; and Davies, *The limits of neoliberalism*.

chains. A form of public–private partnership dominated by a few key actors, the alliance uses faith and free markets to frame modern slavery. It claims that slavery is bad for business and that business can help to eradicate modern slavery. Disclosure requirements and rankings are supposed to enable consumers and investors to align their ethical beliefs with their economic choices without disrupting the existing structures of consumption and accumulation, promoting 'the commodification of ethics'.[104] As Forrest informed the *New York Times* in 2018, 'modern slavery is a First World problem. If you are a chief executive or an investor and you are not prepared to take human rights into account now, you don't deserve to be a chief executive or an investor'.[105] The idea is that the market can be an instrument of ethical consumption and accumulation – if business leaders are encouraged to connect moral norms to corporate policies through managerial practices. This 'ethico-managerial strategy' emerged as belief in global trade (best exemplified by supply chains) as the best road to prosperity (especially in the Global South) began to fade.[106] It attempts to recalibrate and stabilise what a former director of Anti-Slavery International called 'a neo-liberal government alliance with the hyperwealthy' rather than transform it.[107]

The market failure approach to the problem of modern slavery is contested. From a critical political-economy perspective, supply chains are not conduits of unfree labour committed by bad actors located in the Global South; rather, lead firms located in the Global North and their associated management practices are the drivers of modern slavery. Critical scholars argue that lead firms, typically large multinational enterprises, generate intense competition along the supply chains they dominate, which results in labour cost-cutting pressures along the chain.[108] The imperative within the supply chain is to assemble a particular kind of labour force and utilise it in a way that generates the maximum flexibility for the firm, limits the ability of workers to bargain in the labour process, and maximises the return on capital. Research reveals that forced labour and slave-like conditions are not the outcomes of market failure but rather a predictable feature of many sectors and regions of the global political economy.[109]

[104] Mezzadri, *The Sweatshop Regime*, 187.
[105] Wray-Bliss and Michelson, 'Modern slavery and the discursive construction'.
[106] Arnold and Hess, 'Governmentalizing Gramsci', 7.
[107] Dottridge, 'Private donors'.
[108] Phillips and Mieres, 'The governance of forced labour', 244–260.
[109] Mezzadri, 'Class, gender and the sweatshop', 1877–1900; Crane et al., 'Governance gaps in eradicating forced labor', 86–106; LeBaron, 'The coming and current crisis'; Anderson and Rogaly, 'Forced labour and migration to the UK'; Barrientos, *Gender and Work in Global Value Chains*; and Phillips, 'Unfree labour and adverse incorporation', 171–196.

Evidence supporting this critical perspective on global supply chains comes from an unlikely source – the World Bank. Its 2020 flagship report, *Trading for Development in the Age of Global Value Chains*, made the astonishing admission that 'the risk that firms from developing countries experience limited profits after becoming suppliers for global firms mirrors the rise in profits in the developed world'.[110] Higher markups in firms located in developed countries and integrated into global supply chains have reduced labour's share of income worldwide (as well as the share of capital amongst those firms integrated into global supply chains and located in developing countries).[111] The gains are only partly passed on to consumers and suppliers; the real winners from global value chains are large transnational firms, primarily located in the Global North, who have reduced production costs.[112] Despite evidence that gains are not 'trickling down' the supply chain, the World Bank advocates a 'business as usual' approach that promotes international trade agreements and flexible labour markets.

The problem with the 'market failure' story is that it ignores the possibility that profitable business and management practices for key firms in the Global North create the conditions that lead to modern slavery and forced labour lower down the chain in the Global South. It leaves the supporting multiscalar legal framework – which consists of domestic contract and corporate law and international investment, trade, and intellectual property laws – intact.[113]

The perspective that transnational corporations contribute to unfree labour is gaining ground, fuelled in part by what the pandemic revealed about the frailty of global supply chains and how they distributed the greatest risks to the most vulnerable links – workers in the Global South.[114] Indeed, in its 2023 GSI, Walk Free recognises that the purchasing practices of business and governments in wealthy countries 'fuel exploitation in lower-income countries that are at the front line of global supply chains'.[115] Adding to scepticism that the market is the 'solution' to the problem of modern slavery is growing awareness that the use of disclosure legislation has not produced tangible results, despite the energy and money that has gone into promoting firm compliance and refining disclosure and reporting requirements.[116] Research

[110] World Bank, *Trading for Development*, 86.
[111] Ibid., 84–85.
[112] Ibid., 86.
[113] Alessandrini, 'Global value chains, development and the *long durée*'.
[114] BHRRC, 'Wage theft and pandemic profits'.
[115] Walk Free, *Global Slavery Index*, 2023, 146.
[116] Phillips, LeBaron, and Wallin, 'Mapping and measuring', 28. See also Chapter 6.

also reveals that consumers do very little if anything about modern slavery in their consumption, even when they identify it as a significant moral issue.[117]

The shift towards mandatory HRDD reflects growing doubt, even among members of the ethical business alliance, that corporate self-regulation is sufficient to address slavery in supply chains.[118] These laws hardens soft norms like the UNGPS, the ILO's Multinational Enterprises and Social Policies Declaration (MNE Declaration), and the revised OECD Guidelines by requiring companies to engage in some form of due-diligence process to identify, prevent, and address adverse human-rights impacts in their businesses.[119] With the enactment of the French Duty of Vigilance Law in 2017, binding due diligence has become a popular governance mechanism for addressing human rights and environmental abuses that result from transnational business practices.[120] Mandatory HRDD laws have been proliferating in European countries, and the EU has adopted a directive that requires each member to adopt a law imposing due-diligence obligations on corporations and sets out minimum conditions for these laws to meet and, thus, 'level' the playing field.[121]

CONCLUSION

Dissatisfaction with the limited effectiveness of existing disclosure regulations has resulted in Walk Free's support for harder governance mechanisms for addressing modern slavery in supply chains. The 2023 GSI recommended that, among other things, G20 governments (mostly located in the Global North) enact mandatory HRDD legislation requiring large businesses and publicly funded entities to identify and remediate forced labour risks; strengthen existing disclosure laws by adding and implementing penalties and providing a free and accessible repository for modern slavery statements; and take other legal measures such as import controls on products linked to forced labour.[122]

117 Carrington, Chatzidakis, and Shaw, 'Consuming worker exploitation?', 432–450. For a more sanguine assessment of using consumer purchasing power to improve labour standards, see Kolben, 'The consumer imaginary', 839–898.

118 Freedom Fund, 'Freedom in the supply chain'.

119 LeBaron and Rühmkorf, 'The domestic politics of corporate accountability legislation', 710.

120 Duty of Vigilance of Parent and on Its Affiliated Entitles, Law No. 2017-399 (27 March 2017); World Bank, *Trading for Development*; and Evans, 'Overcoming the global despondency trap', 658–685.

121 Dehbi and Martin-Ortega, 'An integrated approach to corporate due diligence'.

122 Walk Free, *Global Slavery Index*, 2023, 150.

Mandatory HRDD laws enlist transnational corporations to enforce human rights and labour standards across national borders, effectively rescaling the sovereignty of states in the Global North. They are 'evolving as a tool for shaping not only corporate conduct, but also the conduct of Global South states with regard to human rights and environmental standards'.[123] So far, none of the mandatory HRDD laws enacted or proposed impose obligations on lead firms to engage in meaningful consultation with actors in the Global South (governments, trade unions, NGOs, and workers) about how their business practices may contribute to modern slavery in supply chains or how to devise effective grievance mechanisms for workers.[124] Indeed, there is a growing literature that is sceptical of the capacity of existing mandatory hrdd laws in Europe to advance the protection of human rights.[125]

Import bans or controls on goods suspected to have used forced labour in their production are a form of trade sanction directed at foreign-made goods.[126] States impose them to protect their citizens' morals from corruption and their markets from unfair competition. Some human-rights advocates see import bans as complementary to mandatory HRDD laws since they can be used to persuade lead firms to exercise their leverage with suppliers to eliminate forced labour in the labour process and as an incentive for suppliers to eliminate forced labour to gain access to markets.[127] However, those who adopt a labour rights perspective caution that bans can be harmful depending on how they are handled; at worst, they can threaten the existence of suppliers with no upside for workers.[128] Under the US import ban, for example, the enforcement agency is not required to consult with workers who are alleged to have been subject to forced labour before issuing a ban, and the law does not

[123] Dehbi and Martin-Ortega, 'An integrated approach to corporate due diligence', 6, references omitted.

[124] Ibid.

[125] Deva, 'Mandatory human rights due diligence in Europe', 390.

[126] At present, only the US, Mexico, and Canada have forced labour import bans in place, and only the US has significant experience enforcing a forced labour import ban. The Mexican and Canadian bans were implemented to meet the requirements enshrined in the US-Mexico-Canada trade agreement. Australia has proposed to introduce a ban on the import of goods made with forced labour through an amendment to its Customs Act, and the European Union has proposed a regulation that would ban the import, sale, and export of products within the EU of goods made with forced labour. Fudge and LeBaron, 'Regulatory design and interactions in worker-driven social responsibility initiatives'; and Pietropaoli, Johnstone, and Balch, 'Effectiveness of forced labour import bans'.

[127] Anti-Slavery International and European Center for Constitutional and Human Rights, *Position on Import Controls*; and LaFianza, 'Threatening ill-gotten gains'.

[128] Fudge and LeBaron, 'Regulatory design and interactions in worker-driven social responsibility initiatives' .

require that provision be made to protect workers or remediate the impacts they might experience because a ban has been imposed.[129]

Mandatory HRDD laws and import bans single out corporations and states in the Global North as the key agents of change. These top-down governance measures tend to reinforce, rather than challenge, the prevailing concentration of power in global economic and political relations. Since these laws do not provide participatory and remedial rights for workers at lower tiers in global supply chains, they treat workers at risk of modern slavery as passive victims rather than as potentially transformative actors.

There is, however, some evidence that key actors in the global antislavery governance network have begun to support governance measures that directly empower workers. Along with these top-down measures, Walk Free's 2023 GSI also advised governments to extend 'labour laws and fundamental labour rights to all groups without exception, including freedom of association and collective bargaining'.[130] The ILO, one of Walk Free's partners in developing the influential Global Slavery Estimates, has made the labour approach a prominent strategy in the global antislavery governance network. As we will see in the next chapter, the ILO used the UN human trafficking protocol's reference to forced labour in its definition of human trafficking to revitalise its mandate and fashion a distinctive labour approach to unfree labour. It acted at the same time as its constituents fought over the scalar dimension of the ILO's distinctive governance instrument, international labour standards.

[129] Ibid.
[130] Walk Free, *The Global Slavery Index*, 2023, 4.

3

The ILO's Governance of Forced Labour

Forced labour represents the underside of globalization.

—ILO, 'More than 12 million are trapped in forced labour worldwide'

It makes less and less sense for the ILO to supervise its standards nation state by nation state, on the basis of freely ratified Conventions, when supply chains are cutting across those nation states.

—'Address by Guy Ryder, Director-General of the International Labour Organization', Paris, France, 20 June 2015

Recruited to the ILO in 2002 to head the newly established Special Action Programme to Combat Forced Labour (SAP-FL), Roger Plant faced a challenge: to 'convince politicians, diplomats, business leaders, and labour unions that slavery truly is a global problem'.[1] He oversaw the preparation and publication of two extremely influential reports on forced labour, which established the ILO as an authoritative source of knowledge about forced labour and human trafficking. What initially set these reports apart from the burgeoning literature produced by regional and international organisations, governments, and NGOs was their use of numbers; they quantified the number of people estimated to toil in conditions of forced labour and measured its economic cost. Quantification is an effective technique for attracting the attention of policy actors because it translates 'complex phenomenon into simplified numerical representations that make modern forms of governance

[1] ILO, 'Roger Plant, winner of the William Wilberforce Award'.

possible'.[2] As Plant declared, 'We've got to persuade public opinion, and this is the importance of that headcount.'[3]

Knowledge production through defining, depicting, and measuring forced labour was part of the ILO's broader shift away from its traditional juridical mode of governance via the production of labour standards.[4] It also accounts, in large part, for the ILO's success in establishing itself as a key player in the global antitrafficking governance network, shifting the focus of the network away from an exclusive preoccupation with trafficking for sexual exploitation to include the labour dimension.

Drawing the border between forced labour and other forms of labour exploitation and mapping forced labour's relationship to human trafficking was critical to the ILO's governance agenda. Like other key actors in the antitrafficking governance network, the ILO treated sexual exploitation differently from labour exploitation. In the 1920s, both the ILO and its sister organisation, the League of Nations, regarded sex trafficking to be 'of a criminal character' and, thus, not within the ILO's jurisdiction. Since then, the ILO's deliberations over sex work have been an amalgam of workers protection, criminalisation, and moralism that has shifted over time and in different contexts.[5] In the 1980s, for example, HIV/AIDS prevention was the entry point for the ILO to treat 'sex work' as a form of labour. Although not explicitly recognised as work, the sale of sexual services was treated as a matter of occupational health and safety. However, for the purposes of legal recognition and standard setting, the ILO legal department was clear: 'Prostitution has never been considered as employment or occupation.'[6]

After making forced labour visible within the antitrafficking network, the ILO's next challenge was to erect a normative foundation for a distinctive labour approach to preventing it. The ILO Forced Labour Convention, 1930, defines forced labour as a crime and obliges states to prohibit it.[7] To utilise the traditional tools of labour law (labour standards, labour inspectors, and joint activities by social partners) to prevent forced labour and to provide redress for its victims, the ILO needed a new standard that would complement the

2 Drubel, 'Regulation by visibility', 190.
3 ILO, 'Roger Plant, winner of the William Wilberforce Award'; and Baccaro and Mele, 'Pathology of path dependency'.
4 Ibid.; Jones, 'A "north star" in governing labour migration?'.
5 Boris and Rodriguez García, '(In)decent work', 211.
6 Ibid.
7 ILO Forced Labour Convention, 1930 (No. 29), 28 June 1930.

prohibition-and-punishment approach of criminal law and add another facet to the overarching multidimensional governance frame.[8]

However, to achieve a new standard, the ILO had to mobilise its tripartite constituents. It overcame the Employers' Group's resistance to new standards by linking forced labour to human trafficking and explaining that the proposed standard would simply extend the existing labour law tools to detecting and preventing forced labour and protecting its victims. In 2014 the ILO adopted the Protocol of 2014 to the Forced Labour Convention, 1930, which provides an alternative legal domain to the carceral one provided in the UN's Protocol to Prevent, Suppress and Punish Trafficking in Persons (2000) (the Trafficking Protocol).[9]

Forced labour poses a scalar-governance dilemma for the ILO. Since two of the key drivers of forced labour – labour migration and global supply chains – are transnational, forced labour is difficult to tackle using only national instruments, which is the ILO's scale of governance. Labour standards and enforcement mechanisms, either through trade unions or public institutions, are primarily treated as a matter of national and territorial jurisdiction. The state in which the employment relationship or work takes place typically has legal jurisdiction to govern it. Labour law's governance domain is employment and work, and employment is understood primarily in bilateral and contractual terms. The ILO's distinctive governance mechanism, the corpus of international standards, exemplifies this approach. The overwhelming majority of conventions apply only to bilateral employment relationships and do not apply to third parties or business and commercial relations. ILO conventions, like international human rights instruments, only apply to states and not to employers and corporations. Moreover, to be given effect, conventions must be 'territorialised by states through ratification and integration into national labour laws'.[10] The problem is that the territorial scale of labour governance creates an incentive for transnational corporations to use their geographic flexibility to engage in regulatory arbitrage. In this way, global supply chains 'transcend territorial nation states and jurisdictions of labour law'.[11] Territorially based jurisdiction also makes it difficult to enforce laws designed to regulate chains of labour recruiters that operate across national borders since cross-border remedies are rare and extraterritorial liability for labour violations is limited.

8 Andrees and Belser, 'Strengthening labor market governance against forced labor'.
9 Kotiswaran, 'From sex panic to extreme exploitation', 31.
10 Prentice, 'Labour rights from labour wrongs?', 1772.
11 Ibid.

Forced labour presented an opportunity for the ILO to rescale its distinctive governance mechanism – labour conventions. However, unlike the ethical business alliance – which, as we saw in Chapter 2, endorses forms of business regulation to promote transnational labour governance – the Secretariat for the Employers' Group at the ILO rejects the principle of mandatory due-diligence regulation, claiming 'it disregards state sovereignty and seeks transnational businesses to fill the on-the-ground governance gaps that exist in many parts of the world'.[12]

How did the ILO use its authority over forced labour to stake a claim in the global antitrafficking network and to steer global governance policy away from criminal and immigration law and towards labour and human rights law? How did scale operate as a contested technique of governance? To answer these questions, this chapter focuses on how the ILO used knowledge production and international labour standards to become a vital actor in the global antislavery network. It explores how and where the ILO draws the borders between free and unfree labour in interpreting and applying its definition of forced labour; how the ILO situates forced labour in relation to other forms of unfree labour such as human trafficking and modern slavery; and what makes the ILO's labour approach to ending modern slavery a distinct governance strategy. It also examines the ILO's attempts to shift scale to govern the activities of transnational supply chains and transnational labour recruiters.

REVITALISING THE ILO'S GOVERNANCE AGENDA

The ILO, whose authority had faded with the rise of neoliberalism, seized on the UN's adoption of Trafficking Protocol in 2000 to increase its visibility in the global governance debates, to deepen its connections with other international organisations, and to establish relations with a broader range of civil society actors.

Created to forestall an international race to the bottom on labour conditions after the First World War, the ILO provided a deliberative tripartite mechanism for adopting international labour standards that would then be ratified, implemented, and enforced by nation-states.[13] The resulting international code of labour standards was supposed to establish a level 'social' playing field, albeit one excluding 'native' workers in the colonies.[14] In 1944, the ILO

[12] IOE, Business at OECD, Business Europe, 'Joint business response to the Revised Draft Legally Binding Instrument'.

[13] Diller, 'Pluralism and privatization in transnational labour regulation', 329

[14] Blackett, 'On the presence of the past', 957; Kawar, 'Assembling an international social protection for the migrant'.

deepened its social justice orientation, exemplified by its motto 'labour is not a commodity', by adopting the Declaration of Philadelphia, which endorsed freedom of association for both workers and employers and the right to collective bargaining, as part of its constitution. In 1946, the ILO became the first specialised agency of the United Nations.

The ILO epitomised embedded liberalism, an international governance regime that prevailed in industrialised capitalist countries until the early 1980s. Coined by John Ruggie, the author of the UN's Guiding Principles on Business and Human Rights (UNGPs), the term refers to a 'form of multilateralism that is compatible with the requirements of domestic stability'.[15] States were persuaded to accept international economic liberalisation and its associated welfare gains because they would retain the ability to intervene to 'tame the socially disruptive effects of markets'.[16]

The ILO is composed of three main bodies – the International Labour Conference (ILC), the Governing Body (GB), and the International Labour Office (Office) – and its tripartite membership sets it apart from other international institutions affiliated with the UN. Known as the International Parliament of Labour, the ILC meets annually to adopt labour standards and to set the ILO's broad policies. Each of its 187 member states sends two government representatives, one representative of a national employers' organization, and one representative of a national trade union. Workers' representatives are drawn from the trade union movement via national federations, which means there is no direct representation of nonunion workers and workers in the informal sector.[17] The International Trade Union Confederation (ITUC) serves as the Workers' Group's secretariat. The International Organization of Employers (IOE), which styles itself as the global voice of business, plays a similar role for the Employers' Group. Its members consist of national business organisations, not actual businesses, and these organisations do not represent transnational corporations.[18] The GB is the ILO's executive. It elects the director-general, takes decisions on ILO policy, sets the annual agenda of the ILC, and establishes the programme and budget, which it then submits to the ILC for adoption. Like the ILC, the GB is tripartite, and just over one-third of the government seats are reserved for the representatives of such key countries as China, India, the Russian

[15] Ruggie, 'International regimes, transactions, and change'.

[16] Ibid., 413. Like the ILO's international labour code with its separate treatment of 'native labour', the compromise of embedded liberalism was never fully extended to the developing countries, most of which were, or recently had been, colonies.

[17] La Hovary, 'A challenging ménage à trois?'

[18] Brudney, 'Hiding in plain sight', 280.

Federation, the UK, and the United States.[19] The Office, which is under the leadership of the director-general, is the ILO's large permanent secretariat and the centre of ILO's activities. Headquartered in Geneva, the ILO also has regional and national offices. Granted a substantial degree of autonomy under the ILO's constitution, the Office and director-general can orchestrate its constituents to endorse labour standards and policies that promote workers' rights.[20] An elaborate supervisory system helps to ensure that countries implement the conventions they ratify and examines member states' application of standards.

The ILO's corporatist structure adds greatly to the normative legitimacy of its international labour standards but makes the organization difficult to pilot. Albert Thomas, the ILO's first director-general, compared the ILO to a car in which the workers acted as the engine, governments as the steering wheel, and employers as the brakes.[21] National governments finance the ILO as well as decide whether to ratify the ILO's conventions. While the Workers' Group strongly supports international labour standards, the Employers' Group is increasingly reluctant to endorse any form of binding labour standard. What Thomas's analogy ignores, however, is the critical role the International Labour Office plays in orchestrating the ILO's tripartite constituents to adopt specific governance agendas and influencing the agendas of international agencies and organisations involved in global economic and social governance.[22] The Office, which is composed of different divisions and departments with distinct but overlapping spheres of authority, expertise, and interests, acts as arbitrator, researcher, and ideas producer. Through its field offices, the Office also provides technical assistance.

The ILO had a marked impact during the heyday of embedded liberalism, but by the 1980s, embedded liberalism was in crisis and neoliberalism promised to 'make markets work to their full potential and thereby rekindle the kind

[19] The GB meets quarterly and is composed of fifty-six titular members (twenty-eight governments, fourteen employers, and fourteen workers) and sixty-six deputy members (twenty-eight governments, nineteen employers, and nineteen workers). Ten of the titular government seats are permanently held by states of chief industrial importance (Brazil, China, France, Germany, India, Italy, Japan, the Russian Federation, the UK, and the US). The other government members are elected by the conference every three years, and the employer and worker members are elected in their individual capacity.

[20] Maupain, *The Future of the International Labour Organization*, 118; Thomas and Turnbull, 'From a "moral commentator" to a "determined actor?"'.

[21] Maupain, *The Future of the International Labour Organization*, 123–124; Thomas and Turnbull, 'From horizontal to vertical labour governance'.

[22] Posthuma and Rossi, 'Coordinated governance in global value chains'; Thomas and Turnbull, 'From a "moral commentator" to a "determined actor?"'.

of economic growth that managed capitalism had failed to deliver in the long 1970s.'[23] The collapse of the Soviet Union in the early 1990s signalled the end of the need for class compromise. Economic liberalisation expanded globally via 'free' trade agreements, and multinational corporations used chains of subsidiaries and suppliers to organise production across the national borders. In this context, the ILO's social justice mandate, its tripartite constituency, and its territorial and national scale of governance were called into question.

The withdrawal of ILO Director-General Michel Hansenne's invitation to the first World Trade Organization (WTO) Ministerial Conference in Singapore in December 1996 revealed the extent to which the ILO had been eclipsed by international economic governance institutions. Labour standards in trade agreements were portrayed as a form of outmoded protectionism. This episode convinced Hansenne, a former Belgian minister of employment and labour, that the ILO needed to align itself better with the prevailing policies of international economic governance. He promoted a new governance approach that emphasised a few key fundamental principles and rights.[24]

The Declaration on Fundamental Principles and Rights at Work (1998) identifies four fundamental rights: (1) freedom from forced labour, (2) freedom from child labour, (3) freedom from discrimination, and (4) freedom of association and the right to collective bargaining.[25] These rights were selected as they enable workers to participate freely in the market rather than imposing substantive standards that interfere with it.[26] The prohibitions against forced and child labour and discrimination were politically appealing on account of their close connection with general human rights discourses, and freedom of association and collective bargaining were already part of the ILO's constitution.[27] The declaration was designed to have a universal effect; countries were expected to respect its principles by virtue of their membership in the ILO, regardless of whether they had ratified the relevant conventions that embodied each of the fundamental freedoms. The ILO provided a distinctive follow-up mechanism that included global reports prepared by the Office, which would cover all four principles of fundamental rights within a four-year cycle. To appease the developing countries, the declaration stated that 'labour standards should not be used for protectionist trade purposes' and

[23] Gerstle, 'The rise and fall (?) of America's neoliberal order', 261.
[24] Ibid., 249.
[25] ILO, ILO Declaration on Fundamental Principles and Rights at Work, June 1998; and Rodgers et al., *The International Labour Organization*, 220.
[26] Maul, *The International Labour Organization*, 260–264.
[27] Ibid., 262.

that it should not be used to call into question 'the comparative advantage of any country.'[28]

Despite the declaration's focus on a few enabling rights that were grounded in the existing conventions, its promotional nature, and its avowal that it should not be used in trade disputes, it barely achieved the required quorum at the 1998 ILC.[29] Throughout the 1990s, heightened normative and epistemic contestation among its constituents had contributed to the ILO's fading authority.[30]

In the process leading up to the UN's adoption of the Trafficking Protocol, the ILO stressed the linkages between human trafficking and existing conventions (especially those pertaining to forced labour) that already covered trafficking in persons for purposes of labour exploitation.[31] Most importantly, it used the declaration's follow-up mechanism and reports to stake out its claim to be recognised as a key actor in the global antitrafficking governance network. Plant, who had worked with the UN and other development agencies and had expertise on modern forms of slavery, was recruited by the ILO to write the first global report on forced labour.[32]

Written in the shadow of the Trafficking Protocol, the ILO's 2001 Global Report, *Stopping Forced Labour*, sought to make forced labour visible within antitrafficking policy.[33] Lamenting that forced labour was not a 'relic of a bygone era', the report characterised it as a widespread and growing problem that occurred primarily in the private sector. Two types predominated. The first involved 'traditional' forms of forced labour, such as bonded labour

[28] Maupain, *The Future of the International Labour Organization*, 145.

[29] Maul, *The International Labour Organization*, 261.

[30] Thomas and Turnbull, 'From horizontal to vertical labour governance', 200.

[31] Andrees and Aikman, 'Raising the bar', 362. Significantly, little emphasis was given by the ILO to the Migrant Workers (Supplementary Provisions) Convention, 1975 (No. 143), which specifically deals with 'illicit and clandestine trafficking in labour' by providing standards aimed at eliminating these abuses. This little-ratified convention is designed 'to suppress clandestine movements of migrants for employment and illegal employment of migrants'(Article 3) by requiring ratifying states to provide for the 'detection of the illegal employment of migrant workers and for the definition and the application of administrative, civil and penal sanctions, which include imprisonment in their range, in respect of the illegal employment of migrant workers, in respect of the organisation of movements of migrants for employment' involving human trafficking (Article 6). Even though Convention 143 is relevant to the UN's protocol against human trafficking, the ILO rarely refers to it in its publications on forced labour. This convention was briefly discussed in the first global report on forced labour (ILO, *Stopping Forced Labour*, 123), mentioned in the second global report (ILO, *A Global Alliance against Forced Labour*), and omitted from the third (ILO, *The Cost of Coercion*). My thanks to Leila Kawar for pointing out the significance of Convention 143.

[32] Plant, 'Foreword', vi.

[33] ILO, *Stopping Forced Labour*, 3.

associated with agrarian feudalism in Asia and Latin America; the second, 'modern', type, involved human trafficking and could be found in every region in the world regardless of the level of development. Referring to human trafficking as the 'underside of globalisation', the report described 'an explosion in the number of persons trafficked across national borders and continents, and then forced into activities including sweatshop labour, domestic service, and even prostitution'.[34]

Although *Stopping Forced Labour* discussed prostitution, sexual exploitation, and trafficking into the sex trade, it did not raise the fraught question of whether the consensual sale of sexual services was a form of work that should be regulated like any other. The ILO simply treated the sale of sexual services differently from the commodification of labour generally, including the commodification of such intimate and gendered forms of labour as domestic work.[35]

The issue of the characterisation of the sale of sexual services was extremely contentious. An attempt in the mid-1990s by an ILO researcher to account for an increase in the number of women working in the commercial sex sector in Southeast Asia led to accusations that the ILO supported the legalisation of prostitution and threats by the United States to cut its funding. Thus, the ILO shied away from any discussion of the legal status of sex work.[36] The 2001 global report simply expressed the view that predominated in the anti-trafficking network: 'Prostitution is sometimes voluntary but overwhelmingly forced' and there is 'widespread regional and international trafficking for this industry'.[37]

The 2001 global report was pivotal for the ILO's governance agenda. By focusing on the private sector and treating labour trafficking as a subset of forced labour, it provided the ILO with a toehold into the prominent and well-resourced global antitrafficking governance network as well as a justification for talking about the need for labour-market regulation to respond to the excesses of economic liberalisation. *Stopping Forced Labour* concluded by calling for more research on forced labour, a task the ILO was eager to undertake. It also proposed 'a holistic approach' to the problem of forced labour that would add labour-market regulation to the criminal prohibition and the launch of a Global Alliance on Forced Labour involving governments and the social partners.

34 Ibid., 14.

35 Boris and Rodriguez García, '(In)decent work'.

36 Ibid., 204–209.

37 ILO, *Stopping Forced Labour*, ix.

The director-general, Juan Somovia, a Chilean diplomat with extensive UN experience who took office in 1999, used the 2001 report to elevate forced labour on the ILO's policy agenda, and the GB authorised a Special Action Programme to Combat Forced Labour (SAP-FL). Modelled on the ILO's International Programme on the Elimination of Child Labour (IPEC), SAP-FL was set up in 2002 and housed in the branch responsible for the follow-up to the declaration.[38] Plant was recruited to spearhead the programme and coordinate the forced labour global reports.

The SAP-FL provided the ILO with the institutional base from which to produce and circulate knowledge about forced labour and to develop a distinctive labour-market approach to trafficking that would complement the existing criminal prohibition and involve labour institutions and actors in coordinated antitrafficking activities.[39] The ILO was mindful of the 'opportunities and dangers of using the label "trafficking"'.[40] On the positive side, 'trafficking' is a rallying call under which resources can be mobilised to tackle forced labour.[41] On the negative side, 'increased attention on trafficking can be used to work against the interests of migrants and the legitimate right of people to move and to seek work', because the current approach to trafficking 'leans heavily on law enforcement, crime prevention and national security' and leads 'to calls for stricter border controls, sanctions on those who seek to move, and deportation for those who do so outside migration laws.'[42] Despite its concern about the collateral damage caused by the predominant carceral approach and its impact on migrants, instead of rejecting the term 'trafficking', the SAP-FL called for expanding the approach to trafficking to include labour regulatory and inspection mechanisms.

MAKING FORCED LABOUR LEGIBLE

The ILO released two more global reports on forced labour, the *Global Alliance against Forced Labour* in 2005 and the *Cost of Coercion* in 2009. These reports established the ILO as the authoritative source of knowledge on

[38] Established in 1992, IPEC became particularly concerned with the trafficking of children after the adoption of the Worst Forms of Child Labour Convention (No. 182) in 1999, under which the trafficking of children is considered a worst form of child labour to be abolished immediately. The SAP-FL worked closely with IPEC. Plant led the SAP-FL between 2002 and 2009.

[39] Plant and O'Reilly, 'The ILO's Special Action Programme to Combat Forced Labour'.

[40] ILO, *Trafficking in Human Beings*, 11.

[41] Ibid.

[42] Ibid.

forced labour in the global economy and put labour trafficking on the global governance agenda.

The 2005 report identified three main types of forced labour. The first, exemplified by the 1996 complaint against the government of Myanmar, was the ILO's traditional focus: forced labour imposed by the state or the military.[43] The second, which was the target of the United States' Trafficking in Persons (TIP) antitrafficking regime and of special concern to the European Union, was forced labour imposed by private agents for commercial sexual exploitation. The third was forced labour imposed by private agents for economic exploitation, the ILO's primary preoccupation. The ILO also distinguished between forced labourers who were trafficked (which involved some form of migration, typically across international borders) and those who were not.

Using this typology, the ILO produced statistics that belied the conventional wisdom that trafficking primarily involved the sexual exploitation of women and children. The 2005 report estimated that 12.3 million people were in forced labour and that trafficking accounted for only 20 per cent (or 2.45 million persons) of this labour. Only 20 per cent of the total cases of forced labour involved state or military coercion; the vast majority, 80 per cent, of forced labourers worked in the private economy. Forced commercial sexual labour, in which women and children predominated at 93 per cent of the victims, made up 11 per cent of all cases in the private sector. In forced economic exploitation, women and girls represented 56 per cent of the victims, while men and boys accounted for 44 per cent.[44] This data fortified the ILO's case for expanding the reach of human-trafficking policy beyond sexual exploitation to include the labour dimension.

Identifying governance deficits in the migration process as a major cause of labour trafficking, the report pointed to private recruiters as posing a particular problem. It estimated that the total profits made by intermediaries who traffic people across borders and the employers who exploit them amounted to US$32 billion in one year.[45] Labour-market deregulation and global competition also contributed to the problem. The report revealed that, to lower costs and speed up supply, retailers and intermediaries put pressure on suppliers, who in turn squeezed labour contractors, who then, in extreme cases, resorted

[43] The ILO's focus on state forms of forced labour, with the exception of Myanmar, dissipated in the 1990s after the breakup of the Soviet Union and the abandonment of labour camps in many countries. Andrees and Aikman, 'Raising the bar', 361; Sweptson, 'Trafficking and forced labour', 411.

[44] ILO, A *Global Alliance against Forced Labour.*

[45] Ibid., 55.

to coercive methods to manage their workers.[46] It portrayed forced labour as the 'combined failure of labour markets, institutions and regulations to provide for more efficient or more equitable outcomes'.[47]

The ILO's 2005 global report was influential within and outside the ILO. The GB called on the Office to develop a plan to build and support a global alliance against forced labour among its constituents. The Bush administration began to consider labour trafficking; for the first time, the 2006 TIP Report identified nonsex trafficking as a major cause for concern.[48]

The ILO's 2005 report also precipitated a debate over where to draw the borders between 'forced labour' and 'trafficking' for legal purposes. The United States rejected the ILO's distinction between forced labour and trafficking, treating them as the same on the ground that as a matter of US law, unlike the definition in the UN protocol, trafficking does not require movement.[49] The GB requested the Committee of Experts on the Application of Conventions and Recommendations (CEACR) to conduct a general survey concerning the two forced labour conventions. The CEACR, a supervisory body of the ILO composed of independent legal experts, has jurisdiction over the application of standards. This supervisory system set the ILO's forced labour conventions apart from the UN's Trafficking Protocol, which does not have a centralised mechanism for determining the interpretation and application of the definition of human trafficking.

The 2007 general survey repeated the CEACR's earlier interpretation that 'trafficking in persons for the purpose of exploitation is encompassed by the definition of forced or compulsory labour' provided in the ILO convention.[50] It also stressed elements in the definition of forced labour – menace of any penalty and voluntarily offer – that turn on coercion and lack of consent, taking care to point out that the employer and the state 'are not accountable for all external constraints or indirect coercion existing in practice: for example, the need to work to earn one's living could become relevant only in conjunction with other factors for which they are answerable'.[51] And, like the UN, the CEACR refused to take a stance on the contentious issue of whether prostitution was a form of exploitation in the absence of coercion.

46 Ibid., 63.

47 Ibid., 64.

48 Chuang, 'Exploitation creep', 619.

49 Ibid., 619–620. The US State Department justified this interpretation in legal terms by emphasising that 'harbouring' was one of the acts in the definition of trafficking.

50 ILO, *Eradication of Forced Labour*, 41.

51 Ibid., 20–21.

Noting that neither the UN's Trafficking Protocol nor the ILO's forced labour convention imposed a duty to criminalise prostitution, it concluded that prostitution should be dealt with by individual countries in accordance with their national laws and policies.[52] By excluding the sale of sexual services from global labour standards, the ILO reflected and reinforced the borders between sexual and labour exploitation and the deployment of different governance strategies against them.

The ILO used the 2005 global report on forced labour to raise its stature in the global antitrafficking governance network. Plant tried to persuade key policy actors to incorporate the ILO's emphasis on labour-market institutions into the emerging multifaced approach to human trafficking.[53] He also reassured the United States that any differences between the United States and ILO over the relationship between human trafficking and forced labour were not fatal to their collaboration, noting that 'the ILO accepts that there will be different views on the best conceptual and legal entry points for tackling such coercive practices today, between forced labour, slavery and slavery-like practices, and trafficking for forced labour exploitation'.[54] Reaching out to US business, Plant stressed the reputational risks to business of being associated with forced labour in its business operations or supply chains and questioned whether voluntary corporate social responsibility initiatives were enough to eliminate forced labour or whether there should be binding legal obligations on companies throughout their supply chains.[55]

The next instalment of the global reports on forced labour, *The Cost of Coercion* in 2009, continued to attract public attention by quantifying the economic cost of forced labour, this time drawing attention to costs borne by the workers, which it estimated to be US$21 billion a year.[56] But its key contribution was to set out the ILO's labour-market approach and explain how it fit in the global governance of trafficking. The report began by addressing the tricky legal question of the relationship between forced labour and other abusive practices such as human trafficking, slavery, slavery-like practices, and debt bondage or bonded labour that hinge on the meaning of labour exploitation and whether coercion is a necessary element in the offence of human trafficking. Deferring to the jurisdiction of the ILO's supervisory bodies to offer an opinion on whether specific actions fall within the prohibition, the

52 However, it was clear that coercive sexual exploitation and forced prostitution fell within the definition of forced labour. Ibid., 41.

53 Plant, 'Forced labour, slavery and poverty reduction'.

54 Plant, 'Trafficking for forced labour', 3.

55 Plant, 'Forced labor: Critical issues for US business leaders'.

56 ILO, *The Cost of Coercion*, 32.

report explained 'that there is a continuum including both what can clearly be identified as forced labour and other forms of labour exploitation and abuse' at one end and freely chosen employment at the other.[57] Between the two extremes exist a variety of employment relationships in which 'the element of free choice by the worker begins at least to be mitigated or constrained and can eventually be cast into doubt'.[58]

The Cost of Coercion set out the ILO's vision of 'the respective roles of criminal and labour justice' in the governance of forced labour and human trafficking.[59] Acknowledging that forced labour is a crime and that individual perpetrators should be punished under the criminal law, the report cast enforceable labour standards combined with effective labour-market institutions, such as public inspectors, as the most effective way of preventing forced labour.[60] While the legal definition of forced labour, with its emphasis on coercion and lack of consent, was narrow, a labour approach to forced labour and labour trafficking would address the broader labour-market failures that result in a continuum of labour exploitation. Calling for the resources allocated to prevention to be increased to match those apportioned to prosecution, Plant stated that 'prevention should be understood as addressing those systemic aspects of labour-market and migration governance which are at the root of much forced labour in the first place'.[61] Forced labour was an opening for the ILO to promote greater labour-market regulation, a matter of pressing concern in the wake of the 2008–09 global economic and financial crisis.

The SAP-FL was very effective in developing the ILO's governance strategy for forced labour and situating it within the antitrafficking governance network. By the end of its first decade, its efforts had established the ILO as the epistemic authority on forced labour and a critical node in the global antitrafficking governance network. In addition to producing statistics pertaining to forced labour, the ILO, along with the European Commission, developed an influential list of indicators, based on surveying experts, for officials to use in the field to assist them in categorising different forms of labour exploitation for legal purposes, and a training manual on forced labour for labour inspectors.[62] The ILO made forced labour legible in the antitrafficking governance network, partnered with a variety of international organisations, and played a

57 Ibid., 8–9.
58 Ibid.
59 Ibid., 25.
60 Ibid., 65.
61 ILO Online, 'Questions and answers on "The cost of coercion"'.
62 ILO, 'Operational indicators of trafficking in human beings'; Andrees, *Forced Labour and Human Trafficking*.

prominent role in the UN Global Initiative to Fight Human Trafficking. It was no longer an 'add-on' at conferences that were concerned almost exclusively with criminal-law enforcement against sex trafficking.[63]

FABRICATING A LABOUR-MARKET APPROACH TO FORCED LABOUR AND TRAFFICKING

In 2012, the Obama administration shifted US antitrafficking policy towards labour exploitation, and 'modern slavery' became the umbrella term used in Anglo-American jurisdictions to capture the different forms of unfree labour.[64] It was a fertile time for the ILO to cultivate a labour-regulation approach and plant it in the global antislavery governance network. The ILO produced knowledge about forced labour and norms for eliminating it, which required the Office to coordinate two different groups of actors: (1) the global governance network of international institutions, leading states (who were also big funders), transnational corporations, and civil society actors and (2) its constituents, the tripartite actors.

The ILO competed with other governance actors – such as Kevin Bales, the International Organization for Migration (IOM), the US TIP regime, and the Walk Free Foundation – to come up with numbers for the victims of human trafficking, forced labour, and modern slavery and the economic cost of all this unfree labour.[65] Indeed, the ILO sought to become the authority on how to measure and quantify forced labour. Its 2012 report, *Hard to See, Harder to Count*, set out a new methodology, which the ILO promoted to other organisations and countries.[66] The ILO estimated the total number of forced labourers across the world at 20.9 million, which was significantly greater than the 2005 estimate of 12.3 million. The overwhelming majority of victims of forced labour, 90 per cent, were exploited by private individuals and enterprises; out of these, forced sexual exploitation accounted for 12 per cent of the victims whereas forced labour exploitation made up 68 per cent of the victims.[67] Unlike earlier reports, the 2012 report did not provide a separate breakdown of the numbers of victims of trafficking within the broader category of forced labour; instead, it presented estimates of the number of people trapped in forced labour as a result of internal or cross-border migration. It estimated that 29 per

[63] Plant, 'Trafficking for labour exploitation'.
[64] Chapter 1, this book.
[65] Chapter 2, this book; Merry, 'Counting the uncountable'.
[66] ILO, *Hard to See, Harder to Count.*
[67] ILO Global Estimate of Forced Labour, 2012, 13.

cent of the victims ended up in forced labour after moving across international borders, with the majority being forced sex workers.[68]

The ILO also sought to draw political attention to fighting forced labour by calculating the economic cost of forced labour to states (through the nonpayment of taxes or diminished remittances, for example) and to the workers who were victimised. Using the 'universally legible' language of dollars and the estimates from its 2012 report, the 2014 report, *Profits and Poverty: The Economics of Forced Labour*, projected the annual profits attributable to forced labour to be US$150 billion, a dramatic rise from its earlier estimate of US$32 billion.[69]

Although there was growing support among key international actors for a labour approach to human trafficking that did not rely exclusively on criminal prosecution and did not focus only on sexual exploitation, the problem was getting the Employers' Group to adopt a new standard authorising a labour-market approach, since the existing conventions simply treated forced labour as a crime. In 2012, the GB elected Guy Ryder, former head of the ITUC, as the ILO's director-general, and his background raised concerns in the Employers' Group about the ILO's direction. As a form of general protest at the ILO's direction, the Employers' Group refused to participate in the final stage of the supervisory process at the 2012 ILC over the legal status of the right to strike in the corpus of international labour standards.[70] It took a great deal of effort by the Office and the support of a tripartite committee of experts to get the issue of a standard to address the gaps in the existing conventions on forced labour on the ILC's 2014 agenda.[71]

When the tripartite committee of experts met in 2013, there was general agreement over the need for a new standard to better address matters relating to prevention, protection, compensation, enforcement, and international cooperation. However, a trio of recurring issues dogged the legislative process: the relationship between forced labour and trafficking; the form the standard should take; and references to global supply chains. The committee simply avoided the definitional quagmire by stating that the standard should focus on forced labour, which included forced labour exacted because of trafficking. The experts also split over whether the new standard should take the form of a protocol or a recommendation, but they agreed that a new convention was not

68 Fifteen per cent became victims of forced labour following movement within their country, whereas the remaining 56 per cent did not leave their place of origin or residence. Ibid., 17.

69 Rittich, 'Representing, counting, valuing', 259; ILO, *Profits and Poverty*, 13.

70 Thomas and Turnbull, 'From a "moral commentator" to a "determined actor"?,' 289; La Hovary, 'A challenging ménage à trois?'

71 Andrees and Aikman, 'Raising the bar', 367–371.

necessary. The employers' spokesperson also insisted that any reference to global supply chains be deleted from the committee's final conclusion, a position that would become the employers' bottom line when it came to the adoption of a new standard for forced labour.[72] The GB considered the expert committee's recommendations and conclusions, and it was persuaded by the Office to hold only one discussion of a standard on forced labour at the 2014 conference, although the normal procedure was to have a discussion at successive conferences.[73]

In a report that summarised the constituents' responses to a questionnaire about a possible new standard and examined member states' laws against forced labour, the Office made the case for a protocol and a recommendation to address the gaps in the existing legal framework on forced labour, claiming that 'a complementary, coordinated, and mutually supportive approach is required between labour and criminal justice systems'.[74] By focusing on prevention, victim protection (including compensation), and labour trafficking, the new standards, it argued, would add value to the existing laws and practices. The Office also prepared a draft protocol and recommendation to accompany its report, which were distributed to constituents in preparation for the 2014 ILC.[75]

At the 2014 ILC, the Committee on Forced Labour had ten days to hammer out new standards based on the Office's draft protocol and recommendation. The United Nations' High Commission for Human Rights and its Office of Drugs and Organised Crime were consulted by the Office and took part in the deliberations.[76] Among the 244 amendments the committee considered, the trio of issues raised at the meeting of tripartite experts was especially contentious. The decision about the ultimate form the standard would take was postponed to the end of committee's deliberations, a delay that was necessary to gain the Employers' Group's support. The Employers' Group also raised the relationship between forced labour and human trafficking as an issue of particular concern given the growth in cross-border labour mobility. This matter was resolved by reaffirming the definition of forced labour contained in the 1930 convention in the protocol and by specifying that measures to eliminate forced labour also include 'action against trafficking in persons for

[72] Ibid., 374–375.
[73] Ibid., 375–376.
[74] ILO, *Strengthening Action to End Forced Labour*, 63.
[75] Sweptson, 'Trafficking and forced labour', 412–413.
[76] Ibid., 404.

the purpose of forced or compulsory labour.'[77] This manoeuvre also resolved the ILO's disagreement with the United States over the legal borders between forced labour and human trafficking.

But the most intractable issue was businesses' role in the fight against forced labour.[78] The Workers' Group, along with some governments, supported an amendment that would require members to promote due diligence by private and public entities to prevent and respond to the risks of forced labour. The Employers' Group opposed the amendment on the ground that the primary duty was on the state, not business, to eliminate forced labour. A compromise was reached whereby members would be required to take preventative measures 'supporting' due diligence by both private and public sectors. However, a proposal by a government member to add a reference to supply chains in the nonbinding recommendation ignited the Employers' Group ire.[79] The Employers' Group claimed that businesses in the informal sector were the source of forced labour, and it disputed that there was evidence linking forced labour to supply chains.[80] Even though the government representatives argued that state obligations were already clearly established and that the principle that business should take measures to address forced labour and other human rights abuses in their supply chains was accepted in the UN's Guiding Principles on Business and Human Rights (UNGPs), the Employers' Group refused to budge. An informal working group eventually devised a compromise in which the term 'supply chain' was not used; instead, language modelled after the UNGPs ('in their operations or in products, services or operations to which they may be directly linked') was adopted. With these changes in place, the Employers' Group, the last holdout, endorsed the protocol and the recommendation, resolving the outstanding issue of the form the standards would take.[81]

Adopted with overwhelming support at the 2014 ILC, the Protocol of 2014 to the Forced Labour Convention, 1930 (No. 29) consists of a short list of general principles (prevention, protection, remedy, and international cooperation) laid out in seven substantive articles, the details of which were to be developed by member states in consultation with employers' and

[77] Andrees and Aikman, 'Raising the bar', 378; Protocol of 2014 to the Forced Labour Convention, 1930 (No. 29), Article 1 (3).

[78] Ibid., 378.

[79] Ibid., 379.

[80] Ibid., 379.

[81] Ibid., 380.

workers' organisations.[82] Guidance on how to implement the principles was provided in the Forced Labour (Supplementary Measures) Recommendation (R203), which accompanied the protocol and was adopted at the same time.

Its preamble situates the protocol in the constellation of international human rights instruments, identifies trafficking in persons for the purposes of forced labour as a subject of growing concern, and states that its purpose is to address gaps in the implementation of the 1930 convention. The protocol provides an institutional framework, through the requirement of national policy and action plans, for states in consultation with the social partners to develop a systematic action to prevent and suppress forced labour (Article 1).[83] The mandatory preventative measures, along with protocol's embrace of tripartism, are its most distinctive labour-related contribution to antitrafficking governance techniques. The measures include ensuring that all workers and all sectors of the economy are covered by labour legislation and enforcement mechanisms, strengthening labour inspection services, protecting migrant and other workers from abusive and fraudulent practices during the recruitment and placement process, and supporting due diligence by both the public and private sectors to prevent and respond to the risks of forced labour (Article 2). The recommendation also identifies promoting freedom of association and collective bargaining to enable at-risk workers to join workers' organisations as a preventive measure.[84]

Protecting the human rights of victims of forced labour is another of the protocol's goals. It builds on earlier statements by the ILO supervisory bodies that cooperation between the labour inspectorate and immigration authorities should be carried out cautiously considering that the main objective of the labour inspection system is to protect the rights and interests of all workers and improve their working conditions, rather than to enforce immigration law.[85] It also advanced the protections offered to workers trafficked into forced labour beyond the existing international trafficking instruments, such as the UN Trafficking Protocol and, as we will see in the next chapter, the EU 2011 directive. The forced labour protocol requires member states to take effective measures to identify and protect victims, including providing them with

82 Since the protocol supplements the forced labour convention, members states are required to ratify the convention before they are entitled to ratify the protocol. Recommendations, which are nonbinding, do not require ratification. The protocol also explicitly deleted the provisions in the 1930 convention permitting colonial practices of forced labour.

83 National action plans are a device used by states to develop their antitrafficking policies. The ILO also adopted this mechanism for addressing the worst forms of child labour.

84 Recommendation 203, 3(b).

85 ILO, *Promoting Fair Migration*, para. 477.

assistance and support (Article 3). Although member states opposed a strict nonpunishment provision prohibiting states from prosecuting people compelled to commit unlawful activities as a consequence of their forced labour, the protocol met the high-water mark for human rights for victims of trafficking by requiring states to give officials the authority not to prosecute (Article 4 (2)).[86] It also imposes an obligation on states to provide 'all victims of forced and compulsory labour, irrespective of their nationality or legal status in the national territory, with access to appropriate and effective remedies, such as compensation' (Article 4(1)). Unlike the UN Trafficking Protocol, these human rights protections are mandatory, and unlike the EU directive (which is discussed in Chapter 4), they do not hinge on a victim assisting a criminal prosecution.

The ILO's forced labour protocol added labour law regulatory techniques to the global antislavery toolbox.[87] It also fed into and reinforced two other items on the 2014 ILC governance agenda: fair migration and a standard designed specifically for global supply chains. These governance initiatives were important not only for tackling the transnational vectors of forced labour but also for addressing a much broader range of decent work deficits.

Although the ILO identified transnational recruiters as a key entry point to forced labour and human trafficking, its governance mechanisms for tackling the problem were weak. In 1997, the Employers' Group's campaign to repeal the previous ban on private recruitment agencies (C97) was successful, and a much weaker convention, C181, which sought to regulate the agencies, by, among other things, banning fees charged to workers for a placement, was adopted. C181 was virtually silent on the regulation of agencies to place migrant workers; it simply requires states 'to provide adequate protection for and prevent abuses of migrant workers recruited or placed in its territory by private employment agencies'.[88] The jurisdictional hook the ILO invoked to address the problem of abusive transnational labour recruiters was the

86 Council of Europe, Council of Europe Convention on Action against Trafficking in Human Beings, 16 May 2005, CETS 197.

87 The ILO promoted ratification of the forced labour protocol through its 50 for Freedom campaign, which was designed to persuade fifty countries to ratify the 2014 protocol by 2019. The Governing Body's governance strategy also included facilitating and supporting partnerships with UN agencies and other organisations to 'enhance impact and policy coherence'. Swepston, 'Trafficking and forced labour', 414.

Following a 2015 decision of the Governing Body, the SAP-FL was amalgamated with the IPEC. The two programs, which offered technical cooperation, were rechristened the IPEC+ Flagship Programme and located in the Fundamental Principles and Rights at Work Branch of the ILO.

88 See Article 8.

nonbinding Private Employment Agencies Recommendation, which accompanied C181, and its requirement that states ensure the elimination of undefined 'unethical recruitment practices'.[89]

The ILO adopted a two-pronged strategy to address the problem of forced labour, which often took the form of debt bondage through the imposition of exorbitant recruitment fees, in transnational labour recruitment. It included provisions on licensing recruiters and banning fees in sector-based conventions where migrant workers predominated: the Maritime Labour Convention, 2006; C188 Work in Fishing, 2007; and C189 Domestic Workers, 2011. To supplement the two hard-law conventions on labour migration, which migrant-receiving states were unwilling to ratify, the ILO developed two soft-law instruments (the Fair Deal for Migrant Workers resolution, in 2004, and the Multilateral Framework on Labour Migration, in 2006), which offered guidance on how to regulate the recruitment process to combat labour trafficking.[90] While these instruments provided some techniques to address some of the practices of transnational labour recruiters associated with forced labour, they did not provide an immediate or holistic solution.[91]

The Fair Recruitment Initiative (FRI) is the ILO's attempt to provide a holistic solution to the problem of transnational labour recruiters. Launched at the 2014 ILC, it is part of the director-general's Fair Migration Agenda, and it reinforces the forced labour protocol's emphasis on measures targeting fraudulent and abusive recruitment practices. Led by the ILO, it is a multistakeholder initiative involving the ITUC, the IOE, governments, agencies of the Global Migration Group (in particular, the International Organization for Migration, the United Nations Office on Drugs and Crime, the Office of the High Commissioner for Human Rights, and the World Bank), and nongovernmental organisations. It is, the director-general explained, 'a more strategic response to address gaps in existing ILO standards and new forms of recruitment-related mistreatment of migrant workers.'[92] The idea is not to adopt new standards but to use existing ones, such as the forced labour protocol's call for states to adopt measures to address fraudulent and abusive recruitment practices, as a basis for developing voluntary guidelines on how to regulate to ensure that recruitment practices are fair. This approach avoided the Employers' Group's objection to new standards and allowed the ILO to

89 Jones, 'A "north star" governing global labour migration?', 304.
90 Ibid., 306.
91 ILO, *The Cost of Coercion*, 9.
92 Jones, 'A 'north star' govening global labour migration?', 304.

concentrate instead on developing a new soft norm of fair recruitment, to be based on the ILO's research on recruitment practices, multistakeholder consultations, and tripartite deliberations.[93]

The Employers' Group was willing to accept multistakeholder and other voluntary initiatives, but it would not countenance a labour standard directed at supply chains. Its objection to any reference to supply chains in the forced labour protocol and recommendation was merely a skirmish in its bigger battle to prevent the ILC from discussing, let alone adopting, a standard directed at global supply chains. Even though the Workers' Group had raised the issue at every GB since 2007, the Employers' Group managed to stave off any consideration of a standard for global supply chains at the ILC until 2014.[94] Its specific concern was the ILO's attempt to shift its governance scale from the territorial to transnational and to impose duties on firms at the top of the global supply chain.

In his first strategic report to the ILC, director-general Ryder indicated that he favoured charting a new governance strategy. He raised the question of whether it was possible to continue to rely solely on state responsibility for labour conditions in global supply chains given 'the fact that private actors are the drivers of the constantly shifting supply chains or production networks that increasingly characterise international trade and investment'.[95] In his view, the situation 'indicated additional opportunities for the ILO to promote decent work' in supply chains.[96] The significance of this governance rescaling was not lost on the tripartite constituents: the ILO was seeking to add to its traditional territorial and national scale of labour regulation 'by "intertwining" a new multiscalar system of labour governance along the supply chain'.[97] This is precisely what the IOE wanted to avoid.

It was not until the Rana Plaza building collapse in 2013, killing over 1,100 garment workers, many of whom had been making garments for global brands and global retailers, that the GB put the issue of a standard for global supply chains on the ILC's 2014 agenda. Even then, the ILO had to contend with the Employers' Group's unrelenting objections to a transnational standard that applied to supply chains.[98] To compensate for the Employers' Group's resistance, the ILO cultivated complementary governance strategies. It developed new and strengthened old voluntary mechanisms to foster transnational

93 Ibid., 313.
94 Thomas and Anner, 'Dissensus and deadlock'.
95 ILO, *Towards the ILO Centenary*, para. 75.
96 Ibid.
97 Thomas and Anner, 'Dissensus and deadlock'.
98 Ibid.

accountability, and it reinforced its position in the global antislavery governance network.

JUMPING GOVERNANCE SCALES AND BUILDING A GLOBAL ALLIANCE

The Rana Plaza tragedy laid bare the failure of private and voluntary corporate social responsibility initiatives to protect workers. It catalysed the discussion of global supply chains and decent work at the 2016 ILO Conference, shaped the nature of the discussion, and influenced its outcomes. In the aftermath of the tragedy, NGOs and unions campaigned to make lead firms in supply chains take greater responsibility for the working conditions of their suppliers' workers. The ILO took on a key role in a legally binding multistakeholder initiative, including over two hundred global brands and retailers, to improve fire and building safety in Bangladesh. An unprecedented number of outside observers attended the supply chain discussion at the 2016 conference, where the central issue boiled down to whether the ILO's existing governance mechanisms adequately addressed the governance challenges posed by global supply chains.[99]

Director-General Ryder observed that the ILO's 'purely nation state approach to the behaviour of the globalized economy' – which depends on each member state ratifying a convention and then enacting laws to regulate employment relationships entered into or taking place in its national territory – 'risked missing the transversal integration of production networks across countries'.[100] A standard that targeted the key actors in global supply chains would help to rescale the ILO's jurisdiction to include cross-border activities. The 2014 protocol on forced labour was one of the ILO's few attempts to codify corporate due-diligence responsibilities in a mandatory standard. With the issue of supply chains and decent work on the 2016 ILC agenda, the ILO had another opportunity to persuade its constituents to adopt a standard that focused on a critical transnational actor.

The Office set out its case for a new governance mechanism for supply chains in the 2016 report to the ILC. Acknowledging that global supply chains can lead to economic and employment upgrading, *Decent Work in Supply Chains* also reported evidence of supply chains leading to decent work

99 Posthuma and Rossi, 'Coordinated governance in global value chain'; Thomas and Anner, 'Dissensus and deadlock'.

100 Ryder, address, quoted in Thomas and Anner, 'Dissensus and deadlock'.

deficits, including forced labour.[101] Some of these deficits, it noted, were linked to lead firms' investment and sourcing decisions. A mismatch between the transnational scale of production and the national scale of the regulation was diagnosed as the source of the problem.[102] Lead firms contract with suppliers located in many countries, and since jurisdiction over labour regulation is primarily territorial and national, national labour laws and institutions govern the suppliers' employment relations. Some governments, according to the report, have been unable 'to cope with the rapid transformation brought about by exposure to the global economy, which has created governance gaps'.[103] Moreover, it explained, in cases where the contracts between a nonresident lead firm and resident suppliers influence the working conditions of the suppliers' workers – through cost pressures, delivery schedules, and penalty clauses, for example – the state where the suppliers and workers reside has no jurisdiction to hold the lead firm accountable. The traditional territorial conception of jurisdiction also restricts the capacity of a state to regulate the extraterritorial conduct of corporations headquartered within its territory.[104]

During the committee discussion of decent work in supply chains at the 2016 ILC, the Employers' Group rejected outright the need for a new governance instrument. Although it disputed the Office's evidence about supply chains leading to decent work deficits, its main objection to the idea of a governance gap was jurisdictional. Declaring 'the question of governance' to be 'at the heart of the debate about cross-border supply chains', the Employers' vice-chairperson went on to claim that it was up to each country to enact and enforce labour standards.[105] The failure of a government 'to meet its duty to protect', he went on, 'did not shift the responsibility to companies'.[106] By contrast, the Workers' Group insisted that it was time to examine whether the current international labour standards addressed the specific challenges posed by global supply chains, holding up the Maritime Labour Convention, 2006, as an example of a new approach to labour governance that went beyond national borders and did not focus on the direct employer.[107] Led by the EU and the United States under the Obama administration, the majority of state members agreed to keep the question of

[101] ILO, *Decent Work in Global Supply Chains*, 2, 7.
[102] Ibid., 2.
[103] Ibid.
[104] Ibid.
[105] ILO, *Reports of the Committee on Decent Work in Global Supply Chains: Summary of Proceedings*, para. 134.
[106] Ibid., para. 135.
[107] Ibid., para. 130.

a new governance mechanism for global supply chains on the ILO's legislative agenda. However, they were not prepared to go so far as to recommend that a new standard be considered, preferring to take a more gradual approach.

With the grudging acceptance of the Employers' Group, the ILC adopted a detailed set of conclusions, which described the ILO as the institution 'best placed to lead global action for decent work in global chains'.[108] The Office was given a mandate to develop a programme of action to address decent work in global supply chains, consisting of research and technical assistance, and to work with other international organisations and provide leadership to drive policy among all multilateral initiatives and processes related to decent work in global supply chains. The GB was instructed, among other things, to convene a meeting to consider standards designed to reduce decent work deficits in global supply chains.

In response to the ILC conclusions, the GB adopted a programme of action, which included a lengthy deliberative process to consider different aspects of the relations between decent work and supply chains.[109] Instead of preserving the fragile consensus achieved at the 2016 ILC, the process gave the Employers' Group time to try to row back the ILO's position on global supply chains as the images of the Rana Plaza collapse faded and the political context changed. Under the Trump administration, for example, the United States did not support regulating supply chains, preferring trade sanctions instead, and this approach resonated with a growing number of right-wing governments.[110]

Throughout the process, tripartite deliberations were adversarial, and they finally broke down at the Technical Meeting on Achieving Decent Work in Supply Chains, held in February 2020. The Employers' Group repeated its refrain that there was no evidence that global supply chains were associated with decent work deficits, identifying the problem as an outgrowth of the informal economy, which was caused by a lack of state capacity to ensure compliance with laws and regulations.[111] Since supply chains were not the source of the problem, the Employers' Group insisted that 'there was no regulatory gap at international level, but rather an implementation challenge at national level'.[112] Remarking on its unhappiness with the 2016 ILC conclusions, the Employers' Group

108 ILO, *Reports of the Committee on Decent Work in Global Supply Chains: Resolution and Conclusions*.

109 ILO, *Follow-Up to the Resolution concerning Decent Work in Global Supply Chains*.

110 See Chapter 1, this book, and Silva, 'The ILO and the future of work'.

111 ILO, *Note on the Proceedings*, para. 14.

112 Ibid.

castigated the Office, declaring that it had 'lost faith' in 'its ability' to conduct an evidence-based and independent review of gaps in the ILO standards when it came to decent work in supply chains.[113] The Employers' Group rejected an attempt by sixteen states, led by the United States, to achieve a consensus on a set of conclusions that simply reiterated in a watered-down form those adopted at the 2016 ILC.[114] A senior ILO official at the technical meeting bemoaned the fact that the ILO was being surpassed by other organisations, such as the UN's Human Rights Council, which was making progress drafting a binding standard to address transnational business and human rights, building on the UNGPs.[115]

Although the 2016 ILC conclusions did not lead to a new standard for global supply chains, they did influence an old mechanism, the ILO Tripartite Declaration of Principles concerning Multinational Enterprises and Social Policy (MNE).[116] A soft-law instrument adopted in 1977, the MNE provides guidance to enterprises (multinational and national) on procedural due-diligence elements to give effect to existing ILO standards. By directly addressing enterprises, the MNE is unique among ILO normative instruments. The 2017 revision incorporated new labour standards and, critically, integrated the UNGPs into the MNE. Among other things, it built on the Protocol of 2014 to the Forced Labour Convention, 1930, by making it clear that both multinational and national enterprises should take effective measures to identify, prevent, mitigate, and account for how they address the risks of forced labour in their operations or in products, services, or operations with which they may be directly linked.[117] Unlike the forced labour protocol, the MNE specifically refers to global supply chains, but it does not provide guidance on how it should be applied to them. It does, however, call on multinational enterprises to use their 'leverage with business partners to

[113] Ibid., para. 134.

[114] Ibid., paras. 112–170.

[115] Ibid., 41. The UN Human Rights Council has jurisdiction over the UNGPs and had established an open-ended intergovernmental working group (IGWG) to draft an international legally binding instrument on transnational corporations and other business enterprises.

[116] The ILC's conclusions on the discussion of supply chains instructed the MNE review process to consider the discussion of supply chains. ILO, *Reports of the Committee on Decent Work in Global Supply Chains: Resolution and Conclusions*. For a discussion of the voluntary compliance mechanism associated with the MNE, see Landau, *Human rights due diligence and labour governance*, 106–108.

[117] ILO, *Tripartite Declaration of Principles Concerning Multinational Enterprises and Social Policy (MNE Declaration)*, para. 25.

encourage them to provide effective means of enabling remediation for abuses of internationally recognised human rights', which would include grievance mechanisms for workers.[118] What distinguishes the ILO's approach to due diligence from other multilateral initiatives, such as the UNGPs, is the MNE's emphasis on 'meaningful consultation with . . . workers' organizations', taking account of the 'central role' of freedom of association, collective bargaining, and social dialogue in identifying and assessing adverse human rights impacts.[119]

The ILO was able quickly to incorporate robust due-diligence procedures into the MNE because it is a voluntary instrument and one that explicitly endorses the primacy of national laws and sovereignty.[120] The soft nature of the Principles and Operational Guidelines on Fair Recruitment also helps to explain their adoption by the ILC in 2016.

Developed through the FRI, the guidelines inform key stakeholders, such as governments, enterprises, public employment agencies, labour recruiters, and employers, about the measures they can take to address the types of recruitment practices that are associated with a variety of different forms of labour exploitation, including forced labour and labour trafficking. Instead of focusing narrowly on prohibiting forced labour, the FRI's approach was to develop guidelines to establish a norm of what is fair. One of the guidelines' key principles is that 'no recruitment fees or related costs should be charged to, or otherwise borne by, workers or jobseekers'.[121]

With the FRI, the ILO engaged its traditional tripartite constituents and brokered a new coalition of partners to develop a norm of fair recruitment.[122] This is an important, albeit limited, accomplishment given the Employers' Group's reluctance to agree to a new binding standard regulating labour recruitment and the states' unwillingness to tolerate restrictions on their sovereignty over immigration. For the IOE and its members, the regulation of international labour recruiters is a small price to pay for the freedom to use private employment and recruitment services domestically and internationally. States are also amenable to the multistakeholder initiative because it does not challenge how they govern temporary labour migration. The FRI focuses on a symptom, abusive private recruiters, of a much bigger problem:

[118] Ibid., para. 65.

[119] Ibid., para. 10(e); Brudney, 'Hiding in plain sight', 336.

[120] ILO, *Tripartite Declaration of Principles Concerning Multinational Enterprises and Social Policy (MNE Declaration)*, para. 8.

[121] ILO, *General Principles and Operational Guidelines on Fair Recruitment.*

[122] Jones, 'A "north star" govening global labour migration?', 317.

transnational modes of production and migration based on low-cost, flexible, and disposable labour.[123]

Another way that the ILO could compensate for the Employers' Group's resistance to transnational labour standards and discord among its constituents was to cement its position in the global antislavery governance network. After the UN adopted its ambitious Sustainable Development Goals (SDGs) in 2015, the ILO played an increasingly prominent role in the network. By placing the elimination of modern slavery, forced labour, and human trafficking by 2030 (target 8.7) firmly under the decent work and economic growth goals, the UN boosted the ILO's authority.[124]

Target 8.7 galvanised the antislavery global governance network, and the ILO took the opportunity to position itself as a key node within it, orchestrating other networks and producing authoritative knowledge about modern slavery. The ILO launched Alliance 8.7, a global partnership of countries, international and regional agencies, workers' organisations, employer and business membership groups, civil society organisations, academic institutions, and other relevant stakeholders and networks to tackle modern slavery. Acting as the alliance's secretariat, the ILO's goal is to coordinate global action among UN agencies and national governments against modern slavery. The alliance also provides a means for the ILO to ensure that its 'value added in the UN – tripartism, normative action, and social dialogue – is fully recognized and incorporated in national, regional, and global SDG processes as well as in UN reform measures'.[125]

The ILO has continued to play a critical role in quantifying the problem of modern slavery. It expanded its influence by collaborating with other Alliance 8.7 partners. In 2017, the Global Estimates of Modern Slavery (GEMS) were released with a great deal of fanfare at the UN's General Assembly.[126] A collaborative effort between the ILO, the Walk Free, and the IOM, each

[123] The ILO is also attempting to broaden the governance debate to include ways to leverage the market power of employers to influence recruitment agencies' practices and for states to consider how their labour migration regimes may contribute to abusive recruitment practices. ILO, *Addressing Governance Challenges in a Changing Labour Migration Landscape*. The complaint against Qatar is a clear example of how a state's immigration policies can lead to forced labour. See Piper, 'The International Labour Organisation as nodal player'.

[124] In addition to targets on economic growth and productivity, the SDG 8 targets require states to take immediate and effective measures to eradicate forced labour, modern slavery, and trafficking (8.7) and to protect the labour rights of all workers, including migrant workers (8.8). UNDP, *The SDGS in Action*; and Kotiswaran, 'Trafficking: A development approach'.

[125] ILO, 'Update on the Alliance 8.7', 1.

[126] Ivanka Trump, representing the US, was flanked by Guy Ryder on one side and Andrew Forest on the other. Klein, 'Ivanka Trump delivers anti-human trafficking speech'.

of which previously had released its own, competing, reports, the GEMS developed a figure to represent the extent of the problem and served as a benchmark for progress toward target 8.7. In 2016, it estimated there were 40.3 million modern slaves, and of these, 24.9 million were in forced labour and 15.4 million in forced marriage.[127] The GEMS adopted the ILO's existing typology of forced labour, separating forced sexual exploitation of adults and commercial sexual exploitation of children from forced labour exploitation and distinguishing between forced labour in the private economy and that imposed by the state. It also broke down the prevalence and types of slavery on a regional basis. But it did not rank countries based on slavery's prevalence or the antislavery initiatives they had undertaken. By contrast, the Global Slavery Index, produced by Walk Free, ranked countries on these two measures.[128] The ILO played no part in the index's production. This kind of ranking exercise could potentially impede future collaboration between the ILO and member states on initiatives to end forced labour.

Target 8.7 elevated modern slavery on the international political agenda. The final communique of the G20 Labour and Employment Ministers' meeting in 2017 embraced SDG target 8.7, calling on governments to consider ratifying and implementing the ILO's Protocol of 2014 to the Forced Labour Convention, 1930, and asking international organisations partnered with the Alliance 8.7 for a report on the worst forms of child labour, forced labour, and modern slavery in global supply chains.[129] In 2019, Alliance 8.7 published the report, the result of a collaboration between the ILO, the IOM, the Organisation for Economic Co-operation and Development, and the United Nations Children's Fund, which provided the first estimates by international organisations of child labour and trafficking for forced labour in global supply chains. It determined that, although child labour and forced labour are more likely to be found in production in the domestic economy, there is a non-negligible risk that such labour contributes to global supply chains.[130] It also reported a strong consensus for responsible business conduct through a comprehensive due-diligence approach, noting that such measures were especially important in the context of insufficient state-based enforcement of labour and human rights standards.[131]

127 ILO and Walk Free Foundation, *Global Estimates of Modern Slavery*, 9, 10.

128 As discussed in Chapter 2.

129 G20 Labour and Employment Ministers Meeting – Germany, 'Ministerial declaration'.

130 ILO, OECD, IOM, and UNICEF, *Ending Child Labour, Forced Labour and Human Trafficking in Global Supply Chains*, 8, 31.

131 Ibid., 48.

A change in the broader political climate in 2021 meant that the Employers' Group was no longer able to stonewall tripartite discussion of a standard for decent work in supply chains. The pandemic revealed the fragility of global supply chains and the failure of lead firms to protect workers in the lower levels who lost wages and their jobs. The Biden administration was much more supportive of labour regulation than its predecessor, and the EU announced its intention to adopt a directive requiring corporations to engage in mandatory human rights due diligence. The GB approved a tripartite working group of ILO constituents to develop options to ensure decent work in supply chains.

Meeting in Geneva from 27 June to 1 July 2022, the experts group hashed out the building blocks of an ILO strategy on supply chains. Initially, the experts from the Employers' Group refused to recognise business 'contribution to weak governance – for example, the way in which enterprise put pressure on governments by making foreign direct investment conditional on low levels of social rights'.[132] However, government experts unanimously agreed that specific problems beset transnational supply chains, and they pressed the Employers' Group to compromise, noting that the Employers' Group had expressed support for the UNGPs and the MNE.[133]

In the end, the tripartite working group released a consensus report that reaffirmed the ILC 2016 Resolution and Conclusions concerning decent work in global supply chains and provided the basis for a five-year strategy for decent work in supply chains that was adopted by the GB in March 2023.[134] The Employers' Group was unable to veto the use of the terms 'supply chain' or 'due diligence', and an ILO standard specifically addressed at supply chains is back on the table. Going forward, the critical question is whether the ILO's Director-General (who since October 2022 is Gilbert F. Houngbo, a former prime minister of Togo with extensive experience working in the international organisations, including the ILO and UN) can steer the ILO's constituents towards a convention designed to regulate supply chains that operate across national borders.

CONCLUSION

The reference to forced labour as an example of exploitation in the UN's definition of human trafficking provided the ILO with an opportunity to

[132] ILO, Meeting of the Tripartite Working Group on Options to Ensure Decent Work in Supply Chains, para 119.

[133] Ibid.

[134] ILO, *ILO Strategy on Decent Work in Supply Chains*.

revitalise its governance role at a time when the dominant neoliberal wisdom treated its traditional governance mechanism (labour standards, public inspections, and worker collective representation through trade unions) with suspicion. The ILO made forced labour legible by producing knowledge about it. On this basis, it reached beyond its traditional constituents to engage with a wider set of powerful new actors on the global antitrafficking stage. By enmeshing itself in the global antitrafficking network, the ILO put labour trafficking on the global governance agenda. The ILO works closely with key actors in the ethical business alliance; indeed, its collaboration with Walk Free on the global estimates of slavery boosted the foundation's credibility and expanded the ILO's sphere of influence.

The ILO developed a labour approach to modern slavery that sees it as rooted in labour market structures and best addressed using labour and market-based tools to enhance workers' bargaining power and capacities.[135] Linking forced labour to labour-market failure, the ILO distinguished between two usages of the term 'labour-market failure'. The first reflected how it is used by the ethical business alliance; 'in strictly economic terms, forced labour is a labour-market failure because it violates key conditions for labour markets to function efficiently, namely the freedom of workers to exercise choice and to receive sufficient remuneration for freely chosen employment'.[136] On this reading, free markets are an antidote to forced labour. However, the ILO has been careful to explain that it was using 'labour-market failure' more broadly 'to encompass the combined failure of labour markets, institutions, and regulations to provide for more efficient or more equitable outcomes'.[137] According to this interpretation, labour markets require institutional supports, including trade unions and embedded social norms, to eliminate labour unfreedom. The ILO advocates strongly in favour of labour-market regulation to increase workers' voice and power in the labour market.

Although the ILO refers to structural factors, such as globalisation, that are driving forced labour, it does not elaborate upon them or offer a critique of global capitalism. The ILO's mandate (employment and work), its tripartite structure, and its need for funding from key donors constrains its governance agenda and narrows its focus. These features distinguish the ILO's approach to forced labour from a broader development approach, which places

[135] Chuang, 'Exploitation creep', 642; Shamir, 'A labor paradigm'; Costello, 'Migrants and forced labour'.
[136] ILO, A *Global Alliance against Forced Labour*, 64.
[137] Ibid.

transnational corporations and their supply chains 'within the global trade, investment, property, and tax regimes we have built'.[138] Such an approach also contemplates interventions 'to address the regulatory structures – the rules on FDI [foreign direct investment], labour migration, trade, and corporate tax law – that are endogenous to the formation and governance of some GVCs'.[139] This approach identifies key features of global capitalism as causing forced labour, and its solution involves reconsidering the social dimension of global trade, reconceptualising development from the perspective of countries in the Global South, and reimagining the role of the state in economic development.[140] The ILO's goal has been more modest: to devise and institutionalise a labour approach to the governance of forced labour.[141]

The ILO stresses the traditional mechanisms of labour regulation – freedom of association and collective bargaining, inclusive systems of social protection, and public labour inspectorates – and this view is gaining traction in the antislavery network (see Chapter 2).[142] Focusing on forced labour made the ILO's programmes more attractive to funders and a new protocol more palatable to its tripartite members.[143]

The Protocol of 2014 to the Forced Labour Convention is an international standard that incorporates the techniques of labour law – labour standards, public enforcement, and collective worker representation – into the governance of forced labour. It also integrates a human rights approach by imposing obligations on states to protect victims and to provide them with effective remedies. The forced labour protocol provides an alternative governance domain, one which tackles labour-market institutions and is preventative in orientation, unlike the criminal law, where the focus is on individual perpetrators and the goal is punishment. These features of the 2014 forced labour protocol help to explain why its rate of ratification is half that of the UN's Trafficking Protocol.[144]

The ILO has not repudiated a carceral approach to human trafficking, although it would limit its sphere of application. Like other international organisations, the ILO is careful to distinguish between protecting victims of

[138] Cockayne, *Developing Freedom*, 75, citing Milberg and Winkler, *Outsourcing Economics*, 123–124.

[139] Ibid.

[140] Ibid., 257; Kotiswaran, 'Trafficking: A development approach'.

[141] ILO, *Ending Forced Labour by 2030*, 27.

[142] ILO, Walk Free, and IOM, *Global Estimates of Modern Slavery*, 6.

[143] Phillips and Mieres, 'The governance of forced labour'.

[144] Six years after the UN adopted the Trafficking Protocol, 111 states had ratified it; in contrast, only 50 states had ratified the ILO's forced labour protocol six years after its adoption.

forced labour and punitive immigration laws. It has also cautioned against 'powerful forces' that seek to 'conflate trafficking for forced labour in the Global North with the legitimate desire of people for migration from poverty and drought and for safe refuge from crisis and conflict'.[145]

The legal definition of forced labour in the ILO's 1930 convention hinges on consent and coercion, and the ILO's supervisory bodies have emphasised individual actors rather than structural factors when it comes to assessing consent. This definition builds upon and reinforces a neoclassical understanding of free wage labour as an individual exchange relationship.[146] By doing so, it excludes the broader structural and institutional factors, such as corporate concentration and immigration policies, for example, that constrain workers' freedom from consideration.[147]

In part, the narrowness of the definition in the 1930 convention can be explained by its purpose, which is to establish the scope of a criminal prohibition. While the borders between free and unfree labour are important for criminal law and victim protection, they are not central to a labour approach that is designed to prevent practices that may deteriorate into forced labour. By promoting labour-market regulation as a preventative measure, the ILO can tackle a broad range of labour exploitation.

Although the regulatory ambit of a labour approach captures a wide range of exploitive practices, it does not benefit sex workers since the ILO does not address the situation of those who sell sexual services. Despite pushing the gendered borders of work when it adopted a standard for domestic workers employed in private households in 2011, the ILO has yet to advocate for labour standards for the sex sector.[148] It has forsaken sex workers in the face of the moral and gendered concerns of the member states.

By requiring states to address fraudulent and abusive labour recruitment and to support due-diligence measures by both the public and private sectors, the forced labour protocol made important gestures to addressing the transnational vectors of forced labour. However, the ILO has only been able to muster its constituents to adopt voluntary norms, such as the FRI and MNE, when it comes to regulating the cross-border dimensions of forced labour. Even though it is the 'epicentre of global social dialogue on labour market issues', the ILO has been unable to sustain a serious tripartite discussion of a

[145] ILO, *Ending Forced Labour by 2030*, 21.
[146] Drubel, 'Regulation by visibility', 196; Fudge, 'Modern slavery, unfree labour and the labour market'.
[147] Lerche, 'A global alliance against forced labour'; Rogaly, 'Migrant workers in the ILO's Global Alliance against Forced Labour'; Phillips and Mieres, 'The governance of forced labour'.
[148] Wijers, 'How we got here'.

labour standard for transnational supply chains. The European Union (as we shall see in the next chapter) has overtaken the ILO when it comes to devising enforceable standards that require a transnational corporation to exercise due diligence to make sure their businesses and supply chains respect human rights. Yet, unlike the ILO, the EU does not come at the task of designing governance mechanisms from the perspective of empowering workers. Thus, the ILO's MNE makes a distinct contribution when it comes to designing due-diligence initiatives. The GB's adoption in March 2023 of a strategy to ensure decent work in supply chains offers some promise that the ILO can develop a normative mechanism able to address one of the transnational vectors of unfree labour.[149]

Scale is a contested technique of governance within the ILO. The IOE, which represents the Employers' Group, has resisted cross-border business regulation to promote labour rights in supply chains, complaining that 'states are seeking to pass the buck onto private entities for their own failure or unwillingness to protect their people's rights'.[150] By contrast, the ethical business alliance promotes business regulation as a way of addressing the challenge that transnational supply chains pose to purely national forms of regulation.[151] In the next chapter, we will see how the key governance actors in the European Union mobilised a dynamic and multiscalar assemblage of jurisdiction to address the different forms of unfree labour that cross national and territorial borders, including mandatory human rights due-diligence legislation and market controls on goods made with forced labour.

[149] ILO, *Note on the Proceedings*, para. 177.

[150] International Organisation of Employers, 'IOE paper on state policy responses on human rights due diligence', 11.

[151] However, business objected to a form of extraterritorial jurisdiction proposed in the 'zero' draft of a legally binding instrument to regulate business regarding human rights on the ground that it would not respect national sovereignty. Krisch, 'Jurisdiction unbound', 510.

4

The EU's Integrated and Holistic Approach

In order to effectively address trafficking, a holistic and integrated approach is needed which builds on the respect and promotion of human rights as its fundament.

—European Commission, *Report of the Experts Group on Trafficking*

The border is the definitive marker of the political, defining in and out, friend and enemy, us and them.

—Longo, *The Politics of Borders*

The most concentrated site of multiscalar governance – the European Union – has led the way in adopting region-wide binding legal norms to address human trafficking. In 1996, the European Commission identified 'trafficking in women for the purpose of sexual exploitation' as 'an increasing type of international organized crime generating high profits with relatively low forms of risk for traffickers'.[1] Initially, the EU's governing institutions approached human trafficking as a problem of organised crime and illegal immigration, focusing almost exclusively on sexual exploitation and prostitution. By 2012, however, labour trafficking was firmly on the agenda. EU governing institutions embraced a multifaceted approach 'based on human rights' and 'systematically embedded in multiple policy instruments' in 'policy areas ranging from security to migration, justice, equality, anti-discrimination, fundamental rights, employment, development, research, humanitarian aid and fisheries, amongst others'.[2] The EU's antitrafficking framework is widely praised for augmenting the human rights of victims and filling the gap surrounding victim protection left in the UN's Human Trafficking

[1] Commission of the European Communities, 'Communication from the Commission to the European Parliament', 3.

[2] Ibid., 14.

Protocol.[3] The overlapping membership between the Council of Europe (whose sole purpose is to protect human rights) and the EU helps to explain the EU's emphasis on the human rights of victims in the context of human trafficking.

The shift in the EU's governance approach to human trafficking occurred at the same time as a similar change in how UN institutions handled the problem and the emergence of the global antislavery network. In both cases, human rights advocates and networks of experts drove the expansion of antitrafficking strategies, which coincided with the interests of governance institutions concerned with protecting and strengthening their institutional domain. Like its international counterparts, EU institutions also adopted highly gendered governance strategies for dealing with different kinds of human trafficking, treating sexual and labour exploitation very differently.

Despite these similarities, there are some critical differences between the EU's and the global antislavery governance network's approaches to human trafficking and unfree labour. Most significantly, the EU has retained the concept of human trafficking with its emphasis on movement as the core of its governance strategies. It is the movement across national borders that gives the EU legislative authority over human trafficking. Another difference is that unlike the global antitrafficking network, EU governance institutions have not embraced the term 'modern slavery'. This difference is more than simply terminological; it signifies different understandings of the nature of the problem to be governed, a difference encapsulated in a 2013 report by two prominent new abolitionists assessing the EU's antitrafficking strategy. Objecting to the EU's use of 'trafficking' as 'an overarching term that includes the concept "slavery"', Kevin Bales and Zoe Trodd argued that since 'trafficking is a process by which slavery can be achieved', trafficking is defined by slavery, not vice versa.[4] In contrast, they identified the problem as a constraint on *freedom*, not movement, urging the EU to adopt the definition of slavery in the Bellagio–Harvard Guidelines, which emphasises controlling a person in such a way as to significantly deprive that person of individual liberty. By pivoting away from human trafficking, with its emphasis on sexual exploitation, to modern slavery, the EU could, they claimed, begin to grapple with the bigger problem, which is forced labour in labour and supply chains.[5]

By late 2020, all EU governance institutions had committed to introducing legislation to tackle the problem of labour exploitation in supply chains;

[3] Jovanovic, 'International law and regional norm smuggling', 808.

[4] Bales and Trodd, 'Addressing contemporary forms of slavery', 7.

[5] Ibid., 13, 14, 16, 17.

however, they did not embrace the overarching frame of modern slavery endorsed by new abolitionists and the ethical business alliance. Instead, the EU adopted a broader notion of sustainability that encompasses the environment, human rights, and decent work.[6] In addition to freedom, the proposed directive on corporate sustainability is intended to protect human dignity and sustainability as core values. The EU's directive will go beyond transparency legislation of the type favoured in the United States, UK, Australia, and Canada (the 'Anglosphere') to impose an obligation on businesses to design and implement processes to identify, prevent, and mitigate any adverse impacts their business may have on human rights. This proposed due-diligence directive is just one dimension of the EU's multifaceted approach to human trafficking, which continues to concentrate on cross-border movement, to emphasise the sexual exploitation of women and children, and to deploy a criminal-law approach.

Understanding the dynamic legal assemblage of jurisdiction between EU institutions and its Member States is critical for understanding how the EU approaches the transnational problems of human trafficking across borders and forced labour in supply chains. The EU disrupts the conventional legal default of jurisdiction that links sovereignty to territory by creating plural and hierarchical borders between Member States of the EU, new accession countries, candidate countries, and countries outside the EU.[7] The treaties that make up the EU allocate governance authority, known in the EU as competences, on a scalar basis between EU institutions and Member States, creating a complex hybrid form of sovereignty.

The treaties also allocate legislative authority between the EU's three main governing institutions: the European Parliament, which is elected by and represents the EU's citizens; the Council of the European Union, which is made up of the heads of each Member State and, as such, tends to represent the interests of individual states; and the European Commission, which acts as the executive and seeks to uphold the interests of the EU as a whole. A key feature of EU integration has been the separation and sorting of different governance authorities (competences) into different scales that are associated with different governance mechanisms and techniques. The treaties assemble the EU's jurisdiction and how its jurisdiction interacts with that of Member States.

From its origins in 1957 as a common market among six nations, the EU evolved, by 2024, into a single market (founded on the four freedoms of

6 Council of the European Union, 'Council conclusions on human rights and decent work'.

7 Andrijasevic, *Migration, Agency and Citizenship*.

movement of goods, capital, services, and people) involving twenty-seven Member States with different economic and political traditions and institutions. In the wake of the breakup of the Soviet Union, the EU intensified its twin projects of transnational governance and market expansion. It responded to the related challenges of integrating new Member States into the single market and enhancing the legitimacy of its decision-making process by attempting to institutionalise a conception of EU citizenship rooted in the 'European values' of free movement, democracy, gender equality, and human rights.[8]

The EU's evolving competences have shaped its approach to human trafficking. Since 1990, the EU has gone through three episodes of significant constitutional change that have altered the scalar and governance dimensions of its competence. The first two episodes (the Maastricht and Amsterdam Treaties), which occurred in the 1990s and are discussed in the following section, triggered a project of criminal-law harmonisation. In contrast, the third constitutional movement, the Lisbon Treaty, which came into effect in 2009 and is the focus of the third section, supported a countermovement, boosted by the Council of Europe's Human Trafficking Convention, to protect the rights of victims of trafficking. The fourth section explains how the dramatic expansion of the EU to include former socialist countries led to increased concerns in 2012 that migrant workers from recent-accession states were subject to exploitation and greater attention to the problem of labour trafficking. The EU's commitment to introducing a mandatory human rights due-diligence (HRDD) directive and a regulation imposing a marketing ban on goods made with forced labour added another facet to the EU's antitrafficking strategy, which is the subject of the final section.

As we will see, trafficking is a problem for the EU to address *because* it is seen as a crime that moves across borders. By contrast, for the EU to address forced labour and modern slavery in supply chains, it must use another source of competence, such as its authority over the internal market or its external power over trade and development. Using different competences (sources of jurisdiction) to deal with different forms of unfree labour has resulted in different governance strategies for what are treated as different problems – the movement of people and the movement of goods across borders. This chapter illustrates how the EU's expanding competence over human trafficking and human rights authorised governance strategies that distinguished between sex and labour trafficking, creating different categories of mobile workers and extending EU values beyond the borders of its Member States.

8 Foret and Grundell, 'European morality politics in the European Union', 1798–1814.

MAKING SEX TRAFFICKING A CRIME

The collapse of the Soviet Union reignited Europe's historical anxiety over sex trafficking. In 1989, the European Parliament adopted a resolution on 'the exploitation of prostitution and the traffic in human beings', urging those Member States that had not already done so to ratify the 1949 UN Convention for the Suppression of the Traffic in Persons and of the Exploitation of the Prostitution of Others.[9] Fears of a 'Natasha' trade in women trafficked from eastern to western Europe harkened back to historical understandings of white slavery centred on European women trafficked in Europe and to the colonies.[10] Noting that the 1949 Convention had declared prostitution *and* human trafficking incompatible with the dignity and worth of the human person, the resolution called for Member States to adopt a common policy to combat prostitution and to eliminate the traffic in persons.

The European Women's Lobby, a feminist umbrella organisation funded by the EU and linked to the influential US-based Coalition Against Trafficking in Women, was crucial in framing human trafficking at the European level as a matter of women's rights and part of the broader agenda to address violence against women and to promote gender equality. Like its international counterpart, the European Women's Lobby viewed prostitution as exploitative per se and advocated its abolition through policies criminalising the demand for sexual services as part of the solution to the problem of human trafficking. Although organisations that supported sex workers' rights distinguished between prostitution and human trafficking by stressing coercion as a critical component of trafficking, the European Women's Lobby exerted a great deal of influence over the EU's antitrafficking policy.[11] Swedish feminists who held influential positions within the commission and Parliament were receptive to the Women's Lobby, and they played an important role in promoting and circulating the Swedish approach to prostitution, which treats it as a form of violence against women antithetical to women's equality and a form of human trafficking.[12]

In the 1990s, all three of the EU's legislative institutions framed human trafficking in terms of sexual exploitation and illegal immigration best tackled by criminal law and securitising borders. Reports of between 200,000 and

9 Resolution on the Exploitation of Prostitution and the Traffic in Human Beings (1989). When capitalised, Member States refers to members of the European Union.

10 Suchland, *Economies of Violence*, 57.

11 Mattson, *The Cultural Politics of European Prostitution Reform*; and Wijers, 'Purity, victimhood and agency', 56–79.

12 Grundell, 'The EU's approach to prostitution', 425–439.

500,000 women and children trafficked each year into the EU circulated widely, and the numbers took on a life of their own.[13] The migrant sex worker came to personify anxieties about national identity and sovereignty in Europe.[14] Since human trafficking was associated with other forms of criminality such as drugs, arms, and prostitution, it was seen as the 'most menacing form of irregular migration'.[15] In turn, the need to combat the horror of sex trafficking affirmed the role of 'the state in maintaining sovereign borders and quelling the anxiety created by European integration and globalization'.[16]

Initially, the EU's antitrafficking actions were restricted by its limited competence over criminal and immigration matters, matters of increasing prominence both for EU institutions and Member States because the Schengen Agreement, once it came into effect in 1995, would abolish internal borders between EU Member States. Effective in 1993, the Maastricht Treaty gave EU institutions authority over police and judicial cooperation in border control, asylum, and migration policy. Indeed, the treaty specifically contemplated the establishment of a European Police Office, and Europol began to operate in 1998. However, since Member States had primary jurisdiction over criminal and immigration matters, EU institutions were relegated to a secondary role, dealing with those matters with a transnational dimension.[17]

Anita Gradin, Sweden's first European commissioner, was pivotal in characterising human trafficking as a policy issue that the EU could and should tackle. Responsible for immigration, home affairs, and justice in the EU from 1995 to 1999, she rejected the idea that there was no legal basis for the EU to take up the issue of human trafficking. Gradin claimed that this 'international slave trade' was clearly a matter of cross-border crime and within the EU's jurisdiction.[18] By focusing on individual criminality, this approach to human trafficking had the effect of cocooning the broader economic and social forces that made women vulnerable to exploitation from scrutiny. While Commissioner Gradin was of the view, which prevailed in Sweden, that prostitution should be abolished as a violation of women's rights, she was

[13] Feingold, 'Trafficking in numbers', 46–74.

[14] Berman, '(Un)popular strangers and crises (un)bounded', 37–86; Aradau, 'The perverse politics of four-letter words', 251–277; and Andrijasevic, *Migration, Agency and Citizenship*.

[15] Laczko and Thompson, *Migrant Trafficking and Human Smuggling in Europe*, 19.

[16] Berman, '(Un)popular strangers and crises (un)bounded', 50.

[17] Officially, European Union, *Treaty on European Union (Consolidated Version), Treaty of Maastricht*. It established the EU (formerly the European Community), laid the foundations for the monetary union (the euro), and set out the criteria for new members to join.

[18] Mattson, *The Cultural Politics of European Prostitution Reform*, 40.

willing to compromise with organisations that promoted sex workers' rights to get antitrafficking policies on the EU's legislative agenda.[19]

The European Parliament urged the EU to address prostitution and take a position on its relationship to human trafficking. A parliamentarian from Sweden, Marianne Eriksson, was very influential in shaping the Parliament's position on prostitution, which equated it with sexual exploitation and human trafficking. She drafted the Parliament's 1997 resolution on violence against women, in which prostitution was defined as a form of violence against women.[20] By contrast, both the commission and council treated prostitution as a matter within the jurisdiction of Member States and, thus, refused to define the relationship between trafficking in human beings and sexual exploitation.[21]

The 1997 Treaty of Amsterdam opened the EU up to the possibility of negotiations for common policies on criminal justice, immigration, and social policy. The treaty also increased the authority of Parliament and reduced that of individual Member States in the legislative process.[22] It accommodated Member States' reluctance to cede their exclusive competence over criminal and immigration law by restricting criminal-law matters to framework decisions that have weaker enforcement powers than directives and by requiring immigration matters to be governed for five more years by the old legislative process.[23] Thus, even though the EU had a legal basis for developing criminal and immigration laws relating to human trafficking, Member States continued to enjoy a great deal of leeway in implementing the former and *de facto* veto power over the latter.

The EU's imminent competence to harmonise criminal law over human trafficking exposed divisions in Member States by bringing opposing conceptions of prostitution as either a form of work or a form of violence against women into direct conflict.[24] The relationship between prostitution and

[19] Ibid., 41.

[20] Grundell, 'The EU's approach to prostitution', 425–439.

[21] Berman, '(Un)popular strangers and crises (un)bounded', 37–86; and Allwood, 'Agenda setting, agenda blocking and policy silence', 126–134.

[22] It gave the EU Parliament co-decision-making power with the Council of Ministers (the heads of members states) and substituted a qualified majority vote for the requirement of unanimity. This legislative process, known as the ordinary process, reduced the power of national authorities and increased that of trans-European organizations that could influence members of Parliament.

[23] Although legally binding on Member States, framework decisions are neither enforceable by EU citizens in Member States' national courts nor by the commission through infringement proceedings at the Court of Justice of the European Union.

[24] Askola, *Legal Responses to Trafficking in Women.*

sexual exploitation fundamentally tied the EU's approach to human trafficking to the criminal laws and policies of Member States. Countries rushed to revise their prostitution laws ahead of the Amsterdam Treaty's coming into force in 1999.[25] The spectrum of state responses to prostitution across the EU ranged from legalisation/regulation (e.g., Germany, Austria, Spain, Luxembourg, Netherlands), to the toleration of prostitution where it was not officially allowed but also not illegal (e.g., Greece, France, Portugal), to full-scale criminalisation in states where prostitution was illegal (e.g., Ireland), to approaches that criminalised the purchase of sexual services (Sweden, Finland).[26] The contention over the best way to regulate prostitution and the sale of sexual services crystallised Member States' concerns about the EU's new, albeit limited, criminal-law competence, raising anxieties about criminality and fears that lack of internal movement controls would, especially with the looming accession of ten states, lead to an influx of desperate migrants. Migrant sex workers epitomised these fears.[27]

In 1999, the European Council asked the commission to prepare legislation on human trafficking. Most EU Member States had no specific legislation addressing trafficking in women, although some maintained that trafficking was dealt with through general provisions criminalising third-party involvement in prostitution.[28] The commission presented a proposal for a council framework decision, which endorsed the UN's broad definition of human trafficking and proposed common penalties to be imposed by Member States.[29] Although the commission included labour exploitation within the definition of human trafficking, its focus was on sex trafficking, especially from central and eastern Europe.[30]

The 2002 framework decision on human trafficking was part of the EU's broader agenda to exercise greater authority over border controls in light of the lifting of internal border controls following the Schengen Agreement.[31] The EU wanted to prevent illegal immigration, which it linked to human trafficking. Following the UN's precedent, the EU adopted two legal instruments, one for human trafficking and the other for human smuggling. The EU's 2002 framework decision on the 'facilitation of illegal immigration', which is

25 Mattson, *The Cultural Politics of European Prostitution Reform*.
26 Locher, 'International norms and European policy making'; Wijers and Lap-Chew, *Trafficking in Women*, 189–210; and Wijers, 'Purity, victimhood and agency', 56–79.
27 Mattson, *The Cultural Politics of European Prostitution Reform*, 32.
28 Locher, 'International norms and European policy making'.
29 Council of the European Union, 'Proposal for a comprehensive plan'.
30 In 2001, the European Commission released 'Trafficking in women'.
31 European Union, 'Council framework decision of 19 July 2002'.

more commonly known as 'smuggling', strengthened the penal framework to prevent the facilitation of unauthorised entry, transit, and residence.[32] The EU gradually expanded its competence over border management, and in 2004 Frontex, the European Agency for the Management of Operational Cooperation at the External Borders, was born.

Despite a recital characterising human trafficking as comprising 'serious violations of fundamental human rights and human dignity', the 2002 framework decision on human trafficking was essentially a criminal-law measure that outlined the elements of the crime of human trafficking and specified minimum penalties; its legal basis was the treaty provisions on police and judicial cooperation in criminal matters.[33] It largely followed the definition of human trafficking in the UN Palermo Protocol, which enabled the EU to avoid getting mired in debates about the relationship between prostitution and human trafficking by delegating the definition of 'exploitation' to Member States.[34] The EU's definition, like that in the protocol, did not require a transnational dimension for the action to be considered human trafficking. However, unlike the UN protocol, the framework decision was silent on matters pertaining to immigration, and the protections it offered to trafficking victims were even weaker than the UN protocol's optional provisions. The EU promised to introduce an instrument more specifically regarding victims' rights.[35]

Concerned with avoiding creating an incentive that would encourage an opportunistic abuse of residence permits by illegal immigrants, Member States were reluctant to agree to legally binding rules to protect the rights of victims of trafficking who were neither their own nationals nor citizens of the EU.[36] It took two years of intense negotiation for the council to adopt a directive on

32 It also contained a framework decision for harmonising EU countries' laws regarding penalties, the liability of legal persons, and jurisdiction for infringements relating to the facilitation of illegal immigration: see European Union, 'Council directive 2002/90/EC' and '2002/946/JHA'.

33 European Union, '2002/629/JHA'; European Union, *Treaty on European Union (Consolidated Version), Treaty of Maastricht*, and Title VI, Articles 29, 31(e) and 34 (2) (b); and Krieg, 'Trafficking in human beings', 775, 778. Although the European Union's 2001 'Council framework decision of 15 March 2001 on the standing of victims in criminal proceedings' (2001/220/JHA) does not refer explicitly to victims of trafficking, but instead addresses victims of any crimes, it sets out the assistance and protection to be provided to victims of trafficking, including the procedure during hearings and the provision of evidence.

34 It expanded the definition of sexual exploitation to include pornography.

35 Askola, *Legal Responses to Trafficking in Women*, 126.

36 Gallagher, 'Recent legal developments in the field of human trafficking', 169; and Askola, *Legal Responses to Trafficking in Women*, 92.

short-term residence permits in 2004 (the Residence Permit Directive).[37] Based on the treaty provisions allowing the EU to adopt legislative measures in relation to illegal immigration and residence, the Residence Permit Directive's aim is to strengthen the fight against trafficking and illegal migration by providing temporary residence permits and encouraging third-country nationals to cooperate with the law enforcement authorities of Member States. It establishes the conditions for granting residence permits of limited duration to EU nationals who are victims of human trafficking or, if the Member State chooses, to those accused of people smuggling who cooperate in prosecuting these crimes. Victims of trafficking are distinguished from third-country nationals smuggled into the EU on the ground that the latter group consented, and the directive creates a small zone of protection for victims. The directive does not require Member States to identify the victims of trafficking, but if they do, Member States are obliged to give victims an unspecified reflection period to allow them to decide whether to cooperate with the authorities. During this period, Member States are prohibited from enforcing expulsion orders against trafficking victims and are required to provide them an unspecified 'appropriate standard' of living and access to emergency medical treatment.[38] Significantly, the directive ties victims' rights to their cooperation with law enforcement initiatives, and even those rights are minimal and discretionary.[39] Not only does this discretion permit wide variation in the way in which Member States treat victims of trafficking, Denmark, Ireland, and the United Kingdom opted out of the residence directive.

The 2002 Framework Decision and the Residence Permit Directive reinforced national sovereignty by giving Member States a great deal of discretion over how to define human trafficking and the rights granted to victims, while at the same time framing human trafficking as a threat to both the EU's and national security, a threat that required stronger borders against illegal migration and greater penalties against transnational crime. The EU's antitrafficking initiatives focused on sexual exploitation and prostitution.

[37] European Union, 'Council directive 2004/81/EC'. The directive requires Member States to bring their national law in line with it by August 2006.

[38] Member States are also required to provide, where appropriate, psychological assistance, free legal assistance (if available to nationals or permanent residents), and translation and interpretation services if needed.

[39] If victims sever relations with their trafficker and decide to cooperate, and if national authorities consider the cooperation to be helpful, Member States (subject to public policy and national security considerations) are required to grant a short-term residence permit of at least six months while they retain the discretion to grant access to work and education during this period.

Migrant prostitution came to be seen as an 'inherent evil to be combatted domestically and internationally'.[40] In part, migrants who are not EU nationals were targeted because the European Court of Justice ruled that EU nationals have the right to work as prostitutes in Member States where the activity is not illegal.[41] The Residence Permit Directive provided a humanitarian rationale for deporting migrant sex workers regardless of the Member State's specific stance on prostitution since they could easily be redefined as victims of trafficking and repatriated to their country of origin. Sex trafficking discourses operated as key elements in the construction of borders in the EU, filtering the flow of people into the EU into different categories, such as EU citizen, illegal migrant, and victim of trafficking, with different rights and entitlements.[42]

HITCHING HUMAN RIGHTS TO A CARCERAL AGENDA

The powerful position of the Council of the European Union in the EU's legislative process and the EU's competence explain the extremely limited protection of the human rights of victims of trafficking in the EU's first two legislative antitrafficking initiatives. Both the commission and Parliament were more open to the human rights approach promoted by international human rights institutions and NGOs than were Member States and the Council of the European Union.

Indeed, for the European Commission, the trafficking directives were another example of the human rights deficit growing in the EU. The commission sought to mediate 'the ongoing tensions between preserving the sovereign right of European states to – individually or collectively within the EU – control their borders and arrivals into their territories, and the desire to preserve Europe's image as a continent that honours its human rights and humanitarian commitments'.[43] It marshalled civil society organisations and experts to persuade Member States and the Council of the European Union to better protect the human rights of victims of trafficking.

Together with the European Parliament and the International Organization for Migration, the commission convened a broad-based

[40] Mattson, *The Cultural Politics of European Prostitution Reform*, 48–49.

[41] Askola, *Legal Responses to Trafficking in Women*, 53n6; and Allwood, 'Agenda setting, agenda blocking and policy silence', 126–134.

[42] Berman, '(Un)popular strangers and crises (un)bounded', 37–86; Aradau, 'The perverse politics of four-letter words', 251–277; Andrijasevic, *Migration, Agency and Citizenship*; and Paul, *The Political Economy of Border Drawing*.

[43] Weinar, Bonjour, and Zhyznomirska, 'Introduction', 6.

conference of a thousand participants in Brussels in September 2002 to take stock of EU antitrafficking policy. This conference issued what came to be known as the Brussels Declaration on Preventing and Combating Trafficking in Human Beings, which characterised human trafficking as a serious violation of the victim's 'human rights as enshrined in international law and the EU Charter on Fundamental Rights'.[44] Announcing its intention to use the Brussels Declaration as the main basis of its future work, in March 2003 the European Commission set up a consultative group known as the Experts Group on Trafficking in Human Beings.

Just months after the EU adopted the Residence Permit Directive, the Experts Group released its report in 2004.[45] The president of the Experts Group, Marjan Wijers, identified two major themes informing the report: a human rights perspective on human trafficking and a holistic, multilevel, and integrated approach to combatting it. Since human rights require states to tackle the root causes of human trafficking, the report argued that any strategy for addressing human trafficking could not be limited to criminal law and immigration controls. Indeed, it cautioned on the need to avoid 'unintended and undesirable side effects of repressive policies that might increase vulnerability for trafficking'.[46]

Essentially, the report offered a critique and alternative to the EU's approach to antitrafficking. Instead of concentrating on the *process* of trafficking, the Experts Group advised the EU to focus on its *outcomes* – 'the exploitation of human beings under forced labour or slavery like conditions, no matter whether such exploitation involves a victim of trafficking, a smuggled person, an illegal migrant or a lawful resident'.[47] Human trafficking was reframed as a problem of labour exploitation rather than a problem of illegal immigration and prostitution. The report identified restrictive border controls, especially when combined with informal and unregulated sectors in the labour markets of EU Member States, as contributing to the problem of human trafficking, and the 'increasing movement of labour and use of contractors and sub-contractors' as making labour and supply chains harder to

[44] European Union, *Brussels Declaration on Preventing and Combating Trafficking in Human Beings*, Annex: Recommendations, Standards and Best Practices.

[45] Eleven experts were drawn from state administrations, five from international and intergovernmental organisations, and four from EU employer associations. Two were academics.

[46] European Commission, *Report of the Experts Group on Trafficking*, 7. Much of the report resembles what Pinto describes as a discourse that challenges the prevailing view that human rights are compatible with penal policies. Pinto, 'Discursive alignment of trafficking, rights and crime control'.

[47] Pinto, 'Discursive alignment of trafficking, rights and crime control'.

regulate.[48] Thus, it recommended legal pathways for labour migration as an essential part of any solution and advocated for the enforcement of labour standards combined with the organisation of workers as critical components of an antitrafficking strategy.[49] Like the ILO, it endorsed a labour approach to trafficking (see Chapter 3).

Blending specific recommendations designed to address clear limitations in victim protection with a far-reaching analysis of the causes of human trafficking, the Experts Group's report urged the commission to initiate a new directive that would better protect the rights of all victims, irrespective of their cooperation in criminal proceedings, and to attend specifically to the position, rights, and needs of children. It also recommended that Member States establish an individual complaint mechanism, national rapporteurs (or their equivalent), and national referral mechanisms, which governments and civil society groups set up to ensure the proper identification and referral of trafficked persons so they could receive adequate assistance.

The 2004 Experts Groups' report was extremely influential in shaping the language the commission used to characterise its approach to antitrafficking policy; the commission's 2005 proposal for an action plan on human trafficking referred to the need to have an 'integrated approach' that has 'as its fundament the respect of human rights'.[50] However, the shared language of 'human rights' and 'integrated approach' obscured different governance strategies based on different approaches to human rights and different conceptions of the harm of human trafficking.[51] Although the proposal emphasised that the EU's Charter of Fundamental Rights prohibited human trafficking and that under international laws and commitments Member States were required to protect the rights of victims of trafficking, it offered little in terms of concrete steps to protect them. In the context of human trafficking, the commission approached human rights from a law enforcement perspective that treats them as a 'justification for a broad range of criminal measures'.[52] It identified labour trafficking as a concern, but it treated the sexual exploitation of women and children as a separate problem warranting particular attention.

The Council of Europe, the leading pan-European human rights organisation, played a critical role in shaping the EU's governance of trafficking. All

48 Ibid., 83, 121.

49 Ibid., 121.

50 Commission of the European Communities, 'Communication from the commission to the European Parliament and the Council: Fighting trafficking', 1.

51 Pinto, 'Discursive alignment of trafficking, rights and crime control'.

52 Ibid.

EU Member States are members of the Council of Europe and bound by the European Convention of Human Rights, which imposes legally enforceable obligations on party states. Like the European Commission, the Council of Europe institutions used experts to develop its human rights approach to trafficking. In 2002, the Council of Europe's Steering Committee for Equality between Men and Women commissioned a study on the feasibility of drawing up a convention on action against human trafficking as part of its attempt to persuade the Council's Committee of Ministers, which is composed of the foreign affairs ministers of its forty-seven member states, to adopt a binding regional instrument.[53] Endorsing the definition of human trafficking provided in the UN protocol, the study claimed that a European convention would add value by making 'human rights its foundation and reference point'.[54]

The Committee of Ministers established an Ad Hoc Committee of Experts on Action Against Trafficking in Human Beings to draft an instrument that better balanced 'matters concerning human rights and prosecution'.[55] The drafting process was tightly controlled, and there were no public hearings, although a coalition of NGOs made submissions and attempted to push the drafting committee in a human rights direction.[56] The Parliamentary Assembly, which consisted of 324 members of Parliament from the 47 member states, was concerned that the protections for the human rights of trafficking victims were being weakened in the negotiation process as states were more concerned 'to protect themselves from illegal immigration'.[57] The European Commission was singled out for attempting to induce the Council of Europe 'to lower its standards to the lowest common denominator of [EU] community law'.[58]

The Council of Europe adopted the Convention on Action against Trafficking in Human Beings in May 2005, which it described as

[53] Council of Europe, 'Council of Europe Convention on Action against Trafficking in Human Beings', 29.

[54] Council of Europe Steering Committee for Equality between Women and Men, *Feasibility Study*.

[55] Council of Europe, 'Council of Europe Convention on Action against Trafficking in Human Beings', 7. Two experts were nominated by every member state of the Council of Europe, and two scientific experts were appointed by the Secretariate General: Scarpa, *Trafficking in Human Beings*, 144.

[56] Gallagher, *The International Law of Human Trafficking*, 112.

[57] Council of Europe, Parliamentary Assembly, 'Recommendation No. 1545 (2002)'.

[58] Scarpa, *Trafficking in Human Beings*, 145–146. See also Raffaelli, 'The European approach to the protection of trafficking victims', 212; and Stoyanova, *Human Trafficking and Slavery Reconsidered*, 28.

supplementing both the UN Protocol and the EU Framework Decision by bringing 'a human rights perspective and its focus on victim protection'.[59] The convention's definition of human trafficking was based on that provided in the UN Protocol, marking a shift away from the Council of Europe's hitherto exclusive focus on the sexual exploitation of women and children. Throughout the convention, however, special reference is made to the importance of guaranteeing gender equality in relation to both prevention and protection. The convention also targeted the demand for services provided by victims of trafficking by requiring parties to consider making it a criminal offence to knowingly use such services.[60]

The convention's victim protection provisions implemented some of the recommendations contained in the EU's 2004 Experts Group report, such as the establishment of a mechanism for identifying victims and detaching the obligation to protect victims from the victim's ability and willingness to cooperate in the prosecution process. Unlike the EU's Residence Permit Directive, the gateway to assistance and protection under the Council of Europe convention is the identification of victims of trafficking and not their cooperation with prosecution. States ratifying the convention are under an obligation to ensure that a national framework is in place for identifying victims and providing them with a period of reflection and recovery. However, the positive obligation to provide assistance depends both on where the individual is in the victim identification procedure and their migration status. Victims who cooperate are entitled to greater assistance, and if a victim who has been identified decides to cooperate, states are required to provide a temporary residence permit, in contrast to the EU's Residence Permit Directive, which leaves the issuance of a residence permit to the discretion of each Member State.

States also have additional obligations under the convention, including the provision of full medical and other assistance, vocational training and education, and access to the labour market to victims with lawful immigration status, although the conditions of access are left to state parties. Moreover, states are obliged to provide victims with a mechanism for seeking compensation and legal redress from their traffickers. Once states have ratified the convention, they are subject to a distinctive monitoring mechanism, the Group of Experts on Action against Trafficking in Human Beings (GRETA), which consists of

59 Council of Europe, Council of Europe Convention on Action against Trafficking in Human Beings. The convention was scheduled to come into force in May 2008.

60 Ibid., paras. 229, 236.

an independent group of fifteen experts.[61] By issuing evaluative reports on a party state's effective implementation of the convention, GRETA exercises soft powers of norm and practice dispersion, which may also involve naming and shaming.

Although the Council of Europe Convention enhances the rights of victims of trafficking beyond what is provided in the UN Protocol and the EU's legislative instruments, states were unwilling to accept key victim protections on the ground that they could be exploited by 'undeserving' victims. The convention does not provide procedural guarantees for challenging a negative determination of an individual's status as a victim. Nor does it prohibit states from prosecuting trafficking victims for other criminal offences, such as illegal immigration or prostitution, that are linked to their status as victims of trafficking.[62] In fact, none of the rights provided to victims in the convention are justiciable and, as such, cannot be enforced by victims via legal actions.[63]

The Council of Europe's convention's emphasis on the human rights of trafficking victims is perfectly compatible with the UN's and EU's emphasis on criminal law. Unlike the 2004 EU Experts Group's report, which cautioned that a carceral approach to human trafficking could undermine the human rights of victims, the Council of Europe interpreted human rights as compatible with an emphasis on security. Its 'victims-first' approach emphasises victim support, while 'acknowledging the role criminal law plays in the fight against human trafficking'.[64] The nexus between human rights and criminal law was reinforced by the European Court of Human Rights' 2005 decision in *Siliadin v. France*, which ruled that the prohibition of slavery, servitude, forced, and compulsory labour in Article 4 of the European Convention on Human Rights gave rise to positive obligations on states to criminalise forms of forced labour, including domestic servitude.[65] Indeed, the law enforcement and victim-rights approaches to human rights in the context of human trafficking were not only compatible, they reinforced one another: 'both frame human rights as dependent upon state-control mechanisms and coercive action, which in turn are regarded as necessary conditions to achieve victims' rights and protection'.[66]

Bolstered by the Council of Europe Convention, the European Commission began to steer the other EU legislative institutions towards a

[61] Planitzer, 'GRETA's first years of work', 31–42.
[62] Stoyanova, *Human Trafficking and Slavery Reconsidered*, 117.
[63] Jovanovic, 'International law and regional norm smuggling', 810.
[64] Pinto, 'Discursive alignment of trafficking, rights and crime control'.
[65] *Siliadin v. France*, 73316/01.
[66] Pinto, 'Discursive alignment of trafficking, rights and crime control', 15.

more victim-oriented human rights approach to human trafficking. This was part of its general concern to strengthen the social dimension of the EU to compensate for its market expansion and cultivate a human rights culture in its new, formerly communist Member States. Emerging out of the failed constitutional project, the Treaty of Lisbon was designed to enhance democracy within the EU and to promote European values, including human rights and gender equality (Article 2). Adopted in December 2007, the treaty introduced co-decision making between the council and Parliament and qualified majority voting over immigration matters, thus limiting the veto power of individual Member States. At the same time, it expanded the EU's competence over the human rights of its citizens. Although the EU had proclaimed the Charter of Fundamental Rights – which enshrines certain political, social, and economic rights for both European Union citizens and residents, including the prohibition against human trafficking in Article 5, in 2000 – the charter's legal effect was weak and uncertain. The Lisbon Treaty required the EU to legislate consistently with the charter and granted the Court of Justice of the European Union the authority to strike down EU legislation that contravenes it.[67] To assist it in exercising its new human rights jurisdiction and to instil a fundamental rights culture, in 2007, the EU established the European Union Agency for Fundamental Rights (FRA), which provides independent advice to EU institutions and Member States on the rights set out in the charter. Moreover, once it came into effect in 2009, the Lisbon Treaty also authorised the EU to adopt directives harmonising substantive criminal law with respect to ten transnational offences, including trafficking in human beings and the sexual exploitation of women and children (Article 83(1)).

In anticipation of the Treaty of Lisbon coming into effect, the commission sought to consolidate and institutionalise a hybrid law enforcement and victims-first approach to human rights in the context of human trafficking within the EU. It set up a second Group of Experts on Trafficking in Human Beings in 2008 to provide its opinion on revising the Framework Decision on Combating Trafficking in Human Beings and specifically directed the group to consider the impact of EU enlargement and the problem of trafficking for labour exploitation. This Group of Experts embraced the first group's 'holistic, coordinated and integrated approach', which became a mantra for the EU's

[67] But the charter does not extend the jurisdiction of the EU beyond that defined in the treaties, and it only applies to EU Member States as regards their implementation of EU. European Union, *Treaty of Lisbon Amending the Treaty on European Union.*

antitrafficking strategy.[68] Many of its recommendations designed to protect victims' rights followed provisions set out in the Council of Europe's Convention, which would also require revising the 2004 Resident Permit. The 2008 Experts Group also underscored the need for a revised framework decision to consider the connection of human trafficking with migration policies and labour market regulation, urging Member States to prevent human trafficking through 'awareness raising, training, and monitoring of the supply chains, and other measures to address demand'.[69]

The commission submitted a proposal for a new directive in March 2010, which was governed by the new 'Lisbon' legislative process that enhanced the power of EU institutions when it came to regulating human trafficking.[70] Under this process, the council was obliged to negotiate the terms of the directive with Parliament, which had just adopted a resolution calling on the commission and council to adopt a 'holistic approach' to human trafficking centred on human rights.[71] The commission identified the value the proposed new directive added to the 2005 Council of Europe Convention as a combination of greater protections for victims and increased coercive powers to tackle human trafficking.[72]

Expressly adopting 'an integrated, holistic, and human rights approach to the fight against human trafficking', 'Directive 2011/36/EU of the European Parliament and the council' repealed the 2002 framework decision (Recital 7 of the Preamble).[73] It went further than the framework decision in protecting the victims of human trafficking and addressing methods of prevention, cleaving closer to the Council of Europe Convention.[74] It required Member States to establish national referral mechanisms to identify victims. It added concern for victims to the law enforcement approach to human rights. However, it ignored the 2004 Experts Group's warnings that a penal approach to human trafficking undermined victims' rights. The directive widened the substantive criminal law definition of trafficking to include begging,

[68] 'Opinion of the Group of Experts on Trafficking in Human Beings set up by the European Commission, On the Commission Proposal for a Council Framework Decision on preventing trafficking in human beings, and protecting victims, repealing Framework Decision 2002/629/JHA, COM (2009) 136 final', https://academic.oup.com/ijrl/article-abstract/21/3/515/1579598?redirectedFrom=fulltext.

[69] Ibid.

[70] In 2009, the commission proposed a new framework decision on human trafficking, but time ran out before the Lisbon Treaty came into force.

[71] European Union, 'European Parliament resolution of 10 February 2010', P7TA(2010)0018.

[72] European Commission, 'Proposal for a directive of the European Parliament'.

[73] European Union, 'Directive 2011/36/EU'.

[74] Stoyanova, *Human Trafficking and Slavery Reconsidered*, 448–449.

exploitation of criminal activities, and removal of organs; clarified the idea of 'vulnerability' in relation to a victim by referring to 'a situation in which the person concerned has no real or acceptable alternative but to submit to the abuse involved' (Article 2 (2)); increased the penalties for human trafficking; added the crime of aggravated trafficking; expanded Member State jurisdiction over human trafficking extraterritorially to include all acts committed by each Member State's nationals anywhere in the world; and added a new provision on the seizure and confiscation of assets. Since the commission's initial proposal to criminalise demand proved to be too controversial, Member States were also urged to consider imposing criminal sanctions on any person who knowingly used the services of a victim of trafficking.

To ensure greater accountability to the EU, Member States were obliged to establish national rapporteurs, responsible for monitoring the implementation of antitrafficking policy at the national level, and to cooperate with the soon-to-be-established EU antitrafficking coordinator, who would be charged with preparing biannual progress reports to the commission assessing efforts to address human trafficking.[75] The deadline for Member States to transpose the directive into national legislation was 6 April 2013.

The 2011 directive is concerned with rectifying the harm to individual victims within an overall criminal law orientation. Its integrated approach to human trafficking hitches victims' rights to a broader carceral agenda that sees human trafficking as a form of organised crime linked to illegal migration. The human rights dimension of the directive is weakened by the fact that many aspects of its transposition into national law are left to the Member States' discretion. For example, the unconditional nature of the protection offered to trafficked persons is limited to the reflection period, after which protection is left to the discretion of Member States. The same is true of the nonpenalisation clause, which only requires Member States to consider the possibility of nonpunishment. In addition, the directive states that its provisions regarding victim protection shall not prejudice the 2004 directive, which means that residence permits are still conditional on victim cooperation in criminal proceedings.

Despite the EU's claim that it was adopting a human rights approach to human trafficking, neither the 2011 antitrafficking directive nor the 2004 Residence Permit Directive is a human rights instrument. It is the

[75] Furthermore, 'Directive 2012/29/EU applies to the victims of trafficking in human beings and ensures that these victims benefit from a range of rights that are not specified in Directive 2011/36/EU': European Union, 'Directive 2012/29/EU'. The legal framework is also complemented by European Union, 'Council Directive 2004/80/EC of 29 April 2004'.

transnational and *criminal* nature of human trafficking that is the legal basis for the EU's jurisdiction to enact antitrafficking legislation. The 2011 directive does not offer trafficked persons from states outside the EU greater protection from deportation than that provided in the 2002 framework decision, although it does provide them with access to a limited suite of social rights. But even these small advances were resisted by Member States; the European Commission repeatedly expressed its unhappiness with their transposition and effective implementation of the directive, especially when it came to victim protection.[76]

TACKLING LABOUR EXPLOITATION AND DEMAND

With the release of its 2012–2016 strategy the year after the 2011 directive was adopted, the EU sought to move beyond its almost exclusive focus on a carceral approach to human trafficking to develop and implement 'a multi-disciplinary, coherent policy'.[77] It also broadened its concern with sex trafficking to give greater attention to labour exploitation, vowing to involve a 'more diverse group of actors', including labour inspectors, trade unions, employers' organisations, temporary job agencies, and recruitment agencies, in policy-making.[78] By widening its focus and adopting a broader range of antitrafficking governance strategies, the EU followed the same path as UN institutions and the United States under the Obama administration (Chapter 1).

The EU's attention to labour trafficking was a response to both the labour market turmoil caused by the 2008 fiscal crisis and a greatly enlarged European labour market composed of Member States with different labour market institutions and outcomes. Stressing the need for labour legislation to regulate migrants working in the EU to prevent human trafficking, the 2012–2016 antitrafficking strategy called for measures to address contractors, subcontractors, and job recruitment agencies in high-risk sectors.[79]

[76] In 2013, the commission began infringement proceedings against thirteen Member States for failing to notify it of their implementation of the directive: European Commission, 'Mid-term Report'. Indeed, it was not until 2016 that they all made the requisite communication. And, even then, the commission found that there remained 'significant room for improvement', especially when it came to victim protection, in Member States' transposition of the directive: European Commission, 'Report from the commission to the European Parliament', COM (2016) 722.

[77] European Commission, 'Communication from the Commission to the European Parliament', COM (2012), 5.

[78] Ibid., 5.

[79] European Commission, 'The EU strategy towards the eradication of trafficking in human beings, 2012–2016', 14.

There were, however, two big impediments to developing a coordinated strategy to address labour trafficking in the EU: the absence of a common understanding or definition of trafficking for labour exploitation in Europe, and Member State competence over most aspects of labour law and regulation.[80] Labour trafficking was neither recognised nor addressed by policy or practice in most European states, which helps explain why the number of individuals identified as victims of labour trafficking in Europe was one-quarter that of the number of victims of sex trafficking in 2010.[81] Two nonlegislative EU institutions, the EU Fundamental Rights Agency (FRA) and the European Foundation for the Improvement of Living and Working Conditions (Eurofound), took up these matters.

In 2015, the FRA released a report on severe labour exploitation, and its goal was to consider human rights as a legal basis for addressing it. Concerned with exploitation, the FRA cited Article 5 of the Charter of Fundamental Rights, which prohibits slavery, forced labour, and trafficking, and Article 31, which grants every worker the right to fair and just working conditions, as sources of competence.[82] By contrast, the focus of the trafficking directive was on transnational movement.

Of specific concern to the FRA was what it called the 'no name' problem: forms of severe exploitation in which working conditions are clearly in breach of legal norms but which do not amount to slavery and forced labour because the worker has 'consented' to the treatment.[83] It proposed to expand the scope of severe labour exploitation operating within EU law beyond forced labour and slavery, the definitions of which hinge on lack of consent and the denial of freedom, to a conception based on human dignity, which is the foundational norm of the EU's human rights system. The 2009 EU employer sanctions directive, designed to deter employers from hiring third-country nationals with irregular migration status by sanctioning such behaviour, offered some guidance for establishing an EU standard. The directive requires Member States to apply criminal penalties against employers who employ undocumented third-country nationals under 'particularly exploitative conditions' or who knowingly employ a victim of human trafficking (Article 9). The

80 Berket, 'Labour exploitation and trafficking for labour exploitation', 359–377; Rijken, 'Trafficking in human beings for labour exploitation', 359–377; and Campana and Varese, 'Exploitation in human trafficking and smuggling', 89–105.

81 GRETA, 'Human trafficking for the purpose of labour exploitation'; and European Commission, 'The EU strategy towards the eradication of trafficking in human beings, 2012–2016', 2.

82 FRA, *Severe Labour Exploitation.*

83 Ibid., 38.

phrase 'particularly exploitative working conditions' is defined as working conditions 'where there is a striking disproportion compared with the terms of employment of legally employed workers which, for example, affects workers' health and safety, and which offends against human dignity' (Article 2).[84]

Like the ILO (Chapter 3), the FRA conceptualised labour exploitation as a continuum spanning from slavery to relatively less serious forms of exploitation covered by labour and or civil law. It defined 'severe labour exploitation' as including 'coercive forms of exploitation, such as slavery, servitude, forced or compulsory labour and trafficking prohibited by Article 5 of the Fundamental Rights Charter *and* employment situations covered by Article 9 (1) of the Employer Sanctions Directive'.[85] This definition includes *non-consensual* and *consensual* forms of exploitation. According to the FRA, the differences in severity between these two forms of exploitation should be reflected in their respective penalties, with situations of 'medium severity', such as those defined in the employers sanctions directive, attracting a lesser penalty than nonconsensual forms of exploitation.[86] To sever the link with illegal immigration, which is the legal basis for the sanctions directive, the FRA advised that the offence of severe labour exploitation apply to EU citizens and third-country nationals regardless of their migration status.

Identifying migrant workers as especially vulnerable to exploitation, the FRA regarded labour market regulation as shaping risk of exposure to severe exploitation. Thus, it urged Member States to implement a comprehensive system of workplace inspections and a mechanism to monitor recruitment agencies. Third parties such as trade unions should, it advised, be enabled to act in support of victims of severe labour exploitation. EU institutions and Member States were encouraged to enact supply-chain-transparency legislation.[87]

Eurofound also focused on the exploitation of migrant workers. Like the ILO (Chapter 3), it adopted a labour approach to the problem of labour trafficking and advocated the regulation of labour market intermediaries through licencing, certifications, and inspections, and the involvement of social partners. However, because most aspects of labour market regulation

[84] European Union, 'Directive 2009/52/EC of the European Parliament and of the council of 18 June 2009'.
[85] FRA, *Severe Labour Exploitation*, 34 [emphasis added].
[86] Ibid., 42.
[87] Ibid., 17, 59.

fell outside the EU's jurisdiction, all the commission could do was pass on these recommendations as policy pointers to Member States.[88]

Since most trafficking victims identified in the EU come from other EU countries, the commission regarded regulating labour markets within EU Member States as extremely important for combatting labour trafficking.[89] In 2017, the president of the European Commission announced the creation of a European Labour Authority, charged with ensuring that EU rules on labour mobility and social-security coordination are enforced fairly and effectively.[90]

The Council of Europe institutions led the way in imposing a duty on states to take positive action beyond simply criminalising specific behaviours to deal with human trafficking. In 2010, the European Court of Human Rights interpreted the prohibition on slavery and forced labour in Article 4 to include human trafficking and imposed a positive obligation on states to ensure that there is a regulatory framework, based primarily in the criminal law but extending beyond it, in place to protect individuals from human trafficking.[91] In 2017, the court made it clear that states must take measures to prevent forced labour when they know it is occurring. It ruled that Greece had failed in its obligations under Article 4 to prevent human trafficking, protect victims, and investigate those responsible.[92] The case involved forty-two undocumented Bangladeshi workers who, among other things, were denied payments for their work at a strawberry farm in southern Greece. When they demanded their unpaid wages, armed guards employed by their employer shot at them, seriously injuring thirty workers. Finding that the workers did not continue to work voluntarily because the employer threatened to expose their undocumented status and have them deported, the court classified their condition as forced labour and as a form of labour trafficking.[93] Noting that state authorities were acquainted with the exploitation of workers in the strawberry plantations, the court emphasised their failure to protect these workers from trafficking. Referring to the Council of Europe's Convention on Human Trafficking, which was not yet in force in Greece, and GRETA's interpretation of state

88 Eurofound, *Regulation of Labour Market Intermediaries*, 45–47.

89 European Commission, 'Report from the commission to the European Parliament', COM (2016) 267, 4.

90 The European Labour Authority was established on 31 July 2019 and since September 2021 has had its permanent seat in Bratislava, Slovakia. See European Labour Authority, 'ELA's mission'.

91 *Rantsev v. Cyprus and Russia*, 25965/04.

92 *Chowdury and Others v. Greece*, 21884/15.

93 Ibid., paras. 95, 101, 115.

obligations, the court held that states are under an obligation to provide an appropriate legislative and administrative framework to address human trafficking, which includes regulating businesses.[94]

The European Parliament advocated for some elements of a labour approach to human trafficking, especially when it came to how immigration status contributed to workers' exposure to extreme labour exploitation. In 2016, it called for Member States to build 'firewalls' between immigration and labour authorities to encourage trafficking victims without lawful immigration status to report abuses and ensure that there is no fear of retaliatory action by immigration authorities. Member States were also reminded of 'the critical distinction' between human trafficking and migrant smuggling, which, the European Parliament noted, require 'different legal and practical responses and involve different State obligations'.[95]

While other EU and Council of Europe institutions were recommending labour law mechanisms to tackle human trafficking, the commission concentrated on how Member States had transposed the provisions in the 2011 anti-trafficking directive having to do with criminalising and discouraging demand.[96] In a 2016 report on Member State legislation, it found that ten of the twenty-seven Members States had established an offence criminalising the use of services of victims of trafficking who suffered any form of exploitation, while fifteen had established only a limited and selective criminalisation for the use of services of victims of sex trafficking.[97] The problem, the commission concluded, was that the 'rather diverse legal landscape' across EU Member States failed to discourage demand and, indeed, may even foster it by cultivating 'a culture of impunity'.[98]

94 Ibid., paras. 104, 105.

95 European Parliament, 'European Parliament resolution of 5 July 2016'.

96 The trafficking directive directs Member States *to consider* criminalising the use of services provided by people who have been trafficked (Article 18.4) and requires them to take measures 'to discourage and reduce the demand that fosters all forms of exploitation related to trafficking in human beings' (Article 18.1). By contrast, the 2009 sanctions directive *requires* Member States to provide for criminal penalties for the employer in the case of particularly exploitative working conditions, if the employer knows that the worker has been trafficked or if a minor has been employed illegally.

97 European Commission, 'Report from the commission to the European Parliament', COM (2016) 719, 3. It also discovered that where national measures have established a criminal offence of knowingly using trafficked services or labour, only those people who directly use the services or labour are deemed to be liable criminally, which, as the commission noted, creates a very high threshold for attributing liability (ibid., 8).

98 Ibid., 10.

Criminalising the use of services performed by a victim of trafficking is tied up with the regulation of prostitution.[99] In 2014, the European Parliament reverted to its historical position of equating prostitution with sexual exploitation when it adopted a nonbinding resolution that would criminalise the purchase of sexual services as a way of combatting human trafficking for sexual exploitation. Characterising 'prostitution as a form of slavery incompatible with human dignity and fundamental human rights', the resolution claimed that 'prostitution in the European Union and across the world is directly linked to the trafficking of women and girls'.[100] That year, the Parliamentary Assembly of the Council of Europe also adopted a similar motion.[101]

Reporting in 2017 on its antitrafficking strategy, the commission referred to the 2015 migration crisis, which Italian prime minister Matteo Renzi had characterised as a 'new slave trade' in the Mediterranean, and called for 'stronger action at both national and EU levels' against human trafficking.[102] It identified three priorities for the EU's future action: stepping up the fight against criminal networks in an effort to disrupt the trafficking chain's business model, guaranteeing victims of trafficking access to their rights, and intensifying a coordinated and consolidated response within and outside the EU.[103] The first two priorities reflected the EU's traditional criminal prosecution and victim protection approaches, while the third covered a range of corporate due diligence, trade, and development initiatives. The commission characterised 'responsible management of global value chains' as one of the ways to discourage the 'demand for all forms of exploitation' and raised the possibility of a new EU instrument that would impose obligations on business to address, among other things, exploitation in supply chains.[104]

SUPPLY CHAINS AND HUMAN RIGHTS

Governing the world's largest single market and committed to the principles of democracy, human rights, and rule of law, the EU was the target of new

99 Campana and Varese, 'Exploitation in human trafficking and smuggling', 89–105; and Ollus and Jokinen, 'Exploitation of migrant workers', 475.

100 European Union, 'European Parliament resolution of 26 February 2014', 6, 15.

101 Council of Europe, Parliamentary Assembly, 'Prostitution, trafficking and modern slavery in Europe'.

102 'Italian PM Matteo Renzi condemns "new slave trade"'; and European Commission, 'Communication from the commission to the European Parliament and the council, reporting on the follow-up to the EU strategy', 2.

103 European Commission, 'Communication from the commission to the European Parliament and the council, reporting on the follow-up to the EU strategy', 3.

104 Ibid., 4.

abolitionists and human rights organisations' campaign for legislation to address modern slavery and labour exploitation in supply chains.[105] However, unlike human trafficking, where the EU's competence is directly provided for in the treaties under provisions dealing with transnational crime and immigration, the commission had to reframe the problem of exploitation in supply chains in order to find a treaty basis for EU competence. Modern slavery laws and trade restrictions on goods made with forced labour were recast as part of a broader sustainable governance measure to promote the freedom of establishments to conduct business in all EU Member States and to ensure the proper functioning of the internal market, which provides the EU with the treaty bases of legislative authority in relation to its internal dimension.[106] The eradication of modern slavery in supply chains was also portrayed by the EU as part of its commitment to protecting and promoting human rights globally.[107]

Corporate transparency requirements were not new to the EU. In the aftermath of the financial crisis, the commission took its first step towards making corporate social responsibility mandatory, and in 2014 the EU adopted the nonfinancial reporting directive, which requires companies to report on matters pertaining to human rights.[108] Complementing and drawing upon corporate social responsibility measures at the international level, the directive allows businesses a great deal of flexibility to accommodate the multidimensional nature of corporate social responsibility and the diversity of businesses. It did not, however, satisfy new abolitionists. Anti-Slavery International complained that the directive was 'inadequate' for resolving specific issues such as forced labour in international supply chains, explaining that it 'is more likely to dissipate attention and action across a range of issues

[105] Anti-Slavery International, 'A call for pan-European action', 7.

[106] The treaty basis for the mandatory human-rights due-diligence directive is European Union, *Consolidated Version of the Treaty on the Future of the European Union*, Article 50(1) and (2) (g), or TFEU, which gives EU competence to coordinate safeguards for the protection of interests of companies' members and other stakeholders to attain freedom of establishment. Article 114, which allows the EU to approximate legislation with the object of ensuring the proper functioning of the internal market, also applies. The key treaty bases for the forced labour regulation are Articles 114 (approximation of laws for the internal market) and 207 (Common Commercial Policy).

[107] Articles 3 and 21 of the *Treaty on European Union (Consolidated Version), Treaty of Maastricht*, commit the EU to protect and promote human rights globally when developing and implementing its external policies, including trade policies, which are the exclusive competence of the EU, and its development policies, which are an area of shared competence with the Member States. Peake and Kenner, 'Slaves to fashion', 192.

[108] European Union, 'Directive 2014/95/EU'.

that will vary from business to business depending on the whims of executives, the company's level of knowledge about the issue and their sense of risk'.[109]

In 2016, the EU faced pressure from some of its members to propose legislation imposing a due-diligence obligation on corporations to respect human rights.[110] Member States with due-diligence legislation were anxious to 'level' the EU market by requiring all members of the internal market to implement such legislation. France, for example, was about to enact its Duty of Vigilance Law, which would impose a duty of care on companies throughout their international supply chains to identify and address environmental and human rights violations.[111] Backed by human rights organisations such as Amnesty International, the European Coalition for Corporate Justice, and CIDSE, an international family of Catholic social justice organisations, this law shifted the debate in the EU away from transparency legislation targeted solely at modern slavery, forced labour, and human trafficking in supply chains to more onerous due-diligence obligations to detect and address a range of environmental and human rights violations.[112]

EU legislative institutions drew closer to the position that mandatory rules requiring some form of corporate social responsibility were necessary to combat modern slavery. Instead of light-touch disclosure obligations, the European Parliament and the commission supported reporting *and* due-diligence obligations encompassing human rights and the UN's Sustainable Development Goals, which included promoting decent work.[113] Dignity and sustainability, and not simply freedom, were the EU's animating values.

In December 2019, one hundred civil society organisations and trade unions, including such prominent actors in the global antislavery network as Anti-Slavery International and the Freedom Fund, released a public call for EU legislation to establish a mandatory human rights and environmental due-diligence framework for businesses operating or offering a product or service

[109] Anti-Slavery International, 'A call for pan-European action', 5.

[110] Eight national parliaments launched a 'green card' initiative, which is a form of enhanced political dialogue through which EU national parliaments can jointly propose to the European Commission new legislation to ensure corporate accountability for human rights abuses. European Union, 'European Parliament resolution of 25 October 2016 on corporate liability', 2015/2315(INI).

[111] Duty of Vigilance of Parent and on Its Affiliated Entities, Law No. 2017-399 (27 March 2017).

[112] European Coalition for Corporate Justice, 'An EU mandatory due-diligence legislation'.

[113] European Parliament, Report A8–0269/2017. By the end of 2020, the Council of the European Union supported mandatory human rights due-diligence legislation for supply chains. Council of the European Union, 'Council conclusions on human rights and decent work'.

within the EU.[114] The commission agreed that EU legislative action was necessary since Member States' action alone is insufficient and inefficient to address the 'global dimension' of the sustainability problem and its 'cross-border effects'.[115] The consultations on the proposed directive revealed a split between business and civil society organisations over the extent of the due-diligence obligations. Individual businesses and their representative, Business Europe, wanted to limit the proposed directive's due-diligence requirements to putting in place a due-diligence process, whereas civil society organisations were overwhelmingly in favour of an enforceable duty of care to mitigate actual and potential harm.[116] In March 2021, the European Parliament threw its weight behind the civil society organisations when it adopted a legislative initiative report (504 votes in favour, 79 against, and 112 abstentions) setting out recommendations to the commission, including a draft directive, which would impose a mandatory corporate due-diligence obligation on corporations to mitigate human rights violations and negative environmental impacts in their supply chains.[117]

On 23 February 2022, the European Commission adopted a proposal for a directive on corporate sustainability due diligence, declaring: 'For businesses these new rules will bring legal certainty and a level playing field. For consumers and investors they will provide more transparency.'[118] Under the ordinary legislative process, the European Parliament and the Council of the EU must agree to formally adopt the directive. The commission and council preferred a measure that would replicate the prevailing model of corporate human rights due diligence, relying heavily on contractual assurances from business partners, third-party auditing, and industry initiatives as measures companies can implement to fulfil their responsibility to respect human rights and the environment in their value chains. By contrast, the European Parliament wanted a much stronger emphasis on stakeholder engagement throughout the due-diligence process. The trialogue was completed in late 2023. However, a lack of consensus between the EU Member States in the Council of the EU delayed the final vote on the directive's text until late April

[114] Anti-Slavery International, 'A call for EU human rights and environmental due diligence legislation'.

[115] European Commission, 'Proposal for a directive amending directive 2011/36/EU', 2022.

[116] Tansey, 'Off the hook?'; European Commission, Directorate-General Justice and Consumers, 'Sustainable corporate governance initiative'; and European Union, 'European Parliament resolution of 10 March 2021'.

[117] European Union, 'European Parliament resolution of 10 March 2021'.

[118] European Commission, Directorate-General for Internal Market Industry, Entrepreneurship and SMEs, 'Just and sustainable economy'.

2024 and it is expected to be adopted in June 2024, after which Member States will be given two years to transpose the directive into national law. The due-diligence directive goes well beyond existing voluntary initiatives .

In 2021, a coalition of human rights groups urged the EU to adopt 'import bans' for products made with forced labour into the EU as a supplement to the sustainable governance directive. They pointed to the 2017 Conflict Minerals Regulation, which requires importers to ensure that certain high-risk minerals and metals do not contribute to forced labour or conflicts, as a precedent.[119] In September 2022, the commission released a proposal for a regulation on prohibiting products made with forced labour (which will follow the ordinary legislative procedure).[120] Unlike the United States (discussed in Chapter 2), the commission's proposal was not designed as an outright import ban. It proposed a more comprehensive approach that includes a marketing ban for products made with forced labour in the internal market, as well as exports out of the EU.[121] In contrast to the due diligence directive, the negotiations among and between the EU governance institutions and Member States on the regulation imposing a market ban on goods made with forced labour was much quicker; Parliament approved the regulation on the import and export of goods made with forced labour in late April 2024.

Trade restrictions, such as an import prohibition, are designed to combat trade in products made with forced labour and are only an indirect tool to tackle the problem of forced labour. The regulation 'is a means to eliminate the unfair competitive advantage enjoyed by businesses and governments exploiting forced labour, and to create a major disincentive for economic operators from using forced labour in their supply chains'.[122] It is seen as a bridge between the 2011 antitrafficking directive's penal approach and the proposed corporate sustainability directive's business regulation orientation. However, the extent to which this kind of trade mechanism can protect workers from forced labour depends on regulatory design and enforcement practices. Unless measures are in place to require remediation, trade restrictions can be very harmful to workers at risk of or engaged in forced labour.[123] The EU's regulation to prohibit goods made with forced labour in the internal

[119] See European Union, 'Regulation (EU) No 2017/821'; Anti-Slavery International et al., 'Key considerations for an EU instrument'.

[120] European Commission, 'Proposal for a regulation of the European Parliament'. Regulations, unlike directives, do not have to be transposed and apply directly to Member States.

[121] Jacob et al., 'Trade-related policy options of a ban on forced labour products'.

[122] Ibid., 38.

[123] Fudge and LeBaron, 'Regulatory design and interactions in worker-driven social responsibility initiatives'.

market does not require companies to undertake remedial action for workers affected by forced labour practices.

CONCLUSION

Describing the 2011 antitrafficking directive as the 'backbone' of the EU's antitrafficking efforts in the 2021–2025 EU antitrafficking strategy, the commission questioned whether the decade old instrument was 'fit for purpose' and announced that it would be launching a study to evaluate it.[124] The evaluation was to focus on strengthening criminal law enforcement and providing better assistance, support, and protection for victims.[125] In December 2022, the commission introduced a proposal to amend the 2011 antitrafficking directive to implement the evaluation's recommendations that the criminal justice aspects of the antitrafficking directive be strengthened, victim identification and protection be improved, and demand be tackled by making the use of services exacted from victims of trafficking a criminal offence.[126] If adopted, the amendments would reinforce the EU's approach to human trafficking of prioritising the criminal law while protecting the rights of victims.

The EU's antitrafficking legislative instruments emphasise *transnational crime* and *movement* across borders because these are the elements over which the EU has competence. With the implementation of the Schengen accord, which lifted internal borders, Member States were concerned that their national borders were only as secure as those of their neighbours. In the face of large migration flows from previous communist states as they opened their borders and the war-torn former Yugoslavia, the EU began to strengthen its external borders. Human trafficking, with its clearly defined victims and villains, underpinned governance strategies 'to strengthen moral capacities of the state by hardening its borders' and by giving state operatives new powers

[124] European Commission, 'Communication from the commission to the European Parliament, the council, the European Economic and Social Committee, and the Committee of the Regions, on the EU Strategy on Combatting Trafficking in Human Beings, 2021–2025', 3, 4.

[125] Ibid., 13.

[126] The commission's amendments propose to expand the definition of human trafficking to include forced marriage, introduce a mandatory sentencing regime, and provide for assets associated with trafficking to be frozen and confiscated. Member States would be required to formally establish national referral mechanisms for identifying and protecting victims and to create new offences concerning the knowing use of services provided by a victim of trafficking. European Commission, 'Proposal for a directive amending directive 2011/36/EU'; European Commission, 'European Commission Working Document, Executive summary of the impact assessment report'.

to surveil and assess third-country migrants.[127] Although the EU's supranational jurisdiction disrupts fixed notions of territorially bounded political units, the rescaling of legislative authority over human trafficking effectively amplifies the power of nation-states to secure their territorial borders.

The EU's turn towards protecting the right of victims of trafficking was driven by human rights organisations and the increasing institutionalisation of European values, such as human rights and gender equality, into EU law. Different actors, however, have different interpretations of these values. The Council of Europe's 2005 Anti-Trafficking Convention (which sought to reinforce the human rights domain when it comes to human trafficking) and the European Court of Human Rights' decisions pertaining to forced labour and human trafficking were very influential on the EU. However, under EU directives, the positive obligations imposed on Member States to protect victims are more limited and most turn on assisting with a criminal investigation. The EU's celebrated 'integrated, holistic, and human rights approach to the fight against human trafficking' has not dislodged criminal and immigration law from the heart of antitrafficking governance. Human rights were incorporated within and subsumed under a governance strategy designed to harden the EU's and Member States' borders to exclude undesirable outsiders. In the process, the EU itself became 'a striking incarnation of the anxieties caused by globalisation: the erosion of the state, the homogenization of national cultures, lost control over domestic politics, and subjugation to distant, uncaring overseers'.[128]

When it comes to the governance of human trafficking, EU legislative institutions and Member States mobilise scalar differentiation in a strategic manner to govern a transnational problem. The borders demarcating the inside and outside of the EU have created a complex division of jurisdiction over different legal categories of mobile workers, such as free-moving EU citizens, illegal migrants, and victims of trafficking, with very different rights and obligations.[129] Instead of operating as barriers, the borders operate as filters that sort desirable migrants from unacceptable ones.[130] Victims of trafficking, especially those who are subject to sexual exploitation, epitomise unfreedom and, thus, they are the antithesis of what the EU with its embrace of free movement is about.[131]

[127] Mattson, *The Cultural Politics of European Prostitution Reform*, 168.
[128] Ibid., 168.
[129] Paul, *The Political Economy of Border Drawing*.
[130] Andrijasevic, 'Beautiful dead bodies', 24–44.
[131] Askola, *Legal Responses to Trafficking in Women*, 43.

Combatting sexual exploitation has been at the heart of the EU's antitrafficking legislative initiatives, which has led to their entanglement with the controversial question about how to regulate prostitution. On the twentieth anniversary of the UN's adoption of the Human Trafficking Protocol, the former president of the European Commission's 2004 Experts Group, Marjan Wijers, confessed that if she and other colleagues who advocated for sex workers' rights 'had known the history and the inherent flaws of the concept of trafficking' back in the 1990s when the protocol was being negotiated, 'we never would have used it'.[132] In hindsight, she saw how by 'falling back on the 19th-century Victorian concept of trafficking with its focus on the purity and victimhood of women and the protection of national borders', she and other sex workers' advocates 'unwittingly imported a highly biased concept, dividing women into innocent victims in need of rescue and guilty ones who can be abused with impunity, but also with racist and nationalistic overtones'.[133]

EU legislative institutions have been slower to address labour trafficking, which is considered a smaller, although growing, problem than trafficking for sexual exploitation. In the 2021–2025 EU strategy, the commission recommended that the criminal justice response to trafficking for labour exploitation be strengthened.[134] To discourage demand, the EU has adopted a directive on sustainable corporate governance to foster responsible corporate behaviour and it adopted a regulation to use trade measures to block products made with forced labour from being marketed inside the EU and exported outside of it. None of these measures use governance techniques based on labour law; instead, they rely on the criminal law and on internal trade and commercial laws – legal domains that reflect the EU's treaty basis.

The EU's legal assemblage of jurisdiction has led to a multifaceted approach to human trafficking that is anchored to a concern to protect society from cross-border organised crime.[135] But even though the EU's antitrafficking governance strategies construct the broad categories of hierarchically organised mobile workers, the bulk of the work of sorting mobile people into different legal categories is performed by Member States. What constitutes exploitation is, for the most part, still defined at the national level.

132 Wijers, 'How we got here'.

133 Ibid.

134 European Commission, 'Communication from the commission to the European Parliament, the council, the European Economic and Social Committee, and the Committee of the Regions, on the EU Strategy on Combatting Trafficking in Human Beings, 2021–2025', 7.

135 Krieg, 'Trafficking in human beings', 790.

5

The UK's Crackdown on Illegal Work and Human Trafficking

The migrant is the political figure of our time.

—Thomas Nail, *The Figure of the Migrant*

Bordering constitutes a principal organising mechanism in constructing, maintaining, and controlling social and political order.

—Nira Yuval-Davis, Georgie Wemyss, and Kathryn Cassidy, *Borders*

In 2001, David Blunkett, the UK's home secretary, released *Secure Borders, Safe Haven*, a white paper explaining the government's immigration policy, in which he promised to get 'tough in tackling, Europe-wide, the people traffickers' and 'illegal working, ending exploitation in the shadow economy and dealing with gangmasters and corrupt businesses who evade taxes and undercut fairness and decency for the rest of society'.[1] Under New Labour, which governed from 1997 to 2010, tackling human trafficking was part of the United Kingdom's strategy of strengthening territorial borders, extending borders beyond the United Kingdom's frontier, and instigating bordering practices to manage migration. As devices that act to filter, sort, and channel the movement of people, borders can take a variety of guises (territorial, technological, and classificatory, for example) and their function is institutional and normative, as borders determine membership and entitlement.[2] Along with 'associated notions of sovereign power, authority and capacity',

[1] UK, Home Office, *Secure Borders, Safe Haven*, Foreword.

[2] Mezzadra and Neilson, *Border as Method*; Balibar, *Politics and the Other Scene*; Dehm, 'Framing international migration'; Van Houtum, 'The geopolitics of borders and boundaries'; Paul, *The Political Economy of Border Drawing*; Nail, *Theory of the Border*; Longo, *The Politics of Borders*; Yuval-Davis, Wemyss, and Cassidy, *Bordering*; and Vaughan-Williams, 'Borders, territory, law'.

borders 'are central to the relationship between Britain and the developing EU common migration and asylum policy'.[3] As we will see, New Labour's governance of human trafficking epitomised its relationship to the EU and its fixation on controlling borders.

One of the first countries to sign the UN's Protocol to Prevent, Suppress and Punish Trafficking in Persons (Trafficking Protocol) and a member of the European Union and Council of Europe, the United Kingdom was deeply enmeshed in a multiscalar web of legal norms and instruments pertaining to human trafficking. To take effect, however, these supranational norms had to be absorbed into national discourses and institutions. 'Human trafficking' is a floating signifier that derives its meaning from its social and political context.

How did the United Kingdom's cultural political economy come together with New Labour's vision of the United Kingdom's place in the EU and global economy to shape the government's approach to human trafficking? To answer this question, this chapter begins by describing the distinctive British conception of sovereignty and setting out the discursive, political, and jurisdictional context that shaped the United Kingdom's policy on human trafficking. Like the EU and the United States, the United Kingdom initially focused almost exclusively on trafficking for sexual exploitation, targeting migrants who engaged in prostitution and ignoring trafficking for labour exploitation. However, from the beginning, combatting human trafficking and its doppelganger, illegal working, played a critical role in the United Kingdom's governance strategy. Trafficking was paired with illegal working, and society was cast as a victim of exploitation along with individuals who had been trafficked. These identifications permeated the United Kingdom's anti-trafficking policies and persisted long after the Labour government was defeated, and modern slavery eclipsed human trafficking in the British political lexicon.

NEW LABOUR, SOVEREIGNTY, AND THE EU

A key theme in British politics has been the exercise of sovereignty through the immigration controls at points of entry rather than checks on internal movement through devices like identity cards, common throughout Europe.[4] The United Kingdom's practice is at odds with the Schengen model of waiving border checks for people entering from other EU member states. It also reflects the British political system with its centralised and powerful executive,

[3] Geddes, 'Getting the best of both worlds?', 740.

[4] Geddes, 'The politics of irregular migration', 375.

'a largely subservient legislature and relatively weak courts'.[5] 'Losing control', the comparative immigration scholar Andrew Geddes explains, would strike 'at the legitimacy of the British state and the elected government'.[6]

Within the United Kingdom, control is institutionalised in the Home Office, where authority over immigration, security, and law and order is lodged in a single umbrella ministry that links the governance of immigration with security and criminal law.[7] The Home Office has authority over anti-trafficking policy and strategy, which falls under the portfolio of the minister for immigration. Policy formation is also restricted to the governmental policy elite, which makes it easy to ignore different perspectives and approaches and for certain discourses and solutions to dominate.[8]

Led by Tony Blair from 1997 to 2007 and Gordon Brown from 2007 to 2010, the Labour government was known as 'New Labour' to signify its amalgam of economic liberalism, defined by 'light-touch' regulation, free trade, and economic globalisation; a commitment to the British social democratic legacy of providing public services and (conditional) redistributive measures; and 'law and order' policies.[9] New Labour wanted to modernise the United Kingdom to adapt to the inexorable globalisation of the economy; it mobilised governance capacities by granting autonomy to individuals and organisations within a system of strengthened control (what Foucault calls biopower).[10] Its decisive victories in 1997 and 2001 insulated the Labour government from 'internal rebellion and attack from the opposition', which allowed it to hasten devolution and forge a new relationship with the EU.[11]

A plurinational state, the United Kingdom comprises England, Northern Ireland, Scotland, and Wales. To placate rumblings of Scottish home rule, New Labour moved further down the path of devolution, creating the Scottish Parliament and the Welsh Assembly in 1999.[12] Devolution raised complex questions about sovereignty and national identity, which would come back to

5 Ibid.

6 Ibid.

7 The Home Office jurisdiction covered immigration and passports, drugs policy, crime, fire, counterterrorism, and police. In 2007, criminal justice, prisons, probation, and legal affairs were moved to the new Ministry of Justice.

8 Broad and Turnbull, 'From human trafficking to modern slavery', 122.

9 Faucher-King and Le Galès, *The New Labour Experiment*, 2; Hopkin, 'When Polanyi met Farage', 465.

10 Faucher-King and Le Galès, *The New Labour Experiment*, 7. Biopower is about managing the population – establishing the 'rules of the game' (the conduct of conduct) in which the individual operates. Foucault, *Society Must Be Defended*, 259–260.

11 Faucher-King and Le Galès, *The New Labour Experiment*, 2.

12 Laffin and Shaw, 'British devolution and the Labour Party'.

haunt the UK government.[13] It also resulted in a multiscalar jurisdiction over human trafficking within the United Kingdom. Criminal law and victim care are devolved matters, whereas border and immigration control, including the identification of trafficking victims, are reserved matters dealt with by the UK government. Scotland, Wales, and Northern Ireland, as devolved administrations, have responsibilities to provide care for victims of trafficking, In Northern Ireland and Scotland, responsibilities also extend to policing and justice. Immigration remains an issue reserved to the UK Parliament, and the UK Parliament has jurisdiction over criminal law in Wales and England; in England, the UK Parliament is also responsible for victim care.

New Labour sought to establish a new relationship with the EU, a form of 'instrumental supranationalism', by which it could demonstrate leadership in the EU, pursue the United Kingdom's national interest, and depoliticise the EU domestically, all to avoid the charge that the EU undermined British sovereignty.[14] Both Labour and Conservative governments retained a strong symbolic commitment to the sovereignty of the traditional British nation-state (with its ideas of parliamentary supremacy, liberal values, and strong separation between the economic and political spheres), which resulted in its 'awkward' relationship with the EU.[15] The Conservatives were riven by intraparty divisions over the EU, and a large and vocal wing of Eurosceptics were supported by the tabloid press.[16] By contrast, New Labour projected a vision of an 'Anglicised Europe', in which the United Kingdom would lead the EU to a more deregulated British neoliberal model.[17] Europe would not only give the United Kingdom access to a much larger market, it could also strengthen the United Kingdom's borders.

As the EU's competence over criminal law and immigration deepened and expanded with the adoption of series of treaties in the 1990s and 2000s, the United Kingdom negotiated a special relationship. The Maastricht Treaty (1992) incorporated immigration and transnational crime within the justice and home affairs pillar as matters of common interest. Under this arrangement, although the EU had no legislative authority, there was a commitment

[13] 'Devolved powers' are statutory powers granted to the parliaments and administrations of Northern Ireland, Scotland, and Wales, while 'reserved powers' are those decisions that remain with the UK Parliament and government, which is also responsible for legislation and policy in England on all the matters devolved to the constituent countries.

[14] Bulmer, 'New labour, new European policy?', 597.

[15] Gifford, 'The UK and the European Union', 321.

[16] Gifford, 'The United Kingdom's Eurosceptic political economy'; Simpson and Startin, 'Tabloid tales'.

[17] Gifford, 'The United Kingdom's Eurosceptic political economy', 779.

to cooperation and coordination. The United Kingdom negotiated a flexible opt-out from justice and home affairs measures, the basis for the EU's competence over human trafficking.[18] Provisions for free movement were made within the Schengen Agreement (1985) and its implementing convention (1990). However, the United Kingdom also opted out from the Schengen acquis, retaining the right to opt in on a selective basis. When the 1997 Amsterdam Treaty brought free movement, immigration, and asylum under EU competence, the United Kingdom opted out of these provisions, again retaining the right selectively to opt in. Thus, for the United Kingdom, immigration controls remained matters for domestic policymakers, confirming 'external frontier controls as the main method to regulate entry, and executive-dominated immigration politics'.[19] And under the Lisbon Treaty (2007), the United Kingdom also held on to the right to opt out from the criminal area, which it did in total, opting into specific instruments on a case-by-case basis.

Prime Minister Blair explained the virtues of the United Kingdom's special relationship with the EU over immigration:

> There is no question of Britain giving up our veto on our border controls. In the Treaty of Amsterdam seven years ago we secured the absolute right to opt into any of the asylum and immigration provisions that we wanted to in Europe. Unless we opt in, we are not affected by it. And what this actually gives us is the best of both worlds. We are not obliged to have any of the European rules here, but where we decide in a particular area, for example to halt the trafficking in people, for example to make sure that there are proper restrictions on some of the European borders that end up affecting our country, it allows us to opt in and take part in these measures.[20]

European integration, as we saw in Chapter 4, can strengthen member states' control over their borders. Under New Labour, the United Kingdom took a leadership role in deterritorialising and extending the EU's borders by making sending-and-transit states responsible for controlling unwanted migrants.[21] In this way, New Labour sought to establish that 'sovereignty is not a zero-sum game' but rather that UK sovereignty can be augmented through the selective adoption of EU European rules.[22] There was, however,

[18] Ibid., 611.
[19] Geddes, 'Getting the best of both words?', 730.
[20] Tony Blair, 25 October 2004, quoted in ibid., 723.
[21] Geddes, 'The politics of irregular migration', 382; Bulmer, 'New labour, new European policy?', 612.
[22] Gifford, 'The UK and the European Union', 326.

a latent contradiction between this idea of a functional sovereignty based on interdependence between the United Kingdom and EU and the British notion of absolute sovereignty that does not countenance any legal limitation on the authority of Parliament.[23]

TRAFFICKING AND MIGRANT SEX WORKERS

In *Secure Borders, Safe Haven* the government set out its immigration policy of managing migration for macroeconomic gain combined with a strong security framework to tackle unauthorised migration and reduce asylum seeking. The goal was an orderly, organised, and enforceable system of entry. Migrants who followed the rules would enjoy economic prosperity and integration into British society.[24] Those who did not would be treated as criminals to be punished or as victims to be rescued and removed. Asylum seekers would be deterred through detention and meagre benefits. Borders would be strengthened by biometric technology, deterritorialised, and extended.[25]

Secure Borders, Safe Haven framed trafficking in terms of fighting illegal immigration and organised crime.[26] It responded to anti-immigration politics fuelled by print media and the Conservative Party.[27] Peter Mandelson, a former Labour Cabinet minister, former director of Labour Party communications, and EU commissioner, explained in *The Times* on 11 June 2002: 'If we don't clamp down on illegals then the Nazi's flourish'.[28] The government sought to combine strict restrictions on the wrong type of migrants with a business-friendly system of open migration for the right kind. Hence its 2002 decision not to impose transitory arrangements on nationals of the eight states that would accede to the EU in 2004.[29]

Secure Borders, Safe Haven distinguished 'people trafficking', where someone is brought to the United Kingdom 'to be exploited', from 'people smuggling', where 'entry is facilitated with their consent'.[30] What constitutes exploitation or consent is ambiguous, even though these concepts are used to distinguish between smugglers and illegal workers, on the one hand, and

[23] Loughlin and Tierney, 'The shibboleth of sovereignty', 989.

[24] The subtitle of the report is *Integration with Diversity in Modern Britain.*

[25] UK, Home Office, *Secure Borders, Safe Haven*, 88–89.

[26] Ibid. Human trafficking is discussed in a chapter titled 'Tackling fraud: People trafficking, illegal entry, and illegal working', in which each of the activities is treated as a form of organised immigration crime.

[27] Geddes, 'The politics of irregular migration', 371; Simpson and Startin, 'Tabloid tales', 3.

[28] Geddes, 'The politics of irregular migration', 380.

[29] Balch, 'Labour and epistemic communities', 617.

[30] UK, Home Office, *Secure Borders, Safe Haven*, 75.

traffickers and their victims, on the other. 'Exploitation' is not defined but is described as harmful, not only to the victim but to the competitiveness of law-abiding employers.[31] The overarching problem is portrayed as illegal working – work performed by people who are in the United Kingdom illegally or in the United Kingdom legally but who have no right to work.[32]

Claiming that the United Kingdom played a pivotal role in the UN's Trafficking Protocol and the EU's Framework Decisions on trafficking and the facilitation of illegal entry, *Secure Borders, Safe Haven* declared the government would strengthen the criminal law against smuggling and introduce legislation to make trafficking internationally and within the country a crime.[33] Trafficking for sexual exploitation was the government's primary target. It would move quickly 'to close the loophole that allows foreign and EU nationals of whatever sex or age to be brought to the UK for the purposes of sexual exploitation' by using the forthcoming immigration legislation to introduce a 'stopgap pending the major reform' of sexual offences law.[34]

Victims could expect only limited hospitality under the regime proposed in *Secure Borders, Safe Havens*. Support would be conditional on assisting the authorities and provided by the voluntary sector. Victims 'must be returned to their own country wherever possible' because 'to do otherwise would undermine the UK's immigration law and open the door for traffickers to exploit more victims'.[35] Trafficking into the United Kingdom would be fought beyond the United Kingdom's frontiers in source and transit countries through a network of immigration liaison officers who would work with other governments to stop criminal gangs. Through the Department for International Development and the Foreign and Commonwealth Office, the United Kingdom would fund antitrafficking projects.[36]

Legislation followed in a piecemeal fashion and distinguished between trafficking for sexual and labour exploitation and demonstrated a preoccupation with prostitution-related migration. Like the EU, the United Kingdom prioritised trafficking for sexual exploitation and focused on women as victims, which prompted a reconsideration of the regulation of prostitution. In 1999, the Home Office commissioned an influential report by two academic researchers, Liz Kelly and Linda Regan. *Stopping Traffic: Exploring the Extent of, and Responses to, Trafficking in Women for Sexual Exploitation in*

31 Ibid., 84.
32 Ibid.
33 Ibid., 83.
34 Ibid., 84.
35 Ibid., 85.
36 Ibid.

the UK, appeared the next year. Its estimates of the extent of trafficking for sexual exploitation were influential, as were its focus on migrant sex workers and its broader framing of the problem.[37]

The location of sex work, the report disclosed, had shifted from the street (treated as a nuisance and patrolled) to off-street work advertised online (simply ignored), and there had been a demographic shift from domestic to 'foreign' sex workers.[38] By surveying police forces, Kelly and Regan identified seventy-one women who were trafficked into prostitution in the United Kingdom in 1998. Arguing that a hidden trafficking problem existed, they estimated that between 142 and 1,420 women were trafficked into the United Kingdom during the same period.[39] Drawing borders between trafficking in women and prostitution, they suggested, is problematic since 'trafficking in women for the purposes of sexual exploitation relies upon, and sustains, prostitution and women's inequality'.[40] They concluded that the government should create a crime of 'sexual exploitation' that would punish those who benefitted from the performance of a sexual act, with enhanced penalties for coerced prostitution that involved a vulnerable person, including a foreign national.[41] Although Kelly and Regan recognised that increased monitoring of off-street sex work could cause collateral damage, especially for migrant women, who could be deported to places with no support, they argued that no monitoring 'would be a dereliction of social and legal responsibility to limit responses to those few trafficked women who themselves come forward for help'.[42]

During the 2001 UK election, the home secretary, Jack Straw, released a consultation paper on reforming the law on sexual offences that recommended creating the offence of human trafficking for sexual exploitation. Referring to Kelly and Regan's study and the International Office of Migration's report that half a million women were trafficked into the EU in 1995, it identified human trafficking as a problem. Noting that there was no law designed to target human trafficking, the paper muddied the border between sexual exploitation and prostitution, not illegal in the United Kingdom, by recommending a trafficking offence 'that relates to the bringing of a person from one place to another for the purposes of gaining reward from

[37] Kenway, *The Truth about Modern Slavery*, 78–82; Munro, 'A tale of two servitudes', 93.
[38] Kelly and Regan, *Stopping Traffic*, 23.
[39] Ibid., 22.
[40] Ibid., 1.
[41] Ibid., 42.
[42] Ibid., 39.

the sexual exploitation of that person or for working as a prostitute'.[43] Deception, coercion, and force would not be required for the offence but would add to its seriousness. Using financial powers to confiscate assets was also recommended. The 'white slavery' narrative linking prostitution to trafficking, once an expression of 'late nineteenth-century British imperial anxiety about population and power', provided a ready-made template for contemporary worries about national identity.[44]

As promised in *Secure Borders, Safe Haven*, the Nationality, Immigration and Asylum Act 2002 created a criminal offence (with up to fourteen years' imprisonment) called 'trafficking into prostitution'. It entailed facilitating the transportation of an individual not a resident of the United Kingdom into, out of, or within the United Kingdom for the purposes of controlling them in prostitution.[45] The legislation also added trafficking offences to the list of lifestyle offences (which included pimping- and brothel-related offences) in the Proceeds of Crime Act 2002 so that the courts, when considering a confiscation order, must assume that all assets derive from criminal conduct unless proved otherwise.[46]

This offence focused on migrants, reflecting the EU's concern that the trafficking of migrant sex workers was a problem. As shown in Chapter 4, migrant sex workers, regardless of whether their movement over borders was voluntary, exemplified the unfree, unwelcome, migrant worker. The UK legislation did not explain what 'control over prostitution' meant, a significant problem since the offence of trafficking includes anyone who facilitates the travel to, within, or out of the United Kingdom of a person they have reason to believe may be controlled into prostitution. The human trafficking offence reflected the assumption that prostitution was the problem, which was itself a form of exploitation. However, this perspective fit uneasily with the United Kingdom's mix of toleration and restriction of prostitution at the time, although historically its governance strategy tilted towards abolition.[47]

The government's second step in bringing its human trafficking laws in line with the Trafficking Protocol and the Framework Decision was extending 'human trafficking' to include persons trafficked in the United Kingdom, whether British citizens or foreign nationals, in the Sexual Offences Act, 2003. Announcing the revision, Home Secretary Blunkett linked human trafficking to prostitution, which he described as a 'sub-world of degradation

43 UK, Home Office, *Setting the Boundaries*, 114.

44 Devereux, 'The Maiden Tribute', 18.

45 Nationality, Immigration and Asylum Act 2002 (2002, c. 41), ss. 145, 146.

46 Proceeds of Crime Act 2002 (2002, c. 29), s. 10, sched. 2.

47 Munro, 'A tale of two servitudes', 103.

and exploitation'.[48] The Sexual Offences Act 2003 repealed the earlier offence and introduced wide-ranging offences covering trafficking into, within, or out of the United Kingdom to commit any relevant sexual offence, including arranging, recruiting, or facilitating the transportation of a person into, out of, or within the United Kingdom, with the intention to cause, incite, or control their prostitution for gain.[49] Although the offence does not specifically obviate consent as a relevant consideration, there is no requirement that a trafficked person be forced, deceived, or coerced.

The UK definition of trafficking is broader than the UN Trafficking Protocol's, which must include an element of force. The '"wrong" of trafficking activity in the United Kingdom is neither a component of control nor a component of coercion but, simply, the exploitation deemed inherent in prostitution itself'.[50] Even though the offence is not one of strict liability (to be convicted, the accused must believe or intend that the trafficked person will be sexually exploited), it makes anyone who helps sex workers migrate to ply their trade at risk of prosecution for human trafficking.[51] Essentially the Sexual Offences Act 2003 made moving a person into, out of, or within the United Kingdom for commercial sexual exploitation an offence.[52] It conflates smugglers with traffickers and forces women who migrate for sex work to move alone or with the assistance of individuals willing to run the risk of law-breaking.[53]

By linking prostitution to human trafficking, the government justified a review of prostitution governance. *Paying the Price*, the Home Office's July 2004 consultation paper, referred to growing levels of trafficking and identified prostitution as a big part of the problem because it 'undermines public order and creates a climate in which more serious crime can flourish'.[54] It also equated prostitution with trafficking when it came to migrant women.[55]

Although the consultation document proposed measures that ranged from regulating prostitution as a form of work to increasing criminal offences and associated penalties relating to the purchase of sexual services, the government

[48] Sexual Offences Act 2003 (2003, c. 42); *Hansard*, HC, vol. 394, col. 507, 19 November 2002.
[49] Sexual Offences Act 2003 (2003, c. 42), ss. 57–60.
[50] Munro, 'A tale of two servitudes', 103.
[51] Hill, 'This modern day slavery', 107.
[52] Scoular and O'Neill, 'Regulating prostitution', 765.
[53] Hill, 'This modern day slavery', 108
[54] UK, Home Office, *Paying the Price*, 74.
[55] Despite its emphasis on exploitation, *Paying the Price* put forth a range of options – from criminalising the demand for sexual services to licensing brothels – to reform how prostitution was governed. Ibid., 75.

simply grafted 'prostitution as a species of sexual offence . . . onto the previous policy edifice of public nuisance'.[56] Steering the governance of prostitution closer towards abolition, the government sorted sex workers into categories determined by their migrant status and location of their work. Street-based sex workers who were permanent residents or citizens of the United Kingdom would be rescued and diverted from the sex trade while off-street migrant sex workers would be rescued and removed or charged as criminals and deported.[57]

The government's approach to rescuing domestic sex workers led to new governance strategies to persuade them to change their circumstances, whereas migrant sex workers were dealt with by carceral force.[58] Despite Kelly and Regan's claim that 'it is not our intention to encourage over monitoring of this group of women', this is precisely (and predictably) what happened.[59] The police engaged in high-profile raids, occasionally inviting media crews to join them, to uncover victims of sex trafficking, and most of the migrant women detected were either returned to their home countries voluntarily, deported, or prosecuted.[60]

Although the United Kingdom made human trafficking for sexual exploitation an offence, it made no commitments regarding the victim's rights, social services, or immigration status. The United Kingdom had opted out of the EU's resident permit directive, which gives limited residence and access to social services to third-country nationals who are victims of trafficking or who have been the subject of an action to facilitate illegal immigration and who cooperate with the competent authorities.[61] A pilot project, known as Poppy, was launched to assist women trafficked into prostitution to escape their circumstances and consider testifying against their traffickers; another programme helped migrant victims return home.[62] However, any protection provided by the UK government was discretionary and depended upon a person meeting the stereotype of a helpful and deserving victim.[63]

56 Scoular, *The Subject of Prostitution*, 69–70.

57 Scoular and O'Neill, 'Regulating prostitution', 771–772; Hubbard, Matthews, and Scoular, 'Regulating sex work', 137.

58 Scoular and O'Neil, 'Regulating prostitution', 764; Munro, 'A tale of two servitudes', 9.

59 Kelly and Regan, *Stopping Traffic*, 39.

60 Hill, 'How to stage a raid', 39; Hubbard, Matthews, and Scoular, 'Regulating sex work', 146.

61 However, the UK was bound by EU Directive 2004/80/EC relating to compensation to crime victims, as well as by EU Council Framework Decision 2001/220/JHA, of 15 March 2001, on the standing of victims in criminal proceedings.

62 UK, Home Office, *Tackling Human Trafficking*, 15, 18.

63 Munro, 'A tale of two servitudes', 108; Hill, 'How to stage a raid', 108.

ILLEGAL WORKING AND TRAFFICKING FOR LABOUR EXPLOITATION

Like migrant sex workers, migrant domestic workers – another female-dominated occupation – were seen as particularly vulnerable to human trafficking, although the Labour government's treatment of them was different. In the mid-1990s, advocacy groups invoked 'domestic servitude' and 'modern slavery' to bring attention to the exploitative conditions of migrant domestic workers who entered the United Kingdom with business people, diplomats, tourists, and returning British residents.[64] Unlike other migrant labour categories, these workers' lawful entry depended on entering the United Kingdom with their employers. To maintain their status, they had to work for their sponsors and reside in their homes. The campaign highlighted domestic workers' vulnerability to abuse on account of their gender and the requirement they live in their employers' home, and not their migrant status, which was critical to its success.[65]

In 1998, the newly elected Labour government responded to these complaints of modern slavery by granting migrant domestic workers from third countries the right to change employers if they suffered abuse at the hands of their sponsoring employer; it allowed family members to accompany them and provided them with a route to settlement. In 2002, this scheme was formally incorporated into the Immigration Rules as the Overseas Domestic Workers (ODW) Visa Scheme with stringent requirements.[66] This response was uniquely protective, in part because this was a discrete and small group of migrant workers who entered under a specific visa category sponsored by 'foreign' employers.[67] The treatment of the overseas domestic workers became emblematic of successive governments' treatment of the victims of human trafficking.[68]

With this exception, exploitation was associated with smuggling, not trafficking, which explains why the government was slow to create the offence of trafficking for labour exploitation. Instead, the government fortified its smuggling laws. The offence of 'assisting unlawful immigration' was amended by Section 143 of the Nationality, Immigration and Asylum Act 2002 to apply to any non-EU citizen, and the penalty was increased to a maximum of fourteen

64 Anderson, 'Mobilizing migrants, making citizens', 636.
65 Anderson, *Us and Them?*, 175.
66 Anderson, 'Mobilizing migrants, making citizens', 636; Mullally and Murphy, 'Migrant domestic workers in the UK', 397.
67 Fudge and Strauss, 'Migrants, unfree labour, and the legal construction', 541.
68 Ibid., 524.

years' imprisonment.[69] The government adopted the 2002 framework decision on the strengthening of the penal framework to prevent the facilitation of unauthorised entry, transit, and residence.[70]

Antislavery and antitrafficking campaigners pressed for legislation to make trafficking for labour exploitation a crime. Because it opted into the 2002 EU Framework Decision on Human Trafficking, the United Kingdom had to address trafficking for both labour and sexual exploitation by 1 August 2005. Campaigners were particularly concerned about the trafficking of children into domestic service. When news of a proposed bill was released to the press, a spokesperson for Anti-Slavery International, the oldest slavery abolitionist organisation in the world, cautioned: 'Unless you have a piece of legislation that covers all conceivable forms of trafficking, there will be loopholes that will be exploited'.[71]

The government's solution was to incorporate forms of exploitation listed in Article 4 of the European Convention on Human Rights (ECHR), which included slavery, servitude, and forced and compulsory labour. One of the Labour government's first legislative acts had been to give effect to the European Convention on Human Rights in English law, through the Human Rights Act 1998, which opened the way to successful Article 4 claims by women trafficked and held in forced domestic labour.[72] Tucked into the 2004 Asylum and Immigration (Treatment of Claimants, etc.) Act (concerned with reducing asylum appeal rights and introducing penal measures pertaining to entering the United Kingdom without a passport or with a forged document) was the offence of 'trafficking people for exploitation'.[73] Unlike the international and EU definitions, the definition of 'exploitation' in England and Wales is categorical and exhaustive and does not include the phrase 'at a minimum'. Although trafficking offences relating to labour and sexual exploitation carried the same penalty, the scope of the former was much narrower, as it applied only to non-EU citizens, whereas trafficking for sexual exploitation applied to any person. Labour trafficking, unlike sex trafficking, required that services be coerced. However, the definition of

69 Other offences concerning fraud, forgery (of documents), and false imprisonment can be used by prosecutors alongside offences of sexual and physical violence. See Immigration Act 1971 (1971, c. 77), ss. 25–25C.

70 European Union, 'Council framework decision of 28 November 2002'.

71 Hill, 'Child slave smugglers will face jail at last'.

72 Human Rights Act 1998 (1998, c. 42); Anderson and Rogaly, 'Forced labour and migration to the UK', 21; Immigration Act 1971, ss. 24, 25, 26.

73 Asylum and Immigration (Treatment of Claimants, etc.) Act 2004 (2004, c. 19), s. 4(3) includes organ removal and benefit fraud.

exploitation in the 2004 Act, when combined with the sexual-trafficking offences in the 2003 Act, met the minimum requirements of the EU Framework Decision, which the United Kingdom adopted in 2004, and the UN Trafficking Protocol, which it ratified on 6 February 2006.[74]

Despite evidence of widespread exploitation of migrant workers – including wage withholding, illegal deductions, unsafe working conditions, and threats, all indicators of forced labour across a range of sectors, including agriculture, food processing, cleaning, catering, and construction – the government's primary concern was illegal working, not labour trafficking, and its object was to remove and deport as much as rescue migrant workers.[75] The abolition of the wage councils in the early 1990s meant that the regulation of employment in the United Kingdom, highly fragmented among different agencies and departments, had no overarching labour inspectorate for low-wage and contract work.[76]

It took a tragedy, the death by drowning of twenty-three undocumented migrant shellfish harvesters (cockle-pickers) trapped by the tide in Morecambe Bay on 5 February 2004, to provoke government into action.[77] Portraying trafficked migrants as victims of 'the modern-day slave trade', the shadow home secretary from the Conservative Party sought to embarrass the government:

> Lured to Britain with little knowledge of English, illegal immigrants are forced to work 12 hours a day, six days a week, for derisory amounts of money. Health and safety regulations don't apply. They are kept outside the confines of society and beyond the reach of the law. By doing nothing, the government is giving tacit consent [to smugglers and traffickers].[78]

In response, the government, which the year before had rejected similar regulation, seized on the Gangmasters (Licensing) Bill, a private member bill introduced in January.[79]

[74] *Hansard*, HL, vol. 667, col. 253, 29 November 2004.

[75] Anderson and Rogally, 'Forced labour and migration to the UK', 20.

[76] Balch, 'Regulation and enforcement to tackle forced labour', 21.

[77] In 2003, the Parliament Select Committee on Environment, Food and Rural Affairs (EFRA) investigated the resurgence of gangmaster activity. The Department for Trade and Industry opposed licensing and registration schemes as 'burdensome for business and public authorities'. EFRA recommended that the government revisit the relationship between the supermarkets and their suppliers. The government established an interdepartmental working group to report to the minister responsible for the Department of Environment, Food and Rural Affairs, which had overall responsibility for policy on gangmasters. EFRA, *Fourteenth Report*, para. 54.

[78] Geddes, 'The politics of irregular migration', 372, quoting *Mail on Sunday*, 15 February 2004.

[79] Strauss, 'Unfree again', 190–191.

That bill was modelled on a nineteenth-century law that licensed gangmasters and gang labour.[80] The term 'gangmaster', used by the home secretary in *Secure Borders, Safe Haven*, dates to the mid-1800s, when labour contractors, known as gangmasters, used coercive mechanisms such as tied housing, the truck system, child labour, coercion, and restrictions on seeking work elsewhere to assemble and control workforces for farms. Moral indignation centred on the substitution of women and children for men as agricultural workers led to the Gang Act 1867.

Enacted with the government's support, the Gangmasters (Licensing) Act 2004 was designed to safeguard the welfare of workers by licensing labour providers in specified sectors (agriculture, shellfish harvesting, and processing and packaging for these sectors), enforcing the conditions of the licences granted, and ensuring that labour users do not enter into arrangements with unlicensed gangmasters. The act did not impose new standards or tackle labour exploitation directly. A new public authority would be set up by 2006 to administer a licensing regime that would impose a range of labour standards on a wide range of labour providers, including employment agencies. The act makes a worker's migration status irrelevant to the question of whether the labour provider has violated the terms of its licence, a departure from UK employment law, where migrants working without authorisation cannot enforce their rights because it is contrary to public policy.[81] Here, the distinction is that the state, not the worker, is enforcing the licence.

After the United Kingdom opened its borders to citizens of the eight eastern and central European nations that acceded to the European Union on 1 May 2004, the spectres of unbridled migration, human trafficking, and exploitation circulated widely.[82] The United Kingdom experienced an 'unprecedentedly intensive and utterly unplanned wave of immigration'.[83] The

80 Gang Act, 1867, 30 & 31 Vict., c. 130; Strauss, 'Unfree again', 187.

81 Gangmasters (Licensing) Act 2004 (2004, c. 11), s. 26(2): 'A person is not prevented from being a worker for the purposes of this act by reason of the fact that he has not right to be, or to work, in the United Kingdom'. And see Bogg, 'Illegality in labour law after Patel v Mirza', 257.

82 Migrants seeking work from these countries did not require a visa but were required to register once they entered the UK if they intended to work for longer than a month. The UK government made this decision in 2002, and along with Ireland and Sweden, it waived the transition period. On 1 May 2004, the fifteen states of the European Union (EU-15) welcomed ten new Member States in what was the largest expansion in the history of European integration. The new Member States included eight countries (also called the A-8) from the former Soviet Union: Czech Republic, Hungary, Poland, Slovakia, Slovenia; and the three Baltic states of Estonia, Latvia, and Lithuania. At the same time, membership was granted to the island states of Cyprus and Malta. Lewis and Waite, 'Migrant illegality, slavery and exploitative work', 229.

83 Bale, 'Putting it right?', 297.

government responded to anti-immigration furore in newspapers by imposing transitional restrictions on citizens of Bulgaria and Romania in the 2007 enlargement of the EU and tightening controls for non-EU citizens known as third-country nationals.[84] Before the May 2005 election, as the Conservative Party exploited New Labour's 'weakness' over immigration, the government tried to persuade the public that the country's borders were under control.[85]

CONTROLLING OUR BORDERS

Published three months before the May 2005 election, *Controlling Our Borders: Making Migration Work for Britain* set out the first of a two-part strategy for immigration – measures designed to strengthen the United Kingdom's borders by extending them into and beyond its territorial frontiers. After it won its third-straight election, the Labour government introduced the second part, A *Points-Based System: Making Migration Work for Britain* in 2006, which proposed a system to attract the best and the brightest after employers had attempted to recruit first from within the expanded EU.[86] This Janus-faced governance strategy deployed coercion against undesirable migrants while utilising market-based criteria (such as education, language, and recognised skill level) to select desirable ones.[87] Victims of trafficking and illegal migrant workers personified the uncontrolled border.

Controlling borders was the hinge needed to make managed migration, which the government regarded as essential for continued prosperity, work. In his foreword, Prime Minister Blair declared that his government would enforce 'strict controls to root out abuse' and promised 'a new drive to prevent illegal entry, to crack down on illegal working and a tough policy of removals for those who should not be here' and 'on-the-spot fines for employers who collude with illegal immigration'.[88] Charles Clark, Blunkett's successor as home secretary, vowed that 'using new technology we will develop an integrated control before people enter the United Kingdom, at our borders, and while they are in the country'.[89] Trafficking was subsumed, along with smuggling, under illegal immigration, and it required tough new penalties and the expansion of the state's carceral apparatus.

84 Balch, 'Labour and epistemic communities', 617.
85 Geddes, 'Getting the best of both worlds?', 728.
86 UK, Home Office, A *Points-Based System.*
87 Bosworth, 'Border control and the limits'.
88 UK, Home Office, *Controlling Our Borders*, 6.
89 Ibid., 8.

After the July 2005 bombings in London, Blair doubled down on the need for the United Kingdom to control its borders and adopted an increasingly coercive approach to law and order.[90] In this context, human trafficking was the perfect cipher. Vulnerable people needed to be protected from criminal gangs and predators who, in turn, needed to be punished. Tackling demand was the best way to combat the problem. For sexual exploitation, this meant eliminating prostitution; for labour exploitation, it meant making it unprofitable for employers to rely on illegal workers. The border between trafficked victims and illegal workers blurred.

The police, media, and politicians focused on human trafficking for sexual exploitation. In January 2006, the government released *A Coordinated Prostitution Strategy*, which sought to eradicate all forms of commercial sexual exploitation through a proactive and sustained approach to policing on- and off-street prostitution. The idea was to create 'a hostile environment for those who seek to traffic individuals, nationally or internationally, for the purposes of sexual exploitation'.[91]

The government established the Human Trafficking Centre (the first agency of its kind in Europe) to coordinate antitrafficking efforts by police, immigration agencies, and non-governmental organisations (NGOs), and the Police Service launched a pilot project called Pentameter I to tackle trafficking for sexual exploitation.[92] It was the first proactive policing operation in the United Kingdom and involved over fifty-five police forces in the United Kingdom and the Republic of Ireland and NGOs like Poppy.[93] Pentameter followed the 'raid and rescue' model, targeting premises associated with 'foreign' prostitutes.[94] The government considered the operation, widely reported in the press, a great success. It sparked Pentameter 2 and shaped the government's demand-reduction approach.[95]

In January 2006, the government released *Tackling Human Trafficking*, which elevated its antitrafficking strategy to the level of a moral crusade. Invoking the Slave Trade Act 1807, which brought about the abolition of the slave trade in the former British Empire, the ministerial foreword noted

90 Bosworth and Guild, 'Governing though migration control'.

91 UK, Home Office, *UK Action Plan on Tackling Human Trafficking*, 39.

92 Its partners include the Crown Prosecution Service, the UK Border Agency, the Serious Organized Crime Agency, and HM Revenue and Customs.

93 Hill, 'This modern day slavery', 91. Over a four-month period, police claimed that Pentameter 1 resulted in 232 people arrested, 134 people charged, 188 women in prostitution rescued, and 88 women as victims of trafficking identified.

94 Ibid., 96.

95 Ibid.

that '2007 will see the bicentenary of that landmark Act' and went on to draw a link between that historic event and the challenge of ending human trafficking.[96] Extolling the United Kingdom's leadership role in making human trafficking a priority internationally, the ministers also claimed that the United Kingdom had driven the EU action plan on human trafficking, which endorsed an approach to human trafficking that integrated protecting victims' rights with fighting organised crime and tackling illegal migration.[97]

Despite analogising human trafficking to the slave trade, the UK government downplayed the rights of victims in the face of influential newspaper columnist complaints that immigration policy was being undermined by human rights laws and lobbyists.[98] The consultation document expressed the government's reluctance to sign on to the Council of Europe's newly adopted convention on human trafficking, which, as we saw in Chapter 4, provides the acme of human rights protection for victims of trafficking. Although it claimed to support the convention's aims, the government was concerned that 'some of the provisions, such as the automatic granting of reflection periods and residence permits for trafficking victims, may act as "pull" factors to the UK'.[99]

The consultation document also reviewed the government's approach to labour exploitation, which was treated differently from trafficking for sexual exploitation. In addition to creating the criminal offence of 'trafficking for labour exploitation' in the Immigration, Asylum and Nationalities Act 2006, the government created an offence for employers to withhold documents (genuine or nongenuine) from their employees in the Identity Cards Act 2006. The government's primary strategy was disrupting employer demand by introducing a civil penalty regime and a new offence of 'knowingly employing an illegal migrant worker' with a maximum two-year custodial sentence. The government claimed that this new system, which had a reverse onus of proof that required the employer to object, would deal swiftly and effectively with employers who were less than diligent in carrying out document checks.[100] It was supposed to

96 UK, Home Office, *Tackling Human Trafficking*, 5.

97 UK, Home Office undersecretary of state and Scottish executive member for justice. Ibid., and Chapter 4, this book.

98 Geddes, 'The politics of irregular migration', 381.

99 UK, Home Office, *Tackling Human Trafficking*, 6.

100 Ryan, 'Employer checks of immigration status', 240. The Immigration, Asylum and Nationalities Act 2006 (2006, c. 13) and the Immigration (Restrictions on Employment) Order 2007 (2007, No. 3290) came into effect on 29 February 2009. The maximum fine was one thousand dollars per worker. See also Identity Cards Act 2006 (2006, c. 15).

encourage employers to comply with their legal obligations without criminalising the careless.[101]

However, framing the crackdown on illegal working as an antitrafficking measure was disingenuous since the civil penalty regime simply punished employers who failed to check documentation; it did not address labour exploitation. Moreover, by targeting illegal working as part of an antitrafficking strategy, the government contributed to the idea that migrant workers were engaged in illegal activities and were not victims of exploitation.

Designed to deal with labour-market exploitation, the Gangmasters (Licencing Act) 2004 was one of two exceptions to an antitrafficking strategy based on exclusion, surveillance, punishment, and removal.[102] Housed in the Department of Environment, Food and Rural Affairs (DEFRA) because it was confined to the food sector, the Gangmasters Licencing Authority (GLA) recruited retired police officers as inspectors and worked closely with the tax authority, which, in the absence of a central labour enforcement body, was responsible for enforcing the minimum wage and payroll taxes. The GLA aligned itself with the International Labour Organisation (ILO) and used its indicators of forced labour to identify labour exploitation. It also developed a strategy of proactive inspection. The licensing regime was designed to prevent, not to remedy, labour exploitation. The GLA could impose conditions on the issuance and revocation of a licence, but it had no authority to vindicate employees' rights, such as retrieving lost wages.[103]

Organisations such as Amnesty International, the International Labour Organization, and Anti-Slavery International criticised the government's refusal to ratify the Council of Europe Convention.[104] The Parliamentary Joint Committee on Human Rights released a report in October 2006 calling on the government to place victim protection 'at the heart of the legislative framework to combat trafficking' and 'review immigration laws and policies in the context of their impact on trafficking victims'.[105] While it endorsed the government's carceral approach, applauding its investigation and law-enforcement efforts, the joint committee urged the government to ratify the Council of Europe Convention on Action against Trafficking. Referring to the

[101] The maximum amount of the civil penalty will be decided following public consultation and parliamentary debate. Balch, 'Defeating "modern slavery", reducing exploitation?', 77–78.

[102] Ibid. The other exception was the continued immigration concession for live-in migrant domestic workers.

[103] Fudge, 'Illegal working', 577.

[104] Balch and Geddes, 'Opportunity from crisis?', 31.

[105] UK, House of Lords and House of Commons, Joint Committee on Human Rights, *Human Trafficking*, Twenty-Sixth Report, para. 118.

evidence and to safeguards contained in the convention, the joint committee rejected the government's claim that its provisions relating to reflection periods and residence permits for trafficking victims could draw those willing to make fraudulent claims of victim status to the United Kingdom.[106] It recommended a reflection period of three months, but recognising the United Kingdom was not bound by the EU Residence Directive, it advised the government to use the directive as a model and provide a residence period of six months.[107] The joint committee also urged the government to establish a UK-wide system for identifying and referring victims of trafficking.

Most significantly, the joint committee endorsed a labour approach to address human trafficking for labour exploitation, advising the government to shift its focus 'from immigration control to the prevention of exploitation of migrants and workers, and care of victims'.[108] It questioned whether the legislation concerning the employment of illegal migrants addressed the circumstances of trafficking and its victims and, instead, endorsed promoting and protecting workers' rights by enforcing labour and employment laws. Moreover, it suggested that the establishment of a single body (such as the Fair Employment Commission) to enforce workers' rights would be a desirable first step.[109]

Civil society organisations together with a group of parliamentarians put pressure on the government to adopt the Council of Europe Convention. Anthony Steen, a Conservative member of Parliament, established an all-party working group on human trafficking, which pushed the government to act.[110] A scandal relating to the release of over a thousand foreign prisoners without considering them for deportation led to the resignation of the home secretary and the appointment of John Reid, who restructured the Home Office, set up a new arms-length immigration agency, and signed on to the convention.[111]

TURNING ANTITRAFFICKING INTO A MORAL CRUSADE

In an act of pure political theatre, in March 2007 on the bicentenary of the 1807 Slave Trade Act, the home secretary signed the Council of Europe

[106] Ibid., paras. 199–200.
[107] Ibid., para. 204.
[108] Ibid., 69.
[109] Ibid., para. 109.
[110] Kenway, *The Truth about Modern Slavery*, 21.
[111] Balch and Geddes, 'Opportunity from crisis?', 30. In 2007, the government announced plans to break the Home Office into two separate departments: a Ministry of Justice and a new streamlined Home Office focused on crime, immigration, and terrorism. In April 2007, the new Border and Immigration Agency began operating. Formerly part of the Home Office, it was an arm's-length agency, providing greater operational freedom.

Convention on Human Trafficking, on the former desk of William Wilberforce, the British politician, philanthropist, and leader of the movement to abolish the slave trade. On the same day, the Home Office, together with the Scottish Executive, released the *UK Action Plan on Tackling Human Trafficking*. By invoking the United Kingdom's leadership on the abolition of the slave trade to frame its plan of action to combat human trafficking, the government declared it would not 'forget the plight of the thousands of people who are still forced to live in slave like conditions as a result of the inhuman criminal practices perpetrated by 21st century traffickers'.[112]

The celebration of the bicentenary of the Act to abolish the slave trade was, as Ben Wellings explains, an exercise in portraying the United Kingdom as a globally engaged and moral actor at a time when the formation of a minority government in the Scottish Assembly by the Scottish National Party detracted from celebration of the 300th anniversary of the political union of Scotland with the United Kingdom.[113] This depiction resonated with the idea of British greatness associated with the British Empire. The government characterised the 1807 Slave Trade Act as an instance of humanitarian intervention, motivated by a moral Parliament 'triumphing over a social evil buttressed by economic interests'.[114] This image appeals to progressives and conservatives alike. Thus, the abolition of the slave trade was a perfect metaphor for the United Kingdom's strategy to combat human trafficking.

Citing the joint committee's concerns, the government announced that victim assistance was necessary for effective enforcement. It promised to develop a national referral mechanism for victim identification and protection and to provide a formal reflection period during which removal action would be held in abeyance for a minimum period of thirty days and residence permits would be granted in certain circumstances to identified victims of trafficking. But instead of establishing an independent agency to monitor the plan and its implementation, the government decided that the Inter-Departmental Ministerial Group (IDMG) on Human Trafficking would be the most suitable monitor, thereby consolidating control over antitrafficking policy in the executive.

The 2007 plan marked the first time the government seriously considered trafficking for labour exploitation. It did not define what it meant by labour exploitation, although it acknowledged that it was difficult to draw a line

[112] An Act for the Abolition of the Slave Trade, 47 Geo. III, Sess. 1, c. 36 (Hansard, 10 February 1807); UK, Home Office, *UK Action Plan on Tackling Human Trafficking*, 2.

[113] Wellings, *English Nationalism, Brexit and the Anglosphere*, 134–135.

[114] Ibid., 134.

between 'poor working conditions and situations involving forced labour' and stressed coercion as an indicator of the latter.[115] Instead of taking the joint committee's advice to shift away from fighting illegal immigration towards strengthening workers' protection, the government intended to 'strengthen the legislation on the employment of illegal workers to deter trafficking for labour exploitation'.[116] To tackle the demand for trafficked labour, the government targeted employers who breached immigration laws, not those who violated labour laws. The concern was that firms using trafficked persons for cheap labour had an unfair advantage.[117] Except for the Gangmasters Licensing Authority, the action plan contained no discussion of labour regulation as a method for preventing trafficking.[118]

The attention paid to labour trafficking did not signal the government's turn away from trafficking for sexual exploitation. In fact, the government proposed to abolish the existence of all forms of prostitution, regardless of location, and shift the focus of enforcement 'onto the users and abusers, and developing routes out for those involved'.[119] This demand-centred approach was authorised by the Council of Europe Convention (Article 6) and reflected the strategy of abolishing prostitution under the guise of tackling human trafficking, which was gaining momentum in Europe.

As the government committed to protecting the rights of victims of trafficking, it placed great weight on strengthening borders. During the debate over the United Kingdom's Border Bill in February 2007, the Conservative shadow minister for immigration, Damien Green, declared: 'We don't have a barrier. We have a sieve'.[120] In response, the government made the immigration rules and border controls even stricter. The UK Borders Act 2007 increased the powers of immigration officials and the enforcement budget doubled.[121] In 2008, the government made private actors responsible for monitoring visa conditions imposed on non-EU citizens. The secondary legislation required 'sponsors' (employers and education providers such as private schools, colleges, and universities) to monitor 'foreign' employees and students, report

[115] UK, Home Office, *UK Action Plan on Tackling Human Trafficking*, 5, 40.
[116] Ibid., 10.
[117] Ibid., 94.
[118] The plan referred to the need to expand enforcement activity to assist victims of forced labour as part of its commitment to implementing and ratifying the Council of Europe's convention. Ibid., 42.
[119] Ibid., 54.
[120] Bosworth, 'Border control and the limits', 200.
[121] The UK Borders Act 2007 (2007, c. 30); Balch and Geddes, 'Opportunity from crisis?', 37.

their behaviour to the Home Office, and dismiss anyone who breached the rules by missing lectures or taking unauthorised absences, for example.[122]

After he took over the leadership of the party and government from Tony Blair in 2007, Gordon Brown appointed Jacqui Smith, a 'staunch opponent of prostitution', as home secretary, the third in a little over a year and the first woman to hold the office.[123] She and Harriet Hartman, a former government minister and deputy leader of the Labour Party, argued that prostitution was a form of violence against women.[124] Support for this position could be found among the opposition. In November 2007, Conservative MP Philip Hollobone proposed an amendment to the Criminal Justice and Immigration Bill to criminalise paying for sex. It was rejected in committee.[125]

In 2008, Smith commissioned a six-month review to assess measures to reduce the demand for prostitution. She was concerned that 'too little attention has been focused on the sex buyer'.[126] In November, the Home Office published *Tackling the Demand for Prostitution*. Although the government favoured the Swedish model of criminalising the purchase of sexual services, stakeholders were divided over having a generic criminal offence for paying for sex.[127] As a compromise, the review proposed to make it easier to prosecute purchasers of sexual services by amending the offences of kerb-crawling and persistent soliciting to eliminate the requirement of proving persistence. It also advised the government to consider 'a specific strict liability offence of paying for sex with someone who is controlled for another person's gain' to protect vulnerable individuals who have been trafficked or exploited.[128]

The government followed through on these recommendations in the Policing and Crime Bill, which proposed two new offences. The first, 'soliciting the sexual services of a prostitute in a public place, whether the customer is in a motor vehicle or not', was uncontroversial and quickly adopted.[129] The second, 'paying for the sexual services of a prostitute being controlled for gain', led to a lengthy debate on the meaning of the phrase 'controlled for gain'.[130] The outcome was a strict-liability offence, committed if someone pays or

[122] Sponsors who failed to comply risked loss of their sponsor licence and freedom to recruit or sponsor workers or students not EU citizens. Griffiths and Yeo, 'The UK's hostile environment', 526–527.

[123] Hill, 'This modern day slavery', 73.

[124] Ibid.

[125] Mulvihill, 'The criminalisation of paying for sex in England and Wales', 179.

[126] Van Dyke, 'The UK's response to modern slavery', 53.

[127] UK, Home Office, *Tackling the Demand for Prostitution*, 15.

[128] Ibid., 15.

[129] Policing and Crime Act 2009, s. 19.

[130] Mulvihill, 'The criminalisation of paying for sex in England and Wales', 175–177.

promises payment for the sexual services of a prostitute who has been subject to exploitative conduct of a kind likely to induce or encourage the provision of sexual services for which the payer has made or promised payment.[131] An offence is committed regardless of whether the person paying or promising payment for sexual services knows or ought to know or be aware that the victim has been subject to exploitative conduct, which goes further than the Council of Europe Convention's recommendation that the buyer have some knowledge of the exploitation. Moreover, under the new offence, it does not matter in which country the sexual services are provided.[132]

Tackling Demand for Prostitution justified taking a harder line on prostitution by linking it to trafficking for sexual exploitation, which it portrayed as a problem in the United Kingdom. It referred to a Home Office analysis that estimated that up to four thousand women had been trafficked for sexual exploitation in 2003. It calculated that this market was worth up to £275 million.[133] Referring to Pentameter 1 and 2, national police operations against sexual exploitation, the review claimed that this these figures underestimated the reality of the problem.[134]

Pentameter 2 combined demand-reduction tactics (such as awareness-raising advertisements in websites and magazines where men would look for massage parlours, saunas, or brothels) with raid and rescue.[135] It was considered a great success by the Home Office, which, together with the UK Human Trafficking Centre, disseminated 'sound-bites and pre-selected statistics' on Pentameter 2 to the media.[136] According to official police statistics, the results of Pentameter 2 were impressive: between October 2007 and March 2008, 822 establishments were raided, resulting in the rescue 167 victims of trafficking and the arrest of 528 people (later reduced to 406) on suspicion of human trafficking.[137]

However, an internal report for the UK Centre on Human Trafficking obtained and circulated by investigative journalist Nick Davies painted a

[131] Section 14 of the Policing and Crime Act 2009, inserting s. 53A of the Sexual Offences Act 2003, which requires that the person responsible for the exploitative conduct must have been acting for or in the expectation of gain for himself or herself or another person, other than the payer or the prostitute.

[132] The maximum penalty for this offence is a fine of £1,000. The offence came into force on 1 April 2010.

[133] UK, Home Office, *Tackling the Demand for Prostitution*, 6.

[134] Ibid.

[135] UK, Home Office, *UK Action Plan on Tackling Human Trafficking*, 31.

[136] Hill, 'This modern day slavery', 93.

[137] Balch, 'Defeating "modern slavery", reducing exploitation?', 80; Hill, 'This modern day slavery', 97.

different picture. Women recovered through Pentameter 2 rarely received protection or support from state agencies. The overwhelming majority were removed from the United Kingdom, declined support, absconded, disappeared, or were charged.[138] Perhaps more damming from the government's perspective was the fact that only fifteen men and women were convicted, of which only five men were convicted of importing women and forcing them to work as prostitutes. Even then, these traffickers were not detected by the Pentameter 2 operation.[139]

Davies' account revealed the cycle of citation that transformed estimates (clearly acknowledged by their authors to be based on poor and not very reliable data) into hard facts. Commissioned and circulated by the Home Office, these estimates were picked up by Christian charities Care and the Salvation Army and an umbrella group of evangelicals called Churches Alert to Sex Trafficking Across Europe (Chaste). Chaste explicitly campaigned for an end to all prostitution and was enlisted as a specialist adviser to the police. Home Office ministers, an array of politicians, and high-ranking police officers repeated these, and even more preposterous figures, to justify devoting more resources to fighting trafficking for sexual exploitation, including further criminalising prostitution.[140] Davies noted the absence of sex workers, who disputed the claims of their widespread exploitation, from the discussion. His exposé of how the moral panic came to be had little impact as the government moved towards abolishing prostitution to prevent human trafficking.[141]

The government had a great deal of support for its approach from the Labour and Conservatives parties, police forces, and antitrafficking NGOs.[142] Its governance strategy resonated with deeply embedded narratives about white slavery, including redeeming unruly and wanton women. It was also supported by the Bush administration, the EU Parliament, and the Council of Europe. The government used its antitrafficking campaign to target a sector associated with degrading treatment and violence against women while ignoring other sectors, such as agriculture and construction, rife with exploitation.

The problem of sex trafficking gave the police licence to target migrant sex workers, raid premises throughout the United Kingdom, and criminalise prostitution, actions that were seen as bringing the United Kingdom in line with its international and EU commitments. As Angela Hill observed:

[138] Davies, 'Prostitution and trafficking'; Hill, 'This modern day slavery', 100.

[139] Hill, 'This modern day slavery', 104.

[140] Davies, 'Prostitution and trafficking'.

[141] Scoular, *The Subject of Prostitution*, 68–71.

[142] Hill, 'This modern day slavery', 111; Turnbull and Broad, 'Bringing the problem home', 200.

> This figure of the sex slave has made immigration a threat not to British citizens, but to a certain class of migrant untarnished by the taint of immigration and asylum. This reconfiguration of the anti-immigrant stance allows the UK to be the liberator, to come to the rescue, of this deserving class of migrants while presenting restrictive immigration policies as based on the interest and protection of others.[143]

The challenge was to develop a mechanism to sort victims of slavery, whose rights should be protected, from migrant sex workers, who should be punished, removed, or deported.

In December 2008, the United Kingdom ratified the Council of Europe Convention on Action against Trafficking. The Home Office adopted a forty-five-day reflection period and the possibility of granting a one-year residence permit for victims of trafficking, both of which were longer than the minimums specified in the convention. The government used these initiatives to demonstrate its 'commitment to putting victim care and protection at the heart of our human trafficking strategy'.[144] In 2009, it established a process, known as the National Referral Mechanism (NRM), to identify victims and refer them to the proper agencies to access protections. The Home Office designated the UK Human Trafficking Centre, first housed in the Police Service and then in the Serious Organised Crime Agency, and the UK Border Agency as competent authorities for assessing trafficking victims even though the Council of Europe Convention proposed that this competence be distributed through frontline agencies. NGOs like the Poppy Project and Salvation Army were incorporated into the NRM as first responders who could refer potential victims to competent authorities for a final determination of their status. When it came to oversight, the government refused to appoint an independent national rapporteur to monitor the state's antitrafficking policies and legislation, as recommended by the convention, claiming that an 'additional layer of bureaucracy may actually hamper our efforts to combat human trafficking'.[145] The executive was unwilling to cede any control over its governance of human trafficking.

In the absence of an independent rapporteur, nine NGOs set up the Anti-Trafficking Monitoring Group (ATMG).[146] Their first report, *Wrong Kind of*

[143] Hill, 'This modern day slavery', 114.

[144] Van Dyke, 'The UK's response to modern slavery', 56.

[145] Hill, 'This modern day slavery', 115, quoting Alan Campbell, parliamentary under-secretary of state.

[146] Amnesty International UK, Anti-Slavery International, End Child Prostitution, Child Pornography and the Trafficking of Children for Sexual Purposes (ECPAT UK), the Helen Bamber Foundation, the Immigration Law Practitioners' Association (ILPA), Kalayaan, the

Victim, released in 2010, revealed how the competent authorities in the NRM sorted trafficking victims from illegal migrants and other criminals. UK and EU citizens were processed by the UK Human Trafficking Centre, which was housed in police services and had experience dealing with victims of crime; third-country nationals were processed by the UK Border Agency, primarily concerned with identifying and removing immigration offenders.[147] Evidence of delayed and discriminatory victim-identification processes and inadequate protections for trafficking victims led the ATMG to conclude that the United Kingdom was not yet meeting its commitments under the Council of Europe Convention on Action Against Trafficking.[148]

Although eastern European women are viewed as the archetypical victim, the ATMG found that only 45 per cent of referrals in 2009 were for sexual exploitation. Between April and December 2009, of the 477 people referred to the NRM, 371 were from states outside the EU (primarily Nigeria, China, and Vietnam), 72 were from the EU (excluding the United Kingdom), and 34 were UK nationals. The ATMG reported an overall positive identification as a trafficking victim in 19 per cent of the 477 cases. But the positive identification rate differed dramatically depending on the immigration status of the potential victim; the rate for UK nationals was 76 per cent and EU nationals 29 per cent, but for nationals from outside the EU, it was only 12 per cent.[149] The UK Border Service appeared to be much more adept at discovering illegal migrant workers than identifying victims of trafficking.[150]

The UK government characterised human trafficking as a foreign problem, and its solution was to stop victims from entering the United Kingdom by deterritorialising and externalising its borders.[151] In the 2007 *Action Plan on Human Trafficking*, the government declared it would extend 'the extraterritorial application of trafficking offences to cover acts of facilitation carried out overseas, irrespective of the nationality of the person carrying out the acts'.[152] The UK Borders Act 2007 also reasserted the position of the Sexual Offences Act 2003 that, regardless of the traditional territorial jurisdiction of the criminal law, trafficking offences 'apply to anything done whether inside or outside

POPPY Project, the Trafficking Awareness Raising Alliance of Glasgow Community and Safety Services (TARA), and the UN International Children's Emergency Fund (UNICEF UK). The Anti-Trafficking Legal Project (ATLEP) also consulted on the research.

[147] Balch and Geddes, 'Opportunity from crisis?', 37.

[148] Ibid., 6.

[149] Anti-Trafficking Monitoring Group, *Wrong Kind of Victim?*, 9.

[150] Balch and Geddes, 'Opportunity from crisis?', 37.

[151] FitzGerald, 'Vulnerable geographies', 181.

[152] UK, Home Office, *UK Action Plan on Tackling Human Trafficking*, 34.

the United Kingdom'.[153] The government allowed the Crown Prosecution Service (CPS) to use powers provided in the Sexual Offences Act 2003, and the Asylum and Immigration (Treatment of Claimants, etc.) Act 2004 was amended as the government promised. The CPS focused on the Caribbean, West Africa, China, and Afghanistan.[154] The government also continued to place international liaison officers in cooperating countries known to be sources or transit routes for human traffickers to advise domestic migration authorities and airlines on how to identify and stop trafficked migrants from leaving their countries of origin.[155] Development aid was deployed to stop trafficking overseas.[156] The United Kingdom's expansion of its criminal-law jurisdiction beyond its territory and the externalisation of its borders were in keeping with the EU strategy of enrolling non-EU neighbours considered 'gatekeeper' and 'buffer' states to implement control measures on behalf of EU states.[157]

As part of its commitment to ratifying the Council of Europe Convention, the government acknowledged that it would have to enforce its prohibition against labour trafficking.[158] The government's concern was illegal movement, not labour exploitation. However, human rights organisations like Liberty and Anti-Slavery International were unhappy that the prohibition in the Asylum and Immigration (Treatment of Claimants, etc.) Act 2004 only applied where there was cross-border movement involving non-EU citizens. In the face of mounting evidence of the existence of EU nationals and other migrants who may not have been trafficked but were still exploited, they pressed for measures to tackle labour exploitation outside of trafficking.[159]

The lack of enforcement of labour legislation contributed to labour exploitation. In its 2009 report on human trafficking, the Home Committee of the House of Commons recounted that outside of GLA sectors 'enforcement was at best patchy and at worst nonexistent' and suggested expanding the GLA's remit to construction.[160] Trade unions and workers' advocates campaigned to bring the construction, cleaning, and catering sectors under the GLA's

[153] FitzGerald, 'Vulnerable bodies, vulnerable borders', 238, discussing ss. 31(2) and (4) of the Act. The exploitation must take place after the victim's arrival in the UK, but facilitation may take place anywhere in the world.

[154] UK, Home Office, *UK Action Plan on Tackling Human Trafficking*, 6.

[155] FitzGerald, 'Vulnerable bodies, vulnerable borders', 236–238.

[156] FitzGerald, 'Vulnerable geographies', 191–193.

[157] O'Connell-Davidson, *Modern Slavery*, 121.

[158] UK, Home Office, *UK Action Plan on Tackling Human Trafficking*, 41.

[159] Van Dyke, 'The UK's response to modern slavery', 52.

[160] UK, House of Commons, Home Affairs Committee, *The Trade in Human Beings*, 27.

authority. Citing the financial crisis, the Labour government refused to bring other sectors under the GLA on the ground that doing so would impose additional regulatory burdens on business.[161]

Human rights organisations turned to the courts, claiming that under Article 4 of the European Convention on Human Rights the government was obliged to criminalise forced labour and domestic servitude.[162] Several NGOs helped bring a case against a police force, arguing that its refusal to investigate an allegation of domestic servitude on the ground that no trafficking was involved was in breach of the United Kingdom's obligation.[163] The case wound up before the European Court of Human Rights, which held that the government had failed to meet its procedural duty to investigate forced labour.[164] The court elaborated that 'domestic servitude is a specific offence, distinct from trafficking and exploitation, which involves a complex set of dynamics and both overt and more subtle forms of coercion, to force compliance'.[165] With no specific offence of domestic servitude, the court concluded that the UK authorities were unable to give due weight to factors, such as the complainant's allegation that her passport had been taken, that her wages were withheld, and that she had been explicitly and implicitly threatened with denunciation to the immigration authorities – all ILO indicators of forced labour.[166]

The government baulked when human rights groups demanded it create a new criminal-law offence targeting forced labour without an element of trafficking; it claimed criminal-law provisions already outlawed such activities. When a Liberty-drafted clause that would criminalise servitude and forced labour was introduced during the House of Lord's consideration of the Coroners and Justice Bill, the government recanted. It finally agreed to address the problem of forced labour outside the context of immigration.[167] However, it substituted its own provisions for those drafted by the human rights group, arguing 'that a slightly different approach is preferable', one that

[161] Balch, 'Defeating "modern slavery", reducing exploitation?', 82; UK, *Government Reply to the Sixth Report from the Home Affairs Committee*, 4.

[162] Liberty brought a successful review against a police force for failing to investigate a case of trafficking for forced labour. Balch, 'Regulation and enforcement to tackle forced labour', 23.

[163] The Equality and Human Rights Commission and AIRE Centre intervened in *CN v. UK*, which was also supported by Anti-Slavery International, Kalayaan, and the Poppy Project.

[164] *CN v. UK* (2013) 56 EHRR 24, paras. 72, 76.

[165] Ibid., para. 80.

[166] Ibid.

[167] UK, Home Office and Scottish Government, *Update to the UK Action Plan on Tackling Human Trafficking*, 5.

draws on 'the offence of trafficking for such purposes without the requirement that the person has been trafficked'.[168]

Section 71 of the Coroners and Justice Act 2009, which came into effect in 2010, created an offence of holding another person in slavery or servitude or requiring them to perform forced or compulsory labour. Significantly, Section 71 did not define slavery, servitude, or forced or compulsory labour, referring instead to Article 4 of the European Convention on Human Rights, thereby delegating the responsibility for defining the scope of the offence to the European Court of Human Rights.[169] The government justified the legislation because it met the UK's positive obligation under Article 4 to 'protect those within its jurisdiction from slavery, servitude and forced or compulsory labour' and because such behaviour, in addition to causing serious harm to individuals, 'creates unfair competition amongst competing businesses'.[170]

The UK's response to the Council of Europe and EU legal instruments was selective. It was bound by the European Convention on Human Rights and, thus, had no option but to abide by the European Court of Human Rights' decisions. The government chose to ratify the Council of Europe Convention on Action Against Human Trafficking, which required it to provide more robust protection for victims. However, the human trafficking convention, unlike the European Convention on Human Rights, was not justiciable, and the only arms-length review mechanism was the Group of Experts on Action against Trafficking in Human Beings, which relies on periodic reports instead of enforceable sanctions.[171] Even as the government ratified the Council of Europe Convention on Action Against Trafficking, it opted out of an EU directive, which is justiciable, that provides undocumented migrant workers with the right to recoup unpaid wages.[172] The government adopted an approach to human trafficking that positioned trafficking as an integral part of border controls and reinforced a criminal-law jurisdiction while it avoided labour law initiatives that could be seen as 'rewarding' breaches of immigration legislation and restricted human rights to a narrow category of victims.

168 Fudge and Strauss, 'Migrants, unfree labour, and the legal construction', 537.

169 Coroners and Justice Act 2009 (2009, c. 25).

170 UK, Ministry of Justice, 'Slavery, servitude and forced or compulsory labour', para. 13.

171 For Foucault, discipline is obtained through imposing precise and detailed norms. Biopower does not displace disciplinary techniques; instead, according to him, it infiltrates and embeds itself in existing disciplinary techniques, operating on a different scale and making use of different instruments. Foucault, *Society Must Be Defended*, 242.

172 European Union, 'Directive 2009/52/EC of the European Parliament and of the Council of 18 June 2009'. Britain opted into EU measures aimed at tackling irregular migration and opted out of measures designed to protect victims of trafficking: Geddes, 'Getting the best of both worlds?', 733.

CONCLUSION

International and European legal instruments prompted the UK government to enter the human trafficking policy space and provided a broad legal framework. Like the EU, the United Kingdom treated human trafficking for labour exploitation very differently from trafficking for sexual exploitation. The United Kingdom moved closer to the strategy favoured by the EU and Council of Europe of combatting sexual exploitation by abolishing prostitution. For governments, migrant sex workers exemplified the problem of porous borders in the United Kingdom and Europe, where criminal laws against trafficking for sexual exploitation did little to protect migrant women caught up in antitrafficking police operations.

Despite these similarities, the United Kingdom's distinctive cultural political economy marked its human trafficking laws and policies.[173] Key elements of the British conception of sovereignty, such as controlling borders at territorial frontiers and concentrating authority within the executive, were prominent, distinctive features of the United Kingdom's antitrafficking discourse and governance strategy. The association of illegal entry and illegal working with human trafficking created an aura of criminality that spilled over to trafficking victims. The government did not want to be seen as too tender in its treatment of illegal migrants and, thus, was reluctant to commit to protecting the human rights of victims who were migrants. The gateway for victim protection was through the NRM, which in the case of non-EU citizens was lodged in the agency with jurisdiction over enforcing immigration controls. The government only grudgingly extended labour exploitation beyond the context of illegal immigration, it regarding labour exploitation first and foremost as a crime against British business and workers. To stamp out human trafficking, illegal working had to be tackled. By equating tackling human trafficking with the abolition of the slave trade, the government elevated its antitrafficking policies to a moral crusade that transcended bipartisan politics. At the same time, it consolidated its authority over the governance of human trafficking, minimising the role of Parliament and refusing independent oversight wherever possible.

New Labour's selective adoption of EU directives pertaining to human trafficking fortified the United Kingdom's external borders and preserved its control over the entry and entitlements of migrants who were non-EU citizens. But the tenson between sharing sovereignty with the EU to strengthen the United Kingdom's capacity to control its borders and pursue its national

[173] See Sum and Jessop, *Towards a Cultural Political Economy*.

interest and the idea of parliamentary sovereignty and executive control as the 'reservoir' of sovereignty could be ignored only if the public accepted the legitimacy of political decision making and political elites tolerated EU constraints on their political freedom. Sovereignty's link with border control and immigration in the United Kingdom also contributed to the volatility of the United Kingdom's relationship with the EU. At the May 2007 Labour Party conference, Gordon Brown responded to reports that EU workers had taken jobs in the United Kingdom by proclaiming, 'British jobs for British workers'.[174]

In 2008, when the United Kingdom's liberal growth model ground to a halt and the UK economy suffered its sharpest contraction since the Great Depression, public opinion hardened against immigration, including the movement of EU citizens into the United Kingdom.[175] The fact that EU treaties trumped the UK Parliament over matters of borders and belonging not only illuminated the contradiction between the different ideas of sovereignty, it also raised the question of popular sovereignty and the political legitimacy of decision making.[176] The Lisbon Treaty, which came into effect in 2009 and was intended to increase the democratic legitimacy of the EU by limiting the power of Members States' governments and increasing the authority of the EU Parliament in the EU's legislative process, was seen by the British political elite, including Prime Minister Gordon Brown, as threatening to British sovereignty. In 2010, David Cameron (the leader of the Opposition) launched the Conservative Party's general election campaign with a promise 'to redistribute power from the political elite to the man and woman in the street'.[177] He declared the Conservatives would take control back from Brussels.[178] New Labour was unsuccessful in depoliticising the EU domestically, and sovereignty became the flashpoint in political discourse.

Instead of a rupture with the Labour government's human trafficking policy, the 2010 election, which resulted in a hung Parliament and the formation of a coalition government between the Conservative and Liberal Democratic parties, amplified the existing themes, including a focus on illegal working, a punitive and restrictive approach to immigration and prostitution, and a suspicion of alleged victims of human trafficking.[179] As we shall see in

174 Bale, 'Putting it right?', 300.
175 Hopkin, 'When Polanyi met Farage', 465.
176 Gifford, 'The UK and the European Union', 326.
177 Batty, 'David Cameron launches election campaign'.
178 Gifford, 'The UK and the European Union', 333.
179 Broad and Turnbull break human trafficking and modern slavery policy in the UK into two phases, from the mid-1990s to 2013 and from 2013 on: see 'From human trafficking to

the next chapter, under the Coalition and Conversative governments, taking control of UK borders extended beyond asylum seekers and refugees to EU citizens. In 2013, the Conservative Party seized on the Labour government's linking of its antitrafficking strategy with the abolition of the slave trade to rechristen 'human trafficking' 'modern slavery'. The beauty of the modern slavery frame, from a political perspective, is that it enabled the UK government to cloak its carceral approach to protecting its borders and restoring order under a moral crusade in which Britain would re-establish itself as a global humanitarian leader. However, unlike the New Labour government, which could rely on its majority to maintain control over antitrafficking policy, the coalition government required Parliament's support. How modern slavery was mobilised in the UK governance agenda between 2010 and 2023 is the subject of the next chapter.

modern slavery', 128. While I agree that the discursive shift to modern slavery is important and that it expands to covers a greater range of unfree labour, I argue that the continuities with New Labour's emphasis on illegal working and its specific understanding of the harm of labour exploitation are as, if not, more important.

6

Global Britain and the Modern Slavery Act 2015

To stamp out a trade that affects 30 million people around the world is not a question of Labour vs Tory, as both sides are committed to the [the Modern Slavery] Bill. The question is how we make this Bill a world leader which other countries will seek to adopt.

—Frank Field, *The Spectator*

Just as it was Britain that took an historic stand to ban slavery two centuries ago, so Britain will once again lead the way in defeating modern slavery and preserving the freedoms and values that have defined our country for generations.

—Theresa May, 'Anti-slavery service'

At an antislavery service held at Westminster Abbey in 2016 to honour the celebrated abolitionist William Wilberforce, Prime Minister Theresa May took up his mantle: 'I want Britain at the forefront of this fight, leading the world with our efforts to stamp out modern day slavery and human trafficking.'[1] She described modern slavery as a crime that 'knows no geographic boundaries' and held up the United Kingdom's Modern Slavery Act 2015 as having some of the toughest penalties in the world. With the help of an elite antislavery policy network, May, as home secretary, had forged a bipartisan consensus on abolition in Parliament in favour of modern slavery legislation and cultivated the support of faith-based organisations. As home secretary (2010–2016) and prime minister (2016–2019), May positioned the United Kingdom as a critical node in the global antislavery governance network and fashioned the United Kingdom's fight against modern slavery as a key plank in her vision of Global Britain.

[1] May, 'Anti-slavery service'.

This chapter explores how modern slavery came to play a central role in the United Kingdom's governance strategy. Initially, the Coalition (Conservatives and Liberal Democrats) government followed New Labour's carceral approach to human trafficking and reluctantly adopted the 2011 EU antitrafficking directive, which it felt demanded too much in the way of victim protection. It also tried to retain executive control over antitrafficking policy, but no party had a majority in Parliament. Parliamentarians gave the policy a distinctively British inflexion through the adoption of the term 'modern slavery'. They also pressured the government to tackle forced labour in supply chains.

As we saw in Chapter 5, the bipartisan All-Party Parliamentary Group (APPG) on Human Trafficking (its name was amended in 2015 to add Modern Slavery) pressured the Labour government to adopt the Council of Europe Convention on Action Against Trafficking in Human Beings. It used the language of slavery to refer to human trafficking and evoked the memory of Britain's leading role in the antislavery campaign. In December 2009, the APPG's founder, Anthony Steen (a Conservative MP), introduced the Anti-Slavery Day Bill. He referred to William Wilberforce's parliamentary campaign against the slave trade as a model to emulate.[2] The private member's bill received royal assent before the May 2010 election.

Reframing human trafficking as slavery enabled new abolitionists to draw on a historical repertoire in which Christian evangelicals, Parliament, and British leaders figured prominently. Cast as a moral issue, modern slavery transcended party politics. Modern slavery, like human trafficking, was mobilised by groups – from Christian abolitionists to antiprostitution campaigners to workers' rights advocates – who held incommensurable views on what modern slavery comprises, its causes, and potential solutions. Employing the language of modern slavery also allowed the government to sidestep the divisive issue of prostitution, which fell under human trafficking.

May's invocation of Wilberforce is telling. Wilberforce's rightly praised abolition work overshadowed other aspects of his politics that were conservative and repressive. He introduced his ninth abolition bill in February 1799 between supporting a bill suspending habeas corpus and introducing a bill to outlaw trade unions, which he denounced as 'a general disease on society'.[3] Wilberforce 'used his moral capital as the hero of abolition' to outlaw trade unions, introduce imprisonment without trial, and reduce freedom of

2 Hansard, HC, vol. 505, col. 536, 5 February 2010.

3 The Combination Act 1799 made it an offence, subject to three months imprisonment or two months hard labour, for a workman to join a trade union. Tomkins, *William Wilberforce*, 146.

speech and freedom of assembly. But there is nothing cynical or contradictory in this blend of freedom and coercion if, according to his biographer Stephen Tomkins, we consider Wilberforce's religion (evangelical Christian) and class (a wealthy importer of Baltic timber and iron). Wilberforce interpreted British radicalism, often coupled with attacks on traditional Christianity, as an attack on Christian values and society.[4] The antislavery movement in Britain in the early 1800s was 'spiritually radical but socially reactionary'.[5] Its challenge was to abolish slavery without upending the social order.

Like Wilberforce's legislation, the Modern Slavery Act 2015 was sandwiched between repressive legislation – the Immigration Acts of 2014 and 2016, designed to make the United Kingdom a 'hostile environment' for illegal migrants. These three interconnected laws are May's political legacy, and for her, as for Wilberforce, there is no contradiction between this mix of freedom and coercion. They are integral components of a legal scheme that sorts out victims and illegal migrants from migrants who are welcome. This system draws on and reinvigorates ideas of control and sovereignty deeply rooted in the United Kingdom's cultural political economy – ideas that were particularly potent as the United Kingdom decided to leave the EU.

SOVEREIGNTY, AUSTERITY, AND BREXIT

The United Kingdom's relationship with the EU became contentious in the context of a fragile governing coalition, the Eurozone financial crisis, and domestic austerity policies.[6] The slogan 'Take Back Control' – associated with border and immigration controls and the rise of the United Kingdom Independent Party (UKIP) – also came to refer to sovereignty, with its links to power, authority, and national identity. Reclaiming sovereignty was a rallying cry for those who sought to leave the EU and chart a new path for 'Global Britain'.[7]

Sovereignty has three dimensions here.[8] In the United Kingdom, sovereignty as a political principle means parliamentary sovereignty, which includes elements of monarchical sovereignty and emphasises centralised power and control.[9] But on its own, parliamentary sovereignty cannot provide political legitimacy. The second dimension, popular sovereignty (equated

4 Tomkins, *William Wilberforce*, 146.

5 Scanlan, *Slave Empire*, 16.

6 Gifford, 'The people against Europe'.

7 Wellings, *English Nationalism, Brexit and the Anglosphere*; and Daddow, 'Globalbritain™'.

8 Gifford, 'The UK and the European Union', 323.

9 Ibid.

with democratic rule exercised by citizens), is required. The third dimension, economic sovereignty, is the separation of the market from the state, and it resonates with 'British' values of liberty and private property.[10] While the border between politics and markets is contested, in the United Kingdom the state has 'historically been quite effective at policing and reinforcing the sovereignty of the market'.[11]

Eurosceptics exploited the contradiction between the economic functionalism of the New Labour's supernationalism and the different dimensions of sovereignty prominent in UK political discourse. Fearing the impact of the Eurozone crisis and the EU's qualified voting majority rules on the United Kingdom's economic autonomy, Prime Minister David Cameron took an increasingly hard stance on the EU.[12] In his version of economic supernationalism, the United Kingdom would obtain greater concessions from the EU, especially over the free movement of EU citizens, and lead the EU in a more liberal market-oriented direction. On 23 January 2013, Cameron set out his position: 'We have the character of an island nation – independent, forthright and passionate in defence of our sovereignty. We can no more change this British sensibility than we can drain the English Channel. And because of this sensibility, we come to the European Union with a frame of mind that is more practical than emotional.'[13] This expression of 'British' exceptionalism was designed to placate the growing Eurosceptic faction in the Conservative Party. To appease them, Cameron announced that a Conservative victory in the 2015 election would mean a referendum on EU membership.[14]

Emboldened by UKIP's populist rhetoric (disseminated in the tabloid press), Eurosceptics championed popular sovereignty as the path to taking back power ceded to bureaucrats in Brussels.[15] Although popular sovereignty and national identity were at the heart of the September 2014 Scottish referendum on independence, nationalism is not straightforward in the United Kingdom's plurinational context. Elite political discourse incorporated political nationalism, in the form of overt populism and tacit nativism, by expressing it in terms of controlling immigration.[16] Since the 1950s,

[10] Ibid., 323–324.
[11] Ibid., 335.
[12] Gifford, 'The United Kingdom's Eurosceptic political economy', 790.
[13] Gifford, 'The people against Europe', 524.
[14] Gifford, 'The UK and the European Union', 332.
[15] Ibid.
[16] Menon and Wager, 'Taking back control', 281.

immigration policy meant controlling the movement of people deemed racially distinct, and controls created different categories of migrants.[17]

Opposition to immigration and the EU were closely linked.[18] An influx of EU citizens after the 2004 enlargement, combined with the financial crisis and austerity policies, fuelled anti-immigration political discourse and opposition to free movement. Cameron did not challenge claims that migration, rather than government cuts, had led to the deterioration of public services such as education, health, and housing.[19] Indeed, he blamed the United Kingdom's 'soft touch' benefits culture for attracting EU and third-country citizens.[20]

In 2015, when the Conservatives won the election with a majority, Cameron announced that the referendum would be held in June 2016. Although the EU made concessions, including a 'brake' on free movement, key proponents of the Leave campaign, including prominent figures in the Conservative Party and the UK Parliament and cabinet, blamed migrants for exhausting public services and the EU for draining the United Kingdom's finances.[21] The slogan 'Take Back Control' elided the idea of 'control over borders', 'designed to resonate amongst those concerned about levels of immigration into the UK', and the 'slightly more esoteric argument about the right form of democracy and representation that ought to pertain to Britain'.[22] In the run-up to the referendum, tabloids claimed that membership in the EU had led to uncontrolled immigration.[23]

The Leave campaign offered a positive economic vision to counter the EU Remainers' 'fearmongering' about the consequences of leaving the EU. Conservative Eurosceptics claimed the EU encumbered the United Kingdom with regulations; the United Kingdom would flourish as a more globally oriented player.[24] Britain's imperial past allowed Brexiters to imagine a global future in which the market was sovereign and extended beyond the United Kingdom's territorial borders. They pointed to London's role as a global financial centre that had the 'capacity, particularly when compared to

[17] Geddes, 'The politics of irregular migration'; Gish, 'Color and skill'. In *Bordering Britain*, El-Enany traces these racialised legal categories back to Britain's colonial and slave-trading past.

[18] Menon and Wager, 'Taking back control'; Goodwin and Milazzo, 'Taking back control'.

[19] Hopkin, 'When Polanyi met Farage', 472.

[20] Ibid.

[21] Such as Iain Duncan Smith, Michael Gove, Boris Johnson, and Jacob Rees-Mogg. Labour Member of Parliament Frank Field, a key policy actor in the modern slavery policy space, also promoted Brexit.

[22] Wellings, *English Nationalism, Brexit and the Anglosphere*, 105.

[23] Simpson and Startin, 'Tabloid tales'.

[24] Menon and Wager, 'Taking back control'.

its European counterparts, to deterritorialise capital'.[25] The Leave campaign working with tabloids blanketed neoliberal globalism – low taxes, deregulation, and minimal state intervention in a 'free' market – with the language of 'sovereignty and symbolism'.[26]

Cameron resigned when the majority of those voting in the referendum favoured leaving the EU. May became prime minister in July 2016 and rebranded the United Kingdom as 'Global Britain'.[27] This governance narrative drew on 'imperial nostalgia' for Britain's past glory as a trading nation and moral leader.[28] In Britain, particularly England, sovereignty had long had an extraterritorial dimension. As Ben Wellings explains, 'English nationalists do not seek to make the state and nation congruent: instead they instinctively defend British sovereignty its existence, operation, and memory', which, as a former empire, is extraterritorial.[29] May had incorporated the 'narrative of moral leadership and the myth of British exceptionalism' into her fight against modern slavery (her personal cause) and governance strategy.[30] Casting the United Kingdom as a world leader in the campaign against modern slavery helped her build cross-party support during the Coalition government's tenure and after the EU referendum. It linked the United Kingdom's post-EU role to its former glory. Invoking William Wilberforce and the abolitionist campaign to end slavery reinforced a narrative of moral authority, liberty, and British exceptionalism, since in the United Kingdom, unlike the United States, slavery ended through acts of Parliament, not war.[31] Despite a shift from the language of human trafficking to that of modern slavery, Coalition and Conservative governments did not discard but incorporated the links New Labour drew between illegal working and human trafficking. The language of modern slavery heralded a revitalised vision of British global sovereignty.

HUMAN TRAFFICKING AND IMMIGRATION

Using terms almost identical to New Labour's, Cameron had defended his government's aggressive approach to illegal migration. It 'is a question of fairness – yes to the British people . . . but also to those who have been shipped over here against their will, kept as slaves and forced to work horrendous

[25] Gifford, 'The United Kingdom's Eurosceptic political economy', 784.
[26] Menon and Wager, 'Taking back control', 281.
[27] Daddow, 'Globalbritain™'; Atkins, 'Rhetoric and audience reception'.
[28] Melhuish, 'Euroscepticism, anti-nostalgic nostalgia'.
[29] Wellings, *English Nationalism, Brexit and the Anglosphere*, 21.
[30] Atkins, '(Re)imagining Magna Carta', 60.
[31] Wellings, *English Nationalism, Brexit and the Anglosphere*, 134.

hours'.[32] The Coalition government, following New Labour's approach to human trafficking, treated EU directives with scepticism and emphasised criminality and illegal immigration as the causes. The government initially refused to opt into the proposed EU antitrafficking directive, which (as we saw in Chapter 4) went further than the framework decision to protect victims of human trafficking and address methods of prevention. It explained that most of the directive's provisions, already in place in the United Kingdom, would require the government to transform discretionary provisions around victim assistance into mandatory entitlements.[33] However, in the face of concerted opposition, the minority government changed its position. The prime minister confirmed the United Kingdom would adopt the 2011 directive and pledged to 'make Britain a "world leader" in the fight against human trafficking'.[34]

On 19 July 2011, the government published *Human Trafficking: The Government's Strategy*, with a foreword by May, then home secretary. She set four priorities: 'a renewed focus on prevention overseas, a stronger border at home, tougher action on the perpetrators, and better identification and care for the victims'.[35] The National Crime Agency (NCA), which would be up and running in 2013, would connect and direct local, national, and overseas action to detect and disrupt human trafficking and strengthen border arrangements. Building on measures New Labour had put in place, it would work with international law enforcement and other UK agencies, such as the Foreign and Commonwealth Office and the Department for International Development. The goal was to stop 'illegal' immigrants before they got to the United Kingdom by putting in place a scheme at the visa application stage that would use markers such as nationality, gender, age, and socioeconomic status to identify potential victims and offenders.[36]

The government promised to revise the primary institution for victim identification and protection, the National Referral Mechanism (NRM). The NRM comprises different agencies (known as first responders) who refer potential victims through the identification and support process (victims cannot refer themselves). As we saw in Chapter 5, the Anti-Trafficking Monitoring Group (ATMG) had criticised the government's decision to make the UK Border Agency (which detected and deported illegal immigrants) a competent authority to determine victim status in the NRM. In response to complaints, the government said it would improve victim identification,

32 Cameron, 'Prime Minister's address to Conservative Party members'.
33 Lipscombe and Beard, *Human Trafficking*, 25.
34 Dugan, 'UK signs trafficking directive after 10-month delay'.
35 Home Office, *Human Trafficking: The Government's Strategy*, 4.
36 Sharapov, 'Traffickers and their victims', 94.

including by increasing the number of government and nongovernmental agencies eligible to refer potential victims to the NRM. Under the EU directive and the Council of Europe's convention, it was obliged to provide specific services to victims of trafficking. It outsourced all service provision for victims to the Salvation Army, an evangelical Christian church and the largest nongovernment provider of social care.[37] In these ways, NGOs and faith-based organisations were incorporated into its antitrafficking system.

To comply with the EU antitrafficking directive, the United Kingdom needed to amend the territorial scope of human trafficking offences; provide a statutory basis for measures to protect victims; and set up a national rapporteur to gather statistics, assess trafficking trends, and measure the results of antitrafficking actions. The government agreed to criminalise human trafficking for the purposes of labour exploitation in the United Kingdom and human trafficking by a UK national outside the United Kingdom.[38] But the government hesitated to introduce even secondary legislation that would transform discretionary victim assistance and support practices into mandatory legal entitlements.[39] It also continued to consolidate authority over the governance of human trafficking in the executive; it appointed the Inter-Departmental Ministerial Group on Human Trafficking (IDMG) national rapporteur.[40]

On the United Kingdom's first antislavery day, 18 October 2012, the IDMG released its first annual report on human trafficking. It used NRM data to provide an assessment and analysis of trends and the United Kingdom's antitrafficking efforts. While the strategy's success would depend on the NCA's effectiveness, a 'fundamental aspect' of the United Kingdom's strategy involved disrupting a priority list of source countries.[41] The report stressed paying more attention to trafficking for labour exploitation and the challenge of distinguishing 'between cases of labour exploitation, where workers are under paid and subjected to poor working conditions, and cases of trafficking for forced labour where work is exacted under the menace of penalty and performed against the will of the person concerned'.[42] It called for more research on labour exploitation but rejected the suggestion that the Gangmasters Licencing Authority's (GLA) remit be extended to licensing

37 Ibid., 11.
38 HM Government, *Report on the Internal Review of Human Trafficking Legislation*, 3.
39 Lipscombe and Beard, *Human Trafficking*, 25–26.
40 It comprises representatives from the UK government, the Scottish government, the Northern Ireland executive, and the Welsh government.
41 HM Government, *First Annual Report of the Inter-Departmental Ministerial Group*, 46.
42 Ibid., 72.

labour providers in other sectors where migrant workers were exploited. The report also outlined the government's response to the criticism of the border agency's involvement in the NRM process. It claimed that only officials acting under the authority of the Home Secretary, such as the UK Border Agency, have the power to grant leave from immigration controls; thus, the border agency would remain a competent authority. Conclusive ground decisions would be reviewed by a senior caseworker outside the asylum case-working management chain.[43] Despite these changes, the structure and operation of the NRM continued to be criticised for failing to identify and support victims and for a perceived bias against migrants without lawful immigration status.

For the Coalition government, human trafficking was part of the bigger challenge of controlling immigration.[44] Under May, almost every immigration stream was restricted (through caps, stringent eligibility requirements, or both), and many 'low-skill' channels were abolished.[45] She sought to create what she labelled 'a really hostile environment for illegal immigrants' to encourage them to leave the United Kingdom or deter them from entering.[46] While the Labour government had enlisted third parties such as employers and education providers to monitor migrants' visa requirements from within the United Kingdom, May's policy took the unpaid outsourcing of immigration controls to a new level.[47] Two immigration acts, in 2014 and 2016, gave legal expression to the hostile environment policy. The latter was also part of the government's modern slavery governance strategy.

The 2012 reform of the Overseas Domestic Worker (ODW) visa was just one example of the Coalition government's immigration restrictions. But, as we saw in the preceding chapter, this visa programme attracted a great deal of attention because domestic workers and their supporters said it contributed to domestic servitude and modern slavery. Unlike the Labour government, which yielded to a civil society campaign to preserve parts of the ODW visa designed to protect migrant women, the Coalition government stuck to its proposal to abolish the ODW visa or make it more restrictive.[48] In February 2012, it announced it would limit the visa to six months and prohibit ODW visa holders from changing employers while in the United Kingdom, claiming that migrants admitted under the ODW visa now had other forms of

43 Ibid., 82.
44 May, 'Immigration: Home secretary's speech'.
45 Gower, *Immigration and Asylum*.
46 Kirkup and Winnett, 'Theresa May interview'.
47 Griffiths and Yeo, 'The UK's hostile environment', 525.
48 Fudge and Strauss, 'Migrants, unfree labour, and the legal construction'.

protection (such as the NRM).[49] As a result, the protections available to migrant workers on these visas diminished.

Like New Labour, the Coalition government blended criminal prohibitions with immigration restrictions and was grudging when it came to victim protection and labour regulation. Members of Parliament, however, preferred the language of modern slavery to human trafficking and supported a broader range of governance mechanisms.

On the same evening that the IDWG released its first antitrafficking report, the APPG on Human Trafficking marked Antislavery Day by hosting a gathering at the House of Commons in support of a private members bill (modelled after a California law) that would require large corporations to disclose measures they were taking to keep their businesses and supply chains free of forced labour and human trafficking. Michael Connarty, the Labour cochair of the APPG and sponsor of the Transparency in UK Company Supply Chains (Eradication of Slavery) Bill, convened the meeting, attended by about twenty leading faith-based and civil society organisations. The bill was backed by a 'transparency collation', composed of multinational enterprises (including IKEA, Amazon, and ManpowerGroup), ethical investment and shareholder groups, and the Global Business Coalition Against Trafficking (composed of transnational corporations).[50] This initiative was precisely the type the ethical business alliance described in Chapter 2 sought to promote.

At the bill's second reading, Connarty made it clear the proposed law was not about human trafficking, which he equated with immigration, but forced labour, found within the United Kingdom's own domestic food chains.[51] He stressed the bill's support among civil society organisations and transnational businesses and assured Parliament that the bill 'represents a challenge, but not a threat' to companies. The bill's Conservative cosponsor described it as having 'a light touch'.[52] Even free traders who opposed business regulation supported some form of transparency legislation. Referring to 'the proud Christian tradition of opposing slavery in all its forms', Jacob Rees-Mogg, a Eurosceptic Conservative MP, asserted there were robust economic and moral reasons for wanting to avoid slave labour.[53] Despite cross-party support, the bill died on the order table. Later, it would be revived as

[49] Home Office, *Impact Assessment of Changes to ODW visa*, 17.
[50] LeBaron and Rühmkorf, 'The domestic politics of corporate accountability legislation', 730.
[51] Hansard, HC, vol. 551, col., 662, 19 October 2012.
[52] Ibid., col., 663, 667.
[53] Ibid., col., 670.

parliamentarians, NGOs, faith-based organisations, and transnational business sought to shape the Coalition government's modern slavery agenda.

MOBILISING AGAINST MODERN SLAVERY

Released in March 2013, the Centre for Social Justice's report *It Happens Here* put modern slavery law on the government's agenda. Inspired by the new abolitionists, it avoided the issue of prostitution, addressed labour and sexual exploitation, and endorsed a broad range of mechanisms to deal with the different types of slavery.[54] The report recommended a single act to address modern slavery (defined as human trafficking, slavery, servitude, and forced labour) and treated it as a crime and human rights violation. Indeed, it identified 'the widespread misperception that modern slavery is an issue of immigration' as a 'dangerous mistake' that made it hard to identify victims.[55] The report recommended that responsibility for human trafficking move from the minister of immigration to the minister of policing and the elimination of immigration authorities from the NRM's victim-determination process. It called for the establishment of an independent Anti-Slavery Commissioner to launch investigations without ministerial permission and promote victims' interests.

The report's aim was effective enforcement and improved victim identification, protection, and reintegration.[56] Criminal law combined with labour and business regulation was considered the best means to address labour exploitation and modern slavery. Because the GLA played an important role in identifying victims and perpetrators in the fresh-produce supply sector, where it regulated labour providers, the report recommended that its remit be extended to sectors with a high volume of cheap labour.[57] It also proposed allowing ODWs to change employers (and restricting their employment to domestic work).[58]

It Happens Here exemplified the ethical business approach to modern slavery, stressing the need for a framework in which the private sector could

[54] Centre for Social Justice, *It Happens Here*, 33–34. The Modern Slavery Working Group was chaired by Andrew Wallis, director of an antitrafficking victim support charity Unseen, and composed of antislavery campaigners, legal experts, police officers, and migrant and human-trafficking service providers. Kevin Bales, who (as we saw in Chapter 2) was a leading abolitionist, was its adviser.

[55] Ibid., 83.

[56] Ibid., 33–34.

[57] Ibid., 89.

[58] Ibid., 94.

'begin to address the integrity of its supply chains without the fear of public, media or NGO censure'.[59] It supported a transparency law similar to the bill the Centre for Social Justice (CSJ) had helped draft and promote the previous year.

By rebranding 'human trafficking' 'modern slavery', *It Happens Here* appealed to a broader political constituency. That and its provenance explain its influence. The CSJ had impeccable conservative credentials. Set up in 2004 by Iain Duncan-Smith, an influential Conservative who was May's mentor, the centre-right think tank focused on poverty-related social issues: 'while secular in its arguments ... [it] was Christian in tone and hiring'.[60] Christian Guy, the centre's managing director, had previously been David Cameron's adviser. To signal that fighting modern slavery was above party politics, Guy invited Frank Field, a maverick Labour MP and member of the centre's advisory council, to speak at the report's launch.[61]

Together with the CSJ, Field persuaded the home secretary to introduce modern slavery legislation; he commented that May's instincts told her that it was not only right, but it 'would be politically good for her'.[62] According to Fields, the cause was 'universally popular' and nonpartisan.[63] It appealed to Conservative MPs.[64] But instead of introducing a white paper, May launched a new process. She appointed a Modern Slavery Bill Evidence Review Panel and a joint committee, adding two extra stages to an already lengthy legislative process. She sought to cultivate a bipartisan consensus and engage a broad array of stakeholders around the problem of modern slavery, while containing the governance agenda within an elite antislavery policy network. The government made it clear that reforming prostitution law was not on the table.[65]

The elite antislavery network May assembled overshadowed other policy actors. It included individuals who were associated with key nodes such as the APPG, the CSJ, and the Home Office. May appointed Field to chair the Evidence Review Panel and the joint committee. The Human Trafficking Foundation, established by Steen, operated as the APPG's secretariat, organised the witnesses, and the CSJ hosted the hearings. Butler-Sloss, a crossbench

59 Ibid., 209, 212.

60 Cook, 'Christian Tories rewrite party doctrine'.

61 Field's Christian faith inspired his socially conservative values. He resigned from the Labour Party in 2018 and was made crossbench peer by the Conservative government in 2020, after campaigning in favour of Brexit.

62 Field, 'Extension to Michael Dottridge's "How did we get the Modern Slavery Act?"'.

63 Field, 'David Cameron could have been an anti-slavery hero'.

64 Peter Bone, the chair of the APPG, introduced a Slavery Bill much less ambitious than the CSJ had recommended. Hansard, HC, vol. 566, col., 395, 10 July 2013.

65 Robinson, 'The problem with the British government's approach to exploitation'.

peer who cochaired the APPG, was vice-chair of the evidence panel and a member of the joint committee. Steen, former chair of the APPG, was the review's adviser and May's special envoy for combating modern slavery. Andrew Wallis, the CEO of Unseen (an antislavery charity), was the chair of the CSJ's Slavery Working Group and an advocate of supply-chain-transparency legislation; his deputy chair, James Ewins, a barrister associated with the International Justice Mission (an evangelical antislavery organisation), provided support. May's adviser, Fiona Hill, was likewise instrumental in shaping legislation and the government's agenda.

The panel (consisting of Field, Butler-Sloss, and Conservative MP John Randall) heard from academics, NGOs, faith-based organisations, and law enforcement officials. Its report, *Establishing Britain as a World Leader in the Fight against Modern Slavery*, supported the CSJ's recommendations on victim identification and protection, the ODW visa, the independent antislavery commissioner, and transparency legislation. Referring to the evidence of David Arkless, cochair of the Global Business Coalition Against Trafficking (GBCAT), a former executive of ManpowerGroup (which, along with the Qatar Foundation, had funded the CJS's slavery report), and a leader of the 'transparency coalition', the panel claimed business supported the move beyond voluntary measures.[66] Although the panel supported mandatory initiatives over voluntary ones to address forced labour in supply chains, it insisted 'that any such legislation must be pro-business'. It recommended legislation similar to the 2012 transparency bill sponsored by Connarty.[67]

The review panel avoided the issue of prostitution's relationship to exploitation.[68] To address labour exploitation, it recommended moving the GLA from the department responsible for agriculture to the Home Office and expanding it into sectors such as construction and catering where contractors engaged in exploitative practices. It asked the joint committee to consider whether the GLA's power should extend beyond licence violations to the more serious offence of forced labour (workers' advocates feared the reform might detract from the GLA's work ensuring that labour contractors observe basic labour standards).[69] The panel also emphasised augmenting state coercive power by increasing the penalties for serious offences from fourteen years to life, using orders to prevent modern slavery offenders from entering the United Kingdom, and extending the United Kingdom's jurisdiction to

66 Modern Slavery Bill Evidence Review, *Establishing Britain as a World Leader*, 33.
67 Ibid., 46.
68 Ibid., 42. It recommended that the antislavery commissioner address the demand for modern slavery, including the domestic market for prostitution, and make recommendations.
69 Ibid., 19.

prosecute British citizens for modern slavery offences committed outside British territory.[70]

On 16 December 2013, the day the review panel released its report, the home secretary introduced a white paper, which included the Modern Day Slavery Bill, in Parliament. May wanted the bill to make it onto the 2014 legislative agenda and promised to introduce a second bill in May 2014 after the joint committee reported on the first bill. As a gesture towards the CSJ's recommendation that modern slavery be separated from immigration, May authorised the police and security minister to shepherd the bill through Parliament. She cautioned that modern slavery should not be conflated with 'immigration crime' but stated that there 'will often be an immigration crime angle'.[71]

The Modern Slavery Bill was lodged in criminal law, and its goal was to boost the state's coercive power. Applying only to England and Wales, it consolidated the offences of slavery, forced labour, and servitude and human trafficking. It increased the maximum sentence from fourteen years to life and introduced slavery and trafficking-prevention orders (which applied to individuals convicted of a trafficking offence) and slavery and trafficking risk orders (for those not convicted but considered a risk to others). Modelled on sexual offence prevention orders, these civil powers allowed courts to prevent individuals from participating in particular types of businesses, operating as gangmasters, visiting a particular place, working with children, or travelling to specified countries for specified periods of time. The antislavery commissioner's independence and mandate were more limited than the review panel had recommended. The bill provided little in terms of victim protection or revisions to the NRM, which were postponed until the review was completed. Thus, the NRM was not subjected to parliamentary scrutiny. The white paper also put supply chain legislation and extending the GLA's remit on the back burner. It ignored the ODW visa altogether.

Before the bill went to the joint committee for review, the political lines were drawn. The review panel supported using the criminal law against slave traders, but it also stressed victim protection, light-touch business regulation, and labour regulation. The government's sole concern was increasing criminal-law enforcement and penalties. As the bill wound its way through review, the government kept its coercive elements and the Opposition made compromises on what it would accept in terms of business and labour regulation.

70 Ibid., 29, 32–33.

71 Home Office, *Draft Modern Slavery Bill*, Foreword.

Field chaired the joint committee, composed of, and advised by, several members of the elite antislavery network.[72] It published its report and a bill on 8 April.[73] The joint committee repeated many of the review panel's recommendations but dialled back its proposals for business and labour regulation. British retailers opposed a full-scale transparency act in favour of adding modern slavery to the list of social, community, and human rights issues companies were required to report on annually under the Companies Act 2006, as required by the EU's 2014 nonfinancial disclosure directive (as discussed in Chapter 4). The joint committee opted for this weak form of transparency obligation.[74] Noting that the government was restricting the GLA's remit and that the GLA's resources were already overstretched, it recommended that the government review rather than extend the GLA.[75]

The government's response came on 10 June 2014, the same day it introduced the Modern Slavery Bill. The bill was virtually identical to the 2013 draft but with minor amendments that nodded towards victim protection. Throughout the lengthy legislative process, the government opposed amendments and debate claiming that this was necessary so the bill could be enacted before the May 2015 election.[76]

In the meantime, the government consolidated antislavery governance in the Home Office. In 2014, the GLA was brought under the Home Office's authority, and the post of minister for preventing abuse, exploitation, and crime, with direct responsibility for driving the modern slavery governance agenda, was created under the home secretary. Karen Bradley was appointed and shepherded the modern slavery bill through Parliament. The government also released its first modern slavery strategy.[77]

Both May and Field cultivated a faith-based antislavery coalition. May announced the formation of 'Santa Marta Group' while attending an

[72] The joint committee was composed of seven members drawn from each house and included members of the review panel and the APPG, who were assisted by specialist advisers and staff involved in the CSJ and review panel reports.

[73] House of Lords, House of Commons, Joint Committee on the Draft Modern Slavery Bill Report.

[74] Ibid., 91. See also LeBaron and Rühmkorf, 'The domestic politics of corporate accountability legislation'.

[75] Ibid., 93. In 2013, the government moved forestry from the licensing regime.

[76] Craig, 'The UK's modern slavery legislation', 21. The Modern Slavery Bill was introduced in the House of Commons on 10 June 2014 and received its second reading on 8 July. The bill was examined by a Public Bill Committee before receiving both its report stage and third reading on 4 November. It was introduced in the House of Lords on 5 November and received its second reading on 17 November. It completed its final stage on 4 March 2015. After ping pong, the bill received royal assent on 26 March 2015.

[77] Home Office, *Modern Slavery Strategy 2014*, 8, 58.

international antislavery conference in the Vatican organised by Catholic bishops and the London Metropolitan police. Cofounded by Kevin Hyland, soon to be appointed by May as the United Kingdom's first independent antislavery commissioner, the group was composed of police chiefs and bishops from around the world committed to working with civil society to combine vigorous criminal law enforcement with pastoral care for victims.[78] Writing in a right-leaning weekly magazine, Field called on Prime Minister Cameron to support an amendment to require businesses to report their efforts to keep their supply chains free of modern slavery. Field summoned the churches – 'Anglican, Roman Catholic, and Nonconformist' – 'to draw inspiration from the great Christian abolitionist, William Wilberforce, and galvanise their followers to stamp out slavery' by targeting marginal seats in the upcoming election.[79] Other faith-based groups rallied around the bill.[80] Once it became law, faith-based antislavery organisations proliferated.[81]

As the bill moved through Parliament, the government faced mounting pressure for greater protection for victims and noncriminal forms of regulation to address forced labour and labour exploitation. It made minor concessions, but it ignored the APPG's recommendation to criminalise the purchase of sexual services to prevent trafficking.[82] In the end, the bill's criminal-law provisions, which made up most of the legislation, remained virtually intact.

Despite the tribute the home secretary paid to 'the campaigners, organisations, and Parliamentarians of all parties' who shined 'a light on this hidden crime', the law, which she described as a 'historic milestone', fell well short of what the review panel and campaigners had recommended.[83] The Modern Slavery Act 2015 (MSA) provides for two general offences: (1) slavery, servitude, and forced or compulsory labour and (2) human trafficking. The first offence is defined according to Article 4 of the European Convention on Human Rights (ECHR), which brings the European Court of Human Right's Article 4 jurisprudence (which relies, in turn, on ILO instruments and the observations of ILO supervisory bodies) into the definition. 'Human trafficking' covers sexual and nonsexual exploitation, and 'exploitation' includes situations involving trafficking for the purposes of slavery, servitude, forced

78 May, 'A model that works'.

79 Field, 'David Cameron could have been an anti-slavery hero'.

80 Unseen (founded by Andrew Wallis) and Justice and Care (Christian Guy, CEO), both set up in 2008, supported by the bill.

81 Waite et al., 'Faith, bordering and modern slavery', 3; Turnbull and Broad, 'Bringing the problem home'.

82 APPG on Prostitution and the Global Sex Trade, *Behind Closed Doors*, 21.

83 Home Office, 'Historic law to end Modern Slavery passed'.

or compulsory labour, sexual exploitation, the removal of organs, securing services by force, threats, or deception, and securing services from children and other vulnerable persons. Consent does not preclude the offence from having taken place, and personal circumstances (such as a family relationship and mental or physical illness) that make a person more vulnerable may be considered relevant. 'Trafficking for labour' and 'sexual exploitation' are treated differently, as the former always requires coercion and intent, whereas the latter does not. Despite repeated urgings, the government refused to introduce a crime of labour exploitation in which coercion does not figure.[84]

The MSA increased sentences for serious offenders and provided a wide range of enforcement tools, including confiscation and forfeiture orders.[85] Maritime enforcement orders empower officers to stop, board, divert, and detain UK ships operating in England and Wales waters, foreign waters, or international waters and a foreign ship in England and Wales waters. The slavery and trafficking prevention and risk orders also give courts wide-ranging powers to restrict individuals convicted or at risk of committing a modern slavery or human trafficking offence for a minimum period of five and two years, respectively.[86]

Although Field, members of the APPG, and NGOs championed victim protection, the government resisted enshrining victims' rights. It refused to make legal aid available to individuals entering the NRM process, to provide a civil remedy to victims, or to put the NRM on a statutory basis. But it did include a new defence for slavery or trafficking victims who commit a crime, protections for victims who are witnesses in criminal proceedings, civil legal aid for victims confirmed through the NRM process, and independent child trafficking advocates.[87]

In the struggle over the independence and mandate of the antislavery commissioner, the government retained the power to approve the commissioner's strategic plan, but its power to redact the commissioner's annual report was limited, and the commissioner's authority was extended from enforcement to include victim identification.[88]

The government's biggest concession was section 54 of the MSA, which required companies to provide an annual statement on their efforts, if any, to

84 Robinson, 'Claiming space for labour rights', 136–137.

85 The MSA increased the maximum sentence for most serious offenders from fourteen years to life; those with previous convictions for a specific sexual or violent offence face an automatic life sentence.

86 Haynes, 'The Modern Slavery Act (2015)', 41–45.

87 MSA 2015, ss. 43–51.

88 Haynes, 'The Modern Slavery Act (2015)', 45–47.

eradicate modern slavery from their business or supply chains. The government overcame its opposition to imposing a disclosure obligation after the British Retail Consortium wrote to the prime minister to press for it.[89] Nothing in the MSA obliges an organisation to specify the steps it may have taken and whether they were effective and there is no penalty for nondisclosure. Nor does the MSA provide a central registry of modern slavery statements or any type of third-party oversight. The only enforcement mechanism is via an application by the secretary of state for an injunction to compel an organisation to disclose. But even these weak transparency provisions were considered a victory by advocates of supply chain regulation because of the government's previous opposition to even such light-touch business regulation.

Pressure from the Lords resulted in two concessions from the government on the ODW visa. The Modern Slavery Bill was amended to permit workers on ODW visas determined by the NRM to be victims of slavery or human trafficking to stay in the United Kingdom for a minimum of six months, during which time they are entitled to change employers so long as they remain employed as a domestic worker in a private household.[90] The government also appointed Ewins, a member of the elite antislavery policy network, to evaluate the impact of restricting ODW visas to a single employer and report by July 2015.

The government continued to resist labour regulation as a method for tackling exploitation. NGOs pushed to have the GLA's licensing provisions expanded to several low-wage sectors and called for a comprehensive labour inspection and enforcement system.[91] Labour MPs tabled a series of amendments in the Commons to require the government to review the GLA's remit and, based on the review, extend it where necessary, which garnered some support from Conservative backbenchers. The Lords supported measures to tackle labour exploitation and an amendment calling for a review of the GLA's remit and resources. The government suggested that the GLA could take on the issue of serious labour exploitation. In the end, the government committed to a paper on the role of the GLA, involving 'an amorphous consultation' that offered an 'opportunity to further divert the GLA from its labour inspection role towards crime control or immigration enforcement'.[92]

89 Berman, 'Shaping the Modern Slavery Act'; LeBaron and Rühmkorf, 'The domestic politics of corporate accountability legislation'.

90 MSA, s. 53.

91 For example, FLEX (Focus on Labour Exploitation), Forced Labour Monitoring Group, Joseph Rowntree Foundation, Trade Union Congress.

92 Robinson, 'Claiming space for labour rights', 138.

Although there was little in the MSA about immigration, it figured in the government's antislavery agenda. The CSJ's second report, written by Fiona Hill (between her stints as May's political adviser in the Home Office and chief of the prime minister's staff), *A Modern Approach to Modern Slavery*, released between the MSA's royal assent on March 26 and the general election on 7 May 2015, anticipated a return to modern slavery being seen as an offshoot of illegal immigration. The report urged European lawmakers to follow Britain and substitute 'modern slavery' for 'human trafficking'.[93] In her foreword, the home secretary praised the report for making it clear that modern slavery 'is a cross-border crime that needs law enforcement in different countries to work together to disrupt and defeat these organised crime groups'.[94] The report called on police and immigration officials across the EU to take a 'joined-up strategic approach' to investigate and prosecute 'organized crime hidden in the immigration system'.[95] The goal was to create 'a hostile environment' for slave traders.[96]

ILLEGAL WORKING AND LABOUR MARKET EXPLOITATION

The Conservative Party's 2015 election manifesto linked modern slavery to exploitation, unscrupulous employers, and illegal working and called for greater labour market regulation.[97] Together with the Immigration Act 2016, the MSA created an integrated regime for dealing with labour exploitation, from chronic violations of labour standards to modern slavery offences.[98]

During the election campaign, both the Conservative and Labour Parties promised to reduce low-skilled migrant workers and to toughen labour market regulation to prevent labour exploitation and illegal work.[99] After winning a majority, the Conservative government deepened and extended the hostile environment for illegal migrants, stressing the connection between labour-market exploitation and illegal migration. In his 21 May 2015 'high-profile' speech on immigration, Prime Minister Cameron identified 'gangmasters' who lure migrant workers to the United Kingdom and then exploit them and businesses by bringing in 'cheap labour that undercuts the wages of local

93 Centre for Social Justice, *A Modern Approach to Modern Slavery*, 10.
94 Ibid., 7.
95 Ibid., 42.
96 Ibid., 10.
97 The Conservative Party Manifesto 2015, *A Strong Leadership*, 31.
98 Fudge, 'Modern slavery, unfree labour and the labour market', 426–429.
99 Bale, 'Putting it right?', 300.

people'.[100] He promised to create 'a new enforcement agency that cracks down on the worst cases of exploitation'.[101]

The Immigration Act 2014 required landlords and banks to check the immigration status of their tenants or clients and prohibited them from providing services to illegal immigrants. The 2015 immigration bill, designed 'to tackle illegal immigration by making it harder to live and work illegally in the United Kingdom', made it a criminal offence to fail to check immigration status.[102] Doctors, landlords, employers, and others were conscripted to conduct immigration checks, moving bordering practices deep inside the United Kingdom. Unless 'lawful' immigration status could be established, an individual would be denied access to employment, education, housing, health care, driving licences, marriage, and financial services.[103] Requiring private actors to police migrants' 'status' inculcates behaviour in one group by requiring them to help to police another. Because lawful migrant status is often difficult to determine (there are a variety of different visa statuses with different rules, and people can slip from one status to another for a variety of reasons), ethnicity or holding a British passport, as many predicted, came to function as proxies for individuals who did not meet the idea of 'white Britishness'.[104]

The government tabled the immigration bill in September 2015, in time for it to be enacted before the referendum on the EU. In the background papers, consultation documents, and debates, the government blamed organised criminal groups who preyed on vulnerable migrant workers for labour exploitation. It also regarded migrants who chose to work without employment authorisation as bearing some responsibility, since 'illegal working encourages illegal immigration, undercuts legitimate businesses, and is often associated with exploitation'.[105] According to the home secretary, it was necessary to treat illegal working as a criminal offence in order 'to seize and confiscate the profits made by those who choose to break our immigration laws'.[106] She

[100] Cameron, 'PM speech on immigration'.
[101] Ibid.
[102] Fudge, 'Illegal working', 571.
[103] Griffiths and Yeo, 'The UK's hostile environment'.
[104] El-Enany, *Bordering Britain*, 20. An internal Home Office review of what later was renamed the 'compliant' environment found that the hostile-environment policy had a 'meaningful differential impact' on the basis of race and nationality, but that the policy was 'a proportionate means of achieving legitimate aim, rational, fair and reasonable because it is based on the existing framework and legislation underpinning immigration control in the UK'. Home Office, 'Overarching equality impact assessment [EIA]', 24, 25.
[105] Fudge, 'Illegal working', 571.
[106] Hansard, HC, vol. 603, col. 269, 1 December 2015.

assured Parliament that the vulnerable, 'such as those who are trafficked here and forced to work illegally', would not be punished because safeguards provided in the MSA will protect them.[107] Protection would be offered, but only to migrants without lawful immigration status who the NRM confirmed as victims.

On the bill's second reading, on 13 October 2015, its two sponsors, the Department for Business Innovation and Skills and the Home Office, released a consultation document 'Tackling Exploitation in the Labour Market', which the government treated as fulfilling its obligation to review the GLA. The government would deal with all forms of forced labour and abuses of employment law to protect 'local workers and responsible businesses affected by those prepared to exploit cheap labour'. Tackling labour market exploitation was as much about creating a level playing field for business as it was about enforcing workers' rights.[108]

The document presented a limited menu of recommendations: introduce a new offence – aggravated breach of labour-market legislation; create a new statutory Office of Director of Labour Market Enforcement (ODLME) to develop a labour-market strategy and coordinate the enforcement activities of the three labour-market-enforcement agencies;[109] strengthen information sharing between the enforcement agencies; and expand the GLA's remit. A central labour standards enforcement agency was off the table.[110]

In January 2016, the government released its response. Although there was broad agreement that a new offence was needed to address labour exploitation that fell short of the coercive behaviour required under the MSA offences, the government decided to create a new type of enforcement order supported by a criminal offence for noncompliance to tackle the exploitation of workers. While the ODLME received broad support, intelligence sharing and reforming the GLA polarised the respondents. Some expressed concern that

[107] Ibid.

[108] Fudge, 'Illegal working', 571.

[109] The three agencies are HM Revenue and Customs (HMRC), responsible for the enforcement of holiday pay and National Minimum and National Living Wage; the GLA, later the GLAA; and the Employment Agency Standards Inspectorate (EAS), responsible for the enforcement of the Employment Agencies Act 1973 and other regulations that apply to recruitment and employment agencies.

[110] In its 2019 report on modern slavery, the Johnson government announced a review of the existing labour-market-enforcement landscape to ensure that workers' rights were protected and businesses were supported to comply with the law. It published a consultation to consider the case for establishing a new enforcement body for employment rights in July 2019 and closed the consultations in October. UK, *2019 UK Annual Report on Modern Slavery*, 20. As of the end of December 2023, there was still no initiative introducing a single labour-enforcement agency.

information sharing with immigration officials could deter undocumented workers at risk of labour exploitation from reporting labour standards violations for fear of being prosecuted for 'illegal working'. Most respondents considered the GLA's licensing regime to be effective, and the majority thought the GLA's role should be expanded to other sectors and licensing criteria updated. Several feared that a grant of police powers and a new mandate to enforce the MSA would transform the GLA from an agency that used licensing to enforce labour standards to one that used criminal law to target a narrow range of egregious forms of labour abuse.[111]

During the immigration bill's final stage in the Lords, peers mounted a last-ditch attempt to implement changes to the ODW visa, as recommended in the Ewins report. Released in December 2015, the report stated that workers with an ODW visa should be permitted to change employers for any reason during their initial six-month stay in the United Kingdom and to extend their visa for a further two years.[112] A universal right to change employers would, according to Ewins, give abused workers a practical way out without risking either a precarious immigration status or loss of income; a maximum stay of two and a half years was the minimum period required for the effective protection of abused ODWs. The government accepted Ewins's recommendation that workers on ODW visas be allowed to change employers but rejected the suggestion that all ODWs should be able to extend their stay in the United Kingdom by a further two years. It expressed concern that workers would be less likely to report abuse if they could change employers *and* extend their stay in the United Kingdom. The government changed the Immigration Rules in March 2016 to permit ODWs to change employers during their six-month visa; however, only those workers identified as victims of slavery would have leave to remain for up to two years as domestic workers (but with no access to public funds). The Commons supported the government and rejected the Lords' proposed amendment.[113]

On 16 May 2016, three weeks before the Brexit referendum, the Immigration Act 2016 received royal assent. The Act made 'illegal working' a crime, empowered state officials to seize the wages of illegal workers, imposed criminal sanctions on employers who had reasonable cause to believe an individual did not have the right to work in the UK, and empowered the government to close workplaces that engaged or had engaged

[111] Fudge, 'Illegal working', 572.
[112] Ewins, *Independent Review of the Overseas Domestic Workers Visa.*
[113] Gower, 'Calls to change overseas domestic worker visa conditions'.

illegal workers.[114] By making illegal working a crime, the government closed the only avenue available to undocumented workers to enforce employment-related rights – anti-discrimination law.[115]

The Immigration Act 2016 also expanded the remit of the GLA, reborn as the Gangmasters Labour Abuse Authority (GLAA), and increased its powers.[116] The GLAA's mission was to prevent, detect, and investigate worker exploitation across all labour sectors, not just in the regulated sectors of agriculture, food, and food processing (where the GLAA continues to license labour providers and set standards). It has the authority to enforce MSA offences, and labour abuse prevention officers, who have investigatory powers under the Police and Criminal Evidence Act, were created for that purpose.[117] The GLAA was also given authority to enforce the offence-related provisions of the Employment Agencies Act 1973 and the Minimum Wage Act 1998 against more serious or persistent offenders and to use its new labour-market-enforcement undertakings and orders. The Act established the ODLME to direct the three organisations responsible for regulating the UK labour market and to determine how to enforce noncompliance across a spectrum, from occasional and unintentional to severe exploitation.

As those who favoured regulating labour to prevent exploitation feared, the Immigration Act 2016 shifted the GLAA away from licensing labour providers to ensure they met basic labour standards to tackling modern slavery and more egregious forms of labour exploitation.[118] The GLAA focused on modern slavery offences instead of using its new enforcement powers to pursue businesses that violate labour standards.[119] Indeed, David Metcalf, the director of labour market enforcement, expressed concern that the GLAA's jurisdiction over modern slavery was 'beginning to crowd out their licensing work'.[120]

Operations to rescue victims of labour exploitation can now be transformed into raids to detect illegal workers. A series of raids targeting modern slavery in

[114] Fudge, 'Illegal working', 572–575. The Immigration Act 2016 also created an incentive for employers to denounce illegal migrant workers to mitigate their own wrongdoing. Bales, 'Immigration raids, employer collusion', 279.

[115] Ibid., 573–574; Guild and Barylska, 'Decent work for migrants?', 295.

[116] Fudge, 'Illegal working', 578–579.

[117] The GLAA can ask assistance from a chief constable, the Director of the National Crime Agency or an immigration officer, and chief constables and immigration officers can ask, but not require, the GLAA to assist them.

[118] Fudge, 'Illegal working'; Guild and Barylska, 'Decent work for migrants?', 285; and Davies, 'Criminological reflections on the regulation and governance', 73.

[119] Barnard and Fraser Butlin, 'Why are criminal offences criminal in labour law?', 90; HM Government, *2018 UK Annual Report on Modern Slavery*, 28.

[120] Metcalf, *United Kingdom Labour Market Enforcement Strategy 2019/20*, 80. This shift in enforcement occurred despite the GLAA's expanded budget and jurisdiction.

nail bars bore many similarities to raids on massage parlours to rescue migrant women from sexual exploitation (see Chapter 5). Not only were the nail bar raids gendered (female Vietnamese nationals were targeted), but many more individuals who were 'rescued' were charged with immigration offences than identified as victims of slavery.[121]

By inserting labour-market-enforcement provisions within the Immigration Act, the government cemented the connection between illegal working and labour exploitation and shifted the GLAA away from forms of labour regulation like licensing (treated as a burden on business) to the enforcement of criminal offences. It even rejected the ODLME's recommendation for a geographically limited pilot of mandatory licensing of nail bars and car handwashes, marginal sectors in the UK economy that the independent antitrafficking commissioner had identified as being riddled with modern slavery; it insisted instead on trying out a voluntary system.[122] The government resisted new forms of labour and business regulation to prevent the full spectrum of labour exploitation.[123]

GLOBAL LEADER IN THE FIGHT AGAINST MODERN SLAVERY?

Modern slavery was a critical component of May's governance agenda. Within a month of taking office, she marked the first anniversary of the MSA by publishing an article in the *Telegraph* (a Conservative-oriented broadsheet) affirming her government's commitment to fighting modern slavery.[124] The landmark MSA was simply the beginning. May announced that she would be setting up a task force on modern slavery to coordinate and drive government efforts. She also set out her government's priorities: (1) making sure the MSA was prosecuting slave drivers, (2) collaborating with law enforcement agencies around the world to track and stop these criminal 'gangs who operate across borders and jurisdictions', and (3) continuing to 'lead this fight on the global

[121] Balch, 'Defeating "modern slavery", reducing exploitation?', 86.

[122] Metcalf, *UK Labour Market Enforcement Strategy 2018/19*, 101–192. Department for Business, Energy and Industrial Strategy and Home Office, *Government Response*. The government postponed considering procurement and other mechanisms to promote compliance in domestic supply chains until after consultation. In March 2020, the government published its first modern slavery statement, and in 2021 ministerial departments began publishing individual modern slavery statements. While a central registry was introduced by the government in March 2021, companies were not required to submit their modern slavery statements to it.

[123] UK, *2019 UK Annual Report on Modern Slavery*, 20.

[124] May, 'My Government will lead the way in defeating modern slavery'.

stage'.[125] The strategy was received differently by global and domestic audiences.

Under May's leadership, the United Kingdom became a key node in the global antislavery governance network. The United Kingdom vigorously promoted tackling modern slavery on a global scale and played a leading role in making the eradication of modern slavery a Sustainable Development Goal.[126] At the UN General Assembly in September 2017, May launched a Call to Action to End Forced Labour, Modern Slavery, and Human Trafficking. The government also cultivated ties with leading antislavery philanthrocapitalists and the ethical business alliance. Indeed, May invited Andrew Forrest of Walk Free to the UN gathering of world leaders.[127] Strengthening its connections with the other members of the Anglosphere (Australia, Canada, New Zealand, and the United States), the United Kingdom brokered an agreement on four principles to tackle modern slavery in global supply chains: (1) encourage business to address modern slavery in supply chains, (2) tackle modern slavery in public procurement processes, (3) advance responsible recruitment practices, and (4) harmonise laws and policies across jurisdictions. In tandem with Walk Free, May promoted antislavery policy among the members of the Commonwealth, the institutional remnant of Britain's former empire.[128] In 2019, she appointed an international migration and modern slavery envoy to help coordinate the United Kingdom's antislavery efforts with other nations. Tellingly, she linked modern slavery to international migration in the envoy's responsibilities.

The United Kingdom used its economic muscle to shape the modern slavery strategy internationally. In 2017, May doubled aid spending on modern slavery to £150 million and increased it to £200 million in 2018.[129] While some of the aid targeted high-risk countries (such as Nigeria) where victims are regularly trafficked to the United Kingdom, £20 million in seed funding went to the Global Fund to End Modern Slavery, a project of the ethical business alliance and another node in the global antislavery governance network (see Chapter 2). The United Kingdom's efforts to address

[125] Ibid.

[126] Gadd and Broad, 'Troubling recognitions'.

[127] Hewett, 'Andrew Forrest and the fight against slavery'; Robertson, 'A mining billionaire takes his war'.

[128] Walk Free, *Towards a common future*; Guilbert, 'Taking UK's lead'.

[129] The Independent Commission for Aid Impact, *The UK's Approach to Tackling Modern Slavery*, 41.

modern slavery were ranked at the top of Walk Free's 2019 *Measurement, Freedom, Action* index of government responses.[130]

The Conservative Party's 2017 election manifesto made much of the United Kingdom's modern slavery strategy, describing the United Kingdom as 'a global leader in fighting the evil trade in human beings – both around the world and in our own country – for sex and labour exploitation'.[131] It promoted the MSA as the first of its kind in Europe and promised to use the United Kingdom's power to push the UN to make modern slavery a thing of the past. However, the snap election backfired; instead of strengthening her hand in the Brexit negotiations, it cost May her government's parliamentary majority, and she had to negotiate a confidence-and-supply agreement with the very conservative Democratic Unionist Party (DUP) based in Northern Ireland. She was faced with a fractious Parliament disgruntled with the slow speed of Brexit negotiations.

The UK was celebrated as a global leader in the fight against modern slavery, but its strategy attracted a great deal of criticism domestically. In 2017, an independent review issued the first in a series of critical reports by government agencies and parliamentary committees.[132] It found inconsistencies between law enforcement and criminal justice agencies and poor-quality intelligence at all levels. A report by Her Majesty's Inspectorate of Constabulary, Fire Rescue Services (HMICFRS) the same year identified the police's lack of knowledge of modern slavery, ineffective investigations, and referral of potential victims to immigration authorities as problems.[133] In December 2017, the National Audit Office (NAO) criticised the Home Office's lack of strategic action, the absence of effective indicators for measuring progress despite extensive public spending on policing operations, the NRM's failure to identify and support victims, and the failure to monitor businesses' efforts to rid their supply chains of modern slavery.[134] In May 2018, a follow-up report by the Public Accounts Committee confirmed the NOA's criticisms and issued a series of recommendations, which the government accepted.[135] That month, Kevin Hyland, the first independent antislavery commissioner resigned, citing government interference.[136] In July 2018, the government commissioned an independent review of the

[130] Walk Free Foundation, *Measurement, Freedom, Action*, 32, 88.
[131] The Conservative and Unionist Party Manifesto 2017, *Forward, Together*, 42.
[132] UK Home Office, *The Modern Slavery Act Review*.
[133] HMICFRS, *Stolen Freedom*, 13, 38.
[134] National Audit Office, *Reducing Modern Slavery*.
[135] HC Committee of Public Accounts, *Reducing Modern Slavery*.
[136] Dearden, 'UK's first Independent anti-slavery commissioner resigns'.

MSA by members of Parliament, and it appointed the usual suspects, Fields and Butler-Sloss, who were joined by Maria Miller (a Conservative MP). Several of the review's advisers were drawn from the elite antislavery epistemic network.[137] The review had a broad mandate; its report was laid before Parliament on 22 May 2019.[138]

The Home Office's research contributed to the idea that modern slavery was a widespread and pressing social problem. It released a series of reports on the extent of modern slavery in the United Kingdom (2014), a typology of modern slavery offences (2017), and their economic costs (2018). The Home Office's chief scientific adviser estimated that there had been between 10,000 and 13,000 cases of modern slavery in 2013.[139] Seventeen types of modern slavery offences under four broad categories (labour exploitation, domestic servitude, social exploitation, and criminal exploitation) were identified using NRM data.[140] The total cost of modern slavery in the United Kingdom in the year ending March 2017 was estimated to be between £3.3 and £4.3 billion.[141] These estimates, based on intelligence reports rather than confirmed crimes, made the 'dark figure' of modern slavery visible.[142]

The hidden nature of the crime was used to explain the discrepancy between estimates and the number of prosecutions and convictions for modern slavery offences.[143] The number of prosecutions peaked in 2017 at 132 and decreased to 68 in 2019. Convictions under the MSA reached a high of 40 in 2019. The average custodial sentence for those convicted was thirty-six months, a far cry from the maximum life sentence.[144] Yet, instead of raising doubt about the extent and nature of the problem of modern slavery, the tiny number of prosecutions was seen as evidence of the need for additional resources to detect and pursue the hidden crime.[145]

Given the breadth of offences and the flexibility given to police and prosecutors to operationalise a broad definition of modern slavery, the low level of prosecutions and convictions is surprising. Modern slavery offences include the sexual abuse of children in care, forced and sham marriages,

[137] HM Government, *Independent Review of the Modern Slavery Act 2015*; Steen and Guy were among the seven advisers.

[138] Ibid., 11.

[139] Silverman, *Modern Slavery*.

[140] Cooper et al., *A Typology of Modern Slavery Offences*.

[141] Reed et al., 'The economic and social costs of modern slavery'. These costs covered prevention and protection measures and law enforcement and criminal justice.

[142] Broad and Gadd, *Demystifying Modern Slavery*, 29–30.

[143] Office for National Statistics, *Modern Slavery in the UK: March 2020*, 2.

[144] Broad and Gadd, *Demystifying Modern Slavery*, 31–32.

[145] Ibid., 5.

domestic servitude, coerced cannabis cultivation, forced labour exploitation, and assisting the movement of adults involved in prostitution within and across national borders, crimes 'few criminologists would suggest share common causes or solutions'.[146] The definition suited the government as it is 'sufficiently flexible to include emerging forms of modern slavery, such as county lines', which frequently involves children, who are used by gangs to transport drugs and money to and from urban areas to suburban areas and market and coastal towns.[147] This flexibility enabled the government to use the MSA's extensive enforcement powers against a wide range of behaviour not typically associated with modern slavery. It also helps to explain the increased number of victims referred under the NRM.

The NRM is a critical, and much-maligned, component of the government's modern slavery system. It has two functions. The first is epistemological: providing authoritative data about victims of modern slavery in the United Kingdom. The other is normative: determining victim status, which is the gateway to victim support. The NRM sorts people into categories with different legal statuses. First responders, ranging from NGOs to the police, refer people who they suspect to be victims to the NRM. After a person is referred, there is a two-step victim-determination process – first, to decide whether there are reasonable grounds to believe the person is a victim of modern slavery and, second, to determine whether there are conclusive grounds. An individual who has received a positive-ground decision has access to state-funded support, provided by charities, for a minimum of forty-five days while the case is worked on and at least until a conclusive decision has been made.[148]

The NRM process has many problems. The first is selection bias. First responders make the referrals, and they must filter out 'real slaves' who are coerced from those whose labour rights are violated.[149] UK Visa and Immigrations and the police provide the largest number of referrals (about 30 per cent each in 2018). Typically, immigration officials identify potential victims in the context of asylum claims. Policing practices, priorities, and

[146] Gadd and Broad, 'Troubling recognitions', 1449.

[147] HM Government, *Independent Review of the Modern Slavery Act 2015*, 17; HM Government, *The UK Government Response to the Independent Review of the Modern Slavery Act 2015*, 17.

[148] In 2018, the High Court ruled that the Home Office's practice of limiting victim support to a maximum of forty-five days was unlawful and incompatible with the European Convention Against Trafficking (Articles 11 and 12). The government conceded that support should be given to victims of modern slavery in line with their needs and not stopped after a specified period. Hodal, 'High Court suspends Home Office policy'; Lewis and Waite, 'Migrant illegality, slavery and exploitative work', 233–234.

[149] Strauss, 'Sorting victims from workers', 153; and Aliverti, 'Law in the margins', 11.

resources influence the numbers and types of victims who the police refer to the NRM; in 2017, for example, police began to refer county-line victims. This change in policing practice increased the number of child victims and influenced the composition of modern slavery offences.[150] Between 2013 and 2018, the number of victim referrals to the NRM increased from 1,745 to 6,993, and the most common form of exploitation reported by victims was labour exploitation (52 per cent) followed by sexual exploitation (33 per cent). But what counts as category labour exploitation or forced labour is not obvious. In 2018, 47 per cent (1,868) of the 3,990 victims of forced labour were also described as victims of forced criminality, like county lines. As the numbers increased, the system became backlogged – in 2018 over half (3,867) of the decisions were pending. Of those decided, 24 per cent received both a positive reasonable and conclusive grounds decision.[151]

A second problem with the NRM was structural bias against unauthorised migrants, an outgrowth of Visa and Immigration being able to determine victim status for individuals who were neither EU nor UK citizens or UK permanent residents. In the first tranche of referrals in 2009, the Antitrafficking Monitoring Group found that there were much higher rates of conclusive grounds decisions for EU and UK nationals than for third-country citizens, a pattern confirmed by subsequent research.[152] There was also a bias against nationals from certain countries. Despite Albania and Nigeria being the two countries with the greatest overall number of citizen referrals for 2014, their portion of conclusive decisions was among the lowest, at 2 and 10 per cent, respectively.[153] The NMR tends to treat potential victims like illegal migrants. In 2018, 507 victims of human trafficking were in detention even though they had received a 'positive reasonable grounds' decision.[154]

To address these widespread criticisms, in 2019 a single unit in the Home Office was created to determine victim status, and an independent expert panel was appointed to review all negative conclusive-ground decisions.[155] However, without statutory footing, the NRM would remain an executive-led policy with no appeal rights and only limited judicial review.[156]

150 HM Government, *2019 Report on Modern Slavery*, 9–11.
151 Ibid., 8–10.
152 Strauss, 'Sorting victims from workers'; Fudge, 'Why labour lawyers should care about the Modern Slavery Act 2015', 382–384.
153 Strauss, 'Sorting victims from workers', 151.
154 Labour Exploitation Advisory Group, *Detaining Victims*, 34.
155 HM Government, *2019 Report on Modern Slavery*, 6.
156 Currie, 'Compounding vulnerability and concealing unfairness', 498.

The government consistently opposed increasing the protection offered to victims of modern slavery. In April 2017, the Work and Pensions Committee (chaired by Frank Field) released a report, *Victims of Modern Slavery*, championing victim support. The committee found that denial of public benefits to victims and the difficulty of obtaining leave to remain in the United Kingdom undermined victim protection and reintegration.[157] It urged the government to provide victims of slavery at least one year's leave to remain and access to public benefits. But the government preferred the status quo where leave is granted only when there are compelling circumstances that justify it.[158] It claimed that automatic leave and benefits would 'incentivis[e] individuals to make false trafficking claims in an attempt to fraudulently obtain leave to remain or delay removals'.[159]

Although proclaimed world-leading by international actors, on the home front the supply-chain-transparency provisions of the MSA were considered virtually ineffective.[160] Section 54 requires commercial organisations that carry out business in the United Kingdom, have a total turnover in excess of £36 million, and supply goods or services to publish a statement each financial year. The Home Office claimed that business transparency would increase supply-chain accountability and 'create a level playing field' between businesses that act responsibly and those that need to do more, thereby driving up standards.[161] Sanctions were unnecessary for businesses that failed to comply. The Home Office respected the sovereignty of the market; it observed that it is up to consumers, investors, and NGOs to apply pressure when they believe a business falls short.[162]

The limitations of the transparency provision were obvious. Analyses of modern slavery statements found that their quality was uneven and that

157 UK, Home Office, House of Commons, Work and Pensions Committee, *Victims of Modern Slavery*. Other problems included victims having no access to legal aid during the NRM process and the absence of appeal rights from negative determinations of victim status.

158 HM Government, *Government Response to the Committee's Twelfth Report of Session 2016–17*. However, in *K (Ghana) v. Secretary of the State for the Home Department* [2018] EWCA Civ 98, the Court of Appeal found that the compelling circumstances test was too high as Article 14 of the Council of Europe Convention on Action against Trafficking in Human Beings requires consideration of personal circumstances. In response, the Home Office offered interim guidance, placing all refusals of discretionary leave to remain to victims of trafficking on hold, Currie, 'Compounding vulnerability and concealing unfairness', 510.

159 HM Government, *Government Response to the Committee's Twelfth Report of Session 2016–17*.

160 Ibid.; Ergon Associates, *Reporting on Modern Slavery*; and Lindsay, Kirkpatrick, and Low, 'Hardly soft law'.

161 UK, Home Office, *Transparency in Supply Chains etc.*, 2.

162 Ibid.

leading companies (those listed on the Financial Times Stock Exchange's 100 Index) did not meet even the minimal requirements of the MSA. Many of the statements lacked adequate detail and provided superficial and broad descriptions of processes and actions.[163] On 23 May 2016, Baroness Young introduced the Modern Slavery (Transparency in Supply Chains) Bill as a remedy.[164] It proposed to amend the MSA by including public bodies in the transparency requirements; requiring companies and public bodies to publish their statements in company reports; requiring the secretary of state to compile a list of companies that should be compliant; and preventing public bodies from procuring services from companies that have not conducted due diligence. The Joint Committee on Human Rights urged the government to adopt the bill and recommended that a criminal offence (along the lines of the UK's Bribery Act) for failing to prevent human rights abuses be introduced.[165] The independent review also recommended establishing a government-run central registry for slavery statements and extending reporting requirements to government departments.[166]

The government responded in a piecemeal fashion. The Home Office wrote to 17,000 organisations governed by the MSA and urged them to publish a statement. It also committed to carrying out an audit of slavery statements at the end of March 2019 and to publishing a list of noncompliant companies. The prime minister announced the government would publish its own modern slavery statement, extend reporting requirements to government departments and public procurement processes, and establish a central registry for transparency statements.[167] However, her government postponed acting on several of the independent review's recommendations until it conducted public consultations.[168] By the time the consultations concluded in September 2019, May had resigned as prime minister, unable to get her bill

[163] Ergon Associates, *Reporting on Modern Slavery*; Lake et al., *Corporate Leadership on Modern Slavery*; Business and Human Rights Resource Centre, 'FTSE 100 at the starting line'. In a five-year follow-up of its assessments of modern slavery reports, the Business and Human Rights Resource Centre concluded that the Modern Slavery Act was 'not fit for purpose' as the reporting requirements were weak, result in poor disclosure, and do not require companies to prevent forced labour and modern slavery. Business and Human Rights Resource Centre, *Modern Slavery Act*, 11.

[164] Modern Slavery (Transparency in Supply Chains) Bill, House of Lords, Sess. 2016–2017.

[165] Joint Committee on Human Rights, *Human Rights and Business 2017*, 41, 58.

[166] HM Government, *Independent Review of the Modern Slavery Act 2015*, 39–47.

[167] HM Government, *The UK Government Response to the Independent Review of the Modern Slavery Act 2015*, 10–11.

[168] Ibid., 53.

to withdraw the United Kingdom from the EU through Parliament, and Boris Johnson had replaced her.

Before leaving office, May sought to consolidate her legacy on modern slavery. She created a £10 million modern slavery research centre to bring together academics, businesses, and charities to drive research and policy.[169] The Modern Slavery and Human Rights Policy and Evidence Centre is a consortium of universities and independent research organisations that includes, among others, Kevin Bales, Andrew Wallis, a former independent antislavery commissioner, and members of the Home Office. This is precisely the kind of epistemic network that the global antislavery governance network promoted.

Like May, for Johnson, modern slavery symbolised Global Britain. According to the Conservative Party's 2019 election manifesto: 'From helping to end the slave trade to tackling modern slavery, the UK has long been a beacon of freedom and human rights – and will continue to be so.'[170] On December 12, Johnson won a resounding victory in the general election on the platform 'Get Brexit Done'. The United Kingdom withdrew from the EU on 31 January 2020. In March, on the fifth anniversary of the MSA, the government published its first modern slavery statement, with a foreword by Johnson, who expressed his hope that by taking action to drive this 'increasingly pervasive evil' out of the government's supply chains, the United Kingdom would set an 'example that will be followed by governments and businesses right around the world'.[171]

To keep modern slavery at the top of the government's agenda, in 2020 Justice and Care UK and the Centre for Social Justice set up the Modern Slavery Policy Unit. In July 2020, it released a report claiming that 'there could be at least 100,000' victims of modern slavery in the United Kingdom.[172] It called for a blend of tougher criminal laws and greater protection for victims.[173]

The Johnson government continued to treat modern slavery as an important part of its governance agenda. In March 2021, it set up a central registry for modern slavery statements and urged (because without statutory authority it

[169] Home Office, 'Government to launch new modern slavery research centre', 'The £10 million policy centre comes as the government responds to the Independent Review into the Modern Slavery Act'.

[170] Conservative and Unionist Party Manifesto 2019, *Get Brexit Done*, 53.

[171] HM Government, *UK Government Modern Slavery Statement*, 1.

[172] Centre for Social Justice, *It Still Happens Here*, 8. This figure is much closer to Walk Free's estimate that there were 136,000 modern slaves in the UK in 2018.

[173] Ibid.

could not require) companies to submit their modern slavery statements. The Queen's Speech on 10 May 2022 outlined the government's intention to introduce a Modern Slavery Bill to strengthen the protection and support for victims of modern slavery and to increase accountability of companies and other organisations to drive out modern slavery from their supply chains.[174]

However, the pandemic and related scandals derailed the government's plans to better protect victims and strengthen reporting obligations.[175] As the political turmoil became entwined with the deteriorating state of the United Kingdom's Brexit economy, fighting modern slavery began to slip down the political agenda as getting tough on illegal migrants rose. The independent antislavery commissioner's position was left empty.[176] Johnson's Home Secretary (Priti Patel) blamed the MSA for encouraging illegal immigrants to come to the United Kingdom and permitting criminals to avail themselves of the NRM. Indeed, she claimed that child rapists (the ultimate embodiment of evil) had sought referral as modern slaves to avoid or delay deportation or removal.[177] Alleged victims have now joined 'evil slave masters as political folk devils' and a key source of illegal migration, which the government blamed as the source of Britain's economic woes. This narrative distracts from the impact years of austerity, Britain's 'lightly' regulated labour markets, and the effect Brexit had on most people's standard of living.[178]

In the context of a tabloid-fuelled panic around small boats loaded with asylum seekers heading towards British shores, the Johnson government introduced the Nationality and Borders Act 2022, which makes the NRM process more restrictive, and 'disapplies' the EU 2011 trafficking directive to the extent that it contradicts this legislation.[179] Although the Act provided a statutory basis for the reflection period for victims, as required under the European Convention against Trafficking, it reduced the length of the reflection period from forty-five to thirty days and limited it to one period, unless the

[174] UK, Prime Minister's Office, *The Queen's Speech 2022*, 83–85.

[175] By the end of December 2023, the government still had not introduced amendments to strengthen the disclosure requirements. By contrast, the legislation to make it more difficult to establish status as a victim of modern slavery had come into effect.

[176] Dugan, 'Home Office accused of deliberately leaving anti-slavery post unfilled'. It had not been filled by the end of September 2023, leaving the position empty for eighteen months. In October 2023, the government announced that Eleanor Lyons, a former special advisor to Boris Johnson with no background in antislavery initiatives, would in December 2023 become the new antislavery commissioner.

[177] UK, Home Office, 'Alarming rise of abuse within modern slavery system'.

[178] Broad and Gadd, *Demystifying Modern Slavery*, 15, 36.

[179] The provisions came into effect on 30 January 2023. They permit asylum seekers who enter the UK as stowaways and on small boats to be processed in Rwanda.

secretary of state considered it appropriate to provide a further period. The threshold for reasonable-grounds decision making within the NRM was also increased from reasonable grounds for believing a person 'may be a victim' to 'is a victim'.[180] Moreover, the act disqualifies victims who have a reasonable-grounds decision from protection if the competent authority is satisfied that they are a 'threat to public order' or have claimed victim status in 'bad faith'.

These changes made it much more difficult to establish victim status in the United Kingdom. In the first quarter of 2023 (the changes to the NRM came into effect on 1 January 2023), the percentage of referrals to the NRM receiving a reasonable-grounds decision was 58 per cent, a significant drop from 88 per cent in 2022.[181] The number of positive final decisions also dropped, from 92 per cent in early 2022 to 75 per cent in early 2023.[182] These are the highest rejection rates from the NRM since at least 2014, the furthest back the available data goes.

The conflation of modern slavery with illegal migration in government rhetoric continued after Johnson resigned in July 2022. His successor as prime minster, Liz Truss (6 September 2022), only had time to transfer authority over modern slavery from the minister for victims and safeguarding to the minister for immigration and appoint Suella Braverman as home secretary.[183] When Rishi Sunak became prime minister on 25 October 2022 after Truss's debacle, he reappointed Suella Braverman as home secretary. She echoed Patel in identifying the protections available to victims of modern slavery as a source of illegal migration. Braverman told the Conservative Party conference that criminals and asylum seekers were 'gaming' the modern slavery system,[184] a claim disputed by the head of the GLAA.[185]

In a statement to the House of Commons on illegal migration the day after a small boat capsized of the coast of England, drowning four asylum seekers, Prime Minister Sunak doubled down on the Johnson government's decision to get tough on victims of modern slavery. In his push to stop illegal migration, he confirmed that his government would 'remove the gold plating in our modern slavery system, including by reducing the cooling off period from

[180] In response to a successful legal challenge brought be two victims of trafficking, the government changed the reasonable grounds threshold back to what it had been before the Nationality and Borders Act 2022 changes went into effect. Taylor, 'Suella Braverman U-turns on new rules targeting trafficking victims'.

[181] Ibid.

[182] Crosby Medlicott, 'Experts blame Suella Braverman's borders act'.

[183] Roberts, 'The UK government is undermining decades of anti-slavery efforts'.

[184] Dearden, 'No evidence of Suella Braverman's claims'.

[185] Dugan, 'Watchdog disputes Braverman's claim modern slavery laws being "gamed"'.

45 to 30 days' – the legal minimum set out in the (nonjusticiable) European Convention against Trafficking.[186] His government went even further and introduced a bill to facilitate the removal of illegal entrants to the United Kingdom, including those who have established reasonable grounds for believing they are victims of modern slavery.

The Illegal Migration Bill was Sunak's flagship measure to remove those who arrive in the United Kingdom illegally, including asylum seekers and victims of modern slavery. Braverman, the bill's sponsor, characterised it as the government's response 'to the waves of illegal migrants breaching our borders'.[187] Robert Jenrick, Sunak's minister of immigration and responsible for guiding the bill through the House of Commons, claimed it would 'crack down on the opportunities to abuse modern slavery protections, by preventing people who come to the UK through illegal and dangerous journeys from misusing modern slavery safeguards to block their removal'.[188]

Antislavery and human rights advocates complained that the government was running roughshod over the European Convention on Human Rights. To downplay these fears, the government characterised the bill as an extraordinary measure to deal with the small-boats crisis and limited its operation to two years.[189] However, the government failed to allay the concerns of some of its own members that it had gone too far in sacrificing the rights of victims of modern slavery. May expressed her 'fear' that this bill will 'drive a coach and horses through the Modern Slavery Act, denying support to those who have been exploited and enslaved, and in doing so making it much harder to catch and stop the traffickers and slave drivers.'[190]

The Illegal Migration Act received royal assent on 23 July 2023. It removes almost all protections for victims of modern slavery and trafficking who are targeted for removal. For example, victims of modern slavery who have established reasonable grounds to believe that they are indeed victims are to be removed from the United Kingdom before a conclusive grounds decision is made unless they are cooperating with investigations or criminal proceedings relating to their exploitation and the home secretary considers it 'necessary for the person to be present in the United Kingdom to provide that cooperation'.[191] To make it even harder to fit into this exception, the government added a presumption that it is not necessary for a person to be

[186] UK, 'PM statement on illegal migration'.
[187] Hansard, HC, vol. 729, col. 152, 7 March 2023.
[188] UK, Parliament, 'Illegal migration bill'.
[189] Illegal Migration Act 2023, c. 37, s. 26.
[190] Ambrose, 'UK's illegal migration bill will force traffickers underground, says May'.
[191] Illegal Migration Act 2023, c. 37, ss. 22.

in the United Kingdom to cooperate with an investigation and/or prosecution unless there are 'compelling circumstances', to be determined with regard to new statutory guidance. Instead of promoting Britain as a global leader in the fight against modern slavery, the Sunak government calculates that there is greater political capital in depicting the MSA as contributing to the 'immigration' problem.[192]

CONCLUSION

The UK government was the first government to embrace the term 'modern slavery' and incorporate new abolitionist discourse into its governance strategy. Its modern slavery governance agenda was initially both a domestic and global success. By evoking Wilberforce's parliamentary campaign against the slave trade, it reminded people of Britain's golden past when it led the world morally and economically. It had a key driver in the person of Theresa May, who as home secretary and prime minister made eliminating modern slavery her personal cause. An elite antislavery network set the terms of the policy debate in ways that downplayed other elements of the government's agenda, such as labour-market deregulation and creating a hostile environment for illegal migration, which increases the vulnerability of all (citizens and migrants, both documented and undocumented) workers to modern slavery.[193] This network avoided divisive issues, such as the relationship between prostitution and exploitation.[194] The term 'modern slavery' helped elide the nature and causes of exploitation since it covered everything from human trafficking for sexual exploitation and county lines to forced labour. By deploying a moral rather than political vocabulary, new abolitionists could accommodate a range of groups with different approaches and perspectives.

May elucidated her conception of modern slavery and her governance agenda in her speech to the ILO's centenary conference, made when she

[192] Contrary to what the Johnson government promised, as of 1 January 2024, Sunak's government has not adopted any measure to protect victims of modern slavery or to strengthen the transparency requirements in the MSA.

[193] Walk Free's *Measurement, Action, Freedom*, 32, found that the UK's hostile environment policy resulted in wrongful detention and deportation and fear and uncertainty. However, it still ranked the UK as the world leader on modern slavery initiatives.

[194] Although the 2018 independent review acknowledged that prostitution was not within its mandate, its final report observed that the UK might be seen as an 'easy target' by sex traffickers since it does not have a 'sex-buyer law'. The reviewers planned to undertake 'a scoping review into laws surrounding prostitution in England and Wales, and their relation to trafficking for sexual exploitation'. UK, *Independent Review of the Modern Slavery Act 2015*, 20.

was preparing to step down as prime minister. Characterising modern slavery as a 'global epidemic' that 'hides in plain sight', she said her goal was to 'put the issue of modern slavery firmly on the domestic and international agenda'.[195] Slavery not only destroys lives and communities, May noted, but it also 'causes illegal immigration – with all the risks that brings for the migrants and the challenges it brings for nation states'. Modern slavery, she continued, undercuts legitimate business and profits. While aid might deal with the supply side, tackling demand is critical. Here, the 'most powerful voice' belongs 'not to business or government, but to the consumer', since 'it is customers who ultimately decide whether a business succeeds or fails'. She called on 'ordinary shoppers the world over to vote with their wallets' and 'shun those companies that do not make the ethical grade'. But, she advised, 'none of this should distract from the central piece of the puzzle: pursuing the criminals at the heart of it all'. She applauded the extraterritorial reach of the law, citing a British court's jailing of British citizen for her part in trafficking five women from Nigeria to Germany – even though none of her crimes took place in the United Kingdom.[196]

In May's rendition, modern slavery is cast as a moral problem that pits 'barbaric individuals', 'gangs', 'people smugglers', and 'child abusers' against 'ethical entrepreneurs', 'responsible businessmen and women', and consumers with a 'conscience'.[197] In this scenario, governments should use the criminal law against traffickers and encourage businesses to be transparent about their efforts to rid themselves and their supply chains of modern slavery.

But not all consumers can 'vote with their wallets', and entrepreneurs often engage in pricing practices that squeeze suppliers. Some product markets, such as agriculture, have been restructured in ways that depend on a supply of precarious migrant workers (many on temporary work visas that bind them to a specific employer) who lack the political and labour-market power to insist on and enforce decent labour standards.[198] Modern slavery offenders are often marginal players, and it is questionable how many are, as the government suggests, 'invested in enduring criminal enterprises' rather than situational actors.[199] Since many of the modern slavery crimes intersect with immigration

[195] UK, 'PM speech at ILO centenary conference'.

[196] The first person convicted of human trafficking for sexual exploitation with no connection to the UK's territory other than citizenship was born in Liberia, became a British citizen in 2009, and was accused of using 'voodoo' to coerce her victims. Cooper, 'UK "voodoo" nurse first person convicted under modern slavery laws'.

[197] UK, 'PM speech at ILO centenary conference'.

[198] Ruhs and Anderson, *Who Needs Migrant Workers?*

[199] Broad and Gadd, *Demystifying Modern Slavery*, 173.

controls, the proliferation of immigration offences creates 'around it a field of illegal practices' that contributes to the growing number of modern slavery offenders.[200] Associating modern slavery with illegal immigration also fosters racial profiling.[201]

The United Kingdom's modern slavery governance strategy is primarily carceral; the MSA provides a plethora of offences and an elastic definition of exploitation, stiff penalties, a variety of enforcement orders, and extraterritorial effect. Legal authority over modern slavery is lodged in the Home Office, which is concerned with ensuring strong borders and internal order. Different governance strategies are deployed for sexual exploitation and forced labour. Illegal working and modern slavery are the manifestations of labour-market exploitation that concern the UK government. Although labour advocates tried to persuade the government to adopt a labour-market-regulation approach, the government did the opposite. It used the language of modern slavery to shift the GLAA away from enforcing labour standards via licensing to using its criminal-law powers to pursue modern slavery offenders.[202] The United Kingdom has not adopted a labour-market-regulation approach to addressing forced labour and labour exploitation, even though it was one of the first countries to ratify the ILO's protocol on forced labour.

Indeed, the United Kingdom has made 'illegal working' a criminal offence to combat labour-market exploitation, which is seen as undercutting decent employers, good migrants, and British workers. The government justifies the wide variety of private and public bordering practices that operate within, outside, and at the edge of the United Kingdom's territory by claiming it protects victims of modern slavery. However, it offers victims limited hospitality for fear that offering more will attract a flood of illegal migrants. Moreover, as Britain's economic and political woes increased with Brexit, the pandemic, and the war in Ukraine, the Sunak government

[200] Foucault, *Discipline and Punish*, 280.

[201] The Windrush scandal (so named after the *Empire Windrush*, the ship that brought one of the first groups of West Indian migrants to the UK in 1948) involved the wrongful detention and deportation of British subjects, many of whom had arrived in the UK before 1973 from Caribbean countries. In 2018, it emerged that in at least eighty-three cases, individuals had been wrongly deported from the UK by the Home Office. In response, Amber Rudd resigned as home secretary, and her successor, Sajid Javid, rebranded the 'hostile environment' 'compliant environment'.

[202] Elysia McCaffrey, the chief executive of the GLAA, was reported as stating that only 12 of its 1,000 inspections of licence holders had been completed by August 2022. Dugan, 'Watchdog disputes Braverman's claim modern slavery laws being "gamed"'.

abandoned any attempt to use the fight against modern slavery to establish moral hegemony and, instead, has increased its vilification of illegal migrants, including those who also happen to be victims of modern slavery. Despite these changes, Walk Free's 2023 Global Slavery Index ranked the UK government's response to modern slavery as the best out of 160 countries in the world.[203]

[203] It did note, however, that the UK's response had declined and that the Illegal Migration Bill put the UK 'at risk of continuing its downward trend'. Walk Free, *The Global Slavery Index* 2023.

Conclusion

Nothing is more misleading than the ambiguity of the word 'freedom' in labour relations.

—Otto Kahn-Freund, *Labour and the Law*

Freedom and its antithesis are both legal-juridical and social and ideological categories, categories fundamentally informed though ideologies of nationalism, racism, and sexism. It is these every day or 'banal' forms of discrimination that organize the legitimacy for their legal coercive consequences.

—Nandita Sharma, *Home Rule*

The 'discovery' in the twentieth-first century that an estimated 50 million people are modern slaves, and that 27.6 million are engaged in forced labour, raises troubling questions about the relationship between global capitalism and unfree labour.[1] The critical political economist Nicola Phillips helpfully identifies two broad and competing explanatory approaches to understanding the persistence of unfree labour in capitalism, which she refers to as residualist and relational.[2] These contrasting approaches inform debates about how best to characterise the problem of unfree labour and the range of different strategies to eradicate it.[3]

The residualist approach sees the persistence of unfree labour as a pre-capitalist remnant rooted in market failure, political corruption, or a failure of democracy. Leading international financial institutions such as the World Bank and key antislavery charities such as the Walk Free Foundation (the

1 ILO and Walk Free Foundation, *Global Estimates of Modern Slavery*, 2022.

2 Phillips, 'Unfree labour and adverse incorporation'.

3 Mezzadri, *The Sweatshop Regime*; Plant, 'Combatting trafficking for labour exploitation in the global economy'; and McGrath and Watson, 'Anti-slavery as development'.

subject of Chapter 2) have adopted this approach and endorsed expanding and deepening markets, thereby incorporating people into free wage labour. Key researchers in the global antislavery governance network have analysed data on the prevalence of slavery and various measures of economic and political globalisation in more than sixty countries to determine whether there is a 'dark side to globalisation'.[4] They found that the prevalence of slavery is lower in wealthier and more globalised countries that have high levels of democracy. On this reading, they claim that it is too early to lay the blame for modern slavery at the feet of globalisation. Indeed, they hypothesise that since tradeable goods are increasingly subject to international scrutiny, globalisation should reduce modern slavery.[5] For residualists, globalised capitalism, properly managed temporary-labour migration programmes, and transnational supply chains are the solution to, and not a cause of, modern slavery. Slavery is cast as a problem that arises outside of the market and then infiltrates it.[6]

By contrast, the relational approach views the persistence of unfree labour as the adverse incorporation into capitalist relations. Here, the focus is on power relations and the terms of incorporation of so many of the world's poor into exploitative and precarious work with few possibilities for accumulation and the achievement of security.[7] On this reading, corporate concentration, outsourcing, and temporary migrant labour are seen as contributing to unfree labour in global production and labour chains and as crucial features of economic accumulation across the global economy. Research in this vein has found that unfree labour does not, as is commonly assumed, occur solely in local, small-scale, or domestic markets but instead persists within global economic activity and is incorporated within global supply chains.[8]

This book reveals that questions about the relationship between global capitalism and unfree labour percolate just beneath the surface of the antislavery governance network. It argues that transnational modern slavery laws are an attempt to shore up the fading legitimacy of global neoliberal capitalism – an economic, political, and social project that promotes profitability and accumulation as *the* measures of economic and social activities, which are

[4] Landman and Silverman, 'Globalization and modern slavery', 285. Todd Landman is the Rights Lab research director at the University of Nottingham, and Bernard Silverman was the UK's head statistician who came up with the UK's estimates of modern slavery.

[5] Ibid. However, they note that their data is very general and not broken down by sector or by tradeable goods.

[6] McGrath and Watson, 'Anti-slavery as development'.

[7] Phillips, 'Unfree labour and adverse incorporation', 172.

[8] Ibid., 190; and LeBaron, *Combatting Modern Slavery*.

encouraged through a core set of policies, including liberalisation, deregulation, privatisation, recommodification, and globalisation.[9] It focuses on labour migration and global supply chains because they are prime examples of the 'fixes' needed to feed the incessant demand for profits and accumulation under neoliberal capitalism.[10]

Modern slavery laws are attempts to mediate the escalating tensions around borders and markets created by neoliberal capitalism's reliance on managed migration and free trade as engines of accumulation. As we saw in Chapter 1, the UN's human trafficking protocol was a response to states' fear that the collapse of the Soviet Union, rapid economic liberalisation, and increasing globalisation were fuelling transnational criminal networks engaged in trafficking in drugs, people, and weapons. The protocol's focus is transnational trafficking involving organised crime, and it explicitly calls on states to strengthen border controls.[11] Its goal was to reinforce state authority and sovereignty over the movement of people across national borders and, thus, to preserve the political legitimacy of the neoliberal order. This book shows how the EU (Chapter 4), the United Kingdom (Chapters 5 and 6), and the United States under Bush and Trump (Chapter 1) used human trafficking laws to fortify national borders and bolster national sovereignty.

The global financial crash of 2008–2009 dealt a blow to neoliberalism's economic credibility, and the pandemic 'further upended' it.[12] Moreover, Trump struck at the heart of neoliberal orthodoxy: free trade. While other US politicians may not endorse his brand of ethno-nationalist populism, none 'can get anywhere by presenting free trade as an expression of freedom'.[13] In their 2021 joint statement on forced labour, the G7 Trade Ministers affirmed that 'there is no place for forced labour in the rules-based multilateral trading system' and recognised the role of trade policy and the importance of the UN Guiding Principles on Business and Human Rights in developing a comprehensive approach to eliminating forced labour in global supply chains.[14]

This book demonstrates the growing political consensus in the Global North (the Global South is much more sceptical) that mandatory human

9 Harvey, *A Brief History of Neoliberalism*; Jessop, 'Neoliberalization, uneven development, and Brexit', 1729–1733; Davies, *The Limits of Neoliberalism*; and Gerstle, *The Rise and Fall of the Neoliberal Order*.

10 Prentice, 'Labour rights from labour wrongs?', 1768.

11 Rodríguez-López, '(De)constructing stereotypes', 61–72.

12 Gerstle, 'A real opening', 19.

13 Offner, 'A durable concept', 21.

14 G7 Trade Ministers' Statement on Forced Labour, London, 22 October 2021.

rights due-diligence laws and import bans on goods made with forced labour are needed to tame some of the worst excesses of business practices in global supply chains.[15] Chapter 2 explains how the Walk Free Foundation cultivated close ties between business, faith, and government leaders to establish an ethical business alliance to promote antislavery initiatives targeting global supply chains. This alliance was extremely influential in the United Kingdom, where antislavery initiatives were championed by Theresa May, first as home secretary and then as prime minister (Chapter 6). Indeed, since resigning as prime minister, May has continued to champion the fight against modern slavery, which she says is 'still the greatest human rights issue of our time'.[16] She announced the launch of the Global Commission on Modern Slavery and Human Trafficking, which she will chair. The Commission's goal is to 'exert high-level political leverage to restore political momentum towards achieving UN Sustainable Development Goal 8.7 to eradicate forced labour, end modern slavery and human trafficking'.[17] The idea, according to May, is to 'fully engage businesses in identifying slavery and forced labour in their supply chains'.[18]

The problem with the current crop of mandatory human rights due diligence laws is that they run the risk of being counterproductive for addressing business practices that lead to human rights violations, including modern slavery, as they can result in 'cosmetic compliance' or institutionalise human rights due diligence as a defence to liability.[19] Moreover, even if redesigned to overcome existing shortcomings, alone they are simply insufficient as they do

[15] UN human-rights experts applauded the G7 Trade Ministers' statement. They noted, however, that while the G20 leaders did recognize the importance of decent work in global supply chains, the majority of their communiqué focused instead on stable supply chains to provide the goods and services that their economies need. They called on the G20 to follow the lead of the G7 in its commitment to rights-respecting supply chains. UN, '"G7 Trade Ministers" strong stance'.

[16] O'Donoghue, 'Headed up by former British prime minister Theresa May'.

[17] On its website, the Commission claims that it will have 'a global membership and leadership, particularly including the Global South, be genuinely independent from any government or international organisation, and look beyond the usual suspects to include fresh voices from outside the modern slavery sector'. The Commission also includes familiar voices from the ethical business alliance, such as Grace Forrest (from the Walk Free Foundation) and representatives of the Freedom Fund and Global Fund to End Modern Slavery. It is funded by the UK government (through UK International Development) and the government of the Kingdom of Bahrain. The Global Commission on Modern Slavery and Human Trafficking, 'About', www.modernslaverycommission.org/about/.

[18] Global Commission on Modern Slavery and Human Trafficking, 'A message from the chair', www.modernslaverycommission.org/message-from-the-rt-hon-theresa-may-mp/.

[19] Landau, 'Human rights due diligence and the risk of cosmetic compliance', 221; Deva, 'Mandatory human rights due diligence in Europe', 390.

not challenge the 'structural and systemic inequalities embedded in international legal frameworks and in companies laws'.[20] By treating these laws as a panacea to the problem of labour exploitation in transnational supply chains, the global antislavery governance network diverts attention away from the enormous economic and political power wielded by transnational corporations, including through their philanthropic organisations.

This book provides a genealogy of the amalgam of legal concepts that form transnational modern slavery law, probing the wider social relations that propelled this law's evolution. The case studies reveal how key legal concepts were interpreted and positioned by influential actors in the global antislavery governance network and how a 'common sense' understanding of modern slavery was constructed. This genealogy answers the questions that animated the book: How did modern slavery emerge on the global political agenda? Where do key actors in the global antislavery network draw the boundary between free and unfree labour? How does the multifaceted approach to modern slavery keep the different legal domains to which unfree labour is assigned from clashing? How do attempts to govern transnational forms of unfree labour reconfigure sovereignty? Finally, what makes labour 'free'?

A PUZZLED UNRAVELLED

The first puzzle that this book unravelled was how modern slavery became prominent on the global governance agenda and how it came to include transnational forms of unfree labour associated with globalisation. I used a sociolegal, genealogical, and multiscalar approach to investigate how unfree labour came to be expressed in legal terms. Chapter 1 traced the emergence of modern slavery as a global governance problem to the UN's Protocol to Prevent, Suppress and Punish Trafficking in Persons Especially Women and Children. Rooted in anxieties caused by the breakup of the Soviet Union and the acceleration of the cross-border movement of people, goods, services, and capital, the UN protocol was designed to strengthen state sovereignty by creating a carceral apparatus to address human trafficking across national borders. This protocol was lodged in criminal law and part of a suite of international law instruments designed to tame the criminal underside of globalisation while preserving its much-celebrated economic outcomes.

To achieve a broad consensus among member states and facilitate the protocol's quick adoption, the UN included a range of different types of

20 Villiers, 'A game of cat and mouse', 416; and Deva, 'Mandatory human rights due diligence in Europe', 389.

human exploitation, such as forced labour and slavery, in the definition of human trafficking, and the protocol gestured towards the protection of victims. This tactic resulted in what Janie Chuang termed 'exploitation creep' – the tendency to sweep an expanding assortment of unacceptable behaviours and practices under 'human trafficking'.[21] Diverse international organisations sought to stake a claim for their jurisdictions within the emerging antitrafficking governance network, and successive US administrations (under Bush, Obama, Trump, and Biden) pursued different governance agendas domestically and internationally.

What emerged from this contest was a multifaceted approach to human trafficking that simply aggregated the different legal domains – criminal, immigration, human rights, and labour law. While new abolitionists like Kevin Bales had been trying since the mid-1990s to popularise the term 'modern slavery', used to encompass human trafficking, it was only when Obama embraced 'modern slavery' as the true name of human trafficking in 2012 that the term gained pre-eminence in Anglo-American nations. In the EU, by contrast, as we saw in Chapter 4, for historical and jurisdictional reasons the term 'human trafficking' was preferred to 'modern slavery'.

Although modern slavery is not defined in law, it is used as an 'umbrella term that focuses attention on commonalities' across a constellation of legal concepts – slavery, forced labour, human trafficking, and forced marriage – that are defined in different international legal instruments.[22] Chapter 2 revealed how an ethical business alliance attempted to stabilise the meaning of modern slavery by identifying two axes – unfreedom and exploitation – and produced and distributed authoritative knowledge about the prevalence of modern slavery (in the form of the *Global Estimates of Modern Slavery*). By ranking the legal, policy, and programmatic actions that 181 governments are taking to respond to modern slavery, Walk Free's Government Response Index portrays a 'global moral order' composed of virtuous states (the United Kingdom, the Netherlands, and the United States) and wicked ones (North Korea, Eritrea, and Libya), a characterisation that is amplified in extensive media reports.[23] Absent from the ranking is any reference to the legacy of colonialism or the global economic governance apparatus that perpetuates economic inequality between and within nation-states.[24] The moral vocabulary of modern slavery obscures and occludes how political economy shapes

[21] Chuang, 'Exploitation creep', 609–649.
[22] ILO, Walk Free, and IOM, *Global Estimates of Modern Slavery*, 12.
[23] Brankovic, 'Measure of shame', 103–125.
[24] LeBaron, *Combatting Modern Slavery*.

the global configuration of unfreedom and exploitation. It also disguises the extent to which capitalism in Europe and North America was built about the legal institution of chattel slavery and an ideology of anti-Black racism.[25]

By examining how transnational forms of unfree labour are named and governed by different actors in the global antislavery network, this book illustrates 'the pliability of legal concepts and the way they shift with the vectors of power and interest'.[26] Legal terms such as 'human trafficking', 'forced labour', and 'slavery' are defined in terms of essentially contested terms such as 'exploitation', 'involuntary', 'consent', 'force', 'fraud', and 'coercion'.[27] By 'essentially contested', I do not mean simply that there is a penumbra of doubt about where to draw the line about what activity is caught by a term or that there are hard cases that do not easily fit under a legal category (although the recurring problem of legal classification arises each time an individual claims to be a victim of modern slavery). Rather, I mean the nature of the activity itself is disputed. Chapter 1 explained how the definition of 'exploitation' in the UN's protocol was left ambiguous so that each state could decide for itself whether the sale of sexual services (prostitution) was exploitative in the absence of coercion; and how, under the Bush administration, the United States put an extraterritorial disciplinary apparatus in place to treat prostitution as a form of exploitation for the purpose of human trafficking.

The problem of characterising commercial sexual service as either a form of labour or an exploitative practice is a recurring one, and the ILO and EU, like the UN, have refused to resolve it, delegating its solution to nation-states. The nature of exploitation in this context is disputed; some groups see commercial sexual services as a moral issue, others as an instance of violence against women, and still others as a livelihood strategy shaped by a range of structural economic and social constraints. This refusal to grapple with the status of the sale of sexual services as a form of work is also reflected in the academic literature on human trafficking and modern slavery, where, with but a few exceptions, sexual and labour exploitation are treated as ontologically distinct.[28] This is so, even though the mechanisms of control used are often the same. Sexual harassment and violence are used to control women (and sometimes men) in a range of employment relations and tactics (personal

[25] Blackett, 'Teaching critical race theory'; Gevers, 'Reconfiguring slavery through international law'.

[26] Mezzadra and Neilson, *Border as Method*, 178.

[27] Rittich, 'Representing, counting, valuing'.

[28] For the exceptions see Andrijasevic, 'Forced labour in supply chains'; Cruz, 'Beyond liberalism'; Theimann, 'Beyond victimhood and beyond employment?'; and Kotiswaran, 'Protocol at the crossroads'.

relations, tied housing, stigma) associated with controlling women in the context of prostitution are used to control workers in the agriculture, garment, and electronics sectors.[29] The difference between commercial sexual exploitation and labour exploitation is an artefact of governance.

As we saw in Chapters 1 and 5, although the United States and United Kingdom have criminalised many aspects of the purchase of sexual services as a way of combatting human trafficking, they have not yet criminalised the purchase of sexual services domestically (although there is growing pressure to do so). While none of the jurisdictions implemented a prohibition on the sale of sexual services as part of a broader antitrafficking strategy, all of them treated sexual and labour exploitation differently – as manifestations of qualitatively different types of problems. So, too, did most international and transnational organisations, advocacy groups, and NGOs. The result: profoundly gendered governance strategies that single out women and children for 'protection', often resulting in restrictions on women's mobility. Moreover, the collateral damage that 'raid and rescue' human trafficking policies caused to migrant sex workers and sex workers more generally was largely ignored, the racial profiling implicit in such policies continued, and, as we saw in the United Kingdom in Chapter 6, these tactics were extended to address instances of labour exploitation, with the result that migrants without lawful immigration status who were rescued were detained and deported.

Although pliable, legal concepts have their own history and must be embedded in a specific cultural political economy to take effect. Chapter 1 explained how the UN's 2000 Human Trafficking Protocol drew on a series of international treaties adopted at the turn of the twentieth century to address the problem of 'white slavery' – European women being procured to work as prostitutes in the colonies – which merged with ongoing moral and public health crusades to stop prostitution. These international laws were informed by a highly gendered and racialised notion of moral purity and a view of migration as a corrupting influence. Many historians have shown how trafficking 'became a way to manage porous borders and empower early immigration bureaus and departments to surveil and police marginalised and racialised women (and the men branded as "traffickers" and "pimps")'.[30] Prostitution and sexual exploitation were at the centre of antitrafficking strategies, particularly in the United States under Bush, the EU, and the

[29] Henry and Adams, *Spotlight on Sexual Violence and Harassment in Commercial Agriculture*; Andrijasevic, 'Forced labour in supply chains', 410–424; and Naved et al., 'Female garment workers' experiences of violence'.

[30] Hetherington and Laite, 'Trafficking, a useless category of historical analysis', 18.

Council of Europe, where eradicating prostitution was seen as a way to combat human trafficking and promote women's equality. This book illustrates how the paternalistic, gendered, racist, and nationalist overtones of anti-human trafficking initiatives continue to permeate the governance strategies designed to eliminate it.

New abolitionists and the international human rights advocacy network – composed of (mostly Christian) faith-based organisations and human rights groups – recast human trafficking as a specific form of modern slavery. Chapter 2 recounts how the bicentenaries of the abolition of the slave trade (in Britain in 1807, and in the United States in 1808) provided an opportunity for new abolitionists to mobilise the iconography and narratives of historical forms of slavery to highlight new forms and emphasise its continued moral repugnance. The United Kingdom was the first country wholeheartedly to embrace the new abolitionist language of modern slavery in 2013, when it introduced draft modern slavery legislation. Chapter 6 explains how the language of modern slavery activated a repertoire of aggrandising historical tropes, portrayed modern slavery as a moral issue that transcended party politics, and heralded a revitalised vision of British global sovereignty as the United Kingdom was on the cusp of leaving the EU. While this discourse appealed to the British political elite and the British press, it had 'negative historic undertones' in former British colonies.[31] More perniciously, it 'mystifie[d] British history' by depicting Britain's role in the abolition of the slave trade as 'driven by a uniquely British commitment to instilling human rights and respecting human dignity, while at the same time rendering it unbecoming and unpatriotic to mention the pivotal role of chattel slavery in the growth of the British Empire'.[32]

Jurisdiction has provided the central analytic framework for understanding the global governance of modern slavery. In this book, I followed Marianna Valverde's lead in treating jurisdiction as a complex legal assemblage with scalar and governance dimensions. It operates as a sorting mechanism that allocates a problem – a particular form of unfree labour, for example – to an authority for resolution.[33] Jurisdiction resolves scalar questions about which institution – international, transnational, nation-state, or subcomponent of a nation-state – has authority. By assigning a subject to a legal domain (criminal, immigration, human rights, or labour law, for example), jurisdiction also fixes the governance institutions and techniques that can be used. Additionally, it

[31] Broad and Gadd, *Demystifying Modern Slavery*, 25.
[32] Ibid., 3.
[33] Valverde, 'Jurisdiction and scale'.

determines whether the delegation of authority to public and private actors is lawful or unlawful.[34]

I argue that cultural political economy drives the assemblage of jurisdiction in the global antislavery governance network. Human trafficking was seen by powerful states and international organisations as a problem of transnational crime, and states came together to adopt an international criminal-law instrument to provide the basis for a criminal-law approach and to encourage international cooperation. As we saw in Chapters 1 and 4, policy actors and stakeholders at the UN and EU endorsed a multifaceted approach to modern slavery and human trafficking that emphasised the alignment of different legal jurisdictions – criminal, immigration, labour, and human rights – to address different aspects of the problem of modern slavery. Under this approach, different agencies and actors drew on their expertise and governance techniques to tackle different dimensions of the problem.

The ILO (a tripartite institution) used the human trafficking protocol to revitalise its governance agenda of labour market regulation at a time when the dominant neoliberal wisdom viewed its traditional governance mechanisms (labour standards, public inspections, and worker collective representation through trade unions) with suspicion. By enmeshing itself in the global governance network, the ILO put labour trafficking on the governance agenda. It also fashioned an international standard, the protocol of 2014 to the Forced Labour Convention, that incorporated the techniques of labour law into the governance of forced labour. It integrated a human rights approach by imposing obligations on states to protect victims and provide them with effective remedies. The forced labour protocol provides an alternative legal domain, one that is structural and preventative in orientation, unlike the criminal law, where the focus is individual and punitive.

This multifaceted approach raises the question: Is it possible to combine a range of different jurisdictions to combat the problem of labour unfreedom, or will one jurisdiction overwhelm the others? Principles of state sovereignty and subsidiarity, combined with the need for states to absorb the norms and obligations of international and transnational law into domestic legal systems, mean that we have to turn to the national scale to answer this question. I use the example of the United Kingdom (Chapters 5 and 6) to show that the political discourses of modern slavery, combined with the process of legal characterisation and assigning legal jurisdiction, have produced overlapping jurisdictions (criminal, immigration, business, and labour law) with differing

[34] Pratt and Templeman, 'Jurisdiction, sovereignties and Akwesasne', 338; and Valverde, *Chronotopes of Law*, 83.

associated techniques of governance. In the United Kingdom, criminal law and immigration law have elective affinities in the case of human trafficking and modern slavery. Authority over immigration, security, and law and order is lodged in a single ministry (the Home Office) that links the governance of immigration jurisdictionally with security and criminal law.

The relationship between these different jurisdictions is crucial for understanding the normative or legal characterisation of unfreedom and why, in the United Kingdom, the relationship between illegal migrants, criminals, and modern slaves is so fraught. The association of illegal entry and illegal working with human trafficking created an aura of criminality that spilled over to trafficking victims. Moreover, the cultural and political environment functions as a conductor that amplifies the force of a particular jurisdiction or an insulator that weakens the influence of one jurisdiction when compared with another. Despite the best efforts of workers' advocates, the UK government did not enhance labour market regulation to prevent modern slavery. More pertinently perhaps, modern slavery pulled existing labour-market institutions in a carceral direction at a time when successive UK governments were committed to deregulated labour markets and blamed illegal migrants for labour-market exploitation. This book illustrates the importance of cultural political economy in explaining how a state uses law to govern modern slavery.

Although the EU was at the forefront of the multifaceted approach to combatting human trafficking, Chapter 4 explains that its antitrafficking legal instruments emphasised *transnational crime* and *movement* across borders because these are the elements that activate EU legislative jurisdiction under the EU treaties.[35] As EU treaties expanded human rights, the EU's antitrafficking instruments provided greater protection to victims. Yet, in a context where migration could potentially undermine the EU, human rights were incorporated within and subsumed under a governance strategy designed to harden both the EU's and Member States' borders to exclude undesirable outsiders, exemplified by migrant sex workers.

Human rights groups and institutions have been the strongest advocates of a multifaceted approach to human trafficking and modern slavery.[36] The Council of Europe Convention on Human Trafficking is, as we saw in Chapter 4, the high-water mark of human rights protection for victims of human trafficking. Indeed, some legal scholars argue that it is possible to use human rights law to dismantle state action, such as extremely restrictive visa

35 Krieg, 'Trafficking in human beings'.

36 Jovanovic, *State Responsibility for Modern Slavery in Human Rights Law*.

conditions, that contributes to modern slavery.[37] While this is legally possible, the case study presented in Chapters 5 and 6 suggest that it is unlikely to be successful in the United Kingdom. Indeed, the Sunak government's Illegal Migration Act, 2023, runs roughshod over the rights of victims of modern slavery, and Suella Braverman (then the United Kingdom's Home Secretary) has launched a 'fresh' attack on the European Convention on Human Rights on the grounds that it protects the rights of illegal migrants.[38] By contrast, as we saw in Chapters 2 and 4, human rights advocates have had greater success in persuading actors in the antislavery governance network to embrace mandatory human rights due-diligence laws and import bans as tools to tackle forced labour in global supply chains. Of course, the difference is that these laws extend and reinforce the sovereignty of states in the Global North.[39] These examples from the United Kingdom and EU demonstrate that the different legal domains that make up a multifaceted approach to modern slavery are not equal; some have much greater influence on antislavery strategies than others.

The scalar dimension of jurisdiction can also operate as a technique of governance: one that challenges territorial notions of national sovereignty. Chapter 2 shows how Walk Free and other members of the ethical business apparatus advocated transparency legislation as a solution to the problem that territorially bound notions of sovereignty pose to regulating forced labour in global supply chains. They argued that mandatory due diligence and disclosure laws can have an extraterritorial effect by creating incentives for business to eradicate slavery transmitted through transnational supply chains. In this way, state sovereignty can be extended beyond territorial borders by requiring multinational enterprises to take steps to ensure that slave-made goods do not infiltrate their supply chains. Governments essentially delegate to multinational corporations the authority to enact extraterritorial borders. Sovereignty is rescaled and made transnational as public and private actors deploy disciplinary mechanisms that operate across national borders.

By contrast, scale is a contested technique of governance within the ILO. Forced labour presented an opportunity for the ILO to rescale its distinctive governance mechanism – labour conventions that are incorporated into national laws – by proposing a convention that applied to transnational corporations and required them to ensure that the links in their supply chains

37 Mantouvalou, *Structural Injustice and Workers' Rights*.

38 Savage, 'Suella Braverman makes fresh attack'.

39 Krisch, 'Jurisdiction unbound', 512; Deva, 'Mandatory human rights due diligence laws in Europe'; and Villiers, 'A game of cat and mouse.

adhered to labour standards. The workers' group supported such an initiative, but the employers' group blocked it, claiming it disregards state sovereignty and illegitimately imposes human rights obligations directly on private actors.[40] The ILO and its constituents engaged in a game of jurisdiction in which scalar differentiation was mobilised strategically to promote specific interests.

The treaties that make up the EU allocate institutional jurisdiction on a scalar basis between EU institutions and Member States. EU legislative institutions and member states engaged in a game of jurisdiction over the governance of human trafficking. Under New Labour, the UK government sought to establish that UK sovereignty can be augmented through the selective adoption of EU rules around trafficking. However, in the context of austerity policies and unanticipated high levels of immigration, Eurosceptics, who wanted to free Britain from the EU, exploited the latent contradiction between this idea of a functional sovereignty based on interdependence between the United Kingdom and EU and the British notion of absolute sovereignty. After Brexit, the United Kingdom began to withdraw from those aspects of the EU's protocol designed to protect victims.

States have not lost sovereign power over human movement. Sovereignty has been reconfigured as states involve a growing number of nonstate actors in bordering practices. The United Kingdom is a clear example. Chapter 6 illustrates how the UK government recruited a growing group of private actors to enforce border controls within UK territory as it expanded its penal and disciplinary power extraterritorially. For migrants, sovereignty and governance intersect at these borders, where they are transformed into subjects with different legal statuses.[41]

International and transnational instruments define the main legal categories of unfree labour, but it is nation-states that implement them and give meaning to the concept of exploitation. This book argues that the border between free and unfree labour is 'largely a contested and ambivalent artefact of governance'.[42] As political economist Nick Bernards claims, this border, which distinguishes between acceptable and unacceptable forms of coercion, is 'a vital step in the normalisation of capitalist production'.[43] If we start with the premise that the commodification of labour takes place in legal and

40 Indeed, the joint business response to the initial draft of a binding UN treaty to 'harden' the UNGPs objected to the form of extraterritorial jurisdiction envisioned in the draft on the ground that is did not 'respect national sovereignty'. Krisch, 'Jurisdiction unbound', 510.

41 Mezzadra and Neilson, *Border as Method*, 204.

42 Bernards, 'The global politics of forced labour', 964.

43 Ibid.

economic spaces, the key question is, What forms of constraint are unacceptable at a particular place and time?

WHAT MAKES LABOUR FREE?

Focusing on forms of unfree labour ignores the analytically prior question: what makes labour free? The classical political economists Adam Smith, James Mills, and Karl Marx and the founder of economic sociology, Max Weber, all grappled with this question because, when they were writing, the concept of 'free' wage labour had not yet come to epitomise freedom for working people.[44]

Part of the answer has to do with how we understand freedom. Since the 1980s, freedom has come to be equated with free markets and free trade. Freedom means noninterference by the state. There has been a kind of neoliberal flattening of a much more complex and robust concept. There are at least three conceptions of freedom: negative, positive, and republican. Negative freedom is noninterference with another,[45] while positive freedom entails some kind of institutional support that enables individuals to effectively select a range of life options. This kind of positive freedom has been theorised by Amartya Sen in terms of capabilities.[46] Republican freedom, by contrast, is the form of freedom that means that no one is dominating you; it is freedom from subordination.[47]

Law provides a particularly helpful lens for understanding the prevailing conception of freedom as it reflects underlying assumptions in neoclassical economics and liberal social contract theory about freedom as consent. Although there is no legal definition of free labour, we can identify its characteristics from instances that the law considers unfree. International, multilateral, and domestic laws provide a good picture of what leading international institutions and liberal nation-states consider free labour to be. For them, free labour is characterised by the absence of coercion, force, and deception in entering, continuing in, and leaving an employment or service relationship.

In legal terms what makes labour free – exchange relations where there is no coercion, force, or deception – reflects a distinction originating in classical political economy. It also resonates with social contract theory – which

44 Fudge, 'What makes labour free'.
45 Nozick, *Anarchy, State, and Utopia*.
46 Sen, *Development as Freedom*.
47 Anderson, *Private Government*.

assumes that free relations take a contractual form – and liberal understandings of self-ownership and self-sovereignty. For liberal political economy, neoclassical economics, and contract law, the voluntariness of the exchange is the distinctive feature of free labour, and consent is the regulative ideal. The assumption is that the labour market is an arena of free exchange in which legally equal parties contract to their mutual advantage. The law simply provides neutral rules of the game. Meanwhile, the state's role should be to ensure a 'level playing field' between market actors. Because slavery, which is the epitome of unfree labour, interferes with individual autonomy, it must be outlawed as a crime. Moreover, the claim is made that forced labour and slavery are bad for development.

Of course, as Adam Smith, Karl Marx, and Max Weber pointed out, this description of free wage labour ignores how the legal regime – and I want to emphasise that all three of these authors saw the legal regime as constructing (and not simply reflecting) this inequality – renders this freedom purely formal for many workers. During the Industrial Revolution, there was no choice but to do wage work, to go to the workhouse or starve. In the Global North, the welfare state cushioned the process of commodification, but the spectre of a wageless life disciplines workers who increasingly must rely on workfare to subsist. In the Global South, workers construct precarious and informal livelihoods as they continue to hope for a truly developmental state.

Alleviating the economic compulsion that requires people to work would provide some measure of positive freedom. However, it would not address the other form of unfreedom that political economists and political theorists have identified – the subordination that resides in the hidden abode of production. Markets are unable to address the problem of subordination at work. Instead, democratic principles of governance are needed to give people voice at work. Voice is about exercising associational or collective power, and it involves democratic self-determination. Voice is what gives effect to the republican notion of freedom as non-domination at work.

Workers' collective voice is essential if labour is to be free. Indeed, for the first time, the 2023 edition of the *Global Estimates of Modern Slavery* elevated respect for the freedoms of workers to associate and to bargain collectively (described 'as indispensable to a world free from forced labour') to the top of the list of measures to counteract unfreedom.[48] Freedom from domination means that people need voice to challenge authority. This kind of freedom is potentially – although only potentially – transformative. Perhaps that is why

[48] ILO, Walk Free, and IOM, *Global Estimates of Modern Slavery*, 6.

substantive freedom of association at work is so strongly resisted even in liberal democracies.

This conception of free labour as including freedom from subordination is profoundly different from the thin, market-oriented version of freedom that animates the ethical business alliance's campaign against modern slavery. But, as Chapter 2 recounts, the alliance has come to accept forms of mandatory human rights due-diligence legislation and import bans and has supported measures to protect freedom of association.

Yet even a republican conception of freedom, which includes voice, does not address two much deeper problems problem: (1) the profoundly skewed power relations of the prevailing global economic order and (2) the restrictions on mobility placed on people by sovereign states through border controls.

A critical political economy perspective discloses the legal domains and practices through which corporate actors exercise power in the global economy. Private law concepts (corporation, property, contract, tort) combine with international investment, trade, and intellectual property law to invest transnational corporations with vast power over the distribution of resources and governance.[49] Indeed, transnational corporations have played a key role in shaping trade policy to their advantage.[50] Moreover, dispossession and expropriation through colonialism have simply been encoded in international law as postcolonial states were treated as sovereigns equal to their former imperial masters.[51]

Borders, as Harald Bauder explains, function as a mechanism that 'controls, disciplines, and in many cases exploits' workers' labour in two ways: first, by geographically dividing the global workforce into countries with different labour standards and, second, by creating migrant workers with legal statuses that trap them in low-wage and poorly regulated sectors of the labour market.[52] Under the existing global economic governance architecture, capital, goods, and services are free to move across borders while labour is constrained.[53] In the context of contemporary globalism, the flip side of capital's movement offshore to seek cheaper, harder-working, and more disciplined labour is the use of temporary migrant labour in labour-intensive sectors in the Global North and more developed states in the Global South. The 'free' and ever-expanding markets that are foundational to globalisation and neoliberal policies undermine the conditions needed to cultivate

49 Danielson, 'Situating human rights approaches', 225; Alessandrini, 'Global value chains, development and the *long durée*'.

50 Anderer, Dür, and Lechner, 'Trade policy in a "GVC world"', 639.

51 Anghie, *Imperialism, Sovereignty, and the Making of International Law*.

52 Bauder, *Migration Borders Freedom*, 25, 28.

53 Fudge, 'Governing global labour migration'.

cohesive and durable communities and societies. Thus, policies that implement and support neoliberal globalisation create both the necessity and the desire for people to migrate across international boundaries in search of work. In turn, this surplus labour that is not 'native' to the receiving nation-state can be hired, fired, and deported to meet demand without providing workers with wages and working conditions that would enable them to sustain themselves or their households on a long-term basis.

For workers to be truly free, we need to dismantle the neoliberal economic and political order. Although resilient, neoliberalism is fading.[54] It persists, in part, for lack of alternatives that challenge economic inequality between and within nation-states *and* provide imaginaries of sustainable development beyond capitalism and political order beyond the nation-state. This task of revisioning, let alone achieving a different social imaginary, is a tall order. However, crusading for the elimination of modern slavery without changing the legal rules that vest unaccountable power in corporations or providing reparation for centuries of colonial dispossession obscures the ongoing and fraught relationship between freedom and power.

[54] Gerstle, *The Rise and Fall of the Neoliberal Order.*

Bibliography

Aaronson, Ely, and Gregory Shaffer, 'Defining crimes in a global age: Criminalization as a transnational legal process' (2021) 46 *Law and Social Inquiry*, 455–486.

Adams, Zoe, *Labour and the Wage: A Critical Perspective* (Oxford: Oxford University Press, 2020).

'A structural approach to labour law' (2022) 46 *Cambridge Journal of Economics*, 447–463.

Alessandrini, Donatella, 'Global value chains, development and the long *durée* of trade and investment' (2022) 35 *Leiden Journal of International Law*, 619–640.

Allain, Jean, 'Contemporary slavery and its definition in law', in Annie Bunting and Joel Quirk (eds.), *Contemporary Slavery: Popular Rhetoric and Political Practice* (Vancouver: University of British Columbia Press, 2017), 36–66.

'The legal definition of slavery into the twenty-first century', in Jean Allain (ed.), *The Legal Understanding of Slavery: From the Historical to the Contemporary* (Oxford: Oxford University Press, 2012), 199–219.

'White slave traffic in international law' (2017) 1 *Journal of Trafficking and Human Exploitation*, 1–40.

Aliverti, Ana, 'Law in the margins: Economies of illegality and contested sovereignties' (2023) 63 *British Journal of Criminology*, 1024–1040.

All-Party Parliamentary Group on Prostitution and the Global Sex Trade, *Behind Closed Doors: Organised Sexual Exploitation in England and Wales* (London: All-Party Parliamentary Group on Prostitution and the Global Sex Trade, 2018).

Bust the Business Model (London: All-Party Parliamentary Group on Commercial Sexual Exploitation, 2021).

Shifting the Burden: Inquiry to Assess the Operation of the Current Legal Settlement on Prostitution in England and Wales (London: All-Party Parliamentary Group on Prostitution and the Global Sex Trade, 2014).

Allwood, Gill, 'Agenda setting, agenda blocking and policy silence: Why is there no EU policy on prostitution?' (2018) 69 *Women's Studies International Forum*, 126–134.

Alsamawi, Ali, Tihana Bule, Claudia Cappa, Harry Cook, Claire Galez-Davis, and Gady Saiovici, 'Measuring child labour, forced labour and human trafficking in global supply chains: A global input–output approach', Technical Paper, ILO,

OECD, IOM, UNCF, 2019, www.ilo.org/wcmsp5/groups/public/—ed_norm/—ipec/documents/publication/wcms_733916.pdf.

Ambrose, Tom, 'UK's illegal migration bill will force traffickers underground, says May', *Guardian*, 28 March 2023.

Anderer, Christin, Andreas Dür, and Lisa Lechner, 'Trade policy in a "GVC world": Multinational corporations and trade liberalization' (2022) 22 *Business and Politics*, 639–666.

Anderson, Bridget, 'Mobilizing migrants, making citizens: Migrant domestic workers as political agents' (2010) 33 *Ethnic and Racial Studies*, 60–74.

Us and Them? The Dangerous Politics of Immigration Control (Oxford: Oxford University Press, 2013).

Anderson, Bridget, and Rutvica Andrijasevic, 'Sex, slaves and citizens: The politics of anti-trafficking' (2008) 40 *Soundings*, 135–145.

Anderson, Bridget, and Ben Rogaly, 'Forced labour and migration to the UK', Trades Union Congress Report, 2005, http://sro.sussex.ac.uk/id/eprint/11418/1/Forced_Labour_TUC_Report.pdf.

Anderson, Elizabeth, *Private Government: How Employers Rule Our Lives (and Why We Don't Talk about It)* (Princeton, NJ: Princeton University Press, 2017).

Andrees, Beate, *Forced Labour and Human Trafficking: A Handbook for Labour Inspectors* (Geneva: International Labour Office, 2008).

Andrees, Beate, and Amanda Aikman, 'Raising the bar: The adoption of new ILO standards against forced labour', in Prabha Kotiswaran (ed.), *Revisiting the Law and Governance of Trafficking: Forced Labor and Modern Slavery* (Cambridge: Cambridge University Press, 2017), 359–394.

Andrees, Beate, and Patrick Belser, *Forced Labor: Coercion and Exploitation in the Private Economy International Labour Office* (Boulder, CO: Lynne Rienner, 2009).

'Strengthening labour market governance against forced labour', in B. Andreas and P. Belser (eds.), *Forced Labor: Coercion and Exploitation in the Private Economy* (Boulder, CO: Lynne Riener, 2009), 109–129.

Andrijasevic, Rutvica, 'Beautiful dead bodies: Gender, migration and representation in anti-trafficking campaigns' (2007) 86 *Feminist Review*, 24–44.

'Forced labour in supply chains: Rolling back the debate on gender, migration and sexual commerce' (2021) 28 *European Journal of Women's Studies*, 410–424.

Migration, Agency and Citizenship in Sex Trafficking (London: Palgrave Macmillan, 2010).

Andrijasevic, Rutvica, and Nicola Mai, 'Trafficking (in) representations: Understanding the recurring appeal of victimhood and slavery in neoliberal times' (2016) 7 *Anti-trafficking Review*, 1–10.

Andrijasevic, Rutvica, and William Walters, 'The International Organization for Migration and the international government of borders' (2010) 28 *Environment and Planning D: Society and Space*, 977–999.

Anghie, Antony, *Imperialism, Sovereignty and the Making of International Law* (Cambridge: Cambridge University Press, 2005).

Anti-Slavery International, 'A call for EU human rights and environmental due diligence legislation', 2 December 2019, www.antislavery.org/wp-content/uploads/2019/12/cso_eu_due_diligence_statement_2.12.19.pdf.

'A call for pan-European action to tackle forced labour and child labour in global supply chains', June 2018, www.antislavery.org/wp-content/uploads/2018/06/EU-Supply-Chains-briefing.pdf.

Anti-Slavery International and European Center for Constitutional and Human Rights, *Position on Import Controls to Address Forced Labour in Supply Chains*, June 2021, www.antislavery.org/wp-content/uploads/2021/06/Anti-Slavery-International-ECCHR-Import-Controls-Position-Paper-1.pdf.

Anti-Slavery International, International Federation for Human Rights (FIDH), European Coalition for Corporate Justice (ECCJ), Clean Clothes Campaign, European Center for Constitutional and Human Rights (ECCHR), Global Witness, 'Key considerations for an EU instrument to control the importation of forced labour products into the EU', NGO Position Paper, July 2021, https://media.business-humanrights.org/media/documents/Import_controls_NGO_Paper_Final_Design.pdf.

Anti-Trafficking Monitoring Group (ATMG), *Wrong Kind of Victim? One Year On: An Analysis of UK Measures to Protect Trafficked Persons* (London: Anti-Slavery International for the Anti-Trafficking Monitoring Group, 2010) www.antislavery.org/wp-content/uploads/2017/01/full_report.pdf.

Aradau, Claudia, 'The perverse politics of four-letter words: Risk and pity in the securitization of human trafficking' (2004) 33 *Millennium: Journal of International Studies*, 251–277.

Arnold, Dennis, and Martin Hess, 'Governmentalizing Gramsci: Topologies of power and passive revolution in Cambodia's garment production network' (2017) 49 *Environment and Planning A*, 2183–2202.

Askola, Heli, *Legal Responses to Trafficking in Women for Sexual Exploitation in the European Union* (Oxford: Hart, 2007).

Atkins, Judi, '(Re)imagining Magna Carta: Myth, metaphor and the rhetoric of Britishness' (2016) 68 *Parliamentary Affairs*, 603–620.

'Rhetoric and audience reception: An analysis of Theresa May's vision of Britain and Britishness after Brexit' (2022) 42 *Politics*, 216–230.

Baccaro, Lucio, and Valentina Mele, 'Pathology of path dependency? The ILO and the challenge of new governance' (2012) 65 *Industrial and Labor Relations Review*, 207–210.

Balch, Alex, 'Defeating "modern slavery", reducing exploitation? The organisational and regulatory challenge', in Gary Craig, Alex Balch, Hannah Lewis, and Louise Waite (eds.), *The Modern Slavery Agenda: Policy, Politics and Practice in the UK* (Bristol: Policy Press, 2019), 75–96.

'Labour and epistemic communities: The case of "managed migration" in the UK' (2009) 11 *British Journal of Politics and International Relations*, 613–633.

'Regulation and enforcement to tackle forced labour in the UK: A systematic response?' Joseph Rowntree Foundation Programme Paper, February 2012, www.jrf.org.uk/report/regulation-and-enforcement-tackle-forced-labour-uk-systematic-response.

Balch, Alex, and Andrew Geddes, 'Opportunity from crisis? Organisational responses to human trafficking in the UK' (2011) 13 *British Journal of Politics and International Relations*, 26–41.

Bale, Tim, 'Putting it right? The Labour Party's big shift on immigration since 2010' (2014) 85 *Political Quarterly*, 296–303.

Bales, Katie, 'Immigration raids, employer collusion and the Immigration Act 2016' (2017) 46 *Industrial Law Journal*, 279–288.

Bales, Kevin, *Blood and Earth: Modern Slavery, Ecocide, and the Secret to Saving the World* (New York: Random House, 2016).

Disposable People: New Slavery in the Global Economy (Berkeley: University of California Press, 1999).

Ending Slavery: How We Free Today's Slaves (Berkeley: University of California Press, 2007).

'Slavery and the human right to evil' (2004) 3 *Journal of Human Rights*, 53–63.

'What predicts human trafficking?' (2007) 31 *International Journal of Comparative and Applied Criminal Justice*, 269–291.

Bales, Kevin, and Austin Choi-Fitzpatrick, 'The anti-slavery movement: Making rights reality', in Alison Brysk and Austin Choi-Fitzpatrick (eds.), *From Human Trafficking to Human Rights: Reframing Contemporary Slavery* (Philadelphia: University of Pennsylvania Press, 2012), 195–215.

Bales, Kevin, and Alison Gardner, 'Free soil, free producers, free communities', in Genevieve LeBaron, Jessica R. Piley, and David W. Blight (eds.), *Fighting Modern Slavery and Human Trafficking: History and Contemporary Policy* (Cambridge: Cambridge University Press, 2021), 73–96.

Bales, Kevin, and Zoe Trodd, 'Addressing contemporary forms of slavery in EU external policy', Briefing Paper, Directorate-General for External Policies of the Union, Directorate B, Policy Department, December 2013, EXPO/B/DROI/2012/20.

Balibar, Etiene, *Politics and the Other Scene* (London: Verso, 2002).

Barkan, Joshua, 'Law and the geographic analysis of economic globalization' (2011) 35 *Progress in Human Geography*, 589–607.

Batty, David, 'David Cameron launches election campaign with economy pledge,' *Guardian*, 2 January 2010.

Barnard, Catherine, and Sarah Fraser Butlin, 'Why are criminal offences criminal in labour law?' in Alan Bogg, Jennifer Collins, Mark Freedland, and Jonathan Herring (eds.), *Criminality at Work* (Oxford: Oxford University Press, 2020), 70–96.

Barrientos, Stephanie, *Gender and Work in Global Value Chains: Capturing the Gains?* (Cambridge: Cambridge University Press, 2019).

Bauder, Harald, *Migration Borders Freedom* (Abingdon: Routledge, 2017).

Berket, Mariyana Radeva, 'Labour exploitation and trafficking for labour exploitation: Trends and challenges for policy-making' (2015) 16 *ERA Forum*, 359–377.

Berman, Cindy, 'Shaping the Modern Slavery Act: A look back beyond trafficking and slavery', *Open Democracy*, 25 September 2016.

Berman, Jacqueline, 'The left, the right, and the prostitute: The making of US antitrafficking in persons policy' (2005) 14 *Tulane Journal of International and Comparative Law*, 269–294.

'(Un)popular strangers and crises (un)bounded: Discourses of sex-trafficking, the European political community and the panicked state of the modern state' (2003) 9 *European Journal of International Relations*, 37–86.

Berman, Paul Schiff, 'From international law to law and globalization' (2005) 43 *Columbia Journal of Transnational Law*, 485–556.

Bernards, Nick, *The Global Governance of Precarity: Primitive Accumulation and the Politics of Irregular Work* (London: Routledge, 2018).

'The global politics of forced labour' (2017) 14 *Globalizations*, 944–957.

Bernstein, Elizabeth, 'Militarized humanitarianism meets carceral feminism: The politics of sex, rights, and freedom in contemporary anti-trafficking campaigns' (2010) 36 *Signs: Journal of Women in Culture and Society*, 45–72.

Beutin, Lyndsey P., *Trafficking in Antiblackness: Modern-Day Slavery, White Indemnity and Racial Justice* (Durham, NC: Duke University Press, 2023).

Biden, Joseph, 'Presidential Proclamation on National Human Trafficking Prevention Month', 2022, 3, White House, Office of the Press Secretary, News release, www.whitehouse.gov/briefing-room/presidential-actions/2021/12/30/a-proclamation-on-national-human-trafficking-prevention-month-2022/.

Bishop, Matthew, and Michael Green, *Philanthro-Capitalism: How the Rich Can Save the World* (London: Bloomsbury, 2008).

Blackett, Adelle, 'On the presence of the past in the future of international labour law' (2020) 43 *Dalhousie Law Journal*, 947–962.

'Following the drinking gourd: Our road to teaching critical race theory and slavery and the law, contemplatively, at McGill' (2017) 62 *McGill Law Journal* 1251–1277.

Blackett, Adelle, and Anne Trebilcock (eds.), *Research Handbook on Transnational Labour Law* (Cheltenham: Edward Elgar, 2015).

Bogg, Alan, 'Illegality in labour law after Patel v Mirza: Retrenchment and restraint', in Sarah Green and Alan Bogg (eds.), *Illegality after Patel v Mirza* (Oxford: Hart, 2018), 255–287.

Bonilla, T., and C. H. Mo, 'The evolution of human trafficking messaging in the United States and its effect on public opinion' (2019) 39 *Journal of Public Policy*, 201–234.

Boris, Eileen, and Magaly Rodríguez García, '(In)decent work: Sex and the ILO' (2021) 33 *Journal of Women's History*, 194–221.

Bosworth, Mary, 'Border control and the limits of the sovereign state' (2008) 17 *Social and Legal Studies*, 199–215.

Bosworth, Mary, and Mhairi Guild, 'Governing through migration control: Security and citizenship in Britain' (2008) 48 *British Journal of Criminology*, 703–719.

Brace, Laura, and Julia O'Connell-Davidson, 'Slavery and the revival of antislavery activism', in Laura Brace and Julia O'Connell-Davidson (eds.), *Revisiting Slavery and Antislavery: Towards a Critical Analysis* (London: Palgrave Macmillan, 2018), 3–34.

Brankovic, Jelena, 'Measure of shame: Media career of the Global Slavery Index', in L. Ringel, W. N. Espeland, M. Sauder, and T. Werron (eds.), *Worlds of Rankings*, Research in the Sociology of Organizations, Vol. 74 (Bingley: Emerald, 2021), 103–125.

Broad, Rose, and David Gadd, *Demystifying Modern Slavery* (London: Routledge, 2023).

Broad, Rose, and Nick Turnbull, 'From human trafficking to modern slavery: The development of anti-trafficking policy in the UK' (2019) 25 *European Journal on Criminal Policy and Research*, 119–133.

Brudney, James, 'Hidden in plain sight: An ILO Convention on labour standards in global supply chains' (2023) 23 *Chicago Journal of International Law*, 272–341.

Bruggeman, Jean, 'Freedom Network USA now supports sex workers' rights', *Open Democracy*, 10 September 2021, www.opendemocracy.net/en/beyond-trafficking-and-slavery/freedom-network-usa-now-supports-sex-workers-rights/.

Brysk, Alison, and Austin Choi-Fitzpatrick (eds.), *From Human Trafficking to Human Rights: Reframing Contemporary Slavery* (Philadelphia: University of Pennsylvania Press, 2012).

Bulmer, Simon, 'New labour, new European policy? Blair, Brown and utilitarian supranationalism' (2008) 61 *Parliamentary Affairs*, 597–620.

Bunting, Annie, and Joel Quirk, 'Contemporary slavery as more than rhetorical strategy? The politics and ideology of a new political cause', in Annie Bunting and Joel Quirk (eds.), *Contemporary Slavery: Popular Rhetoric and Political Practice* (Vancouver: University of British Columbia Press, 2017), 22–52.

Bush, George, 'President Bush Addresses United Nations General Assembly,' White House, Office of the Press Secretary, 23 September 2003, https://georgewbush-whitehouse.archives.gov/news/releases/2003/09/20030923-4.html.

Business and Human Rights Resource Centre (BHRRC), 'EU Commission publishes legislative proposal on corporate accountability', 23 February 2022, www.business-humanrights.org/en/eu-commissioner-for-justice-commits-to-legislation-on-mandatory-due-diligence-for-companies.

'FTSE 100 at the starting line: An analysis of company statements under the UK Modern Slavery Act', January 2017, https://media.business-humanrights.org/media/documents/files/documents/FTSE_100_Modern_Slavery_Act.pdf.

Modern Slavery Act: Five Years of Reporting Conclusions from Monitoring Corporate Disclosure, February 2021, https://media.business-humanrights.org/media/documents/Modern_Slavery_Act_2021.pdf.

Modern Slavery in Company Operations and Modern Supply Chains: Mandatory Transparency, Mandatory Due Diligence and Public Procurement Due Diligence, September 2017, https://media.business-humanrights.org/media/documents/fb7a2e03e33bcec2611655db2276b4a6a086c36c.pdf.

'Wage theft and pandemic profits: The right to a living wage for garment workers', 11 March 2021, www.business-humanrights.org/en/from-us/briefings/wage-theft-and-pandemic-profits-the-right-to-a-living-wage-for-garment-workers/.

Buxbaum, Hannah, 'Territory, territoriality, and the resolution of jurisdictional conflict' (2009) 57 *American Journal of Comparative Law*, 631–676.

Cameron, David, 'PM speech on immigration', *Guardian*, 21 May 2015, www.gov.uk/government/speeches/pm-speech-on-immigration.

'Prime minister's address to *Conservative Party members on the government's immigration policy*', *Guardian*, 14 April 2011.

Campana, Paolo, and Federico Varese, 'Exploitation in human trafficking and smuggling' (2016) 22 *European Journal on Criminal Policy and Research*, 89–105.

Carrington, Michal, Andreas Chatzidakis, and Deirde Shaw, 'Consuming worker exploitation? Accounts and justifications for consumer (in)action to modern slavery' (2021) 35 *Work, Employment and Society*, 432–450.

Centre for Social Justice, *It Happens Here: Equipping the United Kingdom to Fight Modern Slavery* (London: Centre for Social Justice, 2013).

It Still Happens Here: Fighting UK Slavery in the 2020s (London: Centre for Social Justice, 2020).

A *Modern Approach to Modern Slavery* (London: Centre for Social Justice, 2015).
Charnysh, Volha, Paulette Lloyd, and Beth A. Simmons, 'Frames and consensus formation in international relations: The case of trafficking in persons' (2015) 21 *European Journal of International Relations*, 323–351.
Chimni, B. S., 'The international law of jurisdiction: A TWAIL perspective' (2022) 35 (1) *Leiden Journal of International Law*, 29–54.
Choi-Fitzpatrick, Austin, 'From rescue to representation: A human rights approach to the contemporary antislavery movement' (2015) 14 *Journal of Human Rights*, 486–503.
'Rethinking trafficking: Contemporary slavery', in Alison Brysk and Austin Choi-Fitzpatrick (eds.), *From Human Trafficking to Human Rights: Reframing Contemporary Slavery* (Philadelphia: University of Pennsylvania Press, 2012), 13–24.
'To seek and save the lost: Human trafficking and salvation schemas among American evangelicals' (2014) 1 *European Journal of Cultural and Political Sociology*, 119–140.
Christodoulidis, Emilios, 'Labour constitutionalism in a genealogical key' (2018) 9 *Jurisprudence*, 413–417.
Chuang, Janie A., 'Exploitation creep and the unmaking of human trafficking law' (2014) 108 *American Journal of International Law*, 609–649.
'Giving as governance? Philanthrocapitalism and modern-day slavery abolitionism' (2015) 6 *UCLA Law Review*, 1517–1556.
'Rescuing trafficking from ideological capture: Prostitution reform and anti-trafficking law and policy' (2010) 158 *University of Pennsylvania Law Review*, 1655–1728.
'The United States as global sheriff: Using unilateral sanctions to combat human trafficking' (2005–2006) 27 *Michigan Journal of International Law*, 437–494.
Cimino-Isaacs, Cathleen, Christopher A. Casey, and Katarina O'Reagan, Congressional Research Service, 'Section 307 and U.S. imports of products of forced labor: Overview and issues for Congress', Report, 1 February 2021, sgp.fas .org/crs/misc/R46631.pdf.
Coalition to End Forced Labour in the Uyghur Region, 'Coalition statement on European Commission's proposed ban on products made with forced labour', 21 September 2021, https://enduyghurforcedlabour.org/news/coalition-statement-on-european-commissions-proposed-ban-on-products-made-with-forced-labour/.
Cockayne, James, *Developing Freedom: The Sustainable Development Case for Ending Modern Slavery, Forced Labour and Human Trafficking* (New York: United Nations, 2021).
'Working with the financial sector to correct the market failure of modern slavery' (2021) 6 *Business and Human Rights Journal*, 159–162.
Commission of the European Communities, 'Communication from the commission to the council and the European Parliament: On Trafficking in Women for the Purpose of Sexual Exploitation,' Brussels, 20 November 1996, COM(96) 567 final.
'Communication from the commission to the European Parliament and the council: Fighting trafficking in human beings – An integrated approach and proposals for an action plan', Brussels, 18 October 2005, COM(2005) 514 final.

Conservative Party, *A Strong Leadership: The Conservative Party Manifesto 2015*, 2015, www.theresavilliers.co.uk/sites/www.theresavilliers.co.uk/files/conservativemanifesto2015.pdf.

The Conservative and Unionist Party Manifesto 2017, *Forward, Together: Our Plan for a Stronger Britain and a Prosperous Future*, 2017, https://ucrel.lancs.ac.uk/wmatrix/ukmanifestos2017/localpdf/Conservatives.pdf.

The Conservative and Unionist Party Manifesto 2019, *Get Brexit Done Unleash Britain's Potential*, 2019, https://assets.website-files.com/5da42e2cae7ebd3f8bde353c/5dda924905da587992a064ba_Conservative%202019%20Manifesto.pdf.

Cook, Chris, 'Christian Tories rewrite party doctrine', *Financial Times*, 12 February 2010.

Cooper, Christine, Olivia Hesketh, Nicola Ellis, and Adam Fair, *A Typology of Modern Slavery Offences in the UK*, Research Report 93 (London: Home Office, 2017), www.gov.uk/government/publications/a-typology-of-modern-slavery-offences-in-the-uk.

Cooper, Matthew, 'UK "voodoo" nurse first person convicted under modern slavery laws' *Independent*, 28 June 2018.

CORE and Business and Human Rights Resource Centre, 'UK Modern Slavery Act: First 75 statements in', Press release, 7 March 2016.

Costello, Cathryn, 'Migrants and forced labour: A labour law response', in Alan Bogg, Cathryn Costello, A. C. L. Davies, and Jeremias Prassl (eds.), *The Autonomy of Labour Law* (Oxford: Hart, 2013), 189–228.

Council of Europe, 'Council of Europe Convention on Action against Trafficking in Human Beings' (2005) 197 *Council of Europe Treaty Series*, Warsaw, 16. V.2005.

Council of Europe, Parliamentary Assembly, 'Prostitution, trafficking and modern slavery in Europe, Resolution 1983 (2014), Final version', https://assembly.coe.int/nw/xml/XRef/Xref-XML2HTML-en.asp?fileid=20716.

'Recommendation No 1545 (2002) on a campaign against trafficking in women' (21 January 2002).

Council of Europe Steering Committee for Equality between Women and Men, *Feasibility Study for a Convention of the Council of Europe on Trafficking in Human Beings*, Doc. DG-11 (2002).

Council of the European Union, 'Council conclusions on human rights and decent work in global supply chains', Brussels, 1 December 2020 (OR. en), 13512/20 SOC 772, EMPL 542, https://data.consilium.europa.eu/doc/document/ST-13512-2020-INIT/en/pdf.

'Proposal for a comprehensive plan to combat illegal immigration and trafficking of human beings in the European Union', 2002/C 142/02, *Official Journal, C142*, 14 June 2002.

Craig, Gary, 'The UK's modern slavery legislation: An early assessment of progress' (2017) 5 *Social Inclusion*, 16–27.

Craig, Gary, Alex Balch, Hannah Lewis, and Louise Waite (eds.), *The Modern Slavery Agenda: Policy, Politics and Practice in the UK* (Bristol: Policy Press, 2019).

Crane, Andrew, Genevieve LeBaron, Allain Jean, and Behbahani Laya, 'Governance gaps in eradicating forced labor: From global to domestic supply chains' (2019) 13 *Regulation and Governance*, 86–106.

Crosby Medlicott, Lauren, 'Experts blame Suella Braverman's borders act as stats show record number of potential victims being turned away', *Open Democracy*, 26 May 2023.

Cruz, Katie, 'Beyond liberalism: Marxist feminism, migrant sex work, and labour unfreedom' (2018) 26 *Feminist Legal Studies*, 65–92.

Currie, Samantha, 'Compounding vulnerability and concealing unfairness: Decision-making processes in the UK anti-trafficking framework' (2019) 3 *Public Law*, 495–516.

Daddow, Oliver, '"Globalbritain™": The discursive construction of Britain's post-Brexit world role' (2019) 5 *Global Affairs*, 5–22.

Danielson, Dan, 'Situating human rights approaches to corporate accountability in the political economy of supply chain capitalism', in David Brinks, Julia Dehm, Karen Engle, and Kate Taylor (eds.), *Power, Participation, and Private Regulatory Initiatives: Human Rights under Supply Chain Capitalism* (Philadelphia: University of Pennsylvania Press, 2021), 224–241.

Datta, Monti Narayan, and Kevin Bales, 'Slavery is bad for business: Analyzing the impact of slavery on national economies' (2013) 19 *Brown Journal of World Affairs*, 205–223.

Davies, Jon, 'Criminological reflections on the regulation and governance of labour exploitation' (2020) 23 *Trends in Organized Crime*, 57–76.

Davies, Nick, 'Prostitution and trafficking – The anatomy of a moral panic', *Guardian*, 20 October 2009.

Davies, William, *The Limits of Neoliberalism: Authority, Sovereignty and the Logic of Competition* (London: Sage, 2014).

Davis, David Brion 'The problem of slavery in the Age of Revolution, 1770–1823', in Thomas Bender (ed.), *The Antislavery Debate* (Berkeley: University of California Press, 1992), 161–179.

Day, Sophia, 'The re-emergence of "trafficking": Sex work between slavery and freedom' (2010) 16 *Journal of the Royal Anthropological Institute*, 816–834.

Dearden, Lizzie, 'No evidence of Suella Braverman's claims migrants are "gaming" slavery laws, watchdog says', *Independent*, 9 December 2022.

'UK's first independent anti-slavery commissioner resigns citing government interference', *Independent*, 17 May 2018.

Dehbi, Fatimazahra, and Olga Martin-Ortega, 'An integrated approach to corporate due diligence from a human rights, environmental, and TWAIL perspective', *Regulation and Governance*, 19 June 2023, https://doi.org/10.1111/rego.12538.

Dehm, Sara, 'Framing international migration' (2015) 3 *London Review of International Law*, 133–168.

Department for Business, Energy and Industrial Strategy and Home Office, *UK Labour Market Enforcement Strategy 2018/19: Government Response*, December 2018, https://data.parliament.uk/DepositedPapers/Files/DEP2018-1269/Director_of_Labour_Market_Enforcements_Strategy_-_Government_Response.pdf.

Deva, Surya, 'Mandatory human rights due diligence laws in Europe: A mirage for rightsholders?' (2023) 36 *Leiden Journal of International Law*, 389–414.

Devereux, Cecily, '"The Maiden Tribute" and the rise of the white slave in the nineteenth century: The making of an imperial construct' (2000) 26 *Victorian Review*, 1–23.

Diller, Janelle. M, 'Pluralism and privatization in transnational labour regulation: Experience of the International Labour Organization', in A. Blackett and A. Trebilcock (eds.), *Research Handbook on Transnational Labour Law* (Cheltenham: Edward Elgar, 2015), 329–342.

'The role of the state in the exercise of transnational public and private authority over labour standards' (2020) 17 *International Organizations Law Review*, 41–74. https://doi.org/10.1163/15723747-01701003.

Doezema, Jo, 'Loose women or lost women? The re-emergence of the myth of white slavery in contemporary discourses of trafficking in women' (1999) 18 *Gender Issues*, 23–50.

'Now you see her, now you don't: Sex workers at the UN Trafficking Protocol negotiations' (2005) 14 *Social and Legal Studies*, 61–89.

Doonan, Christina, 'A house divided: Humanitarianism and anti-immigration within US anti-trafficking legislation' (2016) 24 *Feminist Legal Studies*, 273–293.

Dorsett, Shaunnagh, and Shaun McVeigh, *Jurisdiction* (London: Routledge, 2012).

Dottridge, Mike, 'Collateral damage provoked by anti-trafficking measures', in Ryszard Piotrowicz, Conny Rijken, and Baerbel Heide Uhl (eds.), *Routledge Handbook of Human Trafficking* (Abingdon: Routledge, 2017), 342–353.

'Eight reasons why we shouldn't use the term "modern slavery"', *Open Democracy*, 17 October 2017.

'Global trafficking prevalence data distorts efforts to stop patterns of human trafficking' (2017) 8 *Anti-trafficking Review*, 161–164.

'Private donors: The pied pipers of 'modern slavery'?' *Open Democracy*, 29 March 2021, www.opendemocracy.net/en/beyond-trafficking-and-slavery/private-donors-the-pied-pipers-of-modern-slavery/.

'Trafficked and exploited: The urgent need for coherence in international law', in Prabha Kotiswaran (ed.), *Revisiting the Law and Governance of Trafficking: Forced Labor and Modern Slavery* (Cambridge: Cambridge University Press, 2017), 59–82.

Drubel, Julia, 'Regulation by visibility: New forms of global social governance' (2019) 19 *Global Social Policy*, 188–206.

Dugan, Emily, 'Home Office accused of deliberately leaving anti-slavery post unfilled', *Guardian*, 29 August 2022.

'UK signs trafficking directive after 10-month delay', *Independent on Sunday*, 27 March 2011.

'Watchdog disputes Braverman's claim modern slavery laws being "gamed"', *Guardian*, 9 October 2022.

Ebert, Franz Christian, Francesca Francavilla, and Lorenzo Guarcello, 'Tackling forced labour in supply chains: The potential of trade and investment governance', in Marva Corley-Coulibaly, Franz Christian Ebert, and Pelin Sekerler Richiardi (eds.), *Integrating Trade and Decent Work, Volume II. The Potential of Trade and Investment Policies to Address Labour Market Issues in Supply Chains* (Geneva: ILO, 2023), 103–142.

Edwards, Alice, 'Traffic in human beings: At the intersection of criminal justice, human rights, asylum/migration and labor' (2007) 36 *Denver Journal of International Law and Policy*, 9–53.

EFRA (Environment, Food and Rural Affairs Committee), *Fourteenth Report* (London: House of Commons, 2003).

El-Enany, Nadine, *Bordering Britain: Law, Race and Empire* (Manchester: Manchester University Press, 2020).

Ergon Associates, *Modern Slavery Statements: One Year On*, April 2017, http://ergonassociates.net/wp-content/uploads/2016/03/MSA_One_year_on_April_2017.pdf?x74739.

Reporting on Modern Slavery: The Current State of Disclosure, May 2016, http://ergonassociates.net/wp-content/uploads/2017/06/Reporting-on-Modern-Slavery2-May-2016.pdf?x74739.

Ethical Trading Initiative, 'Modern slavery statement 2017/18,' 2018, www.ethicaltrade.org/sites/default/files/shared_resources/ETI%20MS%20statement.pdf.

Eurofound, *Regulation of Labour Market Intermediaries and the Role of Social Partners in Preventing Trafficking of Labour* (Luxembourg: Publications Office of the European Union, 2016), www.eurofound.europa.eu/publications/report/2016/labour-market-industrial-relations/regulation-of-labour-market-intermediaries-and-the-role-of-social-partners-in-preventing-trafficking.

European Coalition for Corporate Justice, 'An EU mandatory due-diligence legislation to promote businesses' respect for human rights and the environment', 1 September 2020, https://corporatejustice.org/publications/principal-elements-of-eu-due-diligence-legislation/.

European Commission, 'Communication from the commission to the European Parliament and the council, reporting on the follow-up to the EU strategy towards the eradication of trafficking inhuman beings and identifying further concrete actions', Brussels, 4 December 2017, COM(2017) 728 final.

'Communication from the commission to the European Parliament, the council, the European Economic and Social Committee and the Committee of the Regions: The EU Strategy towards the Eradication of Trafficking in Human Beings, 2012–2016', Brussels, 19 June 2012, COM(2012) 286 final.

'Communication from the commission to the European Parliament, the council, the European Economic and Social Committee, and the Committee of the Regions, on the EU Strategy on Combatting Trafficking in Human Beings, 2021–2025', Brussels, 14 April 2021, COM(2021) 171 final.

'The EU strategy towards the eradication of trafficking in human beings, 2012–2016', 2012, www.khartoumprocess.net/resources/library/download/file?fid=20.68.

'Mid-term report on the implementation of the EU strategy towards the eradication of trafficking in human beings', Brussels, 17 October 2014, COM(2014) 635 final.

'New EU guidance helps companies to combat forced labour in supply chains,' Press release, 13 July 2021, https://ec.europa.eu/commission/presscorner/detail/en/IP_21_3664.

'Proposal for a directive of the European Parliament and of the council on corporate sustainability due diligence and amending directive (EU) 2019/1937,' Brussels, 23 February 2022, COM(2022) 71 final, 2002/0051 (COD).

'Proposal for a directive of the European Parliament and of the council on preventing and combating trafficking in human beings, and protecting victims, repealing

Framework Decision 2002/629/JHA', Brussels, 29 March 2010, COM(2010)95 final, 2010/0065 (COD).

'Report from the commission to the European Parliament and the council assessing the extent to which member states have taken the necessary measures in order to comply with directive 2011/36EU on preventing and combating trafficking in human beings and protecting its victims in accordance with Article 23(1)', Brussels, 2 December 2016, COM(2016) 722 final.

'Report from the commission to the European Parliament and the council assessing the impact of existing national law, establishing as a criminal offence the use of services which are the objects of exploitation of trafficking in human beings, on the prevention of trafficking in human beings, in accordance with Article 23 (2) of the Directive 2011/36/EU', Brussels, 2 December 2016, COM(2016) 719 final.

'Report from the commission to the European Parliament and the council on the progress made in the fight against trafficking in human beings (2016) as required under Article 20 of Directive 2011/36EU on preventing and combating trafficking in human beings and protecting its victims', Brussels, 19 May 2016, COM (2016) 267 final.

Report of the Experts Group on Trafficking in Human Beings, Brussels, 22 December 2004, https://documentation.lastradainternational.org/lsidocs/49%20Report%20of%20the%20Experts%20Group%20on%20Trafficking%20in%20Human%20Beings.pdf.

'Sustainable corporate governance: Inception impact assessment', Ref. Ares(2020) 4034032–30/07/2020, https://ec.europa.eu/info/law/better-regulation/have-your-say/initiatives/12548-Sustainable-corporate-governance_en.

'Trafficking in women: The misery behind the fantasy – From poverty to sex slavery a comprehensive European strategy', Brussels, 6 March 2001, Memo/01/64, https://ec.europa.eu/commission/presscorner/api/files/document/print/en/memo_01_64/MEMO_01_64_EN.pdf.

European Commission, Directorate-General Justice and Consumers, 'Sustainable corporate governance initiative: Summary report – public consultation', Ref. Ares(2021)3297206–18/05/2021.

European Commission, Directorate-General for Internal Market, Industry, Entrepreneurship and SMEs, 'Just and sustainable economy: Commission lays down rules for companies to respect human rights and environment in global value chains', 23 February 2022, https://single-market-economy.ec.europa.eu/news/just-and-sustainable-economy-commission-lays-down-rules-companies-respect-human-rights-and-2022-02-23_en.

European Labour Authority, 'ELA's mission', 2023, www.ela.europa.eu/en/elas-mission.

European Parliament, Report A8–0269/2017, Committee on International Trade, Rapporteur: Maria Arena, 'Report on the impact of international trade and the EU's trade policies on global value chains', 20 July 2017, 2016/2301 (INI), www.europarl.europa.eu/doceo/document/A-8-2017-0269_EN.html.

European Union, '2001/220/JHA: Council framework decision of 15 March 2001 on the standing of victims in criminal proceedings'.

'2002/629/JHA: Council framework decision of 19 July 2002 on combating trafficking in human beings', *Official Journal of the European Communities*, L 203/1.

'2002/946/JHA: Council framework decision of 28 November 2002 on the strengthening of the penal framework to prevent the facilitation of unauthorised entry, transit and residence', *Official Journal of the European Communities*, L 328/1.

'Council directive 2002/90/EC of 28 November 2002 defining the facilitation of unauthorised entry, transit and residence', *Official Journal of the European Communities*, L 328/17.

'Council directive 2004/80/EC of 29 April 2004 relating to compensation to crime victims', *Official Journal of the European Union*, L 261/15.

'Council directive 2004/81/EC of 29 April 2004 on the residence permit issued to third-country nationals who are victims of trafficking in human beings or who have been the subject of an action to facilitate illegal immigration, who cooperate with the competent authorities', *Official Journal of the European Union*, L 261/19.

'Council framework decision of 19 July 2002 on combating trafficking in human beings', *Official Journal of European Communities*, L 203/1.

'Directive 2009/52/EC of the European Parliament and of the council of 18 June 2009 providing for minimum standards on sanctions and measures against employers of illegally staying third-country nationals', *Official Journal of the European Union*, 30 June 2009.

'Directive 2011/36/EU of the European Parliament and of the council of 5 April 2011 on preventing and combating trafficking in human beings and protecting its victims, and replacing Council Framework Decision 2002/629/JHA', *Official Journal of the European Union*, L 101/1, 1–11.

'Directive 2012/29/EU of the European Parliament and of the Council of 25 October 2012 establishing minimum standards on the rights, support, and protection of victims of crime, and replacing Council Framework Decision 2001/220/JHA', *Official Journal of the European Union*, L 315/57.

'Directive 2014/95/EU of the European Parliament and of the council of 22 October 2014 amending Directive 2013/34/EU as regards disclosure of non-financial and diversity information by certain large undertakings and groups', *Official Journal of the European Union*, L 330/1.

'European Parliament resolution of 5 July 2016 on the fight against trafficking in human beings in the EU's external relations', 2015/2340(INI).

'European Parliament resolution of 10 March 2021 with recommendations to the Commission on corporate due diligence and corporate accountability', Brussels, 10 March 2021, 2020/2129(INL).

'European Parliament resolution of 26 February 2014 on sexual exploitation and prostitution and its impact on gender equality', 2013/2103(INI).

'European Parliament resolution of 25 October 2016 on corporate liability for serious human rights abuses in third countries', 2015/2315(INI).

'Regulation (EU) No 2017/821 of the European Parliament and of the council of 17 May 2017', *Official Journal of the European Union*, L 130/1.

Evans, Alice, 'Overcoming the global despondency trap: Strengthening corporate accountability in supply chains' (202) 27 *Review of International Political Economy*, 658–685.

Ewins, James, *Independent Review of the Overseas Domestic Workers Visa*, 16 December 2015, https://assets.publishing.service.gov.uk/media/5a806ecee5274a2e87db9c85/ODWV_Review_-_Final_Report__6_11_15_.pdf.

Faucher-King, Florence, and Patrick Le Galès, *The New Labour Experiment: Change and Reform under Blair and Brown* (Palo Alto, CA: Stanford University Press, 2010).

Feasely, Ashely, 'Eliminating corporate exploitation: Examining accountability regimes as a means to eradicate forced labor from supply chains', (2016) 2 *Journal of Human Trafficking*, 15–31.

Feingold, David, 'Trafficking in numbers: The social construction of human trafficking data', in P. Andreas and K. M. Greenhill (eds.), *Sex, Drugs, and Body Counts: The Politics of Numbers in Global Crime and Conflict* (Ithaca, NY: Cornell University Press, 2010), 46–74.

Field, Frank, 'David Cameron could have been an anti-slavery hero', *Spectator Magazine*, 16 August 2014.

'Extension to Michael Dottridge's "How did we get the Modern Slavery Act"', *Open Democracy*, 14 December 2016.

FitzGerald, Sharron A., 'Vulnerable bodies, vulnerable borders: Extraterritoriality and human trafficking' (2012) 20 *Feminist Legal Studies*, 227–244.

'Vulnerable geographies: Human trafficking, immigration and border control in the UK and beyond' (2016) 23 *Gender, Place and Culture*, 181–197.

Fitzpatrick, Joan, 'Trafficking and a human rights violation: The complex intersection of legal fameworks for conceptualizing and combating trafficking' (2003) 24 *Michigan Journal of International Law*, 1143–1167.

Ford, Richard, 'Law's territory (A history of jurisdiction)' (1999) 97 *Michigan Law Review*, 843–930.

Foret, François, and Lucrecia Rubio Grundel, 'European morality politics in the European Union: The case of prostitution' (2020) 24 *Sexuality and Culture*, 1798–1814.

Foucault, Michel, *Discipline and Punish: The Birth of the Prison* (New York: Vintage, 1995).

Language, Counter-Memory, Practice: Selected Essays and Interviews (Ithaca, NY: Cornell University Press, 1977).

'Society Must Be Defended': Lectures at the Collège de France, 1975–1976 (London: Picador, 2003).

FRA (European Union Agency for Fundamental Rights), *Severe Labour Exploitation: Workers Moving within or into the European Union: States' Obligations and Victims' Rights* (Vienna: European Union Agency for Fundamental Rights, 2015).

Fraser, Nancy, 'From exploitation to expropriation: Historic geographies of racialized capitalism' (2018) 94 *Economic Geography*, 1–17.

Freedom Fund, 'Freedom in the supply chain: Mobilising solutions to address slavery throughout the supply chain ecosystem', 2018, https://d1r4g0yjvcc7lx.cloudfront.net/uploads/20180815142414/FF-supply-chains-strategic-plan-.pdf.

'Our vision is a world free of slavery', 2018, https://freedomfund.org/wp-content/uploads/FF_2PAGE_2018_WEB1.pdf.

Fudge, Judy, 'Bad for business: The construction of modern slavery and the reconfiguration of sovereignty' (2022) 10 *London Review of International Law*, 3–31.

'Governing global labour migration: Compacts and contradictions', in Eileen Boris, Heidi Gottfried, and Julie Green (eds.), *Global Labour Migration* (Champagne: University of Illinois Press, 2022), 280–296.

'Feminist reflections on the scope of labour law: Domestic work, social reproduction, and jurisdiction' (2014) 22 *Feminist Legal Studies*, 1–23.

'Illegal working: Migrants and labour exploitation in the UK' (2018) 38 *Oxford Journal of Legal Studies*, 557–584.

'Migrant domestic workers in British Columbia, Canada Unfreedom, trafficking and domestic servitude', in Johanna Howe and Rosemary Owens (eds.), *Temporary Labour Migration in a Globalised World: The Regulatory Challenges* (Oxford: Hart, 2016), 151–172.

'(Re)Conceptualising unfree labour: Local labour control regimes and constraints on workers' freedoms' (2019) 10 *Global Labour Journal*, 108–122.

'Modern slavery, unfree labour and the labour market' (2018) 27 *Social and Legal Studies*, 414–434.

'What makes labour free? (And why this question matters)' (2019) 7 *Futures of Work*, https://futuresofwork.co.uk/2019/05/24/what-makes-labour-free-and-why-this-question-matters/.

'Why labour lawyers should care about the Modern Slavery Act 2015' (2018) 29 *King's Law Journal*, 377–406.

Fudge, Judy, and Genevieve LeBaron, 'Regulatory design and interactions in worker-driven social responsibility initiatives: The Dindigul agreement' (forthcoming) *International Labour Review*.

Fudge, Judy, and Guy Mundlak, 'Peeling the onion: On choices judges make in transnational labour litigation', in Ann Trebilcock and Brian Langille (eds.), *Global Justice and the World of Work* (Oxford: Hart, 2023), 249–260.

Fudge, Judy, and Kendra Strauss, 'Migrants, unfree labour, and the legal construction of domestic servitude', in Cathryn Costello and Mark Freedland (eds.), *Migrants at Work: Immigration and Vulnerability in Labour Law* (Oxford: Oxford University Press, 2014), 160–179.

Fukushima, Annie Isabel, *Migrant Crossings: Witnessing Human Trafficking in the U.S.* (Stanford, CA: Stanford University Press, 2019).

G7 Trade Ministers' Statement on Forced Labour, London, UK, 22 October 2021, www.g7.utoronto.ca/trade/211022-forced-labour.html.

G20 Labour and Employment Ministers Meeting – Germany, 'Ministerial declaration: Towards an inclusive future – Shaping the world of work', 19 May 2017, www.ilo.org/global/about-the-ilo/how-the-ilo-works/multilateral-system/g20/WCMS_554414/lang–en/index.htm.

Gadd, David, and Rose Broad, 'Troubling recognitions in British responses to modern slavery' (2018) 58 *British Journal of Criminology*, 1440–1461.

Gallagher, Anne, 'Human rights and human trafficking: A reflection on the influence and evolution of the US Trafficking in Persons reports', in Alison Brysk and Austin Choi-Fitzpatrick (eds.), *From Human Trafficking to Human Rights: Reframing Contemporary Slavery* (Philadelphia: University of Pennsylvania Press, 2012), 172–194.

'Human rights and the new UN protocols on trafficking and migrant smuggling: A preliminary analysis' (2001) 23 *Human Rights Quarterly*, 975–1004.

The International Law of Human Trafficking (Cambridge: Cambridge University Press, 2010).

'Recent legal developments in the field of human trafficking: A critical review of the 2005 European Convention and related instruments' (2006) 8 *European Journal of Migration and Law*, 163–189.

'What's wrong with the Global Slavery Index?' (2017) 8 *Anti-trafficking Review*, 90–112.

Gallagher, Anne T., and Joy Ngozi Ezeilo, 'The UN Special Rapporteur on Trafficking: A turbulent decade in review' (2015) 37 *Human Rights Quarterly*, 913–940.

Ganesan, Arvind, 'Business and human rights during Trump' (2018) 3 *Business and Human Rights Journal*, 265–270.

Gangmasters Labour Abuse Authority, *The Nature and Scale of Labour Exploitation across all Sectors within the United Kingdom*, 2018, www.gla.gov.uk/media/3537/external-nature-and-scale-of-labour-exploitation-report-final-version-may-2018.pdf.

García, Magaly Rodríguez, 'The ILO and the oldest non-profession', in Ulbe Bosma and Karin Hofmeester (eds.), *The Lifework of a Labor Historian: Essays in Honor of Marcel van der Linden* (Leiden: Brill, 2018), 90–114.

Geddes, Andrew, 'Getting the best of both worlds? Britain, the EU and Migration Policy' (2005) 81 *International Affairs*, 723–740.

'The politics of irregular migration, human trafficking and people smuggling in the United Kingdom', in Elspeth Guild and Paul Minderhoud (eds.), *Immigration and Criminal Law in the European Union* (Leiden: Martinus Nijhoff, 2006), 371–385.

Gerstle, Gary, 'A real opening', (2023) 3 *Dissent*, 17–19.

'The rise and fall (?) of America's neoliberal order' (2018) 28 *Transactions of the Royal Historical Society*, 241–264.

The Rise and Fall of the Neoliberal Order: America and the World in the Free Market Era (Oxford: Oxford University Press, 2023).

Gevers, Christopher, 'Refiguring slavery through international law: The 1926 Slavery Convention, the 'Native Labor Code' and Racial Capitalism' (2022) 25 *Journal of International Economic Law*, 312–333.

Giammarinaro, Maria Grazia, Report of the Special Rapporteur on Trafficking in Persons, Especially Women and Children, UN GA, 74th Session, 18 July 2019, A/74/189, 12.

Gifford, Chris, 'The people against Europe: The Eurosceptic challenge to the United Kingdom's coalition government' (2014) 52 *Journal of Common Market Studies*, 512–528.

'The UK and the European Union: Dimensions of the sovereignty and problem of Eurosceptic Britishness' (2010) 63 *Parliamentary Affairs*, 321–338.

'The United Kingdom's Eurosceptic political economy' (2016) 18 *British Journal of Politics and International Relations*, 779–794.

Gish, Oscar, 'Color and skill: British immigration, 1955–1968' (1968) 3 *The International*, 19–37.

The Global Commission on Modern Slavery and Human Trafficking, 'About', 2023, www.modernslaverycommission.org/about/.

'A message from the chair', 2023, www.modernslaverycommission.org/message-from-the-rt-hon-theresa-may-mp/.

Global Fund to End Modern Slavery, 'Funding principles', 2018, on file with author.

'Theory of change', 2018, on file with author.

Gómez-Mera, Laura, 'The global governance of trafficking in persons: Toward a transnational regime complex' (2017) 3 *Journal of Human Trafficking*, 303–326.

Goodwin, Matthew, and Caitlin Milazzo, 'Taking back control? Investigating the role of immigration in the 2016 vote for Brexit' (2017) 19 *British Journal of Politics and International Relations*, 450–464.

Gordon, Todd, 'Capitalism, neoliberalism, and unfree labour' (2018) 54 *Critical Sociology*, 921–939.

Gower, Melanie, 'Calls to change overseas domestic worker visa conditions', House of Commons Library, Briefing Paper, No. 4786, 13 May 2016.

Immigration and Asylum: Changes Made by the Coalition Government, 2010–2015, Standard Note: SN/HA/5829, House of Commons Library, 24 March 2015.

Grant, Melissa Gira, 'Beyond strange bedfellows: How the "war on trafficking" as made to unite the left and the right' (Summer 2018) *The Public Eye*, 11–16.

'The Trump administration finally broke the anti-trafficking movement', *New Republic*, 18 February 2020, newrepublic.com/article/156579/trump-administration-finally-broke-anti-trafficking-movement.

GRETA (Group of Experts on Action against Trafficking in Human Beings), 'Human trafficking for the purpose of labour exploitation,' *Thematic chapter of the 7th General Report on GRETA's Activities, 2019 (Covering the Period from 1 January to 31 December 2017)* (Strasbourg: Council of Europe, 2019), https://respect.international/wp-content/uploads/2020/08/Human-Trafficking-for-the-Purpose-of-Labour-Exploitation.pdf.

Report concerning the Implementation of the Council of Europe Convention on Action against Trafficking in Human Beings by the United Kingdom (Strasbourg: Council of Europe, 2012), www.coe.int/t/dghl/monitoring/trafficking/docs/Reports/GRETA_2012_6_FGR_GBR_en.pdf.

Report concerning the Implementation of the Council of Europe Convention on Action against Trafficking in Human Beings by the United Kingdom, Second Evaluation Round, Adopted 8 July 2016 (Strasbourg: Council of Europe, 2016).

Griffiths, Melanie, and Colin Yeo. 'The UK's hostile environment: Deputising immigration control' (2021) 41 *Critical Social Policy*, 521–544.

Gross, Ariela, and Chantal Thomas, 'The new abolitionism, international law, and the memory of slavery' (2017) 35 *Law and History Review*, 99–118.

Grundell, Lucrecia Rubio, 'The EU's approach to prostitution: Explaining the 'why' and 'how' of the EP's neo-abolitionist turn' (2021) 28 *European Journal of Women's Studies*, 425–439.

Guilbert, Kieran, 'Taking UK's lead, Commonwealth lawmakers set sights on modern slavery', *Reuters*, 14 December 2017.

Guild, Elspeth, and Anita Magdalena Barylska, 'Decent work for migrants? Examining the impacts of the UK frameworks of gangmasters legislation and modern slavery on working standards for irregularly present migrants' (2021) 1 *Global Public Policy and Governance*, 279–299.

Guth, Andrew, Robyn Anderson, Kasey Kinnard, and Hang Tran, 'Proper methodology and methods of collecting and analyzing slavery data: An examination of the Global Slavery Index' (2014) 2 *Social Inclusion*, 14–22.

Guy, Christian, 'Prime minster announces new international modern slavery and migration envoy', Justice and Care, 2019, https://justiceandcare.org/new-international-modern-slavery-and-migration-envoy/.

Halliday, Terence, and Gregory Shaffer, 'Transnational legal orders: A theoretical framing', in Terence C. Halliday and Gregory Shaffer (eds.), *Transnational Legal Orders* (Cambridge: Cambridge University Press, 2015), 8–79.

Harvey, David, *A Brief History of Neoliberalism* (Oxford: Oxford University Press, 2007).

Haynes, Jason, 'The Modern Slavery Act (2015): A legislative commentary' (2016) 37 *Statutory Law Review*, 33–56.

Heine, Jorge, and Ramesh Thakar, *The Dark Side of Globalization* (Shibuya-ku: United Nations University Press, 2011).

Henry, Carla, and Jacqueline Adams, *Spotlight on Sexual Violence and Harassment in Commercial Agriculture: Lower and Middle Income Countries*. Research Department Working Paper No. 31 (Geneva: International Labour Office, 2018).

Her Majesty's Inspectorate of Constabulary, Fire and Rescue Service, *Stolen Freedom: The Policing Response to Modern Slavery and Human Trafficking*, October 2017, https://hmicfrs.justiceinspectorates.gov.uk/publications/stolen-freedom-the-policing-response-to-modern-slavery-and-human-trafficking/.

Hetherington, Philippa, and Julia Laite, 'Introduction to the issue: trafficking, a useless category of historical analysis' (2021) 33 *Journal of Women's History*, 7–39.

Hewett, Jennifer, 'Andrew Forrest and the fight against slavery', *Financial Review*, 24 September 2017.

Hill, Angela, '"This modern day slavery": Sex trafficking and moral panic in the United Kingdom', Unpublished Ph.D. thesis, University of California, Berkeley (2011).

Hill, Amelia, 'Child slave smugglers will face jail at last', *Guardian*, 9 November 2003.

Hill, Annie, 'How to stage a raid: Police, media and the master narrative of trafficking' (2016) 7 *Anti-Trafficking Review*, 39–55.

HM Government, *2018 UK Annual Report on Modern Slavery*, HM Government, 2018, https://assets.publishing.service.gov.uk/media/5f2c0263e90e0732e16a7b52/2018_UK_Annual_Report_on_Modern_Slavery.pdf.

2019 Report on Modern Slavery (London: 2019), https://assets.publishing.service.gov.uk/media/5da73f18e5274a5cbodf831f/Modern_Slavery_Report_2019.pdf.

UK Government Modern Slavery Statement, 2020, https://assets.publishing.service.gov.uk/media/5e7c5b5d86650c743bcode95/UK_Government_Modern_Slavery_Statement.pdf.

Victims of Modern Slavery: Government Response to the Committee's Twelfth Report of Session 2016–17, 30 November 2017, https://publications.parliament.uk/pa/cm201719/cmselect/cmworpen/672/67202.htm.

Hodal, Kate, 'High court suspends Home Office policy of limiting support for slavery victims', *Guardian*, 17 April 2019.

Home Office, 'Government to launch new modern slavery research centre', 9 July 2019, www.gov.uk/government/news/government-to-launch-new-modern-slavery-research-centre.

Hopkin, Jonathan, "When Polanyi met Farage: Market fundamentalism, economic nationalism, and Britain's exist from the European Union' (2017) 19 *British Journal of Politics and International Relations*, 465–478.

Hoyle, Carolyn, Mary Bosworth, and Michelle Madden Dempsey, 'Researching trafficked women: On institutional resistance and the limits to feminist reflexivity' (2011) 17 *Qualitative Inquiry*, 769–779.

Hubbard, Phil, Roger Matthews, and Jane Scoular, 'Regulating sex work in the EU: Prostitute women and the new spaces of exclusion' (2008) 15 *Gender, Place and Culture*, 137–152.

Huckerby, Jane, 'Same, but different: Assessing the interaction of the migrant workers' rights and anti-trafficking regimes under international law' (2014–2015) 47 *New York University Journal of International Law and Policy*, 593–645.

Hyland, Kevin, 'Letter to Theresa May', 4 May 2018, https://assets.publishing.service.gov.uk/government/uploads/system/uploads/attachment_data/file/708125/20180504_IASC.PDF.

ILO (International Labour Organization), *Addressing Governance Challenges in a Changing Labour Migration Landscape*. Report IV, International Labour Conference, 106th Session, 2017.

Application of International Labour Standards 2015, International Labour Conference, 104th Session, 2015, ILC.104/III(1A).

The Cost of Coercion: Global Report under the Follow-Up to the ILO Declaration on Fundamental Principles and Rights at Work (Geneva: ILO, 2009).

Decent Work in Global Supply Chains, International Labour Conference, 105th Session, 2016, Report IV, ILC.105/IV.

Ending Forced Labour by 2030: A Review of Policies and Programmes (Geneva: ILO, 2018), www.ilo.org/wcmsp5/groups/public/—ed_norm/—ipec/documents/publication/wcms_653986.pdf.

Follow-Up to the Resolution concerning Decent Work in Global Supply Chains: Roadmap for the Programme of Action, International Labour Office, Governing Body, 329th Session, Geneva, 9–24 March 2017, GB.329/INS/3/2.

General Principles and Operational Guidelines for Fair Recruitment and Definition of Recruitment Fees and Related Costs (Geneva: ILO, 2019).

General Survey concerning the Forced Labour Convention, 1930 (No. 29), and the Abolition of Forced Labour Convention, 1957 (No. 105) *Eradication of Forced Labour Convention*, International Labour Conference, 96th Session, 2007, www.ilo.org/resource/conference-paper/eradication-forced-labour-general-survey-concerning-forced-labour.

A Global Alliance against Forced Labour: Global Report under the Follow-Up to the ILO Declaration on Fundamental Principles and Rights at Work 2005. Report of the Director-General, International Labour Conference, 93rd Session, 2005, ILC93/I(B).

Hard to See, Harder to Count: Survey Guidelines to Estimate Forced Labour of Adults and Children. Special Action Programme to Combat Forced Labour (SAP-FL) International Programme on the Elimination of Child Labour (IPEC), 2012, https://ilo.org/wcmsp5/groups/public/—ed_norm/—declaration/documents/publication/wcms_182096.pdf.

ILO Strategy on Decent Work in Supply Chains, Governing Body, 347th Session, Geneva, 13–23 March 2023, GB.347/INS/8.

Meeting of the Tripartite Working Group on Options to Ensure Decent Work in Supply Chains, Geneva, 27 June–1 July 2022, www.ilo.org/wcmsp5/groups/public/—dgreports/—dcomm/documents/meetingdocument/wcms_858677.pdf.

'More than 12 million are trapped in forced labour worldwide,' 11 May 2005, ILO, News, www.ilo.org/global/about-the-ilo/newsroom/news/WCMS_005162/lang–en/index.htm.

Note on the Proceedings, Technical Meeting on Achieving Decent Work in Global Supply Chains, ILO, Geneva, 25–28 February 2020, TMDWSC/2020/7 (Governance and Tripartism Department, 2020).

'Operational indicators of trafficking in human beings: Results from a Delphi survey implemented by the ILO and the European Commission', March 2009, www.ilo.org/wcmsp5/groups/public/—ed_norm/—declaration/documents/publication/wcms_105023.pdf.

Profits and Poverty: The Economics of Forced Labour (Geneva: ILO, 2014).

Promoting Fair Migration: General Survey Concerning the Migrant Workers Instruments, 2016, ILC.105/III/1B, www.refworld.org/docid/5c77a62b7.html.

Reports of the Committee on Decent Work in Global Supply Chains: Resolution and Conclusions Submitted for Adoption by the Conference, International Labour Conference, Provisional Record, 105th Session, Geneva, May–June 2015, ILC105–14-1 (2016).

Reports of the Committee on Decent Work in Global Supply Chains: Summary of Proceedings, Provisional Record, 105th Session, Geneva, May–June 2015, ILC105-PR14–2(Rev) (2016).

'Roger Plant, winner of the William Wilberforce Award,' 20 August 2010, ILO, News, www.ilo.org/global/topics/forced-labour/news/WCMS_143830/lang–en/index.htm.

Stopping Forced Labour: Report of the Director General – Global Report under the Follow-Up to the ILO Declaration on Fundamental Principles and Rights at Work (Geneva: ILO, 2001).

Strategy on Decent Work in Supply Chains, Governing Body, 347th Session, Geneva, 13–23 March 2023, www.ilo.org/gb/GBSessions/GB347/ins/WCMS_869573/lang–en/index.htm.

Strengthening Action to End Forced Labour, International Labour Conference, 103rd Session 2014, Report IV(1), www.ilo.org/wcmsp5/groups/public/—ed_norm/—relconf/documents/meetingdocument/wcms_217752.pdf.

Towards the ILO Centenary: Realities, Renewal and Tripartite Commitment, Report of the General-Director, International Labour Conference, 102nd Session, 2013, Report 1(A).

Trafficking in Human Beings: New Approaches to Combatting the Problem, May 2003.

Tripartite Declaration of Principles Concerning Multinational Enterprises and Social Policy (MNE Declaration) (Geneva: International Labour Office, 2001).

'Update on the Alliance 8.7 of the 2030 Agenda for Sustainable Development', International Labour Office, Governing Body, 335th Session, Geneva, 14–28 March 2019, GB.335/INS/INF/4.

'Questions and answers on "The cost of coercion"', 11 May 2009, www.ilo.org/global/about-the-ilo/mission-and-objectives/features/WCMS_106206/lang–en/index.htm.

ILO and Walk Free Foundation, *Global Estimates of Modern Slavery* (Geneva: ILO, 2017), www.ilo.org/wcmsp5/groups/public/@dgreports/@dcomm/documents/publication/wcms_575479.pdf.

ILO, Walk Free Foundation, and IOM, *Global Estimates of Modern Slavery* (Geneva: ILO, Walk Free, IOM, 2022), www.ilo.org/wcmsp5/groups/public/—ed_norm/—ipec/documents/publication/wcms_854733.pdf.

Independent Commission for Aid Impact, *The UK's Approach to Tackling Modern Slavery through the Aid Programme: A Review*, October 2020, www.antislaverycommissioner.co.uk/media/1482/icai-report-the-uk-s-approach-to-tackling-modern-slavery-through-the-aid-programme.pdf.

International Justice Mission, 'Trafficking and slavery', 2023, www.ijm.org/slavery.

International Labour Organization (ILO), Organisation for Economic Co-operation and Development (OECD), International Organization for Migration (IOM), United Nations Children's Fund (UNICEF), *Ending Child Labour, Forced Labour and Human Trafficking in Global Supply Chains* (Geneva: ILO, 2019), www.ilo.org/wcmsp5/groups/public/—ed_norm/—ipec/documents/publication/wcms_728062.pdf.

International Labor Rights Forum, 'Trade subcommittee hearing on the global challenge of forced labor in supply chains: Strengthening enforcements and protecting workers,' 21 July 2021, ILRF, News, laborrights.org/blog/archive/202107.

International Organization of Employers (IOE), 'IOE paper on state policy responses on human rights due diligence', May 2018, www.ohchr.org/sites/default/files/Documents/Issues/Business/WGSubmissions/2018/IOE.pdf.

Business at OECD, Business Europe, 'Joint business response to the revised draft legally binding instrument to regulate, in International Human Rights Law, the activities of transnational corporations and other business enterprises ("Revised Draft Treaty")', October 2019, Position paper, www.businesseurope.eu/publications/joint-business-response-revised-draft-legally-binding-instrument-regulate-international.

IOM (International Organization for Migration), *International Response to Trafficking in Migrants and the Safeguarding of Migrant Rights* (Geneva: International Organization for Migration, 1994).

Iossa, Andrea, and Maria Persdotter, 'Cross-border social dumping as a "game of jurisdiction": Towards a legal geography of labour relations in the EU internal market' (2021) 59 *Journal of Common Market Studies*, 1086–1102.

'Italian PM Matteo Renzi condemns "new slave trade" in Mediterranean', *BBC*, 19 April 2015, www.bbc.com/news/av/world-europe-32374027

Jacob, Cécile, Pierre Hausemer, Klaus Friesenbichler, and Birgit Meyer, 'Trade-related policy options of a ban on forced labour product,' In-Depth Analysis, Directorate General for External Policies, EU, November 2022, www.europarl.europa.eu/RegData/etudes/IDAN/2022/702570/EXPO_IDA(2022)702570_EN.pdf.

Jessop, Bob, 'Neoliberalization, uneven development, and Brexit: Further reflections on the organic crisis of the British state and society' (2018) 26 *European Planning Studies*, 1728–1746.

Jones, Katherine, 'A "north star" governing global labour migration? The ILO and the Fair Recruitment Initiative' (2002) 22 *Global Social Policy*, 303–322.

Jovanovic, Marija, 'The essence of slavery: Exploitation in human rights law' (2020) 20 *Human Rights Law Review*, 674–703.

'International law and regional norm smuggling: How the EU and ASEAN redefined the global regime on human trafficking' (2020) 68 *American Journal of Comparative Law*, 801–835.

State Responsibility for Modern Slavery in Human Rights Law: A Right Not to Be Trafficked (Oxford: Oxford University Press, 2023).

Kahn-Freund, Otto. *Labour and the Law. Volume 24 of Hamlyn Lectures* (London: Stevens [for] the Hamlyn Trust, 1972).

Kara, Siddharth, *Sex Trafficking: Inside the Business of Modern Slavery* (New York: Columbia University Press, 2009).

Kaushal, Asha, 'The politics of jurisdiction' (2015) 78 *Modern Law Review*, 759–792.

Kawar, L., 'Assembling an international social protection for the migrant: Juridical categorization in ILO migration standards, 1919–1939' (2022) 22 *Global Social Policy*, 244–262.

Kelly, Liz, and Linda Regan, *Stopping Traffic: Exploring the Extent of, and Responses to, Trafficking in Women for Sexual Exploitation in the UK*, Police Research Series, Paper 125 (London: Home Office Research, Development and Statistics Directorate, 2000).

Kempadoo, Kamala, 'Abolitionism, criminal justice, and transnational feminism: Twenty-first-century perspectives on human trafficking', in Kamala Kempadoo, Jyoti Sanghera, and Bandana Pattaniak (eds.), *Trafficking and Prostitution Reconsidered: New Perspectives on Migration, Sex Work, and Human Rights* (Abbingdon: Routledge, 2012), vii–ix.

'Anti-slavery as development: A global politics of rescue' (2015) 93 *Geoforum*, 22–31.

Kenway, Emily, *The Truth about Modern Slavery* (London: Pluto, 2021).

Kerry, John (US Secretary of State), 'Remarks at the White House Forum on combating human trafficking in supply chains,' 29 January 2015, https://2009-2017.state.gov/secretary/remarks/2015/01/236950.htm.

Kessler, Glen, 'The false claim that human trafficking is a "$9.5 billion business" in the United States', *Washington Post*, 2 June 2015, www.washingtonpost.com/news/fact-checker/wp/2015/06/02/the-false-claim-that-child-sex-trafficking-is-a-9–5-billion-business-in-the-united-states/.

Kirkup, James, and Robert Winnett, 'Theresa May interview: "We're going to give illegal migrants a really hostile reception"', *Telegraph*, 25 May 2012.

Klein, Betsy, 'Ivanka Trump delivers anti-human trafficking speech at UN', CNN, 19 September 2017, www.cnn.com/2017/09/19/politics/ivanka-trump-united-nations-human-trafficking.

Kolben, Kevin, 'The consumer imaginary: Labor rights, human rights, and citizen-consumers in the global supply chain' (2020) 52 *Vanderbilt Journal of Transnational Law*, 839–898.

Kotiswaran, Prahba, 'Beyond sexual humanitarianism: A postcolonial approach to anti-trafficking law' (2014) 4 *University of California Irvine Law Review*, 353–406.

Dangerous Sex, Invisible Labor: Sex Work and the Law in India (Princeton, NJ: Princeton University Press, 2011).

'Protocol at the Crossroads: Rethinking Anti-trafficking Law from an Indian Labour Law Perspective' (2015) *Anti-trafficking Review*, https://doi.org/10.14197/atr.20121543.

'From sex panic to extreme exploitation: Revisiting the law and governance of human trafficking', in Prabha Kotiswaran (ed.), *Revisiting the Law and Governance of Trafficking: Forced Labor and Modern Slavery* (Cambridge: Cambridge University Press, 2017), 1–56.

'The sexual politics of anti-trafficking discourse' (2021) 29 *Feminist Legal Studies*, 43–65.

'Trafficking: A development approach' (2019) 72 *Current Legal Problems*, 375–416.

(ed.), *Revisiting the Law and Governance of Trafficking, Forced Labor and Modern Slavery* (Cambridge: Cambridge University Press, 2017).

Krajeski, Jenna, 'The hypocrisy of Trump's anti-trafficking argument for a border wall', *New Yorker*, 5 February 2019, www.newyorker.com/news/news-desk/the-hypocrisy-of-trumps-anti-trafficking-argument-for-a-border-wall.

Krieg, Sarah H., 'Trafficking in human beings: The EU approach between border control, law enforcement and human rights' (2009) 15 *European Law Journal*, 775–790.

Krisch, Nico, 'Jurisdiction unbound: (Extra)territorial Regulation as Global Governance' (2022) 33 *European Journal of International Law*, 481–514.

Kurasawa, Fukuyi, 'Show and tell: Contemporary Anti-Slavery Advocacy as Symbolic Work', in Annie Bunting and Joel Quirk (eds.), *Contemporary Slavery: Popular Rhetoric and Political Practice* (Vancouver: University of British Columbia Press, 2017), 158–179.

La Hovary, Claire, 'A challenging ménage à trois?' (2015) 12 *International Organizations Law Review*, 204–236.

Labour Exploitation Advisory Group, *Detaining Victims: Human Trafficking and the UK Immigration Detention System* (London: LEAG, 2019).

Laczko, Frank, and David Thompson (eds.), *Migrant Trafficking and Human Smuggling in Europe: A Review of the Evidence with Case Studies from Hungary, Poland and Ukraine* (Geneva: International Organization of Migration, 2000).

Laffin, Martin, and Eric Shaw, 'British devolution and the Labour Party: How a national party adapts to devolution' (2007) 9 *British Journal of Politics*, 55–72.

LaFianza, Josh, 'Threatening ill-gotten gains: Analyzing the effectiveness of a forced labor import ban in the European Union', Stanford-Vienna European Union Law Working Papers No. 60, 2022.

Lake, Quintin, Jamie MacAlister, Matthew Gitsham, and Nadine Page, *Corporate Leadership on Modern Slavery: How Have Companies Responded to the UK Modern Slavery Act One Year On?* (Boston: Hult International Business School/Ethical Trading Initiative, 2016).

Landman, Todd, 'Measuring modern slavery: Law, human rights, and new forms of data' (2020) 42 *Human Rights Quarterly*, 303–331.

Landman, Todd, and Bernard W. Silverman, 'Globalization and modern slavery' (2019) 7 *Politics and Governance*, 275–290.

Landau, Ingrid, 'Human rights due diligence and the risk of cosmetic compliance' (2019) 20 *Melbourne Journal of International Law*, 221–247.

Human Rights Due Diligence and Labour Governance (Oxford: Oxford University Press, 2023).

Leary, Mary, 'Religious organizations as partners in the global and local fight against human trafficking' (2018) 16 *Review of Faith and International Affairs*, 51–60.

LeBaron, Genevieve, *Combatting Modern Slavery: Why Labour Governance Is Failing and What We Can Do* (Cambridge, UK: Polity Press, 2020).

'The coming and current crisis of indecent work', in Colin Hay and Tom Hunt (eds.), *The Coming Crisis* (London: Palgrave Macmillan, 2018), 43–52.

'Introduction', in Genevieve LeBaron (ed.), *Researching Forced Labour in the Global Economy: Methodological Challenges and Advances* (Oxford: Oxford University Press, 2020), 1–22.

'Slavery, human trafficking, and forced labour: Implications for international development', in Jean Grugel and Daniel Hammett (eds.), *The Palgrave Handbook of International Development* (London: Palgrave Macmillan, 2016), 381–398.

'Unfree labour beyond binaries' (2015) 17 *International Feminist Journal of Politics*, 1–19.

LeBaron, Genevieve, and Andreas Rühmkorf, 'The domestic politics of corporate accountability legislation: Struggles over the 2015 UK Modern Slavery Act' (2019) 17 *Socio-economic Review*, 709–43.

'Steering CSR through home state regulation: A comparison of the impact of the UK Bribery Act and Modern Slavery Act on global supply chain governance' (2017) 8 *Global Policy*, 15–18.

LeClercq, Desiree, 'A worker-centered trade policy' (2023) 61 *Columbia Journal of Transnational Law*, 733–797.

Legg, Stephen, 'The life of individuals as well as of nations: International law and the League of Nations' anti-trafficking governmentalities' (2012) 25 *Leiden Journal of International Law*, 647–664.

Prostitution and the Ends of Empire: Scale, Governmentalities, and Interwar India (Durham, NC: Duke University Press, 2014).

'Of scales, networks and assemblages: The League of Nations apparatus and the scalar sovereignty of the Government of India' (2009) 34 *Transactions of the Institute of British Geographers*, 234–253.

Lerche, Jens, 'A global alliance against forced labour? Unfree labour, neo-liberal globalization and the International Labour Organization' (2007) 7 *Journal of Agrarian Change*, 425–452.

Lewis, Hannah, and Louise Waite, 'Migrant illegality, slavery and exploitative work', in Gary Craig, Alex Balch, Hannah Lewis, and Louise Waite (eds.), *The Modern Slavery Agenda: Policy, Politics and Practice in the UK* (Bristol: Policy Press 2019) 219–242.

Liechtenstein Initiative, 'A blueprint for mobilizing finance against slavery and trafficking', 2 September 2019, www.fastinitiative.org/the-blueprint/.

Lindsay, Rae, Anna Kirkpatrick, and Jo En Low, 'Hardly soft law: The Modern Slavery Act 2015 and the trend towards mandatory reporting on human rights' (2017) 18 *Business Law International*, 29–50.

Lipscombe, Sally, and Jacqueline Beard, *Human Trafficking: UK Responses*, House of Commons Library, SN/HA/1324, 13, January 2014.

Lloyd, Paulette, and Beth A. Simmons, 'Framing for a new transnational legal order', in Terrance Halliday and Gregory Shaffer (eds.), *Transnational Legal Orders* (Cambridge: Cambridge University Press, 2015), 400–438.

Lobasz, Jennifer, *Constructing Human Trafficking: Evangelicals, Feminists, and an Unexpected Alliance* (London: Palgrave Macmillan, 2018).

Locher, Birgit, 'International norms and European policy making: Trafficking in women in the EU', CEuS Working Paper No. 2002/6.

Longo, Matthew, *The Politics of Borders: Sovereignty, Security, and the Citizen after 9/11* (Cambridge: Cambridge University Press, 2017).

Loughlin, Martin, 'The shibboleth of sovereignty' (2018) 81 *Modern Law Review*, 989–1016.

Mantouvalou, Virginia, 'Legal construction of structures of exploitation', in Hugh Collins, Gillian Lester, and Virginia Mantouvalou (eds.), *Philosophical Foundations of Labour Law* (Oxford: Oxford University Press, 2018), 188–204.

Structural Injustice and Workers' Rights (Oxford: Oxford University Press, 2023).

Mattson, Greggor, *The Cultural Politics of European Prostitution Reform: Governing Loose Women* (New York: Palgrave MacMillan, 2015).

Maul, Daniel, *The International Labour Organization, One Hundred Years of Global Social Policy* (Berlin: Walter de Gruyter, 2019).

'The International Labour Organization and the struggle against forced labour from 1919 to the present' (2007) 48 *Labor History*, 477–500.

Maupain, Francois, *The Future of the International Labour Organization in the Global Economy* (Oxford: Hart, 2013).

May, Theresa, 'Anti-slavery service: Prime Minister's speech', 12 October 2016, www.gov.uk/government/speeches/anti-slavery-service-prime-ministers-speech.

'Immigration: Home secretary's speech of 5 November 2010', 2010, www.gov.uk/government/speeches/immigration-home-secretarys-speech-of-5-november-2010.

'A model that works: A government's role in combating human trafficking', Speech by Home Secretary Theresa May to the Vatican Conference, 9 April 2014, www.gov.uk/government/speeches/a-model-that-works-a-governments-role-in-combating-human-trafficking.

'My Government will lead the way in defeating modern slavery', *Telegraph*, 30 July 2016, www.telegraph.co.uk/news/2016/07/30/we-will-lead-the-way-in-defeating-modern-slavery/.

McCarthy, Lauren A., 'Human trafficking and the new slavery' (2014) 10 *Annual Review of Law and Social Science*, 221–242.

McGoey, Linsey, 'Philanthrocapitalism and its critics' (2012) 40 *Poetics*, 185–199.

McGrath, Siobhan, and Samantha Watson, 'Anti-slavery as development: A global politics of rescue' (2018) 93 *Geoforum*, 22–31.

Mediavilla, Juanjoj, and Jorge Garcia-Arias, 'Philanthrocapitalism as a neoliberal (development agenda) artefact: Philanthropic discourse and hegemony in (financing for) international development' (2019) 16 *Globalizations*, 857–875.

Melhuish, Francesca, 'Euroscepticism, anti-nostalgic nostalgia and the past perfect post-Brexit Future' (2022) 60 *Journal of Common Market Studies*, 1758–1776.

Members of the Research Network on the Legal Parameters of Slavery, '2012 Bellagio-Harvard Guidelines on the Legal Parameters of Slavery', in Jean Allain (ed.), *The*

Legal Understanding of Slavery: From the Historical to the Contemporary (Oxford: Oxford University Press, 2012), 375, Guideline 2.

Menon, Anand, and Alan Wager, 'Taking back control: Sovereignty as strategy in Brexit politics' (2020) 8 *Territory, Politics, Governance*, 279–284.

Merry, Sally Engel, 'Counting the uncountable: Constructing trafficking through measurement', in Prabha Kotiswaran (ed.), *Revisiting the Law and Governance of Trafficking: Forced Labor and Modern Slavery* (Cambridge: Cambridge University Press, 2017), 273–304.

The Seductions of Quantification: Measuring Human Rights, Gender Violence, and Sex Trafficking (Chicago: University of Chicago Press, 2016).

Metcalf, David, *United Kingdom Labour Market Enforcement Strategy: Introductory Report 1, April 2016–31*, July 2017.

United Kingdom Labour Market Enforcement Strategy 2018/19, May 2018.

United Kingdom Labour Market Enforcement Strategy 2019/20, May 2019.

Mezzadra, Sandro, and Brett Neilson, *Border as Method, or, the Multiplication of Labor* (Durham, NC: Duke University Press, 2013).

Mezzadri, Alessandra, 'Class, gender and the sweatshop: On the nexus between labour commodification and exploitation' (2016) 37 *Third World Quarterly*, 1877–1900.

The Sweatshop Regime: Labouring Bodies, Exploitation and Garments Made in India (Cambridge: Cambridge University Press, 2017).

Milberg, William, and Deborah Winkler, *Outsourcing Economics: Global Value Chains in Capitalist Development* (Cambridge: Cambridge University Press, 2013).

Milivojevic, Sanja, and Sharon Pickering, 'Trafficking in people, twenty years on: Sex, migration, and crime in the global anti-trafficking discourse and the rise of the "global trafficking complex"' (2013) 25 *Current Issues in Criminal Justice*, 585–604.

Miller, Alice, and Tara Zivkovic, 'Orwellian rights and the UN Trafficking Protocol', in Ryszard Piotrowicz, Conny Rijken, and Baerbel Heide Uhl (eds.), *Routledge Handbook of Human Trafficking* (Abingdon: Routledge, 2017), 328–341.

Miller, Rebecca, and Sebastian Baumeister, 'Managing migration: Is border control fundamental to anti-trafficking and anti-smuggling interventions?' (2013) 2 *Anti-trafficking Review*, 15–32.

Morgan, Jamie, and Wendy Olsen, 'Forced and unfree labour: An analysis' (2014) 4 *International Critical Thought*, 21–37.

Mortimer, Caroline, 'US and UK pledge millions for largest-ever fund to fight modern day slavery', *The Independent*, 25 January 2018, www.independent.co.uk/news/world/politics/modern-slavery-global-fund-davos-us-uk-government-a8176801.html.

Mügge, Daniel. '40.3 million slaves? Four reasons to question the new global estimates of modern slavery', *Open Democracy*, BTS Policy Brief No. 1, 2018, 1, https://cdn-prod.opendemocracy.net/media/documents/Mugge_4_reasons_to_question_GEMS.pdf.

Mullally, Siobhán, and Clíodhna Murphy, 'Migrant domestic workers in the UK: Enacting exclusions, exemptions and rights' (2014) 36 *Human Rights Quarterly*, 397–427.

Mulvihill, Natasha, 'The criminalisation of paying for sex in England and Wales: How gender and power are implicated in the making of policy' (2018) 38 *Journal of Public Policy*, 165–189.

Mundlak, Guy, 'De-territorializing labor law' (2009) 3 *Law and Ethics of Human Rights*, 188–222.

Munro, Vanessa E., 'A tale of two servitudes: Defining and implementing a domestic response to trafficking of women for prostitution in the UK and Australia' (2005) 14 *Social and Legal Studies*, 91–114.

Murphy, Laura T., 'The new slave narrative and the illegibility of modern slavery' (2015) 32 *Slavery and Abolition*, 382–405.

Murray, Christine, 'U.S. anti-trafficking groups urge Biden to shift focus from sex to labor', *Reuters*, 10 November 2020.

Nail, Thomas, *The Figure of the Migrant* (Palo Alto, CA: Stanford University Press 2015).

Theory of the Border (New York: Oxford University Press, 2016).

National Audit Office, *Reducing Modern Slavery* (London: Home Office, 2017).

Naved, Ruchira, Tabassum Rahman, Samantha Willan, Rachel Jewkes, and Andrew Gibbs, 'Female garment workers' experiences of violence in their homes and workplaces in Bangladesh: A qualitative study' (2018) 196 *Social Science and Medicine*, 150–157.

Nozick, Robert, *Anarchy, State and Utopia* (New York: Basic Books, 1974).

Obama, Barack, 'Presidential Proclamation: National Slavery and Human Trafficking Prevention Month, 2015', White House, Office of the Press Secretary, News release, 31 December 2014, https://obamawhitehouse.archives.gov/the-press-office/2014/12/31/presidential-proclamation-national-slavery-and-human-trafficking-prevent.

'Presidential Proclamation: National Slavery and Human Trafficking Month, 2017', White House, Office of the Press Secretary, News release, 28 December 2016, https://obamawhitehouse.archives.gov/the-press-office/2016/12/28/presidential-proclamation-national-slavery-and-human-trafficking.

'Remarks by the President to the Clinton Global Initiative', White House, Office of the Press Secretary, News release, 25 September 2012, https://obamawhitehouse.archives.gov/the-press-office/2012/09/25/remarks-president-clinton-global-initiative.

O'Brien, Erin, and Michael Wilson, 'Clinton, Bush and Obama: Changing policy and rhetoric in the United States Annual Trafficking in Persons Report', in M. Dragiewicz (ed.) *Global Human Trafficking: Critical Issues and Contexts* (Abingdon: Routledge, 2015), 123–137.

O'Connell-Davidson, Julia, *Modern Slavery: The Margins of Freedom* (London: Palgrave Macmillan, 2015).

'New slavery, old binaries: Human trafficking and the borders of "freedom"' (2010) 10 *Global Networks*, 244–261.

O'Donoghue, Saskia, 'Headed up by former British prime minister Theresa May, the Global Commission for Modern Slavery and Human Trafficking seeks to eradicate the ever-increasing issue by 2030', *Europe News*, 7 October 2023, www.euronews.com/2023/10/07/new-commission-set-to-tackle-rising-human-slavery-in-europe-and-beyond.

Office for National Statistics, *Modern Slavery in the UK: March 2020*, 2020, www.ons.gov.uk/peoplepopulationandcommunity/crimeandjustice/articles/modernslaveryintheuk/march2020.

Offner, Amy, 'A durable concept' (2023) 3 *Dissent*, 21–22.

Ollus, Natalia, and Anniina Jokinen, 'Exploitation of migrant workers and trafficking in human beings: A Nexus of the demand by employers, workers and consumers', in Ryszard Piotrowicz, Conny Rijken, and Baerbel Heide Uhl (eds.), *Routledge Handbook of Human Trafficking* (London: Routledge 2017), 473–486.

Pahuja, Sundhya, 'Laws of encounter: A jurisdictional account of international law' (2013) 1 *London Review of International Law*, 63–98.

Paul, Regine, *The Political Economy of Border Drawing: Arranging Legality in European Labor Migration Policies* (New York: Oxford Berghahn, 2019).

Paz-Fuchs, Amir, 'Badges of modern slavery' (2016) 79 *Modern Law Review*, 757–785.

Peake, Katrina, and Jeff Kenner, '"Slaves to fashion" in Bangladesh and the EU: Promoting decent work?' (2020) 11 *European Labour Law Journal*, 175–198.

Peksen, Dursun, Shannon Blanton, and Robert Blanton, 'Neoliberal policies and human trafficking for labor: Free markets, unfree workers?' (2017) 70 *Political Research Quarterly*, 673–686.

Peters, Alicia W., *Responding to Human Trafficking: Sex, Gender and Culture in the Law* (Philadelphia: University of Pennsylvania Press, 2015).

Phillips, Nicola, 'The politics of numbers: Beyond methodological challenges in research on forced labour – What is forced labour? A practical guide for humanities and social science research', in Genevieve LeBaron (ed.), *Researching Forced Labour in the Global Economy: Methodological Challenges and Advances* (Oxford: Oxford University Press, 2018), 44–59.

'Unfree labour and adverse incorporation in the global economy: Comparative perspectives from Brazil and India' (2013) 4 *Economy and Society*, 171–196.

Phillips, Nicola, Genevieve LeBaron, and Sara Wallin, 'Mapping and measuring the effectiveness of labour-related disclosure requirements for global supply chains', ILO Working Paper No. 32, Geneva, 2018.

Phillips, Nicola, and Fabiola Mieres, 'The governance of forced labour in the global economy' (2015) 12 *Globalizations*, 244–260.

Pietropaoli, Irene, Owain Johnstone, and Alex Balch, 'Policy brief: Effectiveness of forced labour import bans', Modern Slavery and Human Rights Policy and Evidence Centre, 2021, https://modernslaverypec.org/assets/downloads/PEC-Policy-Brief-Effectiveness-Forced-Labour-Import-Bans.pdf.

Pilkington, Ed, 'Trump labor secretary who cut Epstein deal plans to slash funds for sex trafficking victims', *Guardian*, 10 July 2019.

Pinto, Mattia, 'Discursive alignment of trafficking, rights and crime control' (2023) 19 *International Journal of Law in Context*, 122–142. https://doi.org/10.1017/S1744552322000209.

Piper, Nicola, 'The International Labour Organisation as nodal player on the pitch of networked governance: Shifting the goalposts for migrant workers in Qatar' (2022) 22 *Global Social Policy*, 323–340. https://doi.org/10.1177/14680181211065240.

Planitzer, Julia, 'GRETA's first years of work: Review of the monitoring of implementation of the Council of Europe Convention on Action against Trafficking in Human Beings' (2012) 1 *Anti-trafficking Review*, 31–42.

Plant, Roger, 'Combatting trafficking for labour exploitation in the global economy: The need for a differentiated approach', in Prabha Kotiswaran (ed.), *Revising the*

Law and Governance of Trafficking: Forced Labour and Modern Slavery (Cambridge: Cambridge University Press, 2017), 422–442.

'Forced labor: Critical issues for US business leaders' (Background paper prepared for conference on Engaging Business: Addressing Forced Labor, Atlanta, Georgia, 20 February 2008).

'Forced labour, slavery and poverty reduction: Challenges for development agencies' (Paper presented to UK High-Level Conference to Examine the Links between Poverty, Slavery and Social Exclusion, Foreign and Commonwealth Office and DFID, London, 30 October 2007).

'Foreword', in Beate Andrees and Patrick Belser (eds.), *Forced Labor: Coercion and Exploitation in the Private Economy* (Boulder, CO: ILO/Lynne Rienner, 2009), vii–xi.

'Trafficking for forced labour: ILO approaches', Statement, US Congress Washington, 11 October 2007.

'Trafficking for labour exploitation: Conceptual issues, and challenges for law enforcement' (Paper presented to the Fifth International Law Enforcement Conference, Kiev, 31 March to 2 April 2009).

Plant, Roger, and Caroline O'Reilly, 'The ILO's Special Action Programme to Combat Forced Labour' (2003) 142 *International Labour Review*, 73–85.

Posthuma, Anne, and Arianna Rossi, 'Coordinated governance in global value chains: Supranational dynamics and the role of the International Labour Organization' (2017) 22 *New Political Economy*, 186–202.

Pratt, Anna C., and Jessica Templeman, 'Jurisdiction, sovereignties and Akwesasne: Shiprider and the re-crafting of Canada-US cross-border maritime law enforcement' (2018) 33 *Canadian Journal of Law and Society*, 335–357.

Prentice, Rebecca, 'Labour rights from labour wrongs? Transnational compensation and the spatial politics of labour rights after Bangladesh's Rana Plaza garment factory collapse' *Antipode* (2021) 53, 1767–1786.

Quirk, Joel, *The Anti-Slavery Project: From the Slave Trade to Human Trafficking* (Philadelphia: University of Pennsylvania Press, 2011).

'When human trafficking means everything and nothing', in Annie Bunting and Joel Quirk (eds.), *Contemporary Slavery* (Vancouver: University of British Columbia Press, 2017), 67–96.

Raffaelli, Rosa, 'The European approach to the protection of trafficking victims: The Council of Europe Convention, the EU Directive, and the Italian experience' (2009) 10 *German Law Journal*, 205–221.

Raigrodski, Dana, 'Creative capitalism and human trafficking: A business approach to eliminate forced labor and human trafficking from global supply chains' (2016) 8 *William and Mary Business Law Review*, 71–134.

Ramos, Gabriela, 'Abolish modern slavery!', OECD Observer, 25 January 2018, www.oecd-ilibrary.org/sites/724a5be3-en/index.html?itemId=/content/paper/724a5be3-en.

Reed, Sasha, Stephen Roe, James Grimshaw, and Rhys Oliver, 'The economic and social costs of modern slavery', Research Report 100, Home Office, London, July 2018.

Richland, Justin B., 'Jurisdiction: Grounding law in language' (2013) 42 *Annual Review of Anthropology*, 209–226.

Rijken, Conny, 'Trafficking in human beings for labour exploitation: Cooperation in an integrated approach' (2013) 21 *European Journal of Crime, Criminal Law and Criminal Justice*, 9–35.

Rittich, Kerry, 'Making natural markets: Flexibility as labour market truth' (2019) 65 *Northern Ireland Legal Quarterly*, 323–343.

'Representing, counting, valuing: Managing definitional uncertainty in the law of trafficking', in Prahba Kotiswaran (ed.), *Revisiting the Law and Governance of Trafficking: Forced Labor and Modern Slavery* (Cambridge: Cambridge University Press, 2017), 238–270.

Roberts, Kate, 'The UK government is undermining decades of anti-slavery efforts', *Open Democracy*, 21 October 2022.

Robertson, Katie, 'A mining billionaire takes his war on slavery to the UN', *Bloomberg*, 21 September 2017.

Robinson, Caroline, 'Claiming space for labour rights within the United Kingdom modern slavery crusade' (2015) 5 *Anti-Trafficking Review*, 129–143.

'The problem with the British government's approach to exploitation', *Open Democracy*, 25 September 2016.

Rodgers, Gerry, Lee Swepston, Eddy Lee, and Jasmien van Daele, *The International Labour Organization and the Quest for Social Justice, 1919–2009* (Geneva: International Labour Office, 2009).

Rodríguez-López, Silvia, '(De)constructing stereotypes: Media representations, social perceptions, and legal responses to human trafficking' (2018) 4 *Journal of Human Trafficking*, 61–72.

Roe, Mark, Holger Spamann, Jesse M. Fried, and Charles C. Y. Wang, 'The sustainable corporate governance initiative in Europe' (2021) 38 *Yale Journal on Regulation Bulletin*, 133–153.

Rogaly, Ben, 'Migrant workers in the ILO's global alliance against Forced Labour Report: A critical appraisal' (2008) 29 *Third World Quarterly*, 1431–1447.

Ruggie, John Gerard, 'Global governance and "new governance theory": Lessons from business and human rights" (2014) 20 *Global Governance*, 5–17.

'International regimes, transactions, and change: Embedded liberalism in the post-war international organizations' (1982) 36 *Economic Order*, 379–415.

'"Making economic globalization work for all": Achieving socially sustainable supply', *Chains*, February 2017, https://shiftproject.org/making-economic-globalization-work-for-all-achieving-socially-sustainable-supply-chains/.

Ruhs, Martin, and Bridget Anderson (eds.), *Who Needs Migrant Workers? Labour Shortages, Immigration, and Public Policy* (Oxford: Oxford University Press, 2010).

Ryan, Bernard, 'Employer checks of immigration status and employment law', in Cathryn Costello and Mark Freedland (eds.), *Migrants at Work: Immigration and Vulnerability in Labour Law* (Oxford: Oxford University Press, 2014), 239–256.

Ryder, Guy, "Address by Guy Ryder, Director-General of the International Labour Organization," Paris, France, 20 June 2015.

Ryngaert, Cedric, *Jurisdiction in International Law*, 2nd ed. (Oxford: Oxford University Press, 2015).

Sanford, Rachaelle, Daniel E. Martínez, and Ronald Weitzer, 'Framing human trafficking: A content analysis of recent US newspaper articles' (2016) 2 *Journal of Human Trafficking*, 139–155.

Santa Marta Group, 'About', 2023, https://santamartagroup.com/about-santa-marta-group/.

Santos, Boaventura de Sousa, 'Law: A map of misreading – Toward a post-modern conception of law' (1987) 14 *Journal of Law and Society*, 279–302.

Sarfaty, Galit, 'Shining light on global supply chains' (2015) 56 *Harvard International Law Journal*, 419–446.

Sassen, Saskia, *Territory, Authority, Rights: From Medieval to Global Assemblages* (Princeton, NJ: Princeton University Press, 2008).

'When territory deborders territoriality: Territory, politics, governance' (2013) 1 *Governance*, 21–45.

Savage, Michael, 'Suella Braverman makes fresh attack on European Court of Human Rights', *Guardian*, 24 September 2023.

Scanlan, Padraic, *Slave Empire: How Slavery Built Modern Britain* (London: Robinson, 2020).

Scarpa, Silvia, *Trafficking in Human Beings: Modern Slavery* (Oxford: Oxford University Press, 2008).

Schmitt, Carl, *The Nomos of the Earth in the International Law of the Jus Publicum Europaeum*, translated by G. Ulmen (New York: Telos Press, 2003).

Scoular, Jane, *The Subject of Prostitution: Sex Work, Law and Social Theory* (Abingdon: Routledge, 2015).

Scoular, Jane, and Maggie O'Neill, 'Regulating prostitution: Social inclusion, responsibilization and the politics of prostitution reform' (2007) 47 *British Journal of Criminology*, 764–778.

Sen, Amartya, *Development as Freedom* (New York: Anchor, 1999).

Sereni, Anna, *Real People, Real Lives: Ten Years of Advocacy for Victims of Slavery in the UK*, 2019, www.antislavery.org/wp-content/uploads/2019/09/Real-people-real-lives-ATMG-report-1.pdf.

Shamir, Hila, 'A labor paradigm for human trafficking' (2012) 60 *UCLA Law Review*, 76–136.

Sharapov, Karil, 'Giving us the "biggest bang for the buck" (or not): Anti-trafficking government funding in Ukraine and the United Kingdom' (2014) 3 *Anti-Trafficking Review*, 16–40.

'"Traffickers and their victims": Anti-trafficking policy in the United Kingdom' (2017) 43 *Critical Sociology*, 91–111.

Sharma, Nandita, *Home Rule: National Sovereignty and the Separation of Natives and Migrants* (Durham, NC: Duke University Press, 2020).

Shelley, Louise, *Human Trafficking: A Global Perspective* (Cambridge: Cambridge University Press, 2010).

Silva, Vincente. 'The ILO and the future of work: The politics of global labour policy' (2021) 22 *Global Social Policy*, 341–358.

Silverman, Bernard, *Modern Slavery: An Application of Multiple Systems Estimation*, 27 November 2014, www.gov.uk/government/publications/modern-slavery-an-application-of-multiple-systems-estimation.

Simpson, Kathryn, and Nick Startin, 'Tabloid tales: How the British tabloid press shaped the Brexit vote' (2022) 61 *Journal of Common Market Studies*, 1–22.

Slobodian, Quinn, *Globalists: The End of Empire and the Birth of Neoliberalism* (Cambridge, MA: Harvard University Press, 2018).

Smith, Adam, *An Inquiry into the Nature and Causes of the Wealth of Nations* (London: Methuen, 1776).

Somers, Margaret, *Genealogies of Citizenship: Market, Statelessness and the Right to Have Rights* (Cambridge: Cambridge University Press, 2008).

Stoyanova, Vladislava, *Human Trafficking and Slavery Reconsidered: Conceptual Limits and States' Positive Obligations in European Law* (Cambridge: Cambridge University Press, 2017).

Strauss, Kendra, 'Sorting victims from workers: Forced labour, trafficking, and the process of jurisdiction' (2017) 41 *Progress in Human Geography*, 140–158.

'Unfree again: Social reproduction, flexible labour markets and the resurgence of gang labour in the UK' (2013) 45 *Antipode*, 180–197.

Strauss, Kendra, and Siobhán McGrath, 'Temporary migration, precarious employment and unfree labour relations: Exploring the "continuum of exploitation" in Canada's Temporary Foreign Worker Program' (2017) 78 *Geoforum*, 199–208.

Suchland, Jennifer, *Economies of Violence: Transnational Feminism, Postsocialism, and the Politics of Sex Trafficking* (Durham, NC: Duke University Press, 2015).

Sum, Ngai-Ling, and Bob Jessop, *Towards a Cultural Political Economy: Putting Culture in Its Place in Political Economy* (Cheltenham: Edward Elgar, 2013).

Swepston, Lee, 'Trafficking and forced labour: Filling in the gaps with the adoption of the Supplementary ILO Standards, 2014', in Prabha Kotiswaran (ed.), *Revisiting the Law and Governance of Trafficking: Forced Labor and Modern Slavery* (Cambridge: Cambridge University Press, 2017), 395–421.

Tansey, Rachel, 'Off the hook? How business lobbies against liability for human rights and environmental abuses', *Report for Friends of the Earth, European Coalition for Corporate Justice, and Corporate Observatory Europe*, June 2021, https://corporatejustice.org/wp-content/uploads/2021/06/OffThe-Hook.pdf.

Taylor, Diane, 'Revealed: Just 7% of trafficking victims given leave to remain in UK', *Guardian*, 4 January 2022.

'Suella Braverman U-turns on new rules targeting trafficking victims', *Guardian*, 2 July 2023.

Taylor, Russell, *Impact of 'Hostile Environment' Policy Debate on 14 June 2018*, House of Lords, Library Briefing, 11 June 2018.

Thachuk, Kimberly, *Transnational Threats: Smuggling and Trafficking in Arms, Drugs, and Human Life* (Westport, CT: Praeger Security International, 2007).

Theimann, Inga, 'Beyond victimhood and beyond employment? Exploring avenues for labour law to empower women trafficked into the sex industry' (2019) 48 *Industrial Law Journal*, 199–224.

Thomas, Chantal, 'Convergences and divergences in international legal norms on migrant labor' (2010) 32 *Comparative Labor Law and Policy Journal*, 405–442.

Thomas, Huw, and Mark Anner, 'Dissensus and deadlock in the evolution of labour governance: Global supply chains and the International Labour Organization (ILO)' (2023) 184 *Journal of Business Ethics*, 33–49.

Thomas, Huw, and Peter Turnbull, 'From a "moral commentator" to a "determined actor"? How the International Labour Organization (ILO) orchestrates the field of international industrial relations' (2021) 59 *British Journal of Industrial Relations*, 874–898.

'From horizontal to vertical labour governance: The International Labour Organization (ILO) and decent work in global supply chains' (2018) 71 *Human Relations*, 536–559.

Tomkins, Stephen, *William Wilberforce: A Biography* (Oxford: Lion Books 2007).

Trump, Donald, 'State of the Union Address', CNN, 1 February 2019, www.cnn.com/2019/02/05/politics/donald-trump-state-of-the-union-2019-transcript.

Turnbull, Nick, and Rose Broad, 'Bringing the problem home: The anti-slavery and anti-trafficking rhetoric of UK non-government organisations' (2022) 42 *Politics*, 200–215.

Turner, Ian, 'Human rights, positive obligations, and measures to prevent human trafficking in the United Kingdom' (2015) 4 *Journal of Human Trafficking*, 296–317.

Ucnikova, Martina, 'OECD and modern slavery: How much aid money is spent to tackle the issue?' (2014) 3 *Anti-trafficking Review*, 133–150.

UK, *2019 UK Annual Report on Modern Slavery*, October 2019, https://assets.publishing.service.gov.uk/government/uploads/system/uploads/attachment_data/file/840059/Modern_Slavery_Report_2019.pdf.

The Coalition: Our Program for Government, 2011, https://assets.publishing.service.gov.uk/government/uploads/system/uploads/attachment_data/file/78977/coalition_programme_for_government.pdf/.

Establishing Britain as a World Leader in the Fight against Modern Slavery, Modern Slavery Bill Evidence Review, 2013.

First Annual Report of the Inter-departmental Ministerial Group on Human Trafficking, October 2012, Cm 8421.

Government Reply to the Sixth Report from the Home Affairs Committee Session 2008–09 HC 23: The Trade in Human Beings – Human Trafficking in the UK, August 2009, Cm 7693, https://assets.publishing.service.gov.uk/government/uploads/system/uploads/attachment_data/file/228681/7693.pdf.

Human Trafficking: The Government's Strategy, July 2011, www.gov.uk/government/uploads/system/uploads/attachment_data/file/97845/human-trafficking-strategy.pdf.

Independent Review of the Modern Slavery Act 2015: Final Report (London: HM Government, 2019).

Joint Statement of the Inter-Departmental Ministerial Group (IDMG) on Modern Slavery, 2014, https://assets.publishing.service.gov.uk/media/5a7eb9ac40f0b6230268b24c/IDMG_statement_v5_WEB.PDF.

'PM speech at ILO centenary conference: 11 June 2019', 2019, www.gov.uk/government/speeches/pm-speech-at-ilo-centenary-conference-11-june-2019.

'PM statement on illegal migration: 13 December 2022', 2022, www.gov.uk/government/speeches/pm-statement-on-illegal-migration-13-december-2022.

Report on the Internal Review of Human Trafficking Legislation, 2012, https://assets.publishing.service.gov.uk/media/5a78a22040f0b62b22cbb8de/human-trafficking-legislation.pdf.

Second Annual Report of the Inter-departmental Ministerial Group on Human Trafficking, October 2013, Cm 8731.

The UK Government Response to the Independent Review of the Modern Slavery Act 2015, 2019, https://assets.publishing.service.gov.uk/government/uploads/system/uploads/attachment_data/file/815410/Government_Response_to_Independent_Review_of_MS_Act.pdf.

UK Department for Business, Energy and Industrial Strategy and Home Office, *UK Labour Market Enforcement Strategy 2018/19: Government Response*, December 2018, https://data.parliament.uk/DepositedPapers/Files/DEP2018-1269/Director_of_Labour_Market_Enforcements_Strategy_-_Government_Response.pdf

UK, Department for International Development, 'A call to action to end forced labour, modern slavery and human trafficking', 20 September 2017, www.gov.uk/government/publications/a-call-to-action-to-end-forced-labour-modern-slavery-and-human-trafficking.

UK, Home Office, 'Alarming rise of abuse within modern slavery system', Press release, 20 March 2021.

Changes to Tier 5 of the Points Based System and Overseas Domestic Worker Routes of Entry, Impact Assessment, 15 March 2012, www.legislation.gov.uk/ukia/2012/115/pdfs/ukia_20120115_en.pdf.

Controlling Our Borders: Making Migration Work for Britain – Five Year Strategy for Asylum and Immigration (London: Home Office, 2005).

A Coordinated Prostitution Strategy and a Summary of Responses to Paying the Price (London: Home Office, 2006).

Draft Modern Slavery Bill, Cm 8770 (London: HMSO, 2013), https://assets.publishing.service.gov.uk/media/5a7c8afae5274a0bb7cb7bb6/Draft_Modern_Slavery_Bill.pdf.

'Government to launch new modern slavery research centre', 9 July 2019, www.gov.uk/government/news/government-to-launch-new-modern-slavery-research-centre.

'Historic law to end Modern Slavery passed', www.gov.uk/government/news/historic-law-to-end-modern-slavery-passed.

The Modern Slavery Act Review, 31 July 2016, www.gov.uk/government/publications/modern-slavery-act-2015-review-one-year-on.

Modern Slavery Strategy (London: HMSO, 2014), https://assets.publishing.service.gov.uk/media/5a7e46034of0b62302688a4b1/Modern_Slavery_Strategy_FINAL_DEC2015.pdf.

Paying the Price: A Consultation Paper on Prostitution (London: Home Office, Communication Directorate, 2004).

A Points-Based System: Making Migration Work for Britain (London: Home Office, 2006).

Secure Borders, Safe Haven: Integration with Diversity in Modern Britain (London: Stationary Office, 2002).

Setting the Boundaries: Reforming the Law on Sex Offences, vol. 1 (London: Home Office, 2000).

Tackling Human Trafficking Consultation on Proposals for a UK Action Plan (London: Home Office, 2006).

Tackling the Demand for Prostitution: A Review (London: Home Office, 2008).

Transparency in Supply Chains etc.: A Practical Guide (London: Home Office, 2015).

'Overarching equality impact assessment [EIA] of the compliant environment', 9 February 2023, www.gov.uk/government/publications/compliant-environment-overarching-equality-impact-assessment.

UK, House of Commons, Committee of Public Accounts, *Reducing Modern Slavery*, Thirty-Sixth Report, Sess. 2017–2019.

UK, House of Commons, Home Affairs Committee, *The Trade in Human Beings: Human Trafficking in the UK*, Sixth Report, Sess. 2008–2009, vol. 1.

UK, House of Commons, Work and Pensions Committee, *Victims of Modern Slavery*, Twelfth Report, Sess. 2016–2017.

Human Rights and Business 2017: Promoting Responsibility and Ensuring Accountability, Sess. 2016–2017.

UK, House of Lords, Modern Slavery (Transparency in Supply Chains) Bill, Sess. 2016–2017, http:/bills.parliament.uk/bills/1799.

UK, House of Lords and House of Commons, Joint Committee on Human Rights, *Human Trafficking*, Twenty-Sixth Report, Sess. 2005–2006, vol. 1.

UK, House of Lords, House of Commons, Joint Committee on the Draft Modern Slavery Bill, Sess. 2013–2014, https://publications.parliament.uk/pa/jt201314/jtselect/jtslavery/166/166.pdf.

UK, Home Office and Scottish Executive, *UK Action Plan on Tackling Human Trafficking* (London: Home Office, 2007).

UK, Home Office and Scottish Government, *Update to the UK Action Plan on Tackling Human Trafficking* (London: Home Office, 2009).

UK, Ministry of Justice, 'Slavery, servitude and forced or compulsory labour: Implementation of section 71 of the Coroners and Justice Act 2009', Circular 2010/07, 19 March 2010.

UK, Parliament, 'Illegal migration bill: Question for Home Office', *Written Questions Answers and Statements*, 8 March 2023, Robert Jenrick, Answered on 22 March 2023, https://questions-statements.parliament.uk/written-questions/detail/2023-03-08/161356.

UK, Prime Minister's Office, *The Queen's Speech 2022*, 2022, https://assets.publishing.service.gov.uk/media/627a57f88fa8f57d893d3008/Lobby_Pack_10_May_2022.pdf

UK, Treasury, *Minutes: Government Response to the Committee of Public Accounts on the Thirty First to the Thirty Seventh Reports*, Sess. 2017–2019, Cm 9643.

UN, '"G7 Trade Ministers' strong stance" against forced labour in supply chains is welcome but must be followed by concrete action on forced labour and other human rights abuses, says UN expert group', 2 November 2021, www.ohchr.org/en/statements/2021/11/g7-trade-ministers-strong-stance-against-forced-labour-supply-chains-welcome.

UNDP (United Nations Development Programme), *The SDGS in Action*, 2023, www.undp.org/sustainable-development-goals.

United States, *The National Action Plan to Combat Human Trafficking*, 2021, www.whitehouse.gov/wp-content/uploads/2021/12/National-Action-Plan-to-Combat-Human-Trafficking.pdf.

Trafficking in Persons Report, June 2008, 2009–2017, state.gov/documents/organization/105501.pdf

Trafficking in Persons Report, June 2019, www.state.gov/wp-content/uploads/2019/06/2019-Trafficking-in-Persons-Report.pdf.

United States, Customs and Border Protection, *Withhold Release Orders and Findings List*, 2024, www.cbp.gov/trade/forced-labor/withhold-release-orders-and-findings.

United States, Office of the U.S. Trade Representative, *2022 Trade Policy Agenda & 2021 Annual Report*, March 22, 2022, https://ustr.gov/sites/default/files/2022%20Trade%20Policy%20Agenda%20and%202021%20Annual%20Report%20(1).pdf.

UNODC (United Nations Office on Drugs and Crime), *Global Report on Trafficking in Persons* (Vienna: United Nations, 2021), www.unodc.org/documents/data-and-analysis/tip/2021/GLOTiP_2020_15jan_web.pdf.

Valverde, Marianna, 'Analyzing the governance of security: Jurisdiction and scale' (2008) 1 *Behemoth a Journal on Civilisation*, 3–15.

Chronotopes of Law: Jurisdiction, Scale and Governance (London: Routledge, 2015).

'Jurisdiction and scale: Legal "technicalities" as resources for theory' (2009) 18 *Social and Legal Studies*, 139–157.

Van Dyke, Ruth, 'The UK's response to modern slavery', in Gary Craig, Alex Balch, Hannah Lewis, and Louise Waite (eds.), *The Modern Slavery Agenda: Policy, Politics and Practice in the UK* (Bristol: Policy Press 2019), 47–74.

Van Houtum, Henk, 'The geopolitics of borders and boundaries' (2005) 10 *Geopolitics*, 672–679.

Vaughan-Williams, Nick, 'Borders, territory, law' (2008) 2 *International Political Sociology*, 322–338.

Vigeswaran, Darshan, 'Methodological debates in human rights research: A case study of human trafficking in South Africa', in Annie Bunting and Joel Quirk (eds.), *Contemporary Slavery* (Vancouver: University of British Columbia Press, 2017), 180–201.

Villiers, Charlotte, 'A game of cat and mouse: Human rights protection and the problem of corporate law and power' (2023) 36 *Leiden Journal of International Law*, 415–438.

Waite, Louise, Hannah Lewis, Rebecca Murray, and Emma Tomalin, 'Faith, bordering and modern slavery: A UK case study' (forthcoming) *Environment and Planning C: Politics and Space*, https://doi.org/10.1177/23996544231212208.

Walk Free, 'The Global Freedom Network,' 2023, www.walkfree.org/projects/global-freedom-network/.

Global Slavery Index (Perth: Minderoo Foundation, 2013, 2016, 2018, 2023).

Harnessing the Power of Business to End Modern Slavery (Perth: Minderoo Foundation, 2016).

Measurement, Action, Freedom: An Independent Assessment of Government Progress towards Achieving Sustainable Development Goal 8.7 (Perth: Minderoo Foundation, 2019).

Towards a Common Future: Achieving SDG 8.7 in the Commonwealth (Perth: Minderoo Foundation, 2018), https://cdn.walkfree.org/content/uploads/2020/10/06155017/Commonwealth-Report_PAGES_180405_FNL_Digital-p.pdf.

'What is modern slavery?' 2023, www.walkfree.org/what-is-modern-slavery/.

Weinar, Agnieszka, Saskia Bonjour, and Lyubov Zhyznomirska, 'Introduction: The case for regional approach to study politics of migration', in Agnieszka Weinar, Saskia Bonjour, and Lyubov Zhyznomirska (eds.), *The Routledge Handbook of the Politics of Migration in Europe* (London: Routledge, 2019), 1–12.

Weitzer, Ronald, 'Moral crusade against prostitution' (2006) 43 *Society*, 33–38.

'New directions in research on human trafficking' (2014) 653 *The ANNALS of the American Academy of Political and Social Science*, 6–24.

Wellings, Ben, *English Nationalism, Brexit and the Anglosphere: Wider Still and Wider* (Manchester: University of Manchester Press, 2019).

Wen, Shuangge, 'The cogs and wheels of reflexive law and business disclosure under the Modern Slavery Act' (2016) 43 *Journal of Law and Society*, 327–359.

Wijers, Marjan, 'How we got here: The story of the Palermo protocol on trafficking', *Open Democracy*, 1 February 2021, www.opendemocracy.net/en/beyond-trafficking-and-slavery/how-we-got-here-story-palermo-protocol-trafficking/.

'Purity, victimhood and agency: Fifteen years of the UN Trafficking Protocol' (2015) 4 *Anti-trafficking Review*, 56–79.

Wijers, Marjan, and Lin Lap-Chew, *Trafficking in Women, Forced Labour and Slavery-Like Practices in Marriage, Domestic Labour and Prostitution*, rev. ed. (Utrecht/Bangkok: Foundation Against Trafficking in Women/GAATW, 1999), 189–210.

World Bank, *Trading for Development in the Age of Global Value Chains* (Washington, DC: World Bank Group, 2020).

Wray-Bliss, Edward, and Grant Michelson, 'Modern slavery and the discursive construction of a propertied freedom: Evidence from Australian business' (2022) 179 *Journal of Business Ethics*, 649–663.

Yuval-Davis, Nira, Georgie Wemyss, and Kathryn Cassidy, *Bordering* (Cambridge, UK: Polity, 2019).

Index

For EU product safety concerns, contact us at Calle de José Abascal, 56–1°,
28003 Madrid, Spain or eugpsr@cambridge.org.

www.ingramcontent.com/pod-product-compliance
Lightning Source LLC
LaVergne TN
LVHW011809200926
848484LV00005B/1116

9781108473422